Financial Models with Lévy Processes and Volatility Clustering

The Frank J. Fabozzi Series

Financial Models with Lévy Processes and Volatility Clustering

SVETLOZAR T. RACHEV
YOUNG SHIN KIM
MICHELE LEONARDO BIANCHI
FRANK J. FABOZZI

WILEY

John Wiley & Sons, Inc.

Library of Congress Cataloging-in-Publication Data:

Financial models with Lévy processes and volatility clustering / Svetlozar T. Rachev . . . [et al.].
   p. cm.—(The Frank J. Fabozzi series)
  Includes index.
  ISBN 978-0-470-48235-3 (cloth); 978-0-470-93716-7 (ebk);
  978-0-470-93726-6 (ebk); 978-1-118-00670-2 (ebk)
  1. Capital assets pricing model. 2. Lévy processes. 3. Finance—Mathematical models.
  4. Probabilities. I. Rachev, S. T. (Svetlozar Todorov)
   HG4637.F56 2011
   332′.0415015192—dc22   2010033299

Printed in the United States of America

10 9 8 7 6 5 4 3 2 1

Contents

Preface

Carl Frederick Gauss, born in 1777, is one of the foremost mathematicians the world has known. Labeled the "prince of mathematicians" and viewed by some as on par with Sir Isaac Newton, the various works of Gauss have influenced a wide range of fields in mathematics and science. Although very few in the finance profession are familiar with his great contributions and body of work—which are published by the by the Royal Society of Göttingen in seven quatro volumes—most are familiar with his important work in probability theory that bears his name: the Gaussian distribution. The more popular name for this distribution is the normal distribution and was also referred to as the "bell curve" in 1733 by Abraham de Moivre, who first discovered this distribution based on his empirical work. Every finance professional who has taken a probability and statistics course has had a heavy dose of the Gaussian distribution and probably can still recite some properties of this distribution.

The normal distribution has found many applications in the natural sciences and social sciences. However, there are those who have long warned about the misuse of the normal distribution, particularly in the social sciences. In a 1981 article in *Humanity and Society*, Ted Goertzel and Joseph Fashing ("The Myth of the Normal Curve: A Theoretical Critique and Examination of its Role in Teaching and Research") argue that

> The myth of the bell curve has occupied a central place in the theory of inequality . . . Apologists for inequality in all spheres of social life have used the theory of the bell curve, explicitly and implicitly, in developing moral rationalizations to justify the status quo. While the misuse of the bell curve has perhaps been most frequent in the field of education, it is also common in other areas of social science and social welfare.

A good example is in the best-selling book by Richard Herrnstein and Charles Murray, *The Bell Curve*, published in 1994 with the subtitle *Intelligence and Class Structure in American Life*. The authors argue based on their empirical evidence that in trying to predict an individual's income or job performance, intelligence is a better predictor than the educational level or socioeconomic status of that individual's parents. Even the likelihood to commit a crime or to exhibit other antisocial behavior is better predicted by intelligence, as measured by IQ, than other potential explanatory factors. The policy implications drawn from the book are so profound that they set off a flood of books both attacking and supporting the findings of Herrnstein and Murray.

In finance, where the normal distribution was the underlying assumption in describing asset returns in major financial theories such as the capital asset pricing theory and option pricing theory, the attack came in the early 1960s from Benoit Mandelbrot, a mathematician at IBM's Thomas J. Watson Research Center. Although primarily known for his work in fractal geometry, the finance profession was introduced to his study of returns on commodity prices and interest rate movements that strongly rejected the assumption that asset returns are normally distributed. The mainstream financial models at the time relied on the work of Louis Bachelier, a French mathematician who at the beginning of the 20th century was the first to formulate random walk models for stock prices. Bachelier's work assumed that relative price changes followed a normal distribution. Mandelbrot, however, was not the first to attack the use of the normal distribution in finance. As he notes, Wesley Clair Mitchell, an American economist who taught at Columbia University and founded the National Bureau of Economic Research, was the first to do so in 1914. The bottom line is that the findings of Mandelbrot that empirical distributions do not follow a normal distribution led a leading financial economist, Paul Cootner of MIT, to warn the academic community that Mandelbrot's finding may mean that "past econometric work is meaningless."

The overwhelming empirical evidence of asset returns in real-world financial markets is that they are not normally distributed. In commenting on the normal distribution in the context of its use in the social sciences, "Earnest Ernest" wrote the following in the November 10, 1974, in the *Philadelphia Inquirer*:

> *Surely the hallowed bell-shaped curve has cracked from top to bottom. Perhaps, like the Liberty Bell, it should be enshrined somewhere as a memorial to more heroic days.*

Finance professionals should heed the same advice when using the normal distribution in asset pricing, portfolio management, and risk management.

In Mandelbrot's attack on the normal distribution, he suggested that asset returns are more appropriately described by a non-normal stable distribution referred to as a stable Paretian distribution or alpha-stable distribution (α-stable distribution), so-named because the tails of this distribution have Pareto power-type decay. The reason for describing this distribution as "non-normal stable" is because the normal distribution is a special case of the stable distribution. Because of the work by Paul Lévy, a French mathematician who introduced and characterized the non-normal stable distribution, this distribution is also referred to as the Lévy stable distribution and the Pareto-Lévy stable distribution. (There is another important contribution to probability theory by Lévy that we apply to financial modeling in this book. More specifically, we will apply the Lévy processes, a continuous-stochastic process.)

There are two other facts about asset return distributions that have been supported by empirical evidence. First, distributions have been observed to be skewed or nonsymmetric. That is, unlike in the case of the normal distribution where there is a mirror imaging of the two sides of the probability distribution, typically in a skewed distribution, one tail of the distribution is much longer (i.e., has greater probability of extreme values occurring) than the other tail of the probability distribution. Probability distributions with this attribute are referred to as having fat tails or heavy tails. The second finding is the tendency of large changes in asset prices (either positive or negative) to be followed by large changes, and small changes to be followed by small changes. This attribute of asset return distributions is referred to as volatility clustering.

In this book, we consider these well-established facts about asset return distributions in providing a framework for modeling the behavior of stock returns. In particular, we provide applications to the financial modeling used in asset pricing, option pricing, and portfolio/risk management. In addition to explaining how one can employ non-normal distributions, we also provide coverage of several topics that are of special interest to finance professionals.

We begin by explaining the need for better financial modeling, followed by the basics of probability distributions—the different types of probability distributions (discrete and continuous), specific types of probability distributions, parameters of a probability distribution, and joint probability distributions. The definition of the stable Pareto distribution (we adopted the term α-stable distribution in this book) that Mandelbrot suggested is described. Although this distribution has certain desirable properties and is superior to the normal distribution, it is not suitable in certain financial modeling applications such as the modeling of option prices because the mean, variance, and exponential moments of the return distribution have to exist. For this reason, we introduce distributions that we believe are better suited for financial modeling, distributions obtained by tempering the tail properties of the α-stable distribution: the smoothly truncated stable distribution and various types of tempered stable distributions. Because of their important role in the applications in this book, we review continuous-time stochastic processes with emphasis on Lévy processes.

There are chapters covering the so-called exponential Lévy model, and we study this continuous-time option pricing model and analyze the change of measure problem. Prices of plain vanilla options are calculated with both analytical and Monte Carlo methods.

After examples dealing with the simulation of non-normal random numbers, we study two multivariate settings that are suitable to explain joint extreme events. In the first approach, we describe a multivariate random variable for joint extreme events, and in the second we model the joint behavior of log-returns of stocks by considering a feasible dependence structure together with marginals able to explain volatility clutering.

Then we get into the core of the book where we deal with examples of discrete-time option pricing models. Starting from the classic normal model with volatility clustering, we progress to the more recent models that jointly consider volatility clustering and heavy tails. We conclude with a non-normal GARCH model to price American options.

We would like to thank Sebastian Kring and Markus Höchstötter for their coauthorship of Chapter 9 and Christian Menn for his coauthorship of Chapter 12. We also thank Stoyan Stoyanov for providing the MATLAB code for the skew t-copula.

The authors acknowledge that the views expressed in this book are their own and do not necessarily reflect those of their employers.

SVETLOZAR (ZARI) T. RACHEV
YOUNG SHIN (AARON) KIM
MICHELE LEONARDO BIANCHI
FRANK J. FABOZZI
July 2010

About the Authors

Svetlozar (Zari) T. Rachev completed his Ph.D. Degree in 1979 from Moscow State (Lomonosov) University, and his Doctor of Science Degree in 1986 from Steklov Mathematical Institute in Moscow. Currently, he is Chair-Professor in Statistics, Econometrics and Mathematical Finance at the Karlsruhe Institute of Technology (KIT) in the School of Economics and Business Engineering, and Professor Emeritus at the University of California, Santa Barbara in the Department of Statistics and Applied Probability. Professor Rachev has published 14 monographs, 10 handbooks and special-edited volumes, and more than 300 research articles. His recently coauthored books published by John Wiley & Sons in mathematical finance and financial econometrics include *Financial Econometrics: From Basics to Advanced Modeling Techniques* (2007) and *Bayesian Methods in Finance* (2008). He is cofounder of Bravo Risk Management Group, specializing in financial risk-management software. Bravo Group was acquired by FinAnalytica for which he currently serves as Chief-Scientist.

Young Shin (Aaron) Kim studied at the Department of Mathematics, Sogang University, in Seoul, Korea, where he received his doctorate degree in 2005. Currently, he is a scientific assistant in the Department of Statistics, Econometrics and Mathematical Finance at Karlsruhe Institute of Technology (KIT). His current professional and research interests are in the area of Lévy processes, including tempered stable processes, time-varying volatility models, and their applications to finance.

Michele Leonardo Bianchi is an analyst in the Division of Risk and Financial Innovation Analysis at the Specialized Intermediaries Supervision Department of the Bank of Italy. Dr. Bianchi has authored articles on quantitative finance, probability theory, and nonlinear optimization. He earned an Italian "Laurea" in Mathematics in 2005 from the University of Pisa and completed his Ph.D. in Computational Methods for Economic and Financial Decisions and Forecasting in 2009 from the University of Bergamo.

Frank J. Fabozzi is Professor in the Practice of Finance in the School of Management and Becton Fellow at Yale University. He is an Affiliated Professor at the University of Karlsruhe's Institute of Statistics, Econometrics and Mathematical Finance. Prior to joining the Yale faculty, he was a Visiting Professor of Finance in the Sloan School at MIT. Professor Fabozzi is a Fellow of the International Center for Finance at Yale University and on the Advisory Council for the Department of Operations Research and Financial Engineering at Princeton University. He is the editor of the *Journal of Portfolio Management* and an associate editor of *Quantitative Finance*. He is a trustee for the BlackRock family of closed-end funds. In 2002, he was inducted into the Fixed Income Analysts Society's Hall of Fame and is the 2007 recipient of the C. Stewart Sheppard Award given by the CFA Institute. His recently coauthored books published by Wiley include *Institutional Investment Management* (2009), *Quantitative Equity Investing* (2010), *Bayesian Methods in Finance* (2008), *Advanced Stochastic Models, Risk Assessment, and Portfolio Optimization: The Ideal Risk, Uncertainty, and Performance Measures* (2008), *Financial Modeling of the Equity Market: From CAPM to Cointegration* (2008), *Robust Portfolio Optimization and Management* (2007), and *Financial Econometrics: From Basics to Advanced Modeling Techniques* (2007). Professor Fabozzi earned a doctorate in economics from the City University of New York in 1972. He earned the designations of Chartered Financial Analyst and Certified Public Accountant.

CHAPTER 1

Introduction

1.1 THE NEED FOR BETTER FINANCIAL MODELING OF ASSET PRICES

Major debacles in financial markets since the mid-1990s such as the Asian financial crisis in 1997, the bursting of the dot-com bubble in 2000, the subprime mortgage crisis that began in the summer of 2007, and the days surrounding the bankruptcy of Lehman Brothers in September 2008 are constant reminders to risk managers, portfolio managers, and regulators of how often extreme events occur. These major disruptions in the financial markets have led researchers to increase their efforts to improve the flexibility and statistical reliability of existing models that seek to capture the dynamics of economic and financial variables. Even if a catastrophe cannot be predicted, the objective of risk managers, portfolio managers, and regulators is to limit the potential damages.

The failure of financial models has been identified by some market observers as a major contributor—indeed some have argued that it is the single most important contributor—for the latest global financial crisis. The allegation is that financial models used by risk managers, portfolio managers, and even regulators simply did not reflect the realities of real-world financial markets. More specifically, the underlying assumption regarding asset returns and prices failed to reflect real-world movements of these quantities. Pinpointing the criticism more precisely, it is argued that the underlying assumption made in most financial models is that distributions of prices and returns are normally distributed, popularly referred to as the "normal model." This probability distribution—also referred to as the *Gaussian distribution* and in lay terms the "bell curve"—is the one that dominates the teaching curriculum in probability and statistics courses in all business schools. Despite its popularity, the normal model flies in the face of what has been well documented regarding asset prices and returns. The preponderance of the empirical evidence has led to the following three stylized facts regarding financial time series for asset returns: (1) they have *fat tails* (*heavy tails*), (2) they may be *skewed*, and (3) they exhibit *volatility clustering*.

The "tails" of the distribution are where the extreme values occur. Empirical distributions for stock prices and returns have found that the extreme values are more likely than would be predicted by the normal distribution. This means that between periods where the market exhibits relatively modest changes in prices and returns, there will be periods where there are changes that are much higher (i.e., crashes and booms) than predicted by the normal distribution. This is not only of concern to financial theorists, but also to practitioners who are, in view of the frequency of sharp market down turns in the equity markets noted earlier, troubled by, in the words of Hoppe (1999), the "... compelling evidence that something is rotten in the foundation of the statistical edifice ... used, for example, to produce probability estimates for financial risk assessment." Fat tails can help explain larger price fluctuations for stocks over short time periods than can be explained by changes in fundamental economic variables as observed by Shiller (1981).

The normal distribution is a *symmetric distribution*. That is, it is a distribution where the shape of the left side of the probability distribution is the mirror image of the right side of the probability distribution. For a skewed distribution, also referred to as a *nonsymmetric distribution*, there is no such mirror imaging of the two sides of the probability distribution. Instead, typically in a skewed distribution one tail of the distribution is much longer (i.e., has greater probability of *extreme values* occurring) than the other tail of the probability distribution, which, of course, is what we referred to as fat tails. Volatility clustering behavior refers to the tendency of large changes in asset prices (either positive or negative) to be followed by large changes, and small changes to be followed by small changes.

The attack on the normal model is by no means recent. The first fundamental attack on the assumption that price or return distribution are not normally distributed was in the 1960s by Mandelbrot (1963). He strongly rejected normality as a distributional model for asset returns based on his study of commodity returns and interest rates. Mandlebrot conjectured that financial returns are more appropriately described by a non-normal stable distribution. Since a normal distribution is a special case of the stable distribution, to distinguish between Gaussian and non-Gaussian stable distributions, the latter are often referred to as *stable Paretian* distributions or *Lévy stable* distributions.[1] We will describe these distributions later in this book.

---

[1] The stable Paretian distribution is so-named because the tails of the non-Gaussian stable distribution have Pareto power-type decay. The Lévy stable distribution is

Mandelbrot's early investigations on returns were carried further by Fama (1963a, 1963b), among others, and led to a consolidation of the hypothesis that asset returns can be better described as a stable Paretian distribution. However, there was obviously considerable concern in the finance profession by the findings of Mandelbrot and Fama. In fact, shortly after the publication of the Mandelbrot paper, Cootner (1964) expressed his concern regarding the implications of those findings for the statistical tests that had been published in prominent scholarly journals in economics and finance. He warned that (Cootner, 1964, p. 337):

Almost without exception, past econometric work is meaningless. Surely, before consigning centuries of work to the ash pile, we should like to have some assurance that all our work is truly useless. If we have permitted ourselves to be fooled for as long as this into believing that the Gaussian assumption is a workable one, is it not possible that the Paretian revolution is similarly illusory?

Although further evidence supporting Mandelbrot's empirical work was published, the "normality" assumption remains the cornerstone of many central theories in finance. The most relevant example for this book is the pricing of options or, more generally, the pricing of contingent claims. In 1900, the father of modern option pricing theory, Louis Bachelier, proposed using *Brownian motion* for modeling stock market prices.[2] Inspired by his work, Samuelson (1965) formulated the log-normal model for stock prices that formed the basis for the well-known Black-Scholes option pricing

---

named in honor of Paul Lévy for his seminal work introducing and characterizing the class of non-Gaussian stable distributions.

[2]There are several reasons why Brownian motion is a popular process. First, Brownian motion is the milestone of the theory of stochastic processes. However, more realistic general processes that are better suited for financial modeling such as Lévy, additive or self-similar processes (all of which we discuss in this book) have been developed only since the mid-1990s (see Samorodnitsky and Taqqu, 1994, Sato, 1999, and Embrechhts and Maejima, 2002). Most of the practical problems of mathematical finance can be solved by taking into consideration these new processes. For example, the concept of stochastic integral with respect to Brownian motion was introduced in 1933 and only in the 1990s has the general theory of stochastic integration with respect to semimartingale appeared. From a practical point of view, the second reason for the popularity of Brownian motion is that the normal distribution allows one to solve real-world pricing problems such as option prices as estimations and simulations in a few seconds, and most of the problems have a closed-form solution that can be easily used.

model. Black and Scholes (1973) and Merton (1974) introduced pricing and hedging theory for the options market employing a stock price model based on the *exponential Brownian motion*. The model greatly influences the way market participants price and hedge options; in 1997, Merton and Scholes were awarded the Nobel Prize in Economic Science.

Despite the importance of option theory as formulated by Black, Scholes, and Merton, it is widely recognized that on Black Monday, October 19, 1987, the Black-Scholes formula failed. The reason for the failure of the model particularly during volatile periods is its underlying assumptions necessary to generate a closed-form solution to price options. More specifically, it is assumed that returns are normally distributed and that return volatility is constant over the option's life. The latter assumption means that regardless of an option's strike price, the implied volatility (i.e., the volatility implied by the Black-Scholes model based on observed prices in the options market) should be the same. Yet, it is now an accepted fact that in the options market, implied volatility varies depending on the strike price. In some options markets, for example, the market for individual equities, it is observed that, for options, implied volatility decreases with an option's strike price. This relationship is referred to as *volatility skew*. In other markets, such as index options and currency options, it is observed that at-the-money options tend to have an implied volatility that is lower than for both out-of-the-money and in-the-money options. Since graphically this relationship would show that implied volatility decreases as options move from out-of-the-money options to at-the-money options and then increase from at-the-money options to in-the-money options, this relationship between strike price and implied volatility is called *volatility smile*. Obviously, both volatility skew and volatility smile are inconsistent with the assumption of a constant volatility.

Consequently, since the mid-1990s there has been growing interest in non-normal models not only in academia but also among financial practitioners seeking to try to explain extreme events that occur in financial markets. Furthermore, the search for proper models to price complex financial instruments and to calibrate the observed prices of those instruments quoted in the market has motivated studies of more complex models. There is still a good deal of work to be done on financial modeling using alternative non-normal distributions that have recently been proposed in the finance literature. In this book, we explain these univariate and multivariate models (both discrete and continuous) and then show their applications to explaining stock price behavior and pricing options.

In the balance of this chapter we describe some background information that is used in the chapters ahead. At the end of the chapter we provide an overview of the book.

1.2   THE FAMILY OF STABLE DISTRIBUTION AND ITS PROPERTIES

As noted earlier, Mandelbrot and Fama observed fat tails for many asset price and return data. For assets whose returns or prices exhibit fat-tail attributes, non-normal distribution models are required to accurately model the tail behavior and compute probabilities of extreme returns. The candidates for non-normal distributions that have been proposed for modeling extreme events in addition to the α-stable Paretian distribution include mixtures of two or more normal distributions, Student t-distributions, hyperbolic distributions, and other scale mixtures of normal distributions, gamma distributions, extreme value distributions. The class of stable Paretian distributions (which includes α-stable Paretian distribution as a special case) are simply referred to as *stable distributions*.

Although we cover the stable distribution in considerable detail in Chapter 3, here we only briefly highlight the key features of this distribution.

1.2.1   Parameterization of the Stable Distribution

In only three cases does the density function of a stable distribution have a closed-form expression. In the general case, stable distributions are described by their characteristic function that we describe in Chapter 3. A characteristic function provides a third possibility (besides the cumulative distribution function and the probability density function) to uniquely define a probability distribution. At this point, we just state the fact that knowing the characteristic function is mathematically equivalent to knowing the probability density function or the cumulative distribution function. What is important to understand is that the characteristic function (and thus the density function) of a stable distribution is described by four parameters: μ, σ, α, and β.[3]

The μ and σ parameters are measures of central location and scale, respectively. The parameter α determines the tail weight or the distribution's kurtosis with $0 < \alpha \leq 2$. The β determines the distribution's skewness. When the β of a stable distribution is zero, the distribution is symmetric around μ. Stable distributions allow for skewed distributions when $\beta \neq 0$ and fat tails; this means a high probability for extreme events relative to the normal distribution when $\alpha < 0$. The value of β can range from

---

[3]There are many different possible parameterizations of stable distributions. For an overview the reader is referred to Zolotarev (1986). The parameterization used here is the one introduced by Samorodnitsky and Taqqu (1994).

-1 to $+1$. When β is positive, a stable distribution is skewed to the right; when β is negative, a stable distribution is skewed to the left. Figure 1.1 shows the effect on tail thickness of the density as well as peakedness at the origin relative to the normal distribution (collectively the "kurtosis" of the density) for the case of where $\mu = 0$, $\sigma = 1$, and $\beta = 0$. As the values of α decrease, the distribution exhibits fatter tails and more peakedness at the origin. Figure 1.1 illustrates the influence of β on the skewness of the density function for the case where $\alpha = 1.5$, $\mu = 0$, and $\sigma = 1$. Increasing (decreasing) values of β result in skewness to the right (left).

There are only four stable distributions that possess a closed-form expression for their density function. The case where $\alpha = 2$ (and $\beta = 0$, which plays no role in this case) and with the re-parameterization in the scale parameter σ, yields the normal distribution. Thus, the normal distribution is one of the four special cases of the stable distribution, one that possesses a closed-form expression. The second occurs when $\alpha = 1$ and $\beta = 0$. In this case we have the *Cauchy distribution*, which, although symmetric, is characterized by much fatter tails than the normal distribution. When we have $\alpha = 0.5$ and $\beta = 1$, the resulting density function is the *Lévy distribution*.[4]

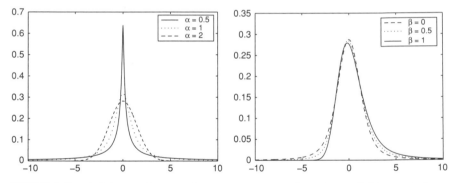

FIGURE 1.1   Stable Density: $\mu = 0$, $\sigma = 1$, $\beta = 0$, and varying α (left); $\alpha = 1.5$, $\mu = 0$, $\sigma = 1$, and varying β (right)

---

[4]The probability mass of the Lévy distribution is concentrated on the interval $(\mu, +\infty)$. The phenomenon that the domain of a stable distribution differs from the whole real line can only occur for values of α strictly less than one and in the case of maximal skewness, that is, for $\beta = +1$ or $\beta = -1$. In the former case, the support of the distribution equals the interval $(\mu, +\infty)$ whereas in the latter case it equals $(-\infty, \mu)$.

And finally, the fourth case with a closed-form density is the *reflected Lévy distribution* with parameters $\alpha = 0.5$ and $\beta = -1$, so-called because this distribution can be obtained from the Lévy distribution by reflecting the graph of the density at the vertical axis.

1.2.2   Desirable Properties of the Stable Distributions

An attractive feature of stable distributions, not shared by other probability distribution models, is that they allow generalization of financial theories based on normal distributions and, thus, allow construction of a coherent and general framework for financial modeling. These generalizations are possible only because of two specific probabilistic properties that are unique to stable distributions (both normal and non-normal): (1) the stability property and (2) the Central Limit Theorem.

The stability property was briefly mentioned before and denotes the fact that the sum of two independent α-stable random variables follows—up to some correction of scale and location—again the same stable distribution. This property, which is well known for the special case of the normal distribution, becomes important in financial applications such as portfolio choice theory or when measuring returns on different time-scales. The second property, also well known for the normal distribution, generalizes to the stable case. Specifically, by the Central Limit Theorem, appropriately normalized sums of independent and identically distributed (i.i.d.) random variables with finite variance converge weakly[5] to a normal random variable, and with infinite variance, the sums converge weakly to a stable random variable. This gives a theoretical basis for the use of stable distributions when heavy tails are present and stable distributions are the only distributional family that has its own domain of attraction—that is, a large sum of appropriately standardized i.i.d. random variables will have a distribution that converges to a stable one. This is a unique feature and its fundamental implications for financial modeling are the following: If changes in a stock price, interest rate, or any other financial variable are driven by many independently occurring small shocks, then the only appropriate distributional model for these changes is a stable model (normal or non-normal stable).

---

[5]Weak converge of a sequence of random variables to a distribution function F means that the distribution functions $F_1, F_2, \ldots$ of $X_1, X_2, \ldots$ converge pointwise in every point of continuity of F to the distribution function F.

1.2.3   Considerations in the Use of the Stable Distribution

Despite the empirical evidence rejecting the normal distribution and in support of the stable distribution, there have been several barriers to the application of stable distribution models, both conceptual and technical. The major problem is that the variance of the stable non-normal distributions equals infinity. This fact can be explained by the tail behavior of stable distributions. One can show that the density function of a stable distribution with index of stability α "behaves like" $|x|^{-\alpha-1}$ and consequently all moments $E|X|^p$ with $p \geq \alpha$ do not exist. In particular, the mean only exists for $\alpha > 1$.

A second criticism of the stable distribution concerns the fact that without a general expression for stable probability densities—except the four cases identified above—one cannot directly implement estimation methodologies for fitting these densities. Today, because of advances in computational finance, there are methodologies for fitting densities for stable distributions that we describe in later chapters. Nevertheless, there remains the problem of using the α-stable distribution in option pricing models because of its infinite moments of order higher than α.

Finally, the empirical evidence of observed market returns, although inconsistent with the normal distribution and better explained by the α-stable distribution, still is not a good fit to that distribution. More specifically, the tails of the distribution for asset returns are heavier than the normal distribution but thinner than the α-stable distribution.[6]

To overcome the drawbacks of the α-stable distribution, the tails of an α-stable random variable can be appropriately tempered or truncated in order to obtain a proper distribution that can be utilized to price derivatives. Several alternatives to the α-stable distribution have been proposed in the literature. One alternative is the *classical tempered stable* (CTS) distribution—introduced under the names truncated Lévy flight, KoBoL, and CGMY[7]—and its extension, the KR distribution. The *modified tempered stable* (MTS) distribution is another alternative.[8] These distributions, sometimes called the *tempered stable distributions*,[9] have not only heavier tails than the

---

[6]See Grabchak and Samorodnitsky (2010).

[7]The truncated Lévyflight, KoBol, and CGMY were introduced by Koponen (1995), Boyarchenko and Levendorskiĭ (2000), and Carr et al. (2002), respectively.

[8]The KR and the MTS distribution are analyzed in Kim et al. (2008) and Kim et al. (2009), respectively.

[9]Rosiński (2007) extended CTS distribution under the name of the tempered stable distribution, and KR distribution is included in this extension, but MTS distribution is not (see Bianchi et al., 2010).

normal distribution and thinner than the α-stable distribution, but also have finite moments for all orders and exponential moments of some order. Thus an exponential Lévy model can be constructed. Recently, Menn and Rachev (2009) introduced the so-called *smoothly truncated stable* (STS) random variable in order to provide a practical framework to extend option pricing theory to the α-stable model.

1.3 OPTION PRICING WITH VOLATILITY CLUSTERING

The arbitrage pricing of options is based on the martingale approach described in Harrison and Kreps (1979) and subsequently by Harrison and Pliska (1981). According to this approach, option prices can be obtained by taking the expectation for the payoff function of the given underlying asset under a so-called *risk-neutral measure* (or *equivalent martingale measure*), which generally differs from the market measure estimated from historical data. The option price is effected by the risk-neutral measure. In the Black-Scholes model, for example, the return distribution is assumed to be a normal distribution and the price of a European call and put option given by a simple explicit form that depends on two main parameters: the risk-free rate and the variance.

Practitioners prefer to use the word *volatility* (the square root of the variance). Two types of volatilities can be observed in the market: (1) the volatility that can be inferred from stock prices, and (2) the so-called *implied volatility* (which we mentioned earlier in this chapter) that is embedded in option prices. The former is the volatility defined under the market measure, and the latter is usually viewed as a predictor of the future stock market volatility, and it can be considered as the risk-neutral volatility. Furthermore, one can assume a constant volatility or a time-varying one, depending on the statistical model one wants to employ. In particular, as observed by Corcuera et al. (2009), the implied volatility, calculated by inverting the formula of a given pricing model, strictly depends on the model selected.

Exponential Lévy models have been proposed to overcome the problems arising from the Black-Scholes model. Unfortunately, in spite of the skewness and the heavy-tail properties of the price-driving process, the exponential Lévy model has been rejected based on empirical evidence because it cannot explain the volatility clustering effect of a time series of observed returns. As noted in section 1.1, volatility clustering behavior refers to the tendency of large changes in asset prices (either positive or negative) to be followed by large changes and small changes to be followed by small changes. Furthermore, Lévy models provide a suitable fit to observed option prices for a single maturity, but not over all the maturities simultaneously.[10] That is, the volatility surface cannot be exactly fit with these kinds of models. In order to overcome this deficiency of Lévy-based models, one can utilize both stochastic volatility models and discrete-time generalized autoregressive conditional heteroscedastic (GARCH) models to price derivatives under the assumption of unknown volatility.

Understanding the behavior of return volatility is important for forecasting as well as pricing option-type derivative instruments since volatility is a proxy for risk. There are two important directions in the literature for modeling for non constant volatility: (1) continuous-time stochastic volatility processes[11] represented in general by a bivariate diffusion process and (2) the discrete-time autoregressive conditionally heteroscedastic (ARCH) model of Engle (1982) or its generalization (GARCH) as first defined by Bollerslev (1986).

There are different ways to construct continuous-time stochastic volatility models. The first way changes the volatility parameter of the Black-Scholes model to a stochastic one and considers a bivariate diffusion process. Hull and White (1987) and Heston (1993) used an Itô process as the volatility process. Recently, Barndorff-Nielsen and Shephard (2001) defined the squared volatility process as an Ornstein-Uhlenbeck process driven by a Lévy subordinator. The second way to build models with dependence in increments is to time change a Lévy process by a positive increasing process with dependent increments. This second way to construct stochastic volatility model goes back to Mandelbrot and Taylor (1967) and Clark (1973) who modeled the asset models price as a geometric Brownian motion subordinated by an independent Lévy subordinator. Mandelbrot and Taylor assumed an α-stable distributed subordinator and Clark a log-normal one.[12]

Based on the previous construction, a stochastic time driven by a positive increasing Lévy process with dependent increments can be taken into consideration.[13] They take homogeneous Lévy processes and generate the desired volatility properties by subordinating them to the time integral of a Cox-Ingersoll-Ross (CIR) process.[14] The randomness of the CIR process induces stochastic volatility, while mean reversion in this process induces volatility clustering.

---

[10]See Corcuera et al. (2009).
[11]Schoutens (2003) examined the performance of various stochastic volatility models. See also Cont and Tankov (2004).
[12]See De Giovanni et al. (2008).
[13]This stochastic volatility model has been proposed in Carr et al. (2002).
[14]This model is introduced in Cox et al. (1985).

The main advantage of the continuous-time models is that a closed-form solution for European option prices is available; in contrast, in general, this is not a property of discrete models. However, in GARCH models, volatility is observable at each time point, thereby making the estimation procedure a much easier task than the one in continuous-time models. Duan (1995) investigated the pricing problem in the presence of lognormal stock returns and a GARCH volatility dynamic. Duan's result relies on the existence of a representative agent with constant relative risk aversion or constant absolute risk aversion. Heston and Nandi (2000), derived a semi-analytical pricing formula for European options for a normal GARCH model. The advantage of their closed-form solution is that the calibration technique is much easier to implement, even if the explanatory power of the model is poor.

Even if GARCH models are a bit mechanical, the methodology is useful since their diffusion limits contain many well-known stochastic volatility models. From an estimation perspective, GARCH models may have distinct advantages over stochastic volatility models. Continuous-time stochastic volatility models are difficult to implement because, with discrete observations on the underlying asset price process, the volatility is not readily identifiable. Furthermore, time-continuity models impose the possibility of continuous trading in order to construct the hedge portfolio this is not feasible in reality. To overcome this problem, implied volatilities are extracted from current option prices. In contrast, GARCH models have the advantage that volatility is observable from the history of asset prices. Consequently, it is possible to price options solely on the basis of observable history of the underlying asset process without requiring information on derivative prices.

In this book, we test performance of option pricing models using the S&P 500 index (SPX) option and the S&P 100 index (OEX) option. The former is a European style option while the latter is American style. Both options are traded on the Chicago Board Options Exchange. All market data are obtained from Option Metrics's Ivy DB in the Wharton Research Data Services.

1.3.1 Non-Gaussian GARCH Models

When fitting GARCH models to return series, it is often found that the residuals still tend to be heavy tailed. One reason is that the normally distributed innovation is insufficient to describe the residual of return distributions. In general, the skewness and leptokurtosis observed for financial data cannot be captured by a GARCH model with innovations that are normally distributed. To allow for particularly heavy-tailed conditional (and unconditional) return distributions, GARCH processes with non-normal distribution have been considered (see Mittnik et al., 1998).

Although asset return distributions are known to be conditionally leptokurtic, only a few studies have investigated the option pricing problem with GARCH dynamics and non-Gaussian innovations. Menn and Rachev (2009) considered *smoothly truncated stable* innovations and Christoffersen et al. (2010) investigated GARCH option pricing with inverse Gaussian and skewed variance-gamma innovations.[15] Kim et al. (2010) studied parametric models based on tempered stable distributions.

Another important direction in the financial literature is to estimate the risk-neutral return distribution and risk-neutral return volatility dependence using nonparametric techniques. Barone-Adesi et al. (2008) proposed the so-called filtered historical simulation method in which a random choice among the observed historical innovation sample is used to simulate the future innovation behavior.[16]

1.4   MODEL DEPENDENCIES

An important topic in quantitative finance is obtaining a reliable estimate of dependencies among financial instruments. This is fundamental in solving portfolio allocation problems or finding a fair price for derivatives whose underlying is a basket of instruments. Multivariate normal distributions are usually considered to model these dependencies, and the correlation matrix becomes the most important parameter to look at. However, correlation cannot explain joint extreme events since it can deal only with linear dependencies. More sophisticated techniques are needed to model the dependency structures observed in financial markets, particularly after the recent financial crisis that highlighted the failure of the Gaussian one-factor copula model in pricing collateralized debt obligations (CDOs).[17]

The more intuitive approach considers non-normal multivariate distributions by looking at a more flexible structure.[18] A second approach considers the copula framework,[19] which involves modeling the joint multivariate distribution in two steps: first by selecting a function to model the dependency structure, and second by selecting a proper model for the marginals. The first approach has its foundation in distribution theory and, in a certain sense, it is more elegant; the second approach offers a framework that can easily be understood by practitioners and offers sufficient flexibility that

---

[15]See also Christoffersen et al. (2006).
[16]See also Ait-Sahalia and Lo (2000), and Badescu and Kulperger (in press).
[17]See Brigo et al. (2010).
[18]See McNeil et al. (2005).
[19]See Embrechts et al. (2003) and references therein.

allows its adaption to stylized empirical facts observed in financial markets. The benefits of the copula framework are that it is quite simple to estimate and simulate, and for this reason in recent years it has become popular among financial practitioners.

A model must have three fundamental characteristics: (1) It has to be sophisticated enough to try to explain the major phenomena observed in financial markets; (2) it has to be simple enough to be calibrated; and (3) it has to be easily understood by practitioners. For these reasons, the normal distribution is a cornerstone in quantitative finance. Even if good a number of researchers found good results in applications to finance, only a few of these models have become market standards for the financial industry. Furthermore, it is not always true that the best model is the most popular. In this book, we will introduce two examples of nonstandard multivariate models for stock returns, with an application to portfolio selection. In particular, in Chapters 9 and 10 we analyze a multi-tail t-distribution and propose an algorithm to calibrate and simulate it, and then employ a skewed-t copula together with a one-dimensional time-series process allowing for volatility clustering in order to take into account the stylized facts of the time series of log-returns.

1.5 MONTE CARLO

Even if we consider the return process of assets modeled by a Brownian motion (that is, the return distribution is assumed to be normal), we do not have a closed-form solution to price complex path-dependent options. In GARCH models, explicit-form solutions are not given for options possessing a complex payoff function and even for European call/put. If we do not have an efficient analytical solution for pricing options, a classical way to price them is to employ the Monte Carlo method.[20]

Monte Carlo integration methods are based on the generation of a large number of simulations. These methods are based on the idea of evaluating an expectation (that is, an integral) by sampling from a set of possible scenarios. For this reason, the generation of random numbers is the fundamental tool used in the Monte Carlo integration method. Algorithms for generating normal and Poisson distributed random numbers are well known and easy to find in the literature. However, more sophisticated methods are required for more complex distributions, such as α-stable and tempered stable distributions. Approximation by a compounded Poisson distribution or a series

---

[20]A detailed introduction is provided in Glasserman (2004).

representation are two possible methods to simulate Lévy processes.[21] In order to be able to price financial instruments in a non-normal setting, in this book we provide an overview of the simulation algorithm that can be utilized to generate random samples starting from simple uniform random variable and ending with more complex infinitely divisible distributions.

1.6   ORGANIZATION OF THE BOOK

In this book we mainly focused on the application of non-normal distributions for modeling the behavior of stock price returns (more specifically, log returns). Both univariate and multivariate models are analyzed from a practical point of view, explaining the necessary theory to to understand these models.

This book includes a brief introduction to fundamental probability distributions that will be used in later chapters. In particular, the α-stable and tempered stable distributions are described in detail from both a theoretical and empirical perspective.

Starting from the notion of a distribution, we describe some fundamental stochastic processes such as Brownian motion and Poisson process. Then, we introduce Lévy processes, giving examples of pure jump processes and time-changed Brownian motion. For these stochastic processes, the change of measure problem is discussed in order to provide a tool to find the link between the market measure and a risk-neutral measure, and thereby for pricing, to price financial derivatives within a Lévy framework.

In Chapters 6 and 7, we go into depth regarding recent results for continuous-time modeling of stock prices with Lévy processes. Commencing with the Black-Scholes model, we investigate time changed, exponential tempered stable, and stochastic volatility models.

Chapter 8 provides a wide spectrum of methods for the simulation of infinitely divisible distributions and Lévy processes with a view toward option pricing.

In Chapters 9 and 10, we investigate two approaches to deal with non-normal multivariate distributions. Both chapters provide insight into portfolio allocation assuming a multi-tail t-distribution and a non-Gaussian multivariate model. The use of a copula function together with time-series analysis needed for modeling joint extreme events and volatility clustering is the subject of Chapter 10.

---

[21]See Asmussen and Glynn (2007) for a complete overview.

The last part is the core of the book: discrete option pricing models with volatility clustering. Non-Gaussian GARCH models for option pricing are investigated in detail. In particular, we critically assess different approaches to price options by using the information content of historical time series for the underling. In the book's final chapter, Chapter 15, we provide an algorithm to price American-style options under non-normal discrete-time models with volatility clustering.

REFERENCES

Ait-Sahalia, Y. & Lo, A. (2000). Nonparametric estimation of state-price densities implicit in financial asset prices. *Journal of Finance 52*, 499–548.

Asmussen, S. & Glynn, P. (2007). *Stochastic simulation: Algorithms and analysis.* New York: Springer.

Badescu, A. & Kulperger, R. (in press). GARCH option pricing: A semiparametric approach. *Insurance: Mathematics and Economics.*

Barndorff-Nielsen, O. E. & Shephard, N. (2001). Non-Gaussian Ornstein-Uhlenbeck-based models and some of their uses in financial economics. *Journal of the Royal Statistical Society, 63*(2).

Barone-Adesi, G., Engle, R., & Mancini, L. (2008). A GARCH option pricing model with filtered historical simulation. *Review of Financial Studies, 21*(3), 1223–1258.

Bianchi, M. L., Rachev, S. T., Kim, Y. S., & Fabozzi, F. J. (2010). Tempered infinitely divisible distributions and processes. *Theory of Probability and Its Applications (TVP), Society for Industrial and Applied Mathematics (SIAM), 55*(1), 59–86.

Black, F. & Scholes, M. (1973). The pricing of options and corporate liabilities. *The Journal of Political Economy, 81*(3), 637–654.

Bollerslev, T. (1986). Generalized autoregressive conditional heteroskedasticity. *Journal of Econometrics, 31*, 307–327.

Boyarchenko, S. I. & Levendorskiĭ, S. Z. (2000). Option pricing for truncated Lévy processes. *International Journal of Theoretical and Applied Finance, 3*(3), 549–552.

Brigo, D., Pallavicini, A., & Torresetti, R. (2010). *Credit models and the crisis: A journey into CDOs, copulas, correlations and dynamic models.* Hoboken, NJ: John Wiley & Sons.

Carr, P., Geman, H., Madan, D., & Yor, M. (2002). The fine structure of asset returns: An empirical investigation. *Journal of Business, 75*(2), 305–332.

Christoffersen, P., Elkamhi, R., Feunou, B., & Jacobs, K. (2010). Option valuation with conditional heteroskedasticity and nonnormality. *Review of Financial Studies, 23*(5), 2139–2183.

Christoffersen, P., Heston, S., & Jacobs, K. (2006). Option valuation with conditional skewness. *Journal of Econometrics, 131*(1-2), 253–284.

Clark, P. (1973). A subordinated stochastic process model with finite variance for speculative prices. *Econometrica*, *41*(1), 135–155.

Cont, R. & Tankov, P. (2004). *Financial modelling with jump processes*. Boca Raton, FL: CRC Press.

Cootner, P. (1964). *The random character of stock market prices*. Cambridge, MA: The MIT Press.

Corcuera, J., Guillaume, F., Leoni, P., & Schoutens, W. (2009). Implied Lévy volatility. *Quantitative Finance*, *9*(4), 383–393.

Cox, J. C., Ingersoll, J. E., & Ross, S. A. (1985). A theory of the term structure of interest rates. *Econometrica*, *53*(2).

De Giovanni, D., Ortobelli, S., & Rachev, S. (2008). Delta hedging strategies comparison. *European Journal of Operational Research*, *185*(3), 1615–1631.

Duan, J. (1995). The GARCH option pricing model. *Mathematical Finance*, *5*(1), 13–32.

Embrechts, P. & Maejima, M. (2002). *Self-similar processes*. Princeton University Press.

Embrechts, P., Lindskog, F., & McNeil, A. (2003). Modelling dependence with copulas and applications to risk management. In S. Rachev (Ed.), *Handbook of heavy-tailed distributions in finance* (pp. 329–384). Amsterdam: Elsevier.

Engle, R. (1982). Autoregressive conditional heteroskedasticity with estimates of the variance of United Kingdom inflation. *Econometrica*, *50*, 987–1007.

Fama, E. (1963a). Mandelbrot and the stable Paretian hypothesis. *Journal of Business*, *36*(4), 420–429.

Fama, E. (1963b). *The distribution of daily differences of stock prices: A test of Mandelbrot's stable Paretian hypothesis*. Ph.D. thesis, Graduate School of Business, University of Chicago.

Glasserman, P. (2004). *Monte Carlo methods in financial engineering*. New York: Springer.

Grabchak, M. & Samorodnitsky, G. (2010). Do financial returns have finite or infinite variance? A paradox and an explanation. *Quantitative Finance*, *10*(8), 883–893.

Harrison, J. M. & Kreps, D. M. (1979). Martingales and arbitrage in multi-period securities markets. *Journal of Economic Theory*, *20*, 381–408.

Harrison, J. M. & Pliska, S. R. (1981). Martingales and stochastic integrals in the theory of continuous trading. *Stochastic Processes and Their Applications*, *11*(3), 215–260.

Heston, S. (1993). A closed form solution for options with stochastic volatility with applications to bond and currency options. *Review of Financial Studies*, *6*, 327–343.

Heston, S. & Nandi, S. (2000). A closed-form GARCH option valuation model. *Review of Financial Studies*, *13*(3), 585–625.

Hoppe, R. (1999). It's time we buried value-at-risk. *Risk Professional*, 14–17.

Hull, J. C. & White, A. (1987). The pricing of options on assets with stochastic volatilities. *Journal of Finance*, *42*, 281–300.

Kim, Y., Rachev, S., Bianchi, M., & Fabozzi, F. (2008). A new tempered stable distribution and its application to finance. In G. Bol, S. T. Rachev, & R. Wuerth

(Eds.), *Risk Assessment: Decisions in Banking and Finance* (pp. 51–84). Heidelberg: Physica Verlag, Springer.

Kim, Y., Rachev, S., Bianchi, M., & Fabozzi, F. (2010). Tempered stable and tempered infinitely divisible GARCH models. *Journal of Banking and Finance*, 34(9), 2096–2109.

Kim, Y., Rachev, S., Chung, D., & Bianchi, M. (2009). The modified tempered stable distribution, GARCH models and option pricing. *Probability and Mathematical Statistics*, 29(1).

Koponen, I. (1995). Analytic approach to the problem of convergence of truncated Lévy flights towards the Gaussian stochastic process. *Physical Review E, 52*.

Mandelbrot, B. (1963). The variation of certain speculative prices. *Journal of Business*, 36, 394–419.

Mandelbrot, B. & Taylor, H. (1967). On the distribution of stock price differences. *Operations Research*, 15(6), 1057–1062.

McNeil, A., Frey, R., & Embrechts, P. (2005). *Quantitative risk management.* Princeton University Press.

Menn, C. & Rachev, S. (2009). Smoothly truncated stable distributions, GARCH-Models, and Option Pricing. *Mathematical Methods of Operations Research*, 63(3), 411–438.

Merton, R. (1974). On the pricing of corporate Debt: The risk structure of interest rates. *Journal of Finance*, 29(2), 449–470.

Mittnik, S., Paolella, M. S., & Rachev, S. T. (1998). A tail estimator for the index of the stable Paretian distribution. *Communications in Statistics: Theory and Methods*, 27, 1239–1262.

Rosiński, J. (2007). Tempering stable processes. *Stochastic Processes and Their Applications*, 117(6), 677–707.

Samorodnitsky, G. & Taqqu, M. (1994). *Stable non-Gaussian random processes: Stochastic models with infinite variance.* Boca Raton, FL: CRC Press.

Samuelson, P. (1965). Proof that properly anticipated prices fluctuate randomly. *Management Review*, 6(2).

Sato, K. (1999). *Lévy processes and infinitely divisible distributions.* Cambridge: Cambridge University Press.

Schoutens, W. (2003). *Lévy processes in finance: Pricing financial derivatives.* West Sussex, England: John Wiley & Sons.

Shiller, R. (1981). Do stock prices move too much to be justified by subsequent changes in dividends? *American Economic Review*, 71(3), 421–436.

Zolotarev, V. (1986). *One-dimensional stable distributions.* Transl. from the Russian by H. H. McFaden, ed. by B. Silver. Translations of Mathematical Monographs, 65. Providence, RI: American Mathematical Society.

CHAPTER 2

Probability Distributions

Will Disney's stock return over the next year exceed 8%? Will 1-month London Interbank Offered Rate (LIBOR) three months from now exceed 4%? Will Walgreen Company default on its debt obligations sometime over the next five years? Disney's stock return over the next year, 1-month LIBOR three months from now, and the default of Walgreen Company on its debt obligations are each variables that exhibit randomness, which is why these variables are referred to as *random variables*.[1] In this chapter, we see how probability distributions are used to describe the potential outcomes of a random variable, the general properties of probability distributions, and the different types of probability distributions.[2] Random variables can be classified as either discrete or continuous.

2.1   BASIC CONCEPTS

An *outcome* for a random variable is the mutually exclusive potential result that can occur. A *sample space* is a set of all possible outcomes. An *event* is a

---

[1]The precise mathematical definition is that a random variable is a measurable function from a probability space into the set of real numbers. In this chapter, the reader will repeatedly be confronted with imprecise definitions. The authors have intentionally chosen this way for a better general understandability and for sake of an intuitive and illustrative description of the main concepts of probability theory. The reader already familiar with these concepts is invited to skip this and some of the following chapters. In order to inform about every occurrence of looseness and lack of mathematical rigor, we have furnished most imprecise definitions with a footnote giving a reference to the exact definition.

[2]For more detailed and/or complementary information, the reader is referred to the textbook by Larsen and Marx (1986) or Shiryaev (1996).

subset of the sample space.[3] For example, consider Disney's stock return over the next year. The sample space contains outcomes ranging from −100% (all the funds invested in Disney's stock will be lost) to an extremely high positive return. The sample space can be partitioned into two subsets: outcomes where the return is less than or equal to 8% and a subset where the return exceeds 8%. Consequently, a return greater than 8% is an event since it is a subset of the sample space. Similarly, 1-month LIBOR three months from now that exceeds 4% is an event.

2.2   DISCRETE PROBABILITY DISTRIBUTIONS

As the name indicates, a *discrete random variable* limits the outcomes where the variable can only take on discrete values. For example, consider the default of a corporation on its debt obligations over the next five years. This random variable has only two possible outcomes: default or nondefault. Hence, it is a discrete random variable. Consider an option contract where for an upfront payment (i.e., the option price) of $50,000, the buyer of the contract receives the following payment from the seller of the option depending on the return on the S&P 500 index:

If S&P 500 return is:	Payment received by option buyer
Less than or equal to zero	$0
Greater than zero but less than 5%	$10,000
Greater than 5% but less than 10%	$20,000
Greater than or equal to 10%	$100,000

In this case, the random variable is a discrete random variable but on the limited number of outcomes.

The probabilistic treatment of discrete random variables is comparatively easy: Once a probability is assigned to all different outcomes, the probability of an arbitrary event can be calculated by simply adding the single probabilities. Imagine that in the above example for the option on the S&P 500 every different payment occurs with the same probability of 25%. Then the probability of losing money by having invested $50,000 to

---

[3]More precisely, only certain subsets of the sample space are called events. In the case where the sample space is represented by a subinterval of the real numbers, the events consist of the so-called "Borel sets." For all practical applications, we can think of Borel sets as containing all subsets of the sample space.

purchase the option is 75%, which is the sum of the probabilities of getting either $0, $10,000, or $20,000 back.

In the following sections, we provide a short introduction to the most important discrete probability distributions: Bernoulli distribution, binomial distribution, and Poisson distribution.[4]

2.2.1 Bernoulli Distribution

We will start the exposition with the *Bernoulli distribution*. A random variable X is said to be *Bernoulli-distributed* with parameter p if it has only two possible outcomes, usually encoded as (which might represent "success" or "default") or (which might represent "failure" or "survival") and if the probability for realizing equals p and the probability for equals $1 - p$.

One classical example for a Bernoulli-distributed random variable occurring in the field of finance is the default event of a company. We observe a company C in a specified time interval I, for example, January 1, 2011, until December 31, 2011. We define

$$X = \begin{cases} 1 & \text{if } C \text{ defaults in } I. \\ 0 & \text{else} \end{cases}$$

The parameter p in this case would be the annualized probability of default of company C.

2.2.2 Binomial Distribution

In practical applications, we usually do not consider only one single company but a portfolio of n companies denoted by $C_1, \ldots, C_n$. Assuming that all n companies have the same annualized probability of default p, this leads to a natural generalization of the Bernoulli distribution, called the binomial distribution. A binomial-distributed random variable Y with parameters n and p is obtained as the sum of n independent[5] and identically Bernoulli-distributed random variables $X_1, \ldots, X_n$. In our example, Y represents the total number of defaults occurring in the year 2011 observed for companies $C_1, \ldots, C_n$. Given the two parameters, the probability of observing

---

[4]A detailed description together with an introduction to several other discrete probability distributions can be found, for example, in the textbook by Johnson et al. (1993).
[5]A definition of what independence means is provided in section 2.6. The reader might think of independence as no-interference between the random variables.

k, $0 \leq k \leq n$ defaults can be explicitly calculated as follows:

$$\mathbf{P}(Y = k) = \binom{n}{k} p^k (1 - p)^{n-k},$$

where

$$\binom{n}{k} = \frac{n!}{(n - k)! k!}.$$

Recall that the factorial of a positive integer n is denoted by $n!$ and is equal to $n(n - 1)(n - 2) \cdots 2 \cdot 1$.

2.2.3   Poisson Distribution

The *Poisson distribution* depends upon only one parameter λ and can be interpreted as an approximation to the binomial distribution. A *Poisson-distributed random variable* is usually used to describe the random number of events occurring over a certain time interval. We used this previously in terms of the number of defaults. One main difference compared to the binomial distribution is that the number of events that might occur is unbounded—at least theoretically. The parameter λ indicates the rate of occurrence of the random events; that is, it tells us how many events occur on average per unit of time.

The probability distribution of a Poisson-distributed random variable N is described by the following equation:

$$\mathbf{P}(N = k) = \frac{\lambda^k}{k!} e^{-\lambda}, \quad k = 0, 1, 2, \ldots,$$

and we denote $N \sim Poiss(\lambda)$. The Poisson distribution occurs in the context of finance as a generic distribution of a stochastic process, called a Poisson process, which we describe in Chapter 4.

2.3   CONTINUOUS PROBABILITY DISTRIBUTIONS

If the random variable can take on any possible value within the range of outcomes, then the probability distribution is said to be a *continuous random variable.*[6] When a random variable is either the price of or the return on a financial asset or an interest rate, the random variable is assumed to be continuous. This means that it is possible to obtain, for example, a price of 95.43231 or 109.34872 and any value in between. In practice, we know that financial assets are not quoted in such a way. Nevertheless, there is no loss in describing the random variable as continuous and in many times treating the return as a continuous random variable means a substantial gain in mathematical tractability and convenience.

For a continuous random variable, the calculation of probabilities works substantially differently from the discrete case. The reason is that if we want to derive the probability that the realization of the random variable lays within some range (i.e., over a subset or subinterval of the sample space), then we cannot proceed in a similar way as in the discrete case: The number of values in an interval is so large, that we cannot just add the probabilities of the single outcomes. The new concept needed will be explained in the next section.

2.3.1 Probability Distribution Function, Probability Density Function, and Cumulative Distribution Function

A *probability distribution function* **P** assigns a probability **P**(*A*) for every event *A*, that is, of realizing a value for the random value in any specified subset *A* of the sample space. For example, a probability distribution function can assign a probability of realizing a monthly return that is negative or the probability of realizing a monthly return that is greater than 0.5% or the probability of realizing a monthly return that is between 0.4% and 1.0%.

To compute the probability, a mathematical function is needed to represent the probability distribution function. There are several possibilities of representing a probability distribution by means of a mathematical function. In the case of a continuous probability distribution, the most popular way is to provide the so-called *probability density function* or simply *density function.*

In general, we denote the density function for the random variable *X* as *f*(*x*). Note that the lowercase *X* is used. This is the convention adopted to denote a particular value for the random variable. The density function

---

[6]More precisely, not every random variable taking its values in a subinterval of the real numbers is continuous. The exact definition requires the existence of a density function such as the one that we will use later in this chapter to calculate probabilities.

of a probability distribution is always non-negative and as its name indicates: Large values for $f(x)$ of the density function at some point x imply a relatively high probability of realizing a value in the neighborhood of x, whereas $f(x) = 0$ for all x in some interval (a, b) implies that the probability for observing a realization in (a, b) is zero.

Figure 2.1 will aid in understanding a continuous probability distribution. The area between an interval on the horizontal axis and the curve is equal to the probability of getting an outcome laying in this specific interval. So, the area under the entire curve is equal to 1 as shown in Figure 2.1(A). In Figure 2.1(B), we see the probability of realizing a return that is less than a. The shaded area is the probability of realizing a return less than or equal to a. In Figure 2.1(C), the shaded area shows the probability of realizing a return between a and b. As probabilities are represented by areas under the density function, it follows that the probability for every single outcome of a continuous random variable always equals zero.

While the shaded areas in Figure 2.1 represent the probabilities associated with realizing a return within the specified range, how does one compute the probability? This is where the tools of calculus are applied. Calculus involves differentiation and integration of a mathematical function. The latter tool is called *integral calculus* and involves computing the area under a curve. Thus the probability that a realization from a random variable is between two real numbers a and b is calculated according to the formula:

$$\mathbf{P}(a \leq X \leq b) = \int_a^b f(x)dx$$

The mathematical function that provides the cumulative probability of a probability distribution, that is, the function that assigns to every real value x the probability of getting an outcome less than or equal to x, is called the *cumulative distribution function* or *cumulative probability function* or simply *cumulative distribution* and is denoted mathematically by $F(x)$. A cumulative distribution function is always non-negative, non-decreasing, and as it represents probabilities it takes only values between zero and one.[7]

The mathematical connection between a probability density function f, a probability distribution $\mathbf{P}$, and a cumulative distribution function F of

---

[7]Negative values would imply negative probabilities. If F decreased, that is, for some $x < y$ we have $F(x) > F(y)$, it would create a contradiction because the probability of getting a value less than or equal to x must be less than or equal to the probability of getting a value less than or equal to y.

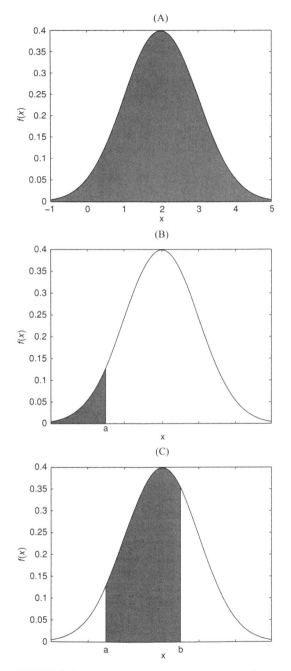

FIGURE 2.1 Probability Density Function of a Two-Dimensional Normal Distribution

some random variable X is given by the following formula:

$$P(X \leq t) = F(t) = \int_{-\infty}^{t} f(x)dx.$$

Conversely, the density equals the first derivative of the distribution function,

$$f(x) = \frac{dF(x)}{dx}.$$

The cumulative distribution function is another way to uniquely characterize an arbitrary probability distribution on the set of real numbers. In terms of the distribution function, the probability that the random variable is between two real numbers a and b is given by

$$P(a \leq X \leq b) = F(b) - F(a).$$

2.3.2   Normal Distribution

The class of *normal distributions*, or *Gaussian distributions*, is certainly one of the most important probability distributions in statistics and, due to some of its appealing properties, also the class that is used in most applications in finance. Here we introduce some of its basic properties.

The random variable X is said to be normally distributed with parameters μ and σ, abbreviated by $X \sim N(\mu, \sigma)$, if the density function of the random variable is given by the formula

$$f(x) = \frac{1}{\sqrt{2\pi\sigma^2}} e^{-\frac{(x-\mu)^2}{2\sigma^2}}, \quad x \in \mathbb{R}.$$

A normal distribution with $\mu = 0$ and $\sigma = 1$ is called a *standard normal distribution*. Notice the following characteristics of the normal distribution. First, the middle of the distribution equals μ. Second, the distribution is symmetric around μ. This second characteristic justifies the name *location parameter* for μ. For small values of σ, the density function becomes more narrow and peaked whereas for larger values of σ the shape of the density widens. These observations lead to the name *shape parameter* or *scale parameter* for σ.

An important property is the so-called *location-scale invariance* of the normal distribution. What does this mean? Imagine you have random variable X, which is normally distributed with the parameters μ and σ. Now we consider the random variable Y, which is obtained as $Y = aX + b$. In general, the distribution of Y might substantially differ from the distribution of X, but in the case where X is normally distributed, the random variable Y is again normally distributed with parameters $\tilde{\mu} = a\mu + b$ and $\tilde{\sigma} = a\sigma$. Thus, we do not leave the class of normal distributions if we multiply the random variable by a factor or shift the random variable. This fact can be used if we change the scale where a random variable is measured: Imagine that X measures the temperature at the top of the Empire State Building on January 1, 2011, at 6 A.M. in degrees Celsius. Then $Y = \frac{9}{5}X + 32$ will give the temperature in degrees Fahrenheit, and if X is normally distributed then Y will be too.

Another interesting and important property of normal distributions is their *summation stability*. If you take the sum of several independent[8] random variables that are all normally distributed with mean μ_i and standard deviation σ_i, then the sum again will be normally distributed. The two parameters of the resulting distribution are obtained as

$$\mu = \mu_1 + \mu_2 + \cdots + \mu_n$$

$$\sigma = \sqrt{\sigma_1^2 + \sigma_2^2 + \cdots + \sigma_n^2}.$$

Why is the summation stability property important for financial applications? Imagine that the daily returns of the S&P 500 are independently normally distributed with $\mu = 0.05\%$ and $\sigma = 1.6\%$. Then the monthly returns again are normally distributed with parameters $\mu = 1.05\%$ and $\sigma = 7.33\%$ (assuming 21 trading days per month), and the yearly return is normally distributed with parameters $\mu = 12.6\%$ and $\sigma = 25.40\%$ (assuming 252 trading days per year). This means that the S&P 500 monthly return fluctuates randomly around 1.05% and the yearly return around 12.6%.

The last important property that is often misinterpreted to justify the nearly exclusive use of normal distributions in financial modeling is the fact that the normal distribution possesses a *domain of attraction*. A mathematical result called the *Central Limit Theorem* states that under certain technical conditions the distribution of a large sum of random variables behaves necessarily like a normal distribution. In the eyes of many, the normal distribution is the unique class of probability distributions having this property. This is wrong and actually it is the class of stable distributions

---

[8]See section 2.6.

(containing the normal distributions), which is unique in the sense that a large sum of random variables can only converge to a stable distribution. We discuss the stable distribution in Chapter 3.

2.3.3 Exponential Distribution

The *exponential distribution* is popular when we want to model the waiting time until a certain event takes place in queuing theory. Examples include the time until the next customer enters the store, the time until a certain company defaults, or the time until a message arriving in my e-mail account.

As it is used to model waiting times, the exponential distribution is defined only in the positive real numbers. Its density function f and cumulative distribution function F possess the following form:

$$f(x) = \lambda e^{-\lambda x}, \quad x > 0$$

$$F(x) = 1 - e^{-\lambda x}, \quad x > 0.$$

When a random variable X follows the gamma distribution with parameter λ, we denote it by $X \sim Exp(\lambda)$.

An interesting fact linked to the exponential distribution is the following connection with the Poisson distribution described earlier. Consider a sequence of independent and identical exponentially distributed random variables $\tau_1, \tau_2, \ldots$ We can think of τ_1, for example, as the time we have to wait until a firm in a high-yield bond portfolio defaults. τ_2 will then represent the time between the first and the second default and so on. These waiting times are sometimes called *inter arrival times*. Now, let N_t denote the number of defaults that have occurred until time $t \geq 0$. One important probabilistic result states that the random variable N_t is Poisson distributed with parameter λt.

2.3.4 Gamma Distribution

The family of *gamma distributions* with parameters (c, λ) forms a two parameter probability distribution family with the following density function:

$$f(x) = \frac{\lambda}{\Gamma(c)} e^{-\lambda x} (\lambda x)^{c-1}, \quad x > 0,$$

where Γ denotes the gamma function.[9] When a random variable X follows the gamma distribution with parameter (c, λ), we denote $X \sim Gamma(c, \lambda)$ For $c = 1$ we obtain the exponential distribution.

2.3.5 Variance Gamma Distribution

Let a random variable X be a random variable defined by

$$X = G_+ - G_-,$$

where $G_+ \sim Gamma(C, \lambda_+)$, $G_- \sim Gamma(C, \lambda_-)$, and G_+ and G_- are independent. Then then the distribution of X is referred to as the *variance gamma distribution*[10] with parameters $(C, \lambda_+, \lambda_-)$, and we denote $X \sim VG(C, \lambda_+, \lambda_-)$. The probability density function of the VG distribution is given by

$$f(x) = \frac{1}{\Gamma(C)} \left(\frac{\lambda_+ \lambda_-}{\lambda_+ + \lambda_-} \right)^C |x|^{C-\frac{1}{2}} e^{-\frac{x}{2}(\lambda_+ + \lambda_-)} \sqrt{\frac{\lambda_+ + \lambda_-}{\pi}} K_{C-\frac{1}{2}} \left(\frac{|x|}{2}(\lambda_+ + \lambda_-) \right)$$

---

[9] The *gamma function* is defined as

$$\Gamma(x) = \lim_{n \to \infty} \frac{n! n^x}{x(x + 1)(x + 2) \cdots (x + n)}.$$

We briefly present four basic properties of the gamma function:

- $\Gamma(x + 1) = x\Gamma(x)$ (the recurrence formula).
- $\Gamma(1) = 1$ and $\Gamma(n + 1) = n!$, $n = 0, 1, 2, \ldots$.
- $\Gamma\left(\frac{1}{2}\right) = \sqrt{\pi}$ and $\Gamma\left(n + \frac{1}{2}\right) = \frac{(2n)!}{2^{2n} n!} \sqrt{\pi}$, $n = 0, 1, 2, \ldots$.

If x is positive, then the integral representation of the gamma function is more useful:

$$\Gamma(x) = \int_0^\infty e^{-t} t^{x-1} dx, \quad x > 0.$$

[10]The class of VG distribution has been used for financial modeling by Madan and Seneta (1990) and Madan et al. (1998).

for real $x \neq 0$, where $K_\nu(x)$ is the modified Bessel function of the second kind.[11]

2.3.6 Inverse Gaussian Distribution

The family of *inverse Gaussian* (IG) *distributions* with parameters (c, λ) forms a two parameter probability distribution family with the following density function:

$$f(x) = \frac{c}{\sqrt{2\pi} x^{\frac{3}{2}}} e^{-\frac{(c-\lambda x)^2}{2x}}, \quad x > 0, .$$

When a random variable X follows the inverse Gaussian distribution with parameter (c, λ), we denote $X \sim IG(c, \lambda)$. The inverse Gaussian distribution developed to model the first hitting time that a Brownian motion[12] reaches a boundary.

2.4   STATISTIC MOMENTS AND QUANTILES

In describing a probability distribution function, it is common to summarize it by using various measures. The five most commonly used measures are:

- Location
- Dispersion
- Asymmetry
- Concentration in tails
- Quantiles

---

[11]The *modified Bessel function of the second kind* is defined that

$$K_p(x) = \frac{\pi}{2 \sin p\pi} \left(\sum_{k=0}^{\infty} \frac{(x/2)^{2k-p}}{k!\Gamma(k-p+1)} - \sum_{k=0}^{\infty} \frac{(x/2)^{2k+p}}{k!\Gamma(k+p+1)} \right).$$

The integral representation of the function is more useful:

$$K_p(x) = \frac{1}{2} \left(\frac{x}{2} \right)^p \int_0^{\infty} e^{-t-\frac{x^2}{4t}} t^{-p-1} \, dt.$$

See Andrews (1998) for details.
[12]See Chapter 4 for a discussion of Brownian motion.

In this section, we describe these measures and the more general notion of statistical moments. We also explain how statistical moments are estimated from real data.

2.4.1 Location

The first way to describe a probability distribution function is by some measure of *central value* or *location*. The various measures that can be used are the mean or average value, the median, or the mode. The relationship among these three measures of location depends on the skewness of a probability distribution function that we describe later. The most commonly used measure of location is the *mean* and is denoted by μ or EX or $E[X]$.

2.4.2 Dispersion

Another measure that can help us to describe a probability distribution function is the dispersion, or how spread out are the values which that random variable can realize. Various measures of dispersion are the range, variance, and mean absolute deviation. The most commonly used measure is the *variance*. It measures the dispersion of the values that the random variable can realize relative to the mean. It is the average of the squared deviations from the mean. The variance is in squared units. Taking the square root of the variance, one obtains the *standard deviation*. In contrast to the variance, the *mean absolute deviation* takes the average of the absolute deviations from the mean.[13] In practice, the variance is used and is denoted by σ^2 or $VarX$ or $Var(X)$ and the standard deviation by σ or $\sqrt{VarX}$.

2.4.3 Asymmetry

A probability distribution may be symmetric or asymmetric around its mean. A popular measure for the asymmetry of a distribution is called its *skewness*. A *negative skewness* measure indicates that the distribution is skewed to the left; that is, compared to the right tail, the left tail is elongated (see Figure 2.2). A *positive skewness* measure indicates that the distribution is skewed to the right; that is, compared to the left tail, the right tail is elongated (see Figure 2.2).

---

[13]It is also common to define the mean absolute deviation from the median because it minimizes the average absolute distance from an arbitrary point x.

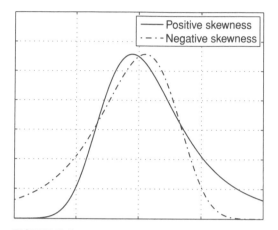

FIGURE 2.2   Density Graphs of a Positively and Negatively Skewed Distribution

2.4.4   Concentration in Tails

Additional information about a probability distribution function is provided by measuring the concentration (mass) of potential outcomes in its tails. The tails of a probability distribution function contain the extreme values. In financial applications, it is these tails that provide information about the potential for a financial fiasco or financial ruin. As we will see, the fatness of the tails of the distribution is related to the peakedness of the distribution around its mean or center. The joint measure of peakedness and tail fatness is called *kurtosis*.

2.4.5   Statistical Moments

In the parlance of the statistician, the four measures described above are called *statistical moments* or simply *moments*. The mean is the *first moment* and is also referred to as the *expected value*. The variance is the *second central moment*, skewness is a rescaled *third central moment*, and kurtosis is a rescaled *fourth central moment*. The general mathematical formulas for the calculation of the four moments is shown in Table 2.1.

The definition of skewness and kurtosis is not as unified as for the mean and the variance. The skewness measure reported in Table 2.1 is the so-called *Fisher's skewness*. Another possible way to define the measure is the *Pearson's skewness*, which equals the square of the Fisher's skewness. The same holds true for the kurtosis, where we have reported the *Pearson's kurtosis*

TABLE 2.1 General Formula for Parameters

Parameter	Discrete Probability Distribution	Continuous Probability Distribution
Mean	$EX = \sum_k x_k P(X = x_k)$	$EX = \int_{-\infty}^{\infty} x f(x) dx$
Variance	$\text{Var} X = \sum_k (x_k - EX)^2 P(X = x_k)$	$\text{Var} X = \int_{-\infty}^{\infty} (x - EX)^2 f(x) dx$
Skewness	$\zeta(X) = \dfrac{E[(X - EX)^3]}{(\text{Var} X)^{\frac{3}{2}}}$	
Kurtosis	$\kappa(X) = \dfrac{E[(X - EX)^4]}{(\text{Var} X)^2}$	

in Table 2.1. *Fisher's kurtosis* (sometimes denoted as *excess kurtosis*) can be obtained by subtracting three from Pearson's kurtosis.

Generally, expectation of a function $g(X)$ of a random variable X is computed by

$$E[g(X)] = \int_{-\infty}^{\infty} g(x) f(x) dx,$$

for a continuous probability distribution. In the case of a discrete probability distribution, the formula is

$$E[g(X)] = \sum_k g(x_k) P(X = x_k).$$

If we consider $g(X) = X^n$ for a positive integer n, we obtain the nth *raw moments* or *raw moments of order n* of random variable X, which denoted by $m_n(X)$ as

$$m_n(X) = EX^n,$$

where $n = 1, 2, \ldots$.

Using the same method, we can define the nth central moment is denoted by $\mu_n(X)$, defined as

$$\mu_n(X) = E[(X - EX)^n],$$

where $n = 1, 2, \ldots$. Therefore, the variance, skewness, and kurtosis can be obtained by:

$$\text{Var}(X) = \mu_2(X), \quad \zeta(X) = \frac{\mu_3(X)}{\mu_2(X)^{\frac{3}{2}}}, \quad \kappa(X) = \frac{\mu_4(X)}{\mu_2(X)^2}.$$

In Table 2.2, we present the expressions of the mean, variance, skewness, and excess kurtosis for some common discrete and continuous distribution functions.

2.4.6 Quantiles

Sometimes in addition to the four statistical moments described above, used to summarize a probability distribution, there is a concept called the α-quantile. The α-quantile gives us information about where the first $\alpha\%$ of the distribution is located. Given an arbitrary observation of the considered probability distribution, this observation will be smaller than the α-quantile q_α in $\alpha\%$ of the cases and larger in $(100 - \alpha)\%$ of the cases.[14] For example,

TABLE 2.2 Statistical Moments

Distribution	Mean	Variance	Skewness	Excess Kurtosis
Bernoulli	p	$p(1-p)$	$\dfrac{1-2p}{\sqrt{p(1-p)}}$	$\dfrac{1-6p(1-p)}{p(1-p)}$
Binomial	np	$np(1-p)$	$\dfrac{1-2p}{\sqrt{np(1-p)}}$	$\dfrac{1-6p(1-p)}{np(1-p)}$
Poisson	λ	λ	$\lambda^{-\frac{1}{2}}$	λ^{-1}
Normal	μ	σ^2	0	0
Gamma	$\dfrac{c}{\lambda}$	$\dfrac{c}{\lambda^2}$	$\dfrac{2}{\sqrt{c}}$	$\dfrac{6}{c}$
VG	$\dfrac{C(\lambda_- - \lambda_+)}{\lambda_+ \lambda_-}$	$\dfrac{C(\lambda_+^2 + \lambda_-^2)}{(\lambda_+ \lambda_-)^2}$	$\dfrac{2\left(\lambda_+^{-3} - \lambda_-^{-3}\right)}{C^{\frac{1}{2}}\left(\lambda_+^{-2} + \lambda_-^{-2}\right)^{\frac{3}{2}}}$	$\dfrac{6\left(\lambda_+^{-4} + \lambda_-^{-4}\right)}{C\left(\lambda_+^{-2} + \lambda_-^{-2}\right)^2}$
IG	$\dfrac{c}{\lambda}$	$\dfrac{c}{\lambda^3}$	$\dfrac{3}{\sqrt{c\lambda}}$	$\dfrac{15}{c\lambda}$

---

[14]Formally, the α-quantile for a continuous probability distribution **P** with strictly increasing cumulative distribution function F is obtained as $q_\alpha = F^{-1}(\alpha)$.

earlier we found that for the normal distribution with mean 7% and standard deviation 2.6%, the value 0% represents the 0.35% quantile.

Some quantiles have special names. The 25%, 50%, and 75% quantile are referred to as the first quartile, second quartile, and third quartile, respectively. The 1%-, 2%-, . . . , 98%, 99% quantiles are called *percentiles*.

2.4.7 Sample Moments

In the previous section, we introduced the four statistical moments: mean, variance, skewness, and kurtosis. Given a probability density function for a probability distribution **P**, we are able to calculate these statistical moments according to the formulae given in Table 2.1. In practical applications, however, we are faced with the situation that we observe realizations of a probability distribution (e.g., the daily return of the S&P 500 index over the last two years), but we do not know the distribution that generates these returns. Consequently, we are not able to apply our knowledge about the calculation of statistical moments. But, having the observations $x_1, \ldots, x_n$, we can try to estimate the "true moments" out of the sample. The estimates are sometimes called *sample moments* to stress the fact that they are obtained out of a sample of observations.

The idea is quite simple: The empirical analogue for the mean of a random variable is the average of the observations:

$$EX \approx \frac{1}{n} \sum_{k=1}^{n} x_k$$

For large n it is reasonable to expect that the average of the observations will not be far from the mean of the probability distribution. Now, we observe that all theoretical formulas for the calculation of the four statistical moments are expressed as "means of something." This insight leads to the expression for the sample moments, summarized in Table 2.3.[15]

2.5 CHARACTERISTIC FUNCTION

Every distribution can be uniquely described by its *characteristic function*. While the density of a distribution may not always exist in a closed form, the

---

[15]A "hat" on a parameter (like $\hat{\kappa}$) symbolizes the fact that the true parameter (in this case the kurtosis κ) is estimated.

TABLE 2.3 Calculation of Sample Moments

Moment	Sample Moment
Mean	$\bar{x} = \dfrac{1}{n} \sum_{k=1}^{n} x_k$
Variance	$s^2 = \dfrac{1}{n} \sum_{k=1}^{n} (x_k - \bar{x})^2$
Skewness	$\hat{\zeta} = \dfrac{\frac{1}{n} \sum_{k=1}^{n} (x_k - \bar{x})^3}{(s^2)^{\frac{3}{2}}}$
Kurtosis	$\hat{\kappa} = \dfrac{\frac{1}{n} \sum_{k=1}^{n} (x_k - \bar{x})^4}{(s^2)^2}$

characteristic function always exists and completely determines the distribution. Therefore, important properties of a random variable may be deducted from the behavior of its characteristic function. In Table 2.4, we present the expressions of the characteristic functions for some common discrete and continuous distribution functions.

A characteristic function is the function that performs a mapping from the real plane to the complex plane: $\phi : \mathbb{R} \to \mathbb{C}$. A characteristic function of the distribution function $F(x)$ around a particular point u ($-\infty < u < \infty$)

TABLE 2.4 Characteristic Functions

Distribution	Characteristic Function
Bernoulli	$1 - p + pe^{iu}$
Binomial	$(1 - p + pe^{iu})^n$
Poisson	$\exp\left(\lambda(e^{iu} - 1)\right)$
Normal	$\exp\left(i\mu u - \dfrac{u^2 \sigma^2}{2}\right)$
Gamma	$\left(\dfrac{\lambda}{\lambda - iu}\right)^c$
VG	$\left(\dfrac{\lambda_+ \lambda_-}{(\lambda_+ - iu)(\lambda_- + iu)}\right)^C$
IG	$\exp\left(-c(\sqrt{\lambda^2 - 2iu} - \lambda)\right)$

for a random variable X is the expectation of a transformed variable e^{iuX}, in which i is the complex number $\sqrt{-1}$:

$$\phi(u) = E\left[e^{iuX}\right] = \int_{-\infty}^{\infty} e^{iux} dF(x).$$

If X is a continuous random variable with density $f(x)$, then

$$\phi(u) = \int_{-\infty}^{\infty} e^{iux} f(x) dx,$$

and if X is discrete with probability mass function $p_n = P(X = x_n)$, $n = 1, 2, \ldots, \sum_{n=1}^{\infty} p_n = 1$, then

$$\phi(u) = \sum_{n=1}^{\infty} e^{iux} p_n.$$

Useful properties of characteristic functions can be found in standard textbooks on probability.[16] We present several properties that are important in practical applications.

- Denote $\phi^{(n)}(0)$ the nth derivative of the characteristic function evaluated around zero. Then, if $E[X^n] < \infty$, the nth raw moment of X can be obtained by

$$E[X^n] = \frac{\phi^{(n)}(0)}{i^n}.$$

- The exponential part of a characteristic function is referred to as the *characteristic exponent* and is denoted by $\psi(u)$. Characteristic exponents are obtained by taking the logarithm of the corresponding characteristic functions, that is,

$$\psi(u) = \log \phi(u).$$

- Let $\psi(u)$ be the characteristic exponent of X, that is, $\psi(u) = \log \phi(u)$, and denote by $\psi^{(n)}(0)$ the nth derivative of $\psi(u)$ evaluated around zero.

---

[16]See, for example, Grimmett and Stirzaker (2001) and Ushakov (1999).

Then, if $E[X^n] < \infty$, the nth *cumulant* of X is defined by

$$c_n(X) = \frac{\psi^{(n)}(0)}{i^n}.$$

The function $\psi(u)$ is called the *characteristic exponent* or the *log characteristic function*. The cumulant can be represented by raw moments and central moments. For example, we have

$$c_1(X) = E[X]$$

$$c_2(X) = E[X^2] - (E[X])^2 = E[(X - E[X])^2] = \text{Var}(X)$$

$$c_3(X) = E[X^3] - 3E[X^2]E[X] + 2(E[X])^3 = E[(X - E[X])^3]$$

$$c_4(X) = E[X^4] - 3(c_2(X))^2.$$

Hence we obtain skewness and kurtosis as

$$\zeta(X) = \frac{c_3(X)}{(c_2(X))^{\frac{3}{2}}}, \qquad \kappa(X) = \frac{c_4(X)}{(c_2(X))^2} + 3.$$

The excess kurtosis is equal to $c_4(X)/(c_2(X))^2$.

- If X and Y are independent random variables with corresponding characteristic functions $\phi_X(u)$ and $\phi_Y(u)$, then the characteristic function of $X + Y$ is

$$\phi_{X+Y}(u) = \phi_X(u)\phi_Y(u).$$

More generally, if $X_1, X_2, \ldots, X_n$ are independent and $X = \sum_{k=1}^{n} X_k$ then

$$\phi_X(u) = \prod_{k=1}^{n} \phi_{X_k}(u).$$

- X and Y are independent if and only if the joint characteristic function is of the following form:

$$\phi_{X,Y}(u, v) = \phi_X(u)\phi_Y(v).$$

- If a and b are real constants and $Y = aX + b$, then

$$\phi_Y(u) = e^{iub}\phi_X(u).$$

As stated earlier, there is a one-to-one correspondence between the distribution function and the characteristic function. The following relation[17] allows one to recover the density function from the characteristic function:

$$f(x) = \frac{1}{2\pi} \int_{-\infty}^{\infty} e^{-iux}\phi(u)du.$$

2.6 JOINT PROBABILITY DISTRIBUTIONS

In the previous sections we explained the properties of a probability distribution of a single random variable (i.e., the properties of a univariate distribution). An understanding of univariate distributions allows us to analyze the time-series characteristics of individual assets. In this section, we move from the probability distribution of a single random variable (*univariate distribution*) to that of multiple random variables (*multivariate distribution*). Understanding multivariate distributions is important because financial theories such as portfolio selection theory and asset-pricing theory involve distributional properties of sets of investment opportunities (i.e., multiple random variables). For example, Markowitz portfolio theory assumes that returns of alternative investments have a joint multivariate distribution whose relevant properties are described by certain parameters.

To explain multivariate distributions, we first introduce the concepts of joint probability distribution, marginal probability distribution, and correlation and covariance. We also discuss the multivariate normal distribution and a special class of distributions that have been used in the theory of finance, the family of elliptical distributions.

2.6.1 Conditional Probability

A useful concept in understanding the relationship between multiple random variables is that of *conditional probability*. Consider the returns on the stocks of two companies in the same industry. The future return X on the stocks of company 1 is not unrelated to the future return Y on the stocks of company 2 because the future economic prospects of the two companies is

---

[17]This relation follows from the Fourier inversion theorem.

driven to some extent by common factors since they are in the same industry. It is a reasonable question to ask what is the probability that the future return X is smaller than a given percentage, for example, $X \leq -2\%$, on condition that Y realizes a huge loss, for example, $Y \leq -10\%$? Essentially, the conditional probability involves calculating the probability of an event provided that another event happens. If we denote the first event by A and the second event by B, then the conditional probability of A provided that B happens, denoted by $\mathbf{P}(A|B)$, is given by the formula,

$$\mathbf{P}(A|B) = \frac{\mathbf{P}(A \cap B)}{\mathbf{P}(B)},$$

which is also known as the *Bayes formula*. According to the formula, we divide the probability that both events A and B occur simultaneously, denoted by $A \cap B$, by the probability of the event B. In the two-stock example, the formula is applied in the following way:

$$\mathbf{P}(X \leq -2\%|Y \leq -10\%) = \frac{\mathbf{P}(X \leq -2\%, Y \leq -10\%)}{\mathbf{P}(Y \leq -10\%)}. \qquad (2.1)$$

Thus, in order to compute the conditional probability, we have to be able to calculate the quantity

$$\mathbf{P}(X \leq -2\%, Y \leq -10\%),$$

which represents the joint probability of the two events.

2.6.2   Joint Probability Distribution Defined

A portfolio or a trading position consists of a collection of financial assets. Thus, portfolio managers and traders are interested in the return on a portfolio or a trading position. Consequently, in real-world applications, the interest is in the *joint probability distribution* or joint distribution of more than one random variable. For example, suppose that a trading position consists of two assets, asset 1 and asset 2. Then there will be a probability distribution for the (1) return of asset 1, (2) return of asset 2, and (3) return of asset 1 and asset 2. The first two distributions are referred to as the *marginal probability distributions* or *marginal distributions*. The distribution for asset 1 and asset 2 is the joint probability distribution.

As in the univariate case, there is a mathematical connection between the probability distribution $\mathbf{P}$, the cumulative distribution function F, and the density function f of a multivariate random variable $X = (X_1, \ldots, X_d)$.

The formula looks similar to the equation we presented in section 2.3.1 showing the mathematical connection between a probability density function, a probability distribution, and a cumulative distribution function of some random variable X:

$$P(X_1 \leq t_1, \ldots, X_d \leq t_d) = F(t_1, \ldots, t_d)$$

$$= \int_{-\infty}^{t_1} \cdots \int_{-\infty}^{t_d} f(x_1, \ldots, x_d)dx_1 \cdots dx_d.$$

The formula can be interpreted as follows: The joint probability that the first random variable realizes a value less than or equal to t_1 and the second less than or equal to t_2 and so on is given by the cumulative distribution function F. The value can be obtained by calculating "the volume" under the density function f. Because there are d random variables, we have now d arguments for both functions: the density function and the cumulative distribution function.

It is also possible to express the density function in terms of the distribution function by computing sequentially the first-order partial derivatives of the distribution function with respect to all variables:

$$f(x_1, \ldots, x_n) = \frac{\partial^n F(x_1, \ldots, x_n)}{\partial x_1 \ldots \partial x_n}. \tag{2.2}$$

2.6.3 Marginal Distribution

In addition to this joint distribution, we can consider the above-mentioned marginal distributions, that is, the distribution of one single random variable X_i. The marginal density f_i of X_i is obtained by integrating the joint density over all variables that are not taken into consideration:

$$f_i(x) = \int_{-\infty}^{\infty} \cdots \int_{-\infty}^{\infty} f(x_1, \ldots, x_{i-1}, x, x_{i+1}, \ldots, x_d)dx_1 \cdots dx_{i-1}dx_{i+1} \cdots dx_d$$

2.6.4 Dependence of Random Variables

Typically, when considering multivariate distributions we are faced with inference between the distributions; that is, large values of one random variable imply large values of another random variable or small values of a third random variable. If we are considering, for example, X_1 the height of a randomly chosen individual and X_2 the weight of this individual, then large values of X_1 tend to result in large values of X_2. This property is referred to as the *dependence of random variables*; a powerful concept to measure dependence will be introduced in a later section where we discuss copulas.

The inverse case of no dependence is denoted as stochastic independence. More precisely, two random variables are *independently distributed* if and only if their joint distribution given in terms of the joint cumulative distribution function F or the joint density function f equals the product of their marginal distribution. That is,

$$F(x_1, \ldots, x_d) = F_1(x_1) \cdots F_d(x_d)$$

or

$$f(x_1, \ldots, x_d) = f_1(x_1) \cdots f_d(x_d).$$

In the special case of $d = 2$, we can say that two random variables are said to be independently distributed if knowing the value of one random variable does not provide any information about the other random variable. For instance, if we assume in the example developed in section 2.6.1 that the two events $X \leq -2\%$ and $Y \leq -10\%$ are independent, then the conditional probability in equation (2.1) equals

$$P(X \leq -2\% | Y \leq -10\%) = \frac{P(X \leq -2\%)P(Y \leq -10\%)}{P(Y \leq -10\%)}$$

$$= P(X \leq -2\%).$$

Indeed, under the assumption of independence, the event $Y \leq -10\%$ has no influence on the probability of the other event.

2.6.5 Covariance and Correlation

There are two strongly related measures among many that are commonly used to measure how two random variables tend to move together: the covariance and the correlation. Letting:

σ_X = standard deviation for X

σ_Y = standard deviation for Y

$\sigma_{X,Y}$ = covariance between X and Y

$\rho_{X,Y}$ = correlation between X and Y

The relationship between the correlation and covariance is as follows:

$$\rho_{X,Y} = \frac{\sigma_{X,Y}}{\sigma_X \sigma_Y},$$

or

$$\sigma_{X,Y} = \rho_{X,Y} \sigma_X \sigma_Y.$$

Here the *covariance*, also denoted by $\sigma_{X,Y} = \text{cov}(X, Y)$, is defined as

$$\sigma_{X,Y} = E[(X - EX)(Y - EY)]$$
$$= E[XY] - EX \cdot EY.$$

It can be shown that the correlation can only have values from -1 to $+1$. When the correlation is zero, the two random variables are said to be *uncorrelated*.

If we add two random variables, $X + Y$, the expected value (first central moment) is simply the sum of the expected value of the two random variables. That is,

$$E[X + Y] = EX + EY.$$

The variance of the sum of two random variables, denoted by σ_{X+Y}^2, is

$$\sigma_{X+Y}^2 = \sigma_X^2 + \sigma_Y^2 + 2\sigma_{X,Y}$$

Here the last term accounts for the fact that there might be a dependence between X and Y measured through the covariance.

2.6.6 Multivariate Normal Distribution

In finance, it is common to assume that the random variables are normally distributed. The joint distribution is then referred to as a *multivariate normal distribution*.[18] We provide an explicit representation of the density function of a general multivariate normal distribution.

---

[18]More precisely, the joint distribution of a random vector $X = (X_1, \ldots, X_n)$ is called a multivariate normal distribution if any linear combination $a_1 X_1 + \ldots + a_n X_n$ of its components is normally distributed. It is not sufficient that only the marginals are normally distributed.

Consider first n independent standard normal random variables $X_1, \ldots, X_n$. Their common density function can be written as the product of their individual density functions and so we obtain the following expression as the density function of the random vector $X = X_1, \ldots, X_n$:

$$f_X(x_1, \ldots, x_n) = \frac{1}{(\sqrt{2\pi})^n} e^{-\frac{x'x}{2}},$$

where the vector notation $x'x$ denotes the sum of the components of the vector x raised to the second power, $x'x = \sum_{i=1}^{n} x_i^2$.

Now consider n vectors with n real components arranged in a matrix A. In this case, it is often said that the matrix A has a $n \times n$ dimension. The random variable

$$Y = AX + \mu, \tag{2.3}$$

in which AX denotes the $n \times n$ matrix A multiplied by the random vector X and μ is a vector of n constants, has a general multivariate normal distribution. The density function of Y can now be expressed as[19]

$$f_Y(y_1, \ldots, y_n) = \frac{1}{(\pi|\Sigma|)^{n/2}} e^{-\frac{(y-\mu)'\Sigma^{-1}(y-\mu)}{2}},$$

where $|\Sigma|$ denotes the determinant of the matrix Σ and Σ^{-1} denotes the inverse of Σ. The matrix Σ can be calculated from the matrix A, $\Sigma = AA'$. The elements of $\Sigma = \{\sigma_{ij}\}_{i,j=1}^{n}$ are the covariances between the components of the vector Y:

$$\sigma_{ij} = \text{cov}(Y_i, Y_j).$$

Figure 2.3 contains a plot of the probability density function of a two-dimensional normal distribution with a covariance matrix,

$$\Sigma = \begin{pmatrix} 1 & 0.8 \\ 0.8 & 1 \end{pmatrix}$$

---

[19]In order for the density function to exist, the joint distribution of Y must be nondegenerate (i.e., the matrix Σ must be positive definite).

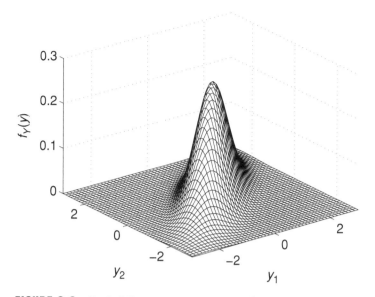

FIGURE 2.3 Probability Density Function of a Two-Dimensional Normal Distribution

and mean $\mu = (0, 0)$. The matrix A from the representation given in formula (2.3) equals

$$A = \begin{pmatrix} 1 & 0 \\ 0.8 & 0.6 \end{pmatrix}.$$

The correlation between the two components of the random vector Y is equal to 0.8 $\text{corr}(Y_1, Y_2) = 0.8$ because in this example the variances of the two components are equal to 1. This is a strong positive correlation that means that the realizations of the random vector Y will cluster along the diagonal splitting the first and the third quadrant. This is illustrated in Figure 2.4, which shows the contour lines of the two-dimensional density function plotted in Figure 2.3. The contour lines are ellipses centered at the mean $\mu = (0, 0)$ of the random vector Y with their major axes lying along the diagonal of the first quadrant. The contour lines indicate that realizations of the random vector Y roughly take the form of an elongated ellipse like the ones shown in Figure 2.4, which means that large values of Y_1 will correspond to large values of Y_2 in a given pair of observations.

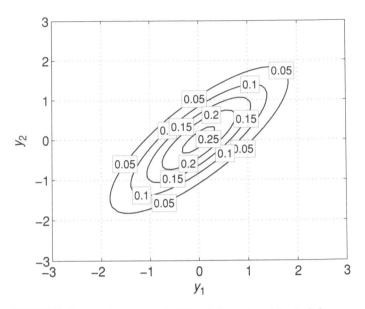

FIGURE 2.4   Level Lines of the Two-Dimensional Probability Density Function Plotted in Figure 2.3

2.6.7   Elliptical Distributions

A generalization of the multivariate normal distribution is given by the class of *elliptical distributions*.[20] We discuss this class because elliptical distributions offer desirable properties in the context of portfolio selection theory. It turns out that in fact it is the class of elliptical distributions where the correlation is the right dependence measure, and that for distributions that do not belong to this family, alternative concepts must be sought.

Simply speaking, a *n*-dimensional random vector X with density function f is called *spherically distributed* if all the level curves,[21] that is, the set of all points where the density function f admits a certain value c, possesses the form of a sphere. In the special case when $n = 2$, the density function can be plotted and the level curves look like circles. Analogously, a

---

[20]This section provides only a brief review of elliptical distributions. Bradley and Taqqu (2003) provide a more complete introduction to elliptical distributions and their implications for portfolio selection.
[21]The reader interested in outdoor activities like hiking or climbing as well as people interested in geography might know the concept of level curves from their hiking maps, where the mountains are visualized by their iso-level lines.

n-dimensional random vector X with density function f is called elliptically distributed if the form of all level curves equals the one of an ellipse.

One can think of elliptical distributions as a special class of symmetric distributions that possess a number of desirable properties. Examples of elliptically distributed random variables include all multivariate normal distributions, multivariate *t*-distributions, logistic distributions, Lapace distributions, and a part of the multivariate stable distributions.[22] Elliptical distributions with existing density function can be described by a triple (μ, Σ, g),[23] where μ and Σ play similar roles as the mean vector and the variance-covariance matrix in the multivariate normal setting. The function g is the so-called *density generator*. All three together define the density function of the distribution as

$$f_X(x) = \frac{c}{\sqrt{|\Sigma|}} g((x - \mu)' \Sigma^{-1} (x - \mu)),$$

where c is a normalizing constant. Compare the similarity between this expression and the density function of a multivariate normal distribution.

2.6.8 Copula Functions

Correlation is a widespread concept in modern finance and risk management and stands for a measure of dependence between random variables. However, this term is very often incorrectly used to mean any notion of dependence. Actually correlation is one particular measure of dependence among many. In the world of multivariate normal distribution and, more generally in the world of spherical and elliptical distributions, it is the accepted measure.

A major drawback of correlation is that it is not invariant under nonlinear strictly increasing transformations. In general

$$\text{corr}(T(X), T(Y)) \neq \text{corr}(X, Y),$$

where $T(x)$ is such transformation.

One example that explains this technical requirement is the following: Assume that X and Y represent the continuous return (log-return) of two

---

[22]For a thorough introduction to the class of elliptical distribution, see Fang et al. (1990).
[23]A "triple" or a "3-tuple" is simply the notation used by mathematicians for a group of three elements.

assets over the period $[0, t]$, where t denotes some point of time in the future. If you know the correlation of these two random variables, this does not imply that you know the dependence structure between the asset prices itself because the asset prices (P and Q for asset X and Y, respectively) are obtained by $P_t = P_0 \exp(X)$ and $Q_t = Q_0 \exp(Y)$, where P_0 and Q_0 denote the corresponding asset prices at time 0. The asset prices are strictly increasing functions of the return but the correlation structure is not maintained by this transformation. This observation implies that the return could be uncorrelated whereas the prices are strongly correlated and vice versa.

A more prevalent approach that overcomes this disadvantage is to model dependency using copulas.[24] As noted by Patton (2004), *copula* comes from Latin for a "link" or "bond." Sklar (1959), who coined the term copula, proved the theorem that a collection of marginal distributions can be "coupled" together by using a copula to form a multivariate distribution. The idea is as follows. The description of the joint distribution of a random vector is divided into two parts:

1. The specification of the marginal distributions.
2. The specification of the dependence structure by means of a special function, called a *copula*.

The use of copulas[25] offers the following advantages:

- The nature of dependency that can be modeled is more general. In comparison, only linear dependence can be explained by the correlation.
- Dependence of extreme events might be modeled.
- Copulas are indifferent to continuously increasing transformations (not only linear as it is true for correlations).

From a mathematical viewpoint, a copula function C is nothing more than a probability distribution function on the n-dimensional hypercube $I_n = [0, 1] \times [0, 1] \times \ldots \times [0, 1]$:

$$C : I_d \to [0, 1]$$

$$(u_1, \ldots, u_n) \to C(u_1, \ldots, u_n)$$

---

[24]For a discussion of applications in finance and insurance, see Embrechts et al. (2002) and Patton (2003a, 2003b, 2004).
[25]Mikosch (2006), Embrechts and Puccetti (2006), and Rüschendorf (2004) provide examples and further references for the application of copulas in risk management.

It has been shown[26] that any multivariate probability distribution function F_Y of some random vector $Y = (Y_1, \ldots, Y_n)$ can be represented with the help of a copula function C in the following form:

$$F_Y(y_1, \ldots, y_n) = \mathbf{P}(Y_1 \leq y_1, \ldots, Y_n \leq y_n) = C(\mathbf{P}(Y_1 \leq y_1), \ldots, \mathbf{P}(Y_n \leq y_n))$$

$$= C(F_{Y_1}(y_1), \ldots, F_{Y_n}(y_n)),$$

where $F_{Y_i}(y_i)$, $i = 1, \ldots, n$ denote the marginal distribution functions of the random variables Y_i, $i = 1, \ldots, n$.

The copula function provides the bridge between the univariate distribution of the individual random variables and their joint probability distribution. This justifies the fact that the copula function creates uniquely the dependence whereas the probability distribution of the random variables involved is provided by their marginal distribution. By fixing the marginal distributions and varying the copula function, we obtain all possible joint distributions with the given marginals.

We present some examples of copulas for a bivariate case:

1. Suppose X and Y are two independent random variables. Then the bivariate copula that explains their dependence is the independence copula:

$$C(u, v) = u \cdot v.$$

2. Elliptical copulas:
   ▪ Gaussian copula:

$$C(u, v) = \int_{-\infty}^{\Phi^{-1}(u)} \int_{-\infty}^{\Phi^{-1}(v)} \frac{1}{2\pi\sqrt{1 - \rho^2}} \exp\left\{-\frac{s^2 - 2\rho st + t^2}{2(1 - \rho^2)}\right\} ds\, dt,$$

where ρ is simply the linear correlation coefficient and Φ is the cumulative distribution function of the standard normal distribution. Gaussian copulas do not have upper tail and lower tail dependence and therefore cannot capture joint extreme observations that are possibly present in financial data.[27]

---

[26]The importance of copulas in the modeling of the distribution of multivariate random variables is provided by Sklar's theorem. The derivation was provided in Sklar (1959).

[27]Let X and Y be random variables with continuous distribution functions F_X and F_Y. The coefficient of upper tail dependence is calculated as $\lambda = \lim_{\alpha \to 1}$.

- *t*-copula:

$$C(u, v) = \int_{-\infty}^{t_d^{-1}(u)} \int_{-\infty}^{t_d^{-1}(v)} \frac{1}{2\pi \sqrt{1 - \rho^2}} \left(1 + \frac{s^2 - 2\rho st + t^2}{d(1 - \rho^2)} \right)^{-\frac{d+2}{2}} ds\, dt,$$

where ρ is simply the linear correlation coefficient, and t_d^{-1} is the inverse cumulative *t*-distribution of the degrees of freedom such that $d > 2$. The *t*-copula has upper and lower tail dependence that is decreasing in d and is therefore useful for modeling tail dependence.

3. Archimedean copulas:

- Gumbel copula:

$$C(u, v) = \exp\left\{ -\left((-\ln u)^\theta + (-\ln v)^\theta \right)^{1/\theta} \right\},$$

where the parameter θ is greater or equal to one and controls the amount of dependence: for example, $\theta = 1$ refers to the case of independence. The Gumbel copula has an upper tail dependence and can be used to model extremes.

- Clayton copula:

$$C(u, v) = (u^{-\theta} + v^{-\theta} - 1)^{-\frac{1}{\theta}},$$

where the parameter θ is greater than zero. Clayton copula has lower tail dependence.

- Frank copula:

$$C(u, v) = -\frac{1}{\theta} \ln\left(1 + \frac{(e^{-\theta u} - 1)(e^{-\theta u} - 1)}{e^{-\theta} - 1} \right),$$

where the parameter θ is between $-\infty$ and $+\infty$. If the two variables are independent, then $\theta = 0$; positive dependence refers to the case when $\theta > 0$, and perfect negative dependence refers to the case when $\theta < 0$. The Frank copula has neither upper nor lower tail dependence.

In the remaining part of this section, we consider several examples that illustrate further the concept behind the copula function. We noted

---

$\mathbf{P}\left[Y > F_Y^{-1}(\alpha) | X > F_X^{-1}(\alpha) \right]$. λ ranges between 0 and 1. For example, if $\lambda = 0$, then X and Y are asymptotically independent. See Embrechts et al. (2002) for details.

that the copula is just a probability distribution function and, therefore, it can be characterized by means of a cumulative distribution function or a probability density function. Given a copula function C, the density is computed according to formula (2.2),[28]

$$c(u_1, \ldots, u_n) = \frac{\partial^n C(u_1, \ldots, u_n)}{\partial u_1 \ldots \partial u_n}.$$

In this way, using the relationship between the copula and the distribution function, the density of the copula can be expressed by means of the density of the random variable. This is done by applying the chain rule of differentiation,

$$c(F_{Y_1}(y_1), \ldots, F_{Y_n}(y_n)) = \frac{f_Y(y_1, \ldots, y_n)}{f_{Y_1}(y_1) \ldots f_{Y_n}(y_n)}. \tag{2.4}$$

In this formula, the numerator contains the density of the random variable Y and in the denominator we find the density of Y but under the assumption that components of Y are independent random variables. Note that the left-hand side corresponds to the copula density but transformed to the sample space by means of the marginal distribution functions $F_{Y_i}(y_i)$, $i = 1, 2, \ldots, n$. The copula density of a two-dimensional normal distribution with covariance matrix

$$\Sigma = \begin{pmatrix} 1 & 0.8 \\ 0.8 & 1 \end{pmatrix}$$

and mean $\mu = (0, 0)$ is plotted in Figure 2.5. The contour lines of the copula density transformed in the sample space through the marginal distribution functions is given in Figure 2.6. Plots of the probability density function and the contour lines of the probability density function are given in Figures 2.3 and 2.4.

Equation (2.4) reveals that, if the random variable Y has independent components, then the density of the corresponding copula, denoted by c_0, is a constant in the unit hypercube

$$c_0(u_1, \ldots, u_n) = 1$$

---

[28]The density of a copula function may not exist since not all distribution functions possess densities. In this discussion, we consider only the copulas with a density.

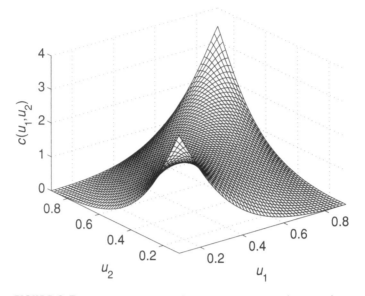

FIGURE 2.5   Copula Density of a Two-Dimensional Normal Distribution

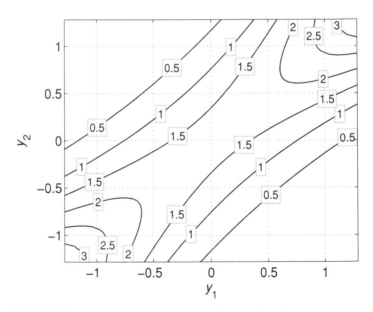

FIGURE 2.6   Contour Lines of a Copula Density of a Two-Dimensional Normal Distribution Transformed in the Sample Space

and the copula C_0 has the following simple form,

$$C_0(u_1, \ldots, u_n) = u_1 \ldots u_n.$$

This copula characterizes stochastic independence.

Now let us consider a density c of some copula C. The formula in equation (2.4) is a ratio of two positive quantities because the density function can only take non negative values. For each value of the vector of arguments $y = (y_1, \ldots, y_n)$, equation (2.4) provides information about the degree of dependence between the events that simultaneously Y_i is in a small neighborhood of y_i for $i = 1, 2, \ldots, n$. That is, the copula density provides information about the *local* structure of the dependence. With respect to the copula density c_0 characterizing the notion of independence, the arbitrary copula density function can be either above 1, or below 1. How is this fact related to the degree of dependence of the corresponding n events? Suppose that for some vector y, the right-hand side of equation (2.4) is close to zero. This means that the numerator is much smaller than the denominator:

$$f_Y(y_1, \ldots, y_n) < f_{Y_1}(y_1) \ldots f_{Y_n}(y_n).$$

As a consequence, the joint probability of the events that Y_i is in a small neighborhood of y_i for $i = 1, 2, \ldots, n$ is much smaller than what it would be if the corresponding events were independent. Therefore, this case corresponds to these events being almost disjoint; that is, with a very small probability of occurring simultaneously.

Suppose that the converse holds, the numerator in equation (2.4) is much larger than the denominator and, as a result, the copula density is larger than 1. In this case,

$$f_Y(y_1, \ldots, y_n) > f_{Y_1}(y_1) \ldots f_{Y_n}(y_n),$$

which means that the joint probability of the events that Y_i is in a small neighborhood of y_i for $i = 1, 2, \ldots, n$ is larger than what it would be if the corresponding events were independent. Therefore, copula density values larger than 1 mean that the corresponding events are more likely to happen simultaneously.

This analysis indicates that the copula density function provides information about the local dependence structure of a multidimensional random variable Y relative to the case of stochastic independence. Figure 2.6 provides an illustration in the two-dimensional case. It shows the contour lines of the surface calculated according to formula (2.4) for the two-dimensional normal distribution considered in section 2.6.6. All points that have an elevation above 1 have a local dependence implying that the events $Y_1 \in (y_1, y_1 + \epsilon)$ and $Y_2 \in (y_2, y_2 + \epsilon)$ for a small $\epsilon > 0$ are likely to occur jointly. This means that in a large sample of observations, we will observe the two events happening together more often than implied by the independence assumption. In contrast, all points with an elevation below 1 have a local dependence implying that the events $Y_1 \in (y_1, y_1 + \epsilon)$ and $Y_2 \in (y_2, y_2 + \epsilon)$ for a small $\epsilon > 0$ are likely to occur disjointly. This means that in a large sample of observations we will observe the two events happening less frequently than implied by the independence assumption.

2.7   SUMMARY

In this chapter, we considered a number of concepts from probability theory that will be used in later chapters in this book. We discussed the notions of a random variable and a random vector. We considered one-dimensional and multidimensional probability density and distributions functions that completely characterize a given random variable or random vector. We discussed statistical moments and quantiles, which represent certain characteristics of a random variable, and the sample moments that provide a way of estimating the corresponding characteristics from historical data. We presented the definition and properties of characteristic functions for random variables. In the multidimensional case, we considered the notion of dependence between the components of a random vector. Finally, we discussed the covariance matrix versus the more general concept of a copula function.

REFERENCES

Andrews, L. D. (1998). *Special functions of mathematics for engineers* (2nd ed.). New York: Oxford University Press.

Bradley, B. & Taqqu, M. S. (2003). Financial risk and heavy tails. In S. T. Rachev (Ed.), *Handbook of heavy-tailed distributions in finance*. Amsterdam: Elsevier. 35–103.

Embrechts, P., McNeil, A., & Straumann, D. (2002). Correlation and dependence properties in risk management: Properties and pitfalls. In M. Dempster (Ed.), *Risk management: Value at risk and beyond*. Cambridge: Cambridge University Press. 176–223.

Embrechts, P. & Puccetti, G. (2006). Bounds for functions of dependent risks. *Journal Finance and Stochastics*, 10(3), 341–352.

Fang, K., Kotz, S., & Ng, K. (1990). *Symmetric multivariate and related distributions*. New York: Chapman and Hall.

Grimmett, G. & Stirzaker, D. (2001). *Probability and random processes*. New York: Oxford University Press.

Johnson, N. L., Kotz, S., and Kemp, A. W. (1993). *Univariate discrete distributions* (2nd ed.). New York: John Wiley & Sons.

Larsen, R. J. & Marx, M. L. (1986). *An introduction to mathematical statistics and its applications*. Englewed Clifs, NJ: Prentice Hall.

Madan, D., Carr, P., and Chang, E. (1998). The variance gamma process and option pricing. *European Finance Review*, 2(1), 79–105.

Madan, D. & Seneta, E. (1990). The variance gamma (VG) model for share market returns. *Journal of Business*, 63, 511–524.

Mikosch, T. (2006). Copulas: Tales and facts. *Extremes*, 9(1), 3–20.

Patton, A. J. (2003a). Estimation of copula models for time series of possibly different lengths. Working paper, London School of Economics.

Patton, A. J. (2003b). On the importance of skewness and asymmetric dependence for asset allocation. *Journal of Financial Econometrics*, 2(1), 130–168.

Patton, A. J. (2004). Modelling asymmetric exchange rate dependence. Working paper, London School of Economics.

Rüschendorf, L. (2004). Comparison of multivariate risks and positive dependence. *Journal of Applied Probability*, 41, 391–406.

Shiryaev, A. N. (1996). *Probability*. New York: Springer.

Sklar, A. (1959). Fonctions de répartition à *n* dimensions et leurs marges. *Publications de l'Institut de Statistique de l'Université de Paris*, 8, 229–231.

Ushakov, N. G. (1999). *Selected topics in characteristic functions*. Utrecht: VSP.

CHAPTER 3

Stable and Tempered
Stable Distributions

Although the normal distribution has been frequently applied in modeling the return distribution of assets, its properties are not consistent with the observed behavior found for asset returns. More specifically, the symmetric and rapidly decreasing tail properties of asset return distributions cannot describe the skewed and fat-tailed properties of the empirical distribution of asset returns. The α-stable distribution has been proposed as an alternative to the normal distribution for modeling asset returns because it allows for skewness and fat tails.[1] The α-stable distribution has been built into some risk and portfolio management software.[2]

While the α-stable distribution has certain desirable properties that were mentioned in Chapter 1 and will be discussed in more detail in this chapter, it is not suitable in certain modeling applications such as the modeling of option prices. In order to obtain a well-defined model for pricing options, the mean, variance, and exponential moments of the return distribution have to exist. For this reason, the smoothly truncated stable distribution and various types of tempered stable distributions have been proposed for financial modeling. Those distributions are obtained by tempering the tail properties of the α-stable distribution. Because they converge weakly to the

---

[1] A summary of the empirical evidence rejecting the normal distribution for various asset classes and financial markets throughout the world is provided in Rachev et al. (2005).

[2] For example, "Cognity" is a risk and portfolio management software product of the U.S.-based FinAnalytica Inc. It is the only commercial system that offers the α-stable Paretian distributions framework. More information regarding the software and products can be obtained from the company's permanent home page: www.finanalytica.com.

α-stable distribution, the α-stable distribution is embedded in the class of the tempered stable distributions.

In this chapter, we discuss the α-stable and tempered stable distributions. The more general distribution, named the infinitely divisible distribution, will be discussed as well. The distributions in this chapter are defined by their characteristic functions. The density functions are not given by a closed-form formula in general but obtained by a numerical method that we discuss in Chapter 6.

3.1 α-STABLE DISTRIBUTION

In this section, we discuss a wide class of α-stable distributions. We review the definition and the basic properties of the α-stable distribution. We further present the class of smoothly truncated stable distributions, which has been proposed by Menn and Rachev (2009) for dealing with the drawbacks of the α-stable distribution.

3.1.1   Definition of an α-Stable Random Variable

We begin with a definition of an α-stable random variable.[3] Suppose that $X_1, X_2, \ldots, X_n$ are independent and identically distributed (i.i.d.) random variables, independent copies of X. Then a random variable X is said to follow an α-stable distribution if there exist a positive constant C_n and a real number D_n such that the following relation holds:

$$X_1 + X_2 + \cdots + X_n \overset{\mathrm{d}}{=} C_n X + D_n.$$

The notation $\overset{\mathrm{d}}{=}$ denotes equality in distribution. The constant $C_n = n^{\frac{1}{\alpha}}$ dictates the stability property, which we will discuss later. When $\alpha = 2$, we have the Gaussian (normal) case. In subsequent discussions of the α-stable distributions in this chapter, we restrict ourselves to the non-Gaussian case in which $0 < \alpha < 2$.

For the general case, the density of the α-stable distribution does not have a closed-form solution. The distribution is expressed by its

---

[3]Extensive analysis of α-stable distributions and their properties can be found in Samorodnitsky and Taqqu (1994), Rachev and Mittnik (2000), and Stoyanov and Racheva-Iotova (2004a, b).

characteristic function:

$$\phi_{\text{stable}}(u; \alpha, \sigma, \beta, \mu) = E[e^{iuX}]$$

$$= \begin{cases} \exp\left(i\mu u - |\sigma u|^\alpha \left(1 - i\beta(\text{sign } u)\tan\frac{\pi\alpha}{2}\right)\right), & \alpha \neq 1 \\ \exp\left(i\mu u - \sigma|u|\left(1 + i\beta\frac{2}{\pi}(\text{sign } u)\ln|u|\right)\right), & \alpha = 1 \end{cases}$$, (3.1)

where

$$\text{sign } t = \begin{cases} 1, & t > 0 \\ 0, & t = 0 \\ -1, & t < 0 \end{cases}$$

The distribution is characterized by four parameters:

- α: the index of stability or the shape parameter, $\alpha \in (0, 2)$.
- β: the skewness parameter, $\beta \in [-1, +1]$.
- σ: the scale parameter, $\sigma \in (0, +\infty)$.
- μ: the location parameter, $\mu \in (-\infty, +\infty)$.

When a random variable X follows the α-stable distribution characterized by those parameters, then we denote $X \sim S_\alpha(\sigma, \beta, \mu)$.

The three special cases where there is a closed-form solution for the densities are (1) the Gaussian case ($\alpha = 2$), (2) the Cauchy case ($\alpha = 1$, $\beta = 0$), and (3) the Lévy case ($\alpha = 1/2$, $\beta = \pm 1$) with the following respective densities:

- Gaussian: $f(x) = \dfrac{1}{2\sigma\sqrt{\pi}}e^{-\frac{(x-\mu)^2}{4\sigma^2}}$, $\quad -\infty < x < \infty$
- Cauchy: $f(x) = \dfrac{\sigma}{\pi\left((x-\mu)^2 + \sigma^2\right)}$, $\quad -\infty < x < \infty$
- Lévy: $f(x) = \dfrac{\sqrt{\sigma}}{\sqrt{2\pi}(x-\mu)^{3/2}}e^{-\frac{\sigma}{2(x-\mu)}}$, $\quad \mu < x < \infty$

Because of the four parameters, the α-stable distribution is highly flexible and suitable for modeling nonsymmetric, highly kurtotic, and heavy-tailed data. Figure 3.1 and Figure 3.2 illustrate the effects of the shape and skewness parameters, respectively, on the shape of the distribution, other parameters

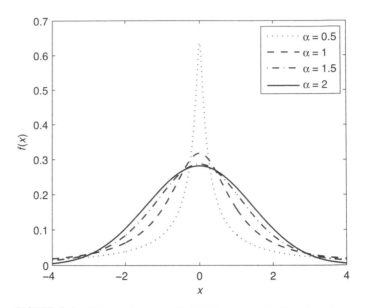

FIGURE 3.1 Illustration of α-Stable Densities for Varying α's, with $\beta = 0$, $\sigma = 1$, and $\mu = 0$

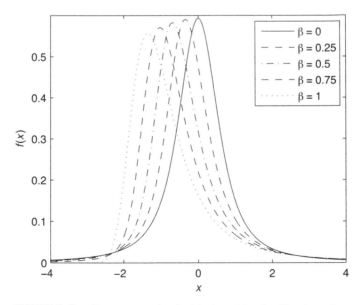

FIGURE 3.2 Illustration of α-Stable Densities for Varying β's, with $\alpha = 1.25$, $\sigma = 0.5$, and $\mu = 0$

kept constant. As is evident from part a of Figure 3.1, a lower value for α is attributed to heavier tails and higher kurtosis.

3.1.2 Useful Properties of an α-Stable Random Variable

We briefly describe four basic properties of the α-stable distribution:

- *Property 1.* The *power tail decay* property means that the tail of the density function decays like a power function (slower than the exponential decay), which is what allows the distribution to capture extreme events in the tails:

$$\mathbf{P}(|X| > x) \propto C \cdot x^{-\alpha}, x \to \infty$$

for some constant C. More precisely, if $X \sim S_\alpha(\sigma, \beta, \mu)$ with $0 < \alpha < 2$ then

$$\begin{cases} \lim_{\lambda \to \infty} \lambda^\alpha \mathbf{P}(X > \lambda) = C_\alpha \dfrac{1+\beta}{2} \sigma^\alpha \\[3mm] \lim_{\lambda \to \infty} \lambda^\alpha \mathbf{P}(X < -\lambda) = C_\alpha \dfrac{1-\beta}{2} \sigma^\alpha \end{cases}$$

where

$$C_\alpha = \begin{cases} \dfrac{1-\alpha}{\Gamma(2-\alpha)\cos(\pi\alpha/2)} & \text{if } \alpha \neq 1 \\[4mm] \dfrac{2}{\pi} & \text{if } \alpha = 1 \end{cases}.$$

- *Property 2.* Raw moments satisfy the property:

$$E|X|^p < \infty \text{ for any } 0 < p < \alpha$$
$$E|X|^p = \infty \text{ for any } p \geq \alpha$$

- *Property 3.* Because of Property 2, the mean is finite only for $\alpha > 1$:

$$E[X] = \mu \text{ for } \alpha > 1$$
$$E|X| = \infty \text{ for } 0 < \alpha \leq 1$$

The second and higher moments are infinite, leading to infinite variance together with the skewness and kurtosis coefficients.

- *Property 4.* The *stability property* is a useful and convenient property and dictates that the distributional form of the variable is preserved under linear transformations. The stability property is governed by the stability parameter α in the constant C_n (which appeared earlier in the definition of an α-stable random variable): $C_n = n^{1/\alpha}$. As was stated earlier, smaller values of α refer to a heavier-tailed distribution. The standard Central Limit Theorem does not apply to the non-Gaussian case: An appropriately standardized large sum of i.i.d. random variables converges to an α-stable random variable instead of a normal random variable.

The following examples illustrate the stability property. Suppose that $X_1, X_2, \ldots, X_n$ are i.i.d. random variables with $X_i \sim S_\alpha(\sigma_i, \beta_i, \mu_i)$, $i = 1, 2, \ldots, n$ and a fixed α. Then:

- The distribution of $Y = \sum_i^n X_i$ is α-stable with the index of stability α and parameters:

$$\beta = \frac{\sum_i^n \beta_i \sigma_i^\alpha}{\sum_i^n \sigma_i^\alpha}, \quad \sigma = \left(\sum_i^n \sigma_i^\alpha \right)^{1/\alpha}, \quad \mu = \sum_i^n \mu_i$$

- The distribution of $Y = X_1 + a$ for some real constant a is α-stable with the index of stability α and parameters:

$$\beta = \beta_1 \quad \sigma = \sigma_1 \quad \mu = \mu_1 + a$$

- The distribution of $Y = a X_1$ for some real constant $a(a \neq 0)$ is α-stable with the index of stability α and parameters:

$$\beta = (\text{ sign } a)\beta_1$$

$$\sigma = |a|\sigma_1$$

$$\mu = \begin{cases} a\mu_1 & \text{for } \alpha \neq 1 \\ a\mu_1 - \dfrac{2}{\pi}a(\ln a)\sigma_1\beta_1 & \text{for } \alpha = 1 \end{cases}$$

- The distribution of $Y = -X_1$ is α-stable with the index of stability α and parameters:

$$\beta = -\beta_1 \quad \sigma = \sigma_1 \quad \mu = \mu_1$$

3.1.3 Smoothly Truncated Stable Distribution

In some special cases of financial modeling it might occur that the infinite variance of stable distributions makes their application impossible. We see one example in Chapter 7 when we discuss the Black-Scholes type no-arbitrage models for the pricing of options. In many cases, the infinite variance of the return might lead to an infinite price for derivative instruments such as options, clearly contradicting reality and intuition. The modeler is confronted with a dilemma. On the one hand, the skewed and heavy-tailed return distribution disqualify the normal distribution as a suitable candidate; on the other hand, theoretical restrictions in option pricing do not allow the application of the stable distribution due to its infinite moments of order higher than α. For this reason, Menn and Rachev (2009) have suggested the use of appropriately truncated stable distributions.

The exact definition of truncated stable distributions is not that important at this point; that is why we restrict ourselves to a brief description of the idea. The density function of a smoothly truncated stable distribution (STS distribution) is obtained by replacing the heavy tails of the density function g of some stable distribution with parameters $(\alpha, \beta, \sigma, \mu)$ by the thin tails of two appropriately chosen normal distributions h_1 and h_2:

$$f(x) = \begin{cases} h_1(x), & x < a \\ g(x), & a \leq x \leq b \\ h_2(x), & x > b \end{cases}$$

The parameters of the normal distributions are chosen such that the resulting function is the continuous density function of a probability measure on the real line. If it is possible to choose the cutting points a and b in a way that the resulting distribution possesses zero mean and unit variance, then we have found an easy way to characterize standardized STS distributions. In Figure 3.3, the influence of the stable parameters on the appropriate cutting points is examined. As α approaches 2 (i.e., when the stable distribution approaches the normal distribution), we observe that the cutting points move to infinity. For small values of α, in contrast, the interval $[a, b]$ shrinks, reflecting the increasing heaviness of the tails of the stable distribution in the center.

Due to the thin tails of the normal density functions, the STS distributions admit finite moments of arbitrary order but nevertheless are able to explain extreme observations. Table 3.1 provides a comparison of tail probabilities for an arbitrarily chosen STS distribution with zero mean and

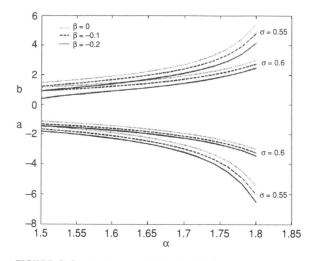

FIGURE 3.3   Influence of the Stable Parameters on the Cutting Points a and b

unit variance and the standard normal distribution. As can be seen from the table, the probability of extreme events is much higher under the assumption of an STS distribution. STS distributions allow for skewness in the returns. Moreover, the tails behave like fat tails but are light tails in the mathematical sense. Hence, all moments of arbitrary order exist and

TABLE 3.1   Comparison of Tail Probabilities for a Standard Normal and a Standardized STS Distribution

x	$P(X_1 \leq x)$ with $X_1 \sim N(0, 1)$	$P(X_2 \leq x)$ with $X_2 \sim STS$
-1	15.866%	11.794%
-2	2.275%	2.014%
-3	0.135%	0.670%
-4	0.003%	0.356%
-5	$\approx 10^{-5}$%	0.210%
-6	$\approx 10^{-8}$%	0.120%
-7	$\approx 10^{-10}$%	0.067%
-8	$\approx 10^{-14}$%	0.036%
-9	$\approx 10^{-17}$%	0.019%
-10	$\approx 10^{-22}$%	0.010%

are finite. For this reason, advocates of the class of STS distribution argue that it is an appropriate class for modeling the return distribution of various financial assets.

3.2 TEMPERED STABLE DISTRIBUTIONS

In this section, we discuss six types of tempered stable distributions. These distributions will be used to construct various Lévy processes in Chapter 3. Asset pricing models using tempered stable distributions will be discussed in Chapters 6, 7, and 13.

3.2.1 Classical Tempered Stable Distribution

Let $\alpha \in (0, 1) \cup (1, 2)$, $C, \lambda_+, \lambda_- > 0$, and $m \in \mathbb{R}$. X is said to follow the *classical tempered stable* (CTS) distribution if the characteristic function of X is given by

$$
\begin{aligned}
\phi_X(u) &= \phi_{CTS}(u; \alpha, C, \lambda_+, \lambda_-, m) \\
&= \exp(ium - iuC\Gamma(1 - \alpha)(\lambda_+^{\alpha-1} - \lambda_-^{\alpha-1}) \\
&\quad + C\Gamma(-\alpha)((\lambda_+ - iu)^\alpha - \lambda_+^\alpha + (\lambda_- + iu)^\alpha - \lambda_-^\alpha)),
\end{aligned} \tag{3.2}
$$

and we denote $X \sim CTS(\alpha, C, \lambda_+, \lambda_-, m)$.

Using the nth derivative of $\psi(u) = \log \phi_X(u)$ evaluated around zero (see section 2.5), the cumulants of X are obtained by

$$
c_1(X) = m
$$
$$
c_n(X) = C\Gamma(n - \alpha)(\lambda_+^{\alpha-n} + (-1)^n \lambda_-^{\alpha-n}), \text{ for } n = 2, 3, \ldots.
$$

The role of the parameters is as follows:

- The parameter m determines the location of the distribution.
- The parameter C is the scale parameter. Figure 3.4 shows the density function of the CTS distributions dependence on C.
- The parameters λ_+ and λ_- control the rate of decay on the positive and negative tails, respectively. If $\lambda_+ > \lambda_-$ ($\lambda_+ < \lambda_-$), then the distribution is skewed to the left (right), and if $\lambda_+ = \lambda_-$, then it is symmetric. Figure 3.5 illustrates left and right skewed density functions of the CTS distribution, as well as the symmetric case.

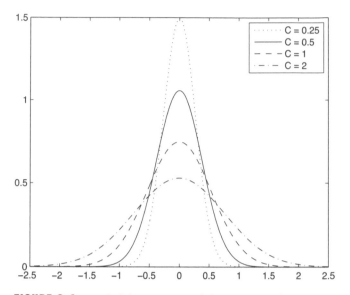

FIGURE 3.4   Probability Density of the CTS Distributions
Dependence on C
Note: $C \in \{0.25, 0.5, 1, 2\}, \alpha = 1.4, \lambda_+ = 50, \lambda_- = 50, m = 0.$

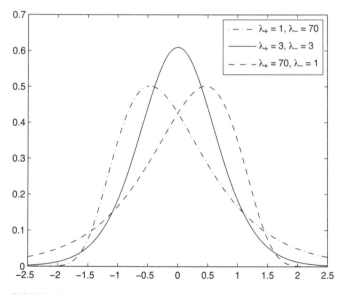

FIGURE 3.5   Probability Density of the CTS Distributions
Dependence on λ_+ and λ_-
Note: $(\lambda_+, \lambda_-) \in \{(1, 70), (3, 3), (70, 1)\}, \alpha = 0.8, C = 1,$
$m = 0.$

- The parameters λ_+, λ_-, and α are related to tail weights. Figure 3.6 and Figure 3.7 illustrate this fact. We will discuss another role of α in section 3.1.1.
- If α approaches to 0, the CTS distribution converges to the VG distribution in distribution sense.

If we take a special parameter C defined by

$$C = \left(\Gamma(2 - \alpha)(\lambda_+^{\alpha-2} + \lambda_-^{\alpha-2})\right)^{-1} \tag{3.3}$$

then $X \sim \text{CTS}(\alpha, C, \lambda_+, \lambda_-, 0)$ has zero mean and unit variance. In this case, X is called the *standard CTS distribution* with parameters $(\alpha, \lambda_+, \lambda_-)$ and denoted by $X \sim \text{stdCTS}(\alpha, \lambda_+, \lambda_-)$. Let m be a real number, σ be a positive real number, and $X \sim \text{stdCTS}(\alpha, \lambda_+, \lambda_-)$. Then

$$Y = \sigma X + m \sim \text{CTS}\left(\alpha, \frac{\sigma^\alpha}{\Gamma(2 - \alpha)(\lambda_+^{\alpha-2} + \lambda_-^{\alpha-2})}, \frac{\lambda_+}{\sigma}, \frac{\lambda_-}{\sigma}, m\right).$$

The random variable Y is the CTS distributed, and its mean and variance are m and σ^2, respectively.

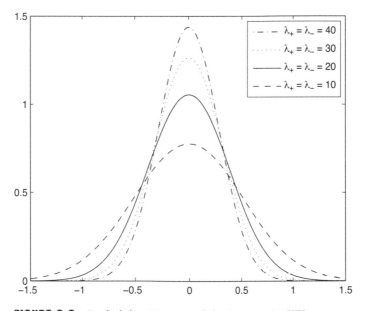

FIGURE 3.6 Probability Density of the Symmetric CTS Distributions Dependence on Parameters λ_+, λ_-
Note: $\lambda_+ = \lambda_- \in \{10, 20, 30, 40\}$, $\alpha = 1.1$, $C = 1$, $m = 0$.

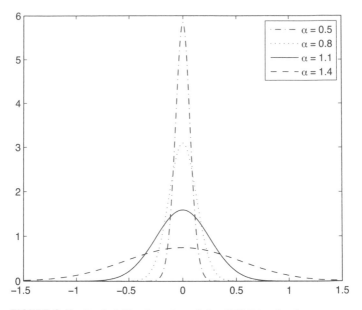

FIGURE 3.7   Probability Density of the CTS Distributions
Dependence on α
Note: $\alpha \in \{0.5, 0.8, 1.1, 1.4\}$, $C = 1$, $\lambda_+ = 50$, $\lambda_- = 50$, $m = 0$.

3.2.2   Generalized Classical Tempered Stable Distribution

A more general form of the characteristic function for the CTS distribution is

$$
\begin{aligned}
\phi_X(u) = \exp(ium &- iu\Gamma(1-\alpha)(C_+\lambda_+^{\alpha_+-1} - C_-\lambda_-^{\alpha_--1}) \\
&+ C_+\Gamma(-\alpha_+)((\lambda_+ - iu)^{\alpha_+} - \lambda_+^{\alpha_+}) \\
&+ C_-\Gamma(-\alpha_-)((\lambda_- + iu)^{\alpha_-} - \lambda_-^{\alpha_-})),
\end{aligned}
\tag{3.4}
$$

where $\alpha_+, \alpha_- \in (0, 1) \cup (1, 2)$, $C_+, C_-, \lambda_+, \lambda_- > 0$, and $m \in \mathbb{R}$. This distribution has been referred to as the *generalized classical tempered stable* (GTS) *distribution* and we denote it by $X \sim \text{GTS}(\alpha_+, \alpha_-, C_+, C_-, \lambda_+, \lambda_-, m)$.[4]

---

[4]The KoBoL distribution (see Boyarchenko and Levendorskiĭ, 2000) is obtained by substituting $\alpha = \alpha_+ = \alpha_-$, the truncated Lévy flight is obtained by substituting $\lambda = \lambda_+ = \lambda_-$ and $\alpha = \alpha_+ = \alpha_-$, while the CGMY distribution (see Carr et al., 2002) is obtained by substituting $C = C_+ = C_-$, $G = \lambda_-$, $M = \lambda_+$ and $Y = \alpha_+ = \alpha_-$.

The cumulants of X are $c_1(X) = m$ and

$$c_n(X) = C_+\Gamma(n - \alpha_+)\lambda_+^{\alpha_+ - n} + (-1)^n C_-\Gamma(n - \alpha_-)\lambda_-^{\alpha_- - n},$$

for $n = 2, 3, \ldots$. If we substitute

$$C_+ = \frac{p\lambda_+^{2-\alpha_+}}{\Gamma(2 - \alpha_+)}, \quad C_- = \frac{(1 - p)\lambda_-^{2-\alpha_-}}{\Gamma(2 - \alpha_-)}, \tag{3.5}$$

where $p \in (0, 1)$, then $X \sim \text{GTS}(\alpha_+, \alpha_-, C_+, C_-, \lambda_+, \lambda_-, 0)$ has zero mean and unit variance. In this case, X is called the *standard GTS distribution* with parameters $(\alpha_+, \alpha_-, \lambda_+, \lambda_-, p)$ and denoted by $X \sim \text{stdGTS}(\alpha_+, \alpha_-, \lambda_+, \lambda_-, p)$.

3.2.3 Modified Tempered Stable Distribution

Let $\alpha \in (0, 1) \cup (1, 2)$, $C, \lambda_+, \lambda_- > 0$, and $m \in \mathbb{R}$. X is said to follow the modified tempered stable (MTS) distribution[5] if the characteristic function of X is given by

$$\begin{aligned}\phi_X(u) &= \phi_{MTS}(u; \alpha, C, \lambda_+, \lambda_-, m) \\ &= \exp(ium + C(G_R(u; \alpha, \lambda_+) + G_R(u; \alpha, \lambda_-)) \\ &\quad + iuC(G_I(u; \alpha, \lambda_+) - G_I(u; \alpha, \lambda_-))), \end{aligned} \tag{3.6}$$

where, for $u \in \mathbb{R}$,

$$G_R(x; \alpha, \lambda) = 2^{-\frac{\alpha+3}{2}}\sqrt{\pi}\Gamma\left(-\frac{\alpha}{2}\right)\left((\lambda^2 + x^2)^{\frac{\alpha}{2}} - \lambda^\alpha\right)$$

and

$$G_I(x; \alpha, \lambda) = 2^{-\frac{\alpha+1}{2}}\Gamma\left(\frac{1 - \alpha}{2}\right)\lambda^{\alpha-1}\left[{}_2F_1\left(1, \frac{1 - \alpha}{2}; \frac{3}{2}; -\frac{x^2}{\lambda^2}\right) - 1\right],$$

where $_2F_1$ is the hypergeometric function. More details about the hypergeometric function are presented in section 3.5.1. We denote an MTS distributed random variable X by $X \sim \text{MTS}(\alpha, C, \lambda_+, \lambda_-, m)$.

---

[5]See Kim et al. (2009).

The role of the parameters of the MTS distribution is the same as the case of the CTS distribution. For example, the parameters λ_+ and λ_- control the rate of decay on the positive and negative tails, respectively, and if $\lambda_+ = \lambda_-$, then it is symmetric. The characteristic function of the symmetric MTS distribution is defined not only for the case $\alpha \in (0, 1) \cup (1, 2)$ but also for the case $\alpha = 1$. The form of the characteristic function for the symmetric case is given by

$$\phi_X(u) = \phi_{MTS}(u; \alpha, C, \lambda, \lambda, m)$$

$$= \exp\left(ium + C2^{-\frac{\alpha+1}{2}}\sqrt{\pi}\Gamma\left(-\frac{\alpha}{2}\right)\left((\lambda^2 + x^2)^{\frac{\alpha}{2}} - \lambda^\alpha\right)\right).$$

The mean of X is m, and the cumulants of X are equal to

$$c_n(X) = 2^{n - \frac{\alpha+3}{2}}C\Gamma\left(\frac{n+1}{2}\right)\Gamma\left(\frac{n-\alpha}{2}\right)(\lambda_+^{\alpha-n} + (-1)^n\lambda_-^{\alpha-n}),$$

for $n = 2, 3, \ldots$.

If we substitute

$$C = 2^{\frac{\alpha+1}{2}}\left(\sqrt{\pi}\Gamma\left(1 - \frac{\alpha}{2}\right)(\lambda_+^{\alpha-2} + \lambda_-^{\alpha-2})\right)^{-1}, \qquad (3.7)$$

then $X \sim \text{MTS}(\alpha, C, \lambda_+, \lambda_-, 0)$ has zero mean and unit variance. In this case, the random variable X is called the *standard MTS distribution* and denoted by $X \sim \text{stdMTS}(\alpha, \lambda_+, \lambda_-)$. Let m be a real number, σ be a positive real number, and $X \sim \text{stdMTS}(\alpha, \lambda_+, \lambda_-)$. Then

$$Y = \sigma X + m \sim \text{MTS}(\alpha, \sigma^\alpha C, \lambda_+/\sigma, \lambda_-/\sigma, m),$$

where C is equal to (3.7). The random variable Y is MTS distributed, and its mean and variance are m and σ^2, respectively.

3.2.4 Normal Tempered Stable Distribution

Let $\alpha \in (0, 2)$, $C, \lambda > 0$, $|\beta| < \lambda$, and $m \in \mathbb{R}$. X is said to follow the *normal tempered stable* (NTS) *distribution*.[6] If the characteristic function of X is

---

[6] The NTS distribution was originally obtained using a time-changed Brownian motion with a tempered stable subordinator by Barndorff-Nielsen and Levendorskiĭ (2001). Later, Kim, Rachev, Chung, and Bianchi (2008a) define the NTS distribution by the exponential tilting for the symmetric MTS distribution.

given by

$$\phi_X(u) = \phi_{NTS}(u; \alpha, C, \lambda, \beta, m)$$
$$= \exp\left(ium - iu2^{-\frac{\alpha-1}{2}} \sqrt{\pi} C\Gamma\left(1 - \frac{\alpha}{2}\right) \beta(\lambda^2 - \beta^2)^{\frac{\alpha}{2}-1} \right.$$
$$\left. + 2^{-\frac{\alpha+1}{2}} C\sqrt{\pi}\Gamma\left(-\frac{\alpha}{2}\right)\left((\lambda^2 - (\beta + iu)^2)^{\frac{\alpha}{2}} - (\lambda^2 - \beta^2)^{\frac{\alpha}{2}}\right)\right). \quad (3.8)$$

We denote an NTS distributed random variable X by $X \sim \text{NTS}(\alpha, C, \lambda, \beta, m)$.

The mean of X is m. The general expressions for cumulants of X are omitted since they are rather complicated. Instead of the general form, we present three cumulants

$$c_2(X) = \bar{C}(\lambda^2 - \beta^2)^{\frac{\alpha}{2}-2}\alpha(\alpha\beta^2 - \lambda^2 - \beta^2),$$
$$c_3(X) = -\bar{C}\alpha\beta(\lambda^2 - \beta^2)^{\frac{\alpha}{2}-3}(\alpha^2\beta^2 - 3\alpha\lambda^2 - 3\alpha\beta^2 + 6\lambda^2 + 2\beta^2),$$
$$c_4(X) = \bar{C}\alpha(\alpha - 2)(\lambda^2 - \beta^2)^{\frac{\alpha}{2}-4}$$
$$\times (\alpha^2\beta^4 - 6\alpha\lambda^2\beta^2 - 4\alpha\beta^4 + 3\beta^4 + 18\lambda^2\beta^2 + 3\lambda^4),$$

where $\bar{C} = 2^{-\frac{\alpha+1}{2}}C\sqrt{\pi}\Gamma\left(-\frac{\alpha}{2}\right)$.

The roles of parameters α, C, and λ are the same as in the case of the symmetric MTS distribution. The parameter β is related to the distribution's skewness. If $\beta < 0$ ($\beta > 0$), then the distribution is skewed to the left (right). Moreover, if $\beta = 0$, then it is symmetric. This fact is illustrated in Figure 3.8.

If we substitute

$$C = 2^{\frac{\alpha+1}{2}}\left(\sqrt{\pi}\Gamma\left(-\frac{\alpha}{2}\right)\alpha(\lambda^2 - \beta^2)^{\frac{\alpha}{2}-2}(\alpha\beta^2 - \lambda^2 - \beta^2)\right)^{-1} \quad (3.9)$$

then $X \sim \text{NTS}(\alpha, C, \lambda, \beta, 0)$ has zero mean and unit variance. In this case, X is called the *standard NTS distribution* and denoted by $X \sim \text{stdNTS}(\alpha, \lambda, \beta)$. Let m be a real number, σ be a positive real number, and $X \sim \text{stdNTS}(\alpha, \lambda, \beta)$. Then

$$Y = \sigma X + m \sim \text{NTS}(\alpha, \sigma^\alpha C, \lambda/\sigma, \beta/\sigma, m),$$

where C is equal to (3.9). The random variable Y is NTS distributed, and its mean and variance are m and σ^2, respectively.

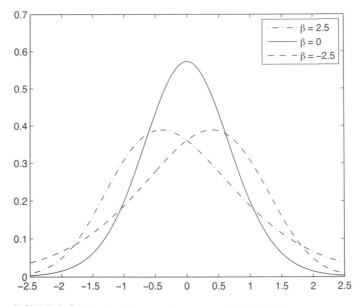

FIGURE 3.8   Probability Density of the NTS Distributions
Dependence on β
Note: $\beta \in \{-2.5, 0, 2.5\}$, $\alpha = 0.8$, $C = 1$, $\lambda = 4$, $m = 0$.

If we substitute $\alpha = 1$ and $C = \frac{c}{\pi}$ into the definition of NTS distribution, we obtain the *normal inverse Gaussian* (NIG) *distribution.*[7] That is, if random variable $X \sim \text{NTS}(1, c/\pi, \lambda, \beta, m)$, then X becomes an NIG distributed random variable. In this case, we denote $X \sim \text{NIG}(c, \lambda, \beta, m)$.

By substituting $\alpha = 1$ and $C = \frac{c}{\pi}$ into (3.8), we obtain the characteristic function of the NIG distributed X as

$$\phi_X(u) = \phi_{NIG}(u; c, \lambda, \beta, m) \tag{3.10}$$

$$= \exp\left(ium - \frac{iuc\beta}{\sqrt{\lambda^2 - \beta^2}} - c\left(\sqrt{\lambda^2 - (\beta + iu)^2} - \sqrt{\lambda^2 - \beta^2}\right)\right).$$

If we substitute

$$c = \frac{(\lambda^2 - \beta^2)^{\frac{3}{2}}}{\lambda^2} \tag{3.11}$$

---

[7]The NIG distribution has been used for financial modeling by Barndorff-Nielsen (1998, 1997) and Rydberg (1997).

then $X \sim \text{NIG}(c, \lambda, \beta, 0)$ has zero mean and unit variance. In this case, X is called the *standard NIG distribution* and denoted by $X \sim \text{stdNIG}(\lambda, \beta)$.

3.2.5 Kim-Rachev Tempered Stable Distribution

Let $\alpha \in (0, 1) \cup (1, 2)$, $k_+, k_-, r_+, r_- > 0$, $p_+, p_- \in \{p > -\alpha \mid p \neq -1, p \neq 0\}$, and $m \in \mathbb{R}$. X is said to follow the *Kim-Rachev tempered stable* (KRTS) *distribution* [8] if the characteristic function of X is given by

$$
\begin{aligned}
\phi_X(u) &= \phi_{KRTS}(u; \alpha, k_+, k_-, r_+, r_-, p_+, p_-, m) \\
&= \exp\left(ium - iu\Gamma(1-\alpha) \left(\frac{k_+ r_+}{p_+ + 1} - \frac{k_- r_-}{p_- + 1} \right) \right. \\
&\qquad \left. + k_+ H(iu; \alpha, r_+, p_+) + k_- H(-iu; \alpha, r_-, p_-) \right)
\end{aligned}
\tag{3.12}
$$

where

$$
H(x; \alpha, r, p) = \frac{\Gamma(-\alpha)}{p} \left({}_2F_1(p, -\alpha; 1+p; rx) - 1 \right).
$$

We denote a KRTS distributed random variable X by $X \sim \text{KRTS}(\alpha, k_+, k_-, r_+, r_-, p_+, p_-, m)$.

The KRTS distribution is an extension of the CTS distribution. Indeed, the distribution $\text{KRTS}(\alpha, k_+, k_-, r_+, r_-, p_+, p_-, m)$ converges weakly to the CTS distribution as $p_\pm \to \infty$ provided that $C_\pm = c(\alpha + p_\pm)r_\pm^{-\alpha}$ where $c > 0$.[9] Figure 3.9 shows that the KRTS distribution converges to the CTS distribution when parameter $p = p_+ = p_-$ increases to infinity.

The cumulants of the KRTS distributed random variable X are $c_1(X) = m$ and

$$
c_n(X) = \Gamma(n - \alpha) \left(\frac{k_+ r_+^n}{p_+ + n} + (-1)^n \frac{k_- r_-^n}{p_- + n} \right), \quad \text{for } n = 2, 3, \ldots.
$$

If we substitute

$$
k_+ = C \frac{\alpha + p_+}{r_+^\alpha},
$$

$$
k_- = C \frac{\alpha + p_-}{r_-^\alpha},
$$

---

[8]See Kim et al. (2007)
[9]See Kim et al. (2008b, 2007).

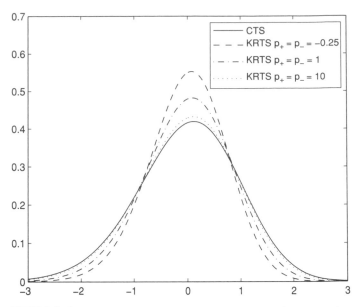

FIGURE 3.9   Probability Density of the CTS Distribution with Parameters $C = 1$, $\lambda_+ = 10$, $\lambda_- = 2$, $\alpha = 1.25$, and the KRTS Distributions with $k_\pm = C(\alpha + p)r_\pm^{-\alpha}$, $r_+ = 1/\lambda_+$, $r_- = 1/\lambda_-$, where $p = p_+ = p_- \in \{ -0.25, 1, 10 \}$

where

$$C = \frac{1}{\Gamma(2 - \alpha)} \left(\frac{\alpha + p_+}{2 + p_+} r_+^{2-\alpha} + \frac{\alpha + p_-}{2 + p_-} r_-^{2-\alpha} \right)^{-1}, \qquad (3.13)$$

then $X \sim \mathrm{KRTS}(\alpha, k_+, k_-, r_+, r_-, p_+, p_-, 0)$ has zero mean and unit variance. In this case, X is said to be a *standard KRTS distribution* and denoted by $X \sim \mathrm{stdKRTS}(\alpha, r_+, r_-, p_+, p_-)$. Let m be a real number, σ be a positive real number, and $X \sim \mathrm{stdKRTS}(\alpha, r_+, r_-, p_+, p_-)$. Then

$$Y = \sigma X + m$$

$$\sim \mathrm{KRTS}\left(\alpha, C(\alpha + p_+)(\sigma r_+)^{-\alpha}, C(\alpha + p_-)(\sigma r_-)^{-\alpha}, \sigma r_+, \sigma r_-, p_+, p_-, m \right),$$

where C is equal to (3.13). The random variable Y is KRTS distributed, and its mean and variance are m and σ^2, respectively.

3.2.6 Rapidly Decreasing Tempered Stable Distribution

Let $\alpha \in (0, 1) \cup (1, 2)$, $C, \lambda_+, \lambda_- > 0$, and $m \in \mathbb{R}$. A random variable X is said to follow the *rapidly decreasing tempered stable* (RDTS) *distribution*[10] if the characteristic function of X is given by

$$\phi_X(u) = \phi_{RDTS}(u; \alpha, C, \lambda_+, \lambda_-, m) \qquad (3.14)$$

$$= \exp\left(ium + C(G(iu; \alpha, \lambda_+) + G(-iu; \alpha, \lambda_-))\right),$$

where

$$G(x; \alpha, \lambda) = 2^{-\frac{\alpha}{2}-1}\lambda^\alpha \Gamma\left(-\frac{\alpha}{2}\right)\left(M\left(-\frac{\alpha}{2}, \frac{1}{2}; \frac{x^2}{2\lambda^2}\right) - 1\right)$$

$$+ 2^{-\frac{\alpha}{2}-\frac{1}{2}}\lambda^{\alpha-1}x\Gamma\left(\frac{1-\alpha}{2}\right)\left(M\left(\frac{1-\alpha}{2}, \frac{3}{2}; \frac{x^2}{2\lambda^2}\right) - 1\right),$$

and M is the confluent hypergeometric function. Further details of the confluent hypergeometric function are presented in section 3.5.2. In this case, we denote $X \sim \text{RDTS}(\alpha, C, \lambda_+, \lambda_-, m)$. The role of the parameters are the same as for the case of the CTS distribution.

The mean of X is m, and the cumulants of X are

$$c_n(X) = 2^{\frac{n-\alpha-2}{2}} C\Gamma\left(\frac{n-\alpha}{2}\right)\left(\lambda_+^{\alpha-n} + (-1)^n\lambda_-^{\alpha-n}\right), \text{ for } n = 2, 3, \ldots.$$

If we substitute

$$C = 2^{\frac{\alpha}{2}}\left(\Gamma\left(1 - \frac{\alpha}{2}\right)\left(\lambda_+^{\alpha-2} + \lambda_-^{\alpha-2}\right)\right)^{-1} \qquad (3.15)$$

then $X \sim \text{RDTS}(\alpha, C, \lambda_+, \lambda_-, 0)$ has zero mean and unit variance, and X is called the *standard RDTS distribution* and denoted by $X \sim \text{stdRDTS}(\alpha, \lambda_+, \lambda_-)$. Let m be a real number, σ be a positive real number, and $X \sim \text{stdCTS}(\alpha, \lambda_+, \lambda_-)$. Then

$$\sigma X + m \sim \text{RDTS}(\alpha, \sigma^\alpha C, \lambda_+/\sigma, \lambda_-/\sigma, m),$$

---

[10] See Bianchi et al. (2010) and Kim et al. (2010).

where C is equal to (3.15). The random variable Y is RDTS distributed, and its mean and variance are m and σ^2, respectively.

3.3   INFINITELY DIVISIBLE DISTRIBUTIONS

A random variable Y is referred to as *infinitely divisible* if for each positive integer n, there are i.i.d. random variables $Y_1, Y_2, \ldots, Y_n$ such that $Y \overset{d}{=} \sum_{k=1}^{n} Y_k$, that is, the distribution of Y is the same as the distribution of $\sum_{k=1}^{n} Y_k$.

For example the normal distribution is infinitely divisible. Using the characteristic function for the normal distribution, we can easily check the property. Suppose $Y \sim N(\mu, \sigma^2)$. For any positive integer n, consider a sequence of i.i.d. random variable $Y_1, Y_2, \ldots, Y_n$ such that $Y_k \sim N(\mu/n, \sigma^2/n)$. Since Y_k's are independent we have

$$E\left[\exp\left(iu \sum_{k=1}^{n} Y_k\right)\right] = \prod_{k=1}^{n} E\left[iu Y_k\right].$$

The characteristic function of Y_k is given by

$$E\left[iu Y_k\right] = \exp\left(\frac{iu\mu}{n} - \frac{\sigma^2 u^2}{2n}\right).$$

Hence, the characteristic function of $\sum_{k=1}^{n} Y_k$ is

$$E\left[\exp\left(iu \sum_{k=1}^{n} Y_k\right)\right] = \exp\left(iu\mu - \frac{\sigma^2 u^2}{2}\right),$$

which is the same as the characteristic function of Y. Therefore, $Y \overset{d}{=} \sum_{k=1}^{n} Y_k$.

Using similar arguments, we can show that the Poisson, gamma, VG, IG, α-stable, CTS, GTS, MTS, NTS (NIG), RDTS, and KRTS distributions are infinitely divisible. The relations of Y and Y_k, $k = 1, \ldots n$ for those distributions are presented in Table 3.2. We can show that the sum of infinitely divisible random variables is again infinitely divisible.

TABLE 3.2 Infinitely Divisible Distributions

	$Y \overset{d}{=} \sum_{k=1}^{n} Y_k$	Y_k
Poisson	$Poiss(\lambda)$	$Poiss(\frac{\lambda}{n})$
Gamma	$Gamma(c, \lambda)$	$Gamma(\frac{c}{n}, \lambda)$
VG	$VG(C, \lambda_+, \lambda_-)$	$VG(\frac{C}{n}, \lambda_+, \lambda_-)$
IG	$IG(c, \lambda)$	$IG(\frac{c}{n}, \lambda)$
Normal	$N(\mu, \sigma^2)$	$N(\frac{\mu}{n}, \frac{\sigma^2}{n})$
α-stable	$S_\alpha(\sigma, \beta, \mu)$	$S_\alpha(\frac{\sigma}{n}, \beta, \frac{\mu}{n})$
CTS	$CTS(\alpha, C, \lambda_+, \lambda_-, m)$	$CTS(\alpha, \frac{C}{n}, \lambda_+, \lambda_-, \frac{m}{n})$
GTS	$GTS\begin{pmatrix} \alpha_+ \, \alpha_-, C_+, C_-, \\ \lambda_+, \lambda_-, m \end{pmatrix}$	$GTS\begin{pmatrix} \alpha_+ \, \alpha_-, \frac{C_+}{n}, \frac{C_-}{n}, \\ \lambda_+, \lambda_-, \frac{m}{n} \end{pmatrix}$
MTS	$MTS(\alpha, C, \lambda_+, \lambda_-, m)$	$MTS(\alpha, \frac{C}{n}, \lambda_+, \lambda_-, \frac{m}{n})$
NTS	$NTS(\alpha, C, \lambda, \beta, m)$	$NTS(\alpha, \frac{C}{n}, \lambda, \beta, \frac{m}{n})$
KRTS	$KRTS\begin{pmatrix} \alpha, \, k_+, k_-, r_+, \\ r_-, p_+, p_-, m \end{pmatrix}$	$KRTS\begin{pmatrix} \alpha, \frac{k_+}{n}, \frac{k_-}{n}, r_+, \\ r_-, p_+, p_-, \frac{m}{n} \end{pmatrix}$
RDTS	$RDTS(\alpha, C, \lambda_+, \lambda_-, m)$	$RDTS(\alpha, \frac{C}{n}, \lambda_+, \lambda_-, \frac{m}{n})$

In the literature, the characteristic function of the one-dimensional infinitely divisible distribution is generalized by the Lévy-Khinchin formula:

$$\exp\left(i\gamma u - \frac{1}{2}\sigma^2 u^2 + \int_{-\infty}^{\infty}(e^{iux} - 1 - iux1_{|x|\leq 1})v(dx)\right). \qquad (3.16)$$

In the formula, the measure v is referred to as the *Lévy measure*. The measure is a Borel measure satisfying the conditions that $v(0) = 0$ and $\int_{\mathbb{R}}(1 \wedge |x^2|)v(dx) < \infty$. The parameters γ and σ are real numbers. The variable γ is referred to as the *center* or *drift* and determines the location. This triplet (σ^2, v, γ) is uniquely defined for each infinitely divisible distribution, and called a *Lévy triplet*.

TABLE 3.3 Lévy Measures

Distributions	Lévy Measure
Poisson	$\nu_{\text{Poisson}}(dx) = \lambda\delta_\lambda(dx)$ [11]
Gamma	$\nu_{\text{gamma}}(dx) = \dfrac{ce^{-\lambda x}}{x}1_{x>0}dx$
VG	$\nu_{\text{VG}}(dx) = \left(\dfrac{Ce^{-\lambda_+ x}}{x}1_{x>0} + \dfrac{Ce^{-\lambda_-|x|}}{x}1_{x<0}\right)dx$
IG	$\nu_{\text{IG}}(dx) = \dfrac{ce^{-\frac{\lambda^2}{2}x}}{\sqrt{2\pi}x^{\frac{3}{2}}}1_{x>0}dx$

If $\nu(dx) = 0$, then the characteristic function equals the characteristic function of the normal distribution. That is, the infinitely divisible distribution with $\nu(dx) = 0$ becomes the normal distribution with mean γ and variance σ^2.

If $\sigma = 0$, then the distribution is referred to as a *purely non-Gaussian distribution*. The characteristic functions of purely non-Gaussian distributions are computed by

$$\exp\left(i\gamma u + \int_{-\infty}^{\infty}(e^{iux} - 1 - iux1_{|x|\leq1})\nu(dx)\right).$$

Hence, except for the location determined by γ, all the properties of the distribution are characterized by the Lévy measure $\nu(dx)$. The Poisson, gamma, VG, IG α-stable, CTS, GTS, MTS, NTS, RDTS, and KRTS distributions are purely non-Gaussian distributions. The Lévy measure of the Poisson, gamma, VG, and IG distributions are given in Table 3.3.

The Lévy measure of the α-stable distribution is given by

$$\nu_{\text{stable}}(dx) = \left(\frac{C_+}{x^{1+\alpha}}1_{x>0} + \frac{C_-}{|x|^{1+\alpha}}1_{x<0}\right)dx. \tag{3.17}$$

Using the Lévy Khinchine formula we can obtain the characteristic function in (3.1).[12]

The Lévy measure of the CTS, MTS, NTS, KRTS, and RDTS distributions can be obtained by multiplying *tempering function* to the Lévy measure of α-stable distribution. For example, if we take $q(x) = e^{-\lambda_+ x}1_{x>0} + $

---

[12] More details about the calculation can be found in Samorodnitsky and Taqqu (1994) and Sato (1999).

TABLE 3.4 Tempering Functions

	Tempering Function $q(x)$
CTS	$e^{-\lambda_+ x}1_{x>0} + e^{-\lambda_-|x|}1_{x<0}$
MTS	$(\lambda_+ x)^{\frac{\alpha+1}{2}} K_{\frac{\alpha+1}{2}}(\lambda_+ x)1_{x>0} + (\lambda_-|x|)^{\frac{\alpha+1}{2}} K_{\frac{\alpha+1}{2}}(\lambda_-|x|)1_{x<0}$
NTS	$e^{\beta x}(\lambda|x|)^{\frac{\alpha+1}{2}} K_{\frac{\alpha+1}{2}}(\lambda|x|)$
KRTS	$r_+^{-p_+}\int_0^{r_+} e^{-x/s} s^{\alpha+p_+-1}ds\,1_{x>0} + r_-^{-p_-}\int_0^{r_-} e^{-|x|/s} s^{\alpha+p_--1}ds\,1_{x<0}$
RDTS	$e^{-\frac{\lambda_+ x^2}{2}}1_{x>0} + e^{-\frac{\lambda_-|x|^2}{2}}1_{x<0}$

$e^{-\lambda_-|x|}1_{x<0}$ as the tempering function, then we obtain the Lévy measure of the CTS distribution as

$$\nu(dx) = q(x)\nu_{\text{stable}}(dx) = \left(\frac{C_+ e^{-\lambda_+ x}}{x^{1+\alpha}}1_{x>0} + \frac{C_- e^{-\lambda_-|x|}}{|x|^{1+\alpha}}1_{x<0}\right) dx.$$

Tempering functions of the other distributions are presented in Table 3.4. For this reason, they are referred as the *tempered stable distributions*. The GTS distribution is also a purely non-Gaussian distribution, but not a tempered stable distribution in this sense. Indeed, its Lévy measure is given by

$$\nu(dx) = \left(\frac{C_+ e^{-\lambda_+ x}}{x^{1+\alpha_+}}1_{x>0} + \frac{C_- e^{-\lambda_-|x|}}{|x|^{1+\alpha_-}}1_{x<0}\right) dx.$$

In this book however, we will refer to the GTS distribution as a tempered stable distribution for convenience. Using the Lévy measures and the Lévy-Khinchin formula, we can obtain the characteristic functions (3.1), (3.2), (3.4), (3.6), (3.8), (3.12), and (3.14).

Generalization of the tempering function and the tempered stable distribution have been studied in the literature.[13]

---

[13] The tempered stable distribution has been generalized by Rosiński (2007) and Bianchi et al. (2010). Rosiński (2007) defined the tempering function as the completely monotone function. The complete monotonicity of the tempering function

3.3.1   Exponential Moments

The *exponential moment* of a random variable X is defined by $E[e^{uX}]$ for some real number u. Existence of the exponential moment is important for modeling an asset price process in option pricing theory.

The exponential moment of the normal distribution is given by

$$E[e^{uX}] = \exp\left(\mu u + \frac{\sigma^2 u^2}{2}\right),$$

where $X \sim N(\mu, \sigma)$.

Using the Lévy measure we can check the existence of the exponential moment for an infinitely divisible random variable. The following theorem (see Sato, 1999) provides a useful tool to verify the existence of an exponential moment of an infinitely divisible distribution.

Theorem. *Let X be an infinitely divisible random variable with the Lévy triplet (σ^2, ν, γ) and let $u \in \mathbb{R}$. Then $E[e^{uX}] < \infty$ if and only if*

$$\int_{|x|>1} e^{ux} \nu(dx) < \infty. \tag{3.18}$$

In this case,

$$E[e^{uX}] = \phi_X(-iu)$$

where ϕ is the characteristic function of X and $i = \sqrt{-1}$.

The existence of exponential moments in the tempered stable distributions is as following:

- For the α-stable random variable X, the exponential moment of X generally does not exist. However, if $X \sim S_\alpha(\sigma, 1, 0)$, then $E[e^{uX}] < \infty$ for $u < 0$. In this case,

$$E[e^{uX}] = \begin{cases} \exp\left(-\dfrac{\sigma^\alpha}{\cos\frac{\pi\alpha}{2}} u^\alpha\right), & \alpha \neq 1 \\[4mm] \exp\left(\dfrac{2\sigma}{\pi} u \ln u\right), & \alpha = 1 \end{cases}.$$

$q(x)$ means that $(-1)^n \frac{d^n}{dx^n} q(x) > 0$ for all $n = 0, 1, 2, \ldots$ and $x \in \mathbb{R}$ with $x \neq 0$. The CTS and the KRTS distributions are included in Rosiński's generalization. In Bianchi et al. (2010), the tempering function is defined by the positive definite radial function. The RDTS and the MTS distributions are subclasses of the class of the tempered infinitely divisible (TID) distributions that we introduce in Chapter 8.

- For the CTS, GTS, and MTS distributions, the condition (3.18) satisfies if and only if $-\lambda_- \leq u \leq \lambda_+$. Hence, $E[e^{uX}] < \infty$ for $u \in [-\lambda_-, \lambda_+]$.
- For the KRTS distribution, $E[e^{uX}] < \infty$ for $u \in [-1/r_-, 1/r_+]$.
- For the NTS and the NIG distributions, $E[e^{uX}] < \infty$ for $u \in [-\lambda - \beta, \lambda - \beta]$.
- For the RDTS distribution, (3.18) is satisfied for the entire real number u. Hence, $E[e^{uX}] < \infty$ for all $u \in \mathbb{R}$.

If $E[e^{uX}] < \infty$, then we can define the *log-Laplace transform* for the random variable X. The log-Laplace transform is given by

$$L(u) = \log E[e^{uX}] = \log \phi(-iu),$$

where u is satisfied (3.18).

For example, let $X \sim \text{stdCTS}(\alpha, \lambda_+, \lambda_-)$. The log-Laplace transform L_{CTS} of X is defined on $u \in [-\lambda_-, \lambda_+]$, and is given by

$$L_{CTS}(u; \alpha, \lambda_+, \lambda_-) = \log \phi_{CTS}(-iu; \alpha, C, \lambda_+, \lambda_-, 0)$$

$$= \frac{(\lambda_+ - u)^\alpha - \lambda_+^\alpha + (\lambda_- + u)^\alpha - \lambda_-^\alpha}{\alpha(\alpha - 1)(\lambda_+^{\alpha-2} + \lambda_-^{\alpha-2})} - \frac{u(\lambda_+^{\alpha-1} - \lambda_-^{\alpha-1})}{(1 - \alpha)(\lambda_+^{\alpha-2} + \lambda_-^{\alpha-2})},$$

where C is satisfied (3.3). Using the same method, we can obtain the log-Laplace transform of the other standard tempered stable distributions as follows:

- Standard GTS distribution:

$$L_{GTS}(u; \alpha_+, \alpha_-, \lambda_+, \lambda_-) = \log \phi_{GTS}(-iu; \alpha_+, \alpha_-, C_+, C_-, \lambda_+, \lambda_-, 0)$$

on $u \in [-\lambda_-, \lambda_+]$ where C_+ and C_- satisfy (3.5).
- Standard MTS distribution:

$$L_{MTS}(u; \alpha, \lambda_+, \lambda_-) = \log \phi_{MTS}(-iu; \alpha, C, \lambda_+, \lambda_-, 0)$$

on $u \in [-\lambda_-, \lambda_+]$ where C satisfies (3.7).
- Standard NTS distribution:

$$L_{NTS}(u; \alpha, \lambda, \beta) = \log \phi_{NTS}(-iu; \alpha, C, \lambda, \beta, 0)$$

on $u \in [-\lambda - \beta, \lambda - \beta]$ where C satisfies (3.9).

- Standard NIG distribution:

$$L_{NIG}(u; \lambda, \beta) = \log \phi_{NIG}(-iu; C, \lambda, \beta, 0)$$

on $u \in [-\lambda - \beta, \lambda - \beta]$ where C satisfies (3.11).
- Standard KRTS distribution:

$$L_{KRTS}(u; \alpha, r_+, r_-, p_+, p_-) = \log \phi_{KRTS}(-iu; \alpha, k_+, k_-, r_+, r_-, p_+, p_-, 0)$$

on $u \in [-\lambda_-, \lambda_+]$ where k_+ and k_- satisfy (3.13).
- Standard RDTS distribution:

$$L_{RDTS}(u; \alpha, \lambda_+, \lambda_-) = \log \phi_{RDTS}(-iu; \alpha, C, \lambda_+, \lambda_-, 0)$$

on $u \in \mathbb{R}$ where C satisfies (3.15).

The log-Laplace transform of the tempered stable distributions will be used for the infinitely divisible GARCH model in Chapter 13.

3.4 SUMMARY

In this chapter, we defined and described the properties of α-stable, STS, and six tempered stable distributions. We explained the notion of an infinitely divisible distributions that contains the α-stable and the tempered stable distribution as special cases. We presented the characteristic functions that completely characterize those distributions. We discussed the cumulants and standardized distributions for the tempered stable distributions. Finally, we discussed log-Laplace transforms of tempered stable distributions.

3.5 APPENDIX

In this Appendix, we provide details for two special functions: the hypergeometric function and the confluent hypergeometric function.[14]
Before discussing these two special functions, we will introduce the following useful notation:

$$(a)_0 = 1, \quad (a)_n = a(a + 1) \cdots (a + n - 1), \quad n = 1, 2, 3, \ldots, \quad a \in \mathbb{R}, \quad (3.19)$$

---

[14] See Andrews (1998) for more details.

and we refer to the notation as the *Pochhammer symbol*. By properties of the gamma function, the Pochhammer symbol can also be defined by

$$(a)_n = \frac{\Gamma(a+n)}{\Gamma(a)}, \quad n = 0, 1, 2, 3, \ldots.$$

From (3.19), we obtain

$$(2n+1)! = 2^{2n} n! \left(\frac{3}{2}\right)_n. \tag{3.20}$$

3.5.1 The Hypergeometric Function

The function

$$_2F_1(a, b; c; x) = \sum_{n=0}^{\infty} \frac{(a)_n (b)_n}{(c)_n} \frac{x^n}{n!}, \quad |x| < 1 \tag{3.21}$$

is called the *hypergeometric function*. If $c \neq 0, -1, -2, \ldots$, the function $F(a, b; c; x)$ is a solution to the linear second-order differential equation

$$x(1-x)y'' + (c - (a+b+1)x)y' - aby = 0, \tag{3.22}$$

referred to as the hypergeometric equation. Moreover, if $c \neq 0, \pm 1, \pm 2, \ldots$,

$$y = C_1 \, _2F_1(a, b; c; x) + C_2 x^{1-c} \, _2F_1(1 + a - c, 1 + b - c; 2 - c; x),$$

for any constants C_1 and C_2, is a general solution to equation (3.22). For $k = 1, 2, 3 \ldots$, kth derivatives are obtained from the following equation:

$$\frac{d^k}{dx^k} \, _2F_1(a, b; c; x) = \frac{(a)_k (b)_k}{(c)_k} \, _2F_1(a + k, b + k; c + k; x).$$

3.5.2 The Confluent Hypergeometric Function

The function

$$M(a; c; x) = \sum_{n=0}^{\infty} \frac{(a)_n}{(c)_n} \frac{x^n}{n!}, \quad -\infty < x < \infty \tag{3.23}$$

is called the *confluent hypergeometric function* and is obtained by the limit of the hypergeometric function as follows:

$$M(a; c; x) = \lim_{b \to \infty} F(a, b; c; x/b).$$

The function $M(a; c; x)$ is a solution of the linear second-order differential equation

$$xy'' + (c - x)y' - ay = 0, \tag{3.24}$$

referred to as the confluent hypergeometric equation. Moreover, if $c \neq 0, \pm 1, \pm 2, \ldots,$

$$y = C_1 M(a; c; x) + C_2 x^{1-c} F(1 + a - c; 2 - c; x),$$

for any constants C_1 and C_2, is a general solution of equation (3.24). For $k = 1, 2, 3 \ldots,$ kth derivatives are obtained by the following equation:

$$\frac{d^k}{dx^k} M(a; c; x) = \frac{(a)_k}{(c)_k} M(a + k; c + k; x).$$

REFERENCES

Andrews, L. D. (1998). *Special functions of mathematics for engineers* (2nd ed.). New York: Oxford University Press.

Barndorff-Nielsen, O. E. (1997). Normal inverse Gaussian distributions and stochastic volatility modelling. *Scandinavian Journal of Statistics*, 24, 1–13.

Barndorff-Nielsen, O. E. (1998). Processes of normal inverse Gaussian type. *Finance and Stochastics*, 41–68.

Barndorff-Nielsen, O. E. & Levendorskiĭ, S. (2001). Feller processes of normal inverse Gaussian type. *Quantitative Finance, 1*.

Bianchi, M. L., Rachev, S. T., Kim, Y. S., & Fabozzi, F. J. (2010). Tempered infinitely divisible distributions and processes. *Theory of Probability and Its Applications (TVP), Society for Industrial and Applied Mathematics (SIAM)*, 55(1), 59–86.

Boyarchenko, S. I. & Levendorskiĭ, S. Z. (2000). Option pricing for truncated Lévy processes. *International Journal of Theoretical and Applied Finance, 3*.

Carr, P., Geman, H., Madan, D., & Yor, M. (2002). The fine structure of asset returns: An empirical investigation. *Journal of Business*, 75(2), 305–332.

Kim, Y., Rachev, S. T., Bianchi, M. L., & Fabozzi, F. J. (2007). A new tempered stable distribution and its application to finance. In G. Bol, S. T. Rachev, &

R. Wuerth (Eds.), *Risk assessment: Decisions in banking and finance* (pp. 77–110). Heidelberg: Physica-Verlag, Springer.

Kim, Y., Rachev, S. T., Bianchi, M. L., & Fabozzi, F. J. (2008). Financial market models with Lévy processes and time-varying volatility. *Journal of Banking and Finance, 32*(7), 1363–1378.

Kim, Y., Rachev, S., Bianchi, M., & Fabozzi, F. (2010). Tempered stable and tempered infinitely divisible GARCH models. *Journal of Banking and Finance, 34*(9), 2096–2109.

Kim, Y., Rachev, S., Chung, D., & Bianchi, M. (2008). A modified tempered stable distribution with volatility clustering. In J. O. Soares, J. P. Pina, and M. Catalaõ-Lopes (Eds.), *New Developments in Financial Modelling.* Newcastle upon Tyne: Cambridge Scholars Publishing, 344–365.

Kim, Y. S., Rachev, S., Chung, D., & Bianchi, M. (2009). The modified tempered stable distribution, GARCH-models and option pricing. *Probability and Mathematical Statistics, 29*(1), 91–117.

Menn, C. & Rachev, S. (2009). Smoothly truncated stable distributions, GARCH-models, and option pricing. *Mathematical Methods of Operations Research, 63*(3), 411–438.

Rachev, S. T. & Mittnik, S. (2000). *Stable Paretian models in finance.* New York: John Wiley & Sons.

Rachev, S. T., Stoyanov, S. V., Biglova, A., & Fabozzi, F. J. (2005). An empirical examination of daily stock return distributions for U.S. stocks. In D. Baier, R. Decker, & L. Schmidt-Thieme (Eds.), *Data analysis and decision support* (pp. 286–281). Berlin: Springer.

Rosiński, J. (2007). Tempering stable processes. *Stochastic Processes and Their Applications, 117*(6), 677–707.

Rydberg, T. (1997). The normal inverse Gaussian Lévy process: Simulation and approximation. *Communications in Statistics. Stochastic Models, 13*, 887–910.

Samorodnitsky, G. & Taqqu, M. (1994). *Stable non-Gaussian random processes: Stochastic Models with Infinite Variance.* Boca Raton, FL: CRC Press.

Sato, K. (1999). *Lévy processes and infinitely divisible distributions.* Cambridge: Cambridge University Press.

Stoyanov, S. & Racheva-Iotova, B. (2004a). Univariate stable laws in the field of finance: Approximation of density and distribution functions. *Journal of Concrete and Applicable Mathematics, 2*(1), 37–58.

Stoyanov, S. & Racheva-Iotova, B. (2004b). Univariate stable laws in the field of finance: Parameter estimation. *Journal of Concrete and Applicable Mathematics, 2*(4), 24–49.

CHAPTER 4

Stochastic Processes in Continuous Time

In the previous chapter, we discussed the infinitely divisible distributions including α-stable and tempered stable distributions. Using those distributions, we can define a continuous sequence of independently divisible random variables, which will be referred to as the *continuous-time stochastic processes*.[1]

The two basic classes of continuous-time stochastic processes are Brownian motion and the Poisson process. The name of the former is due to the botanist Robert Brown who in 1827 described the movement of pollen suspended in water. Brownian motion was later examined and applied by Bachelier (1990) to modeling stock price dynamics. The theory of Brownian motion was founded by the work of Norbert Wiener who was the first to prove its existence and, as a result, Brownian motion is sometimes also referred as a Wiener process. The Poisson process generated by the Poisson distribution is the building block of pure jump processes. Both processes are fundamentally different concerning their path properties and they belong to the larger class of *Lévy processes*.[2]

In this chapter, we discuss continuous-time stochastic processes. We will first consider processes consisting of jumps and then we will discuss continuous processes without jumps. We then turn our focus on processes having random time instead of physical time. Finally, we discuss a general process that contains all of these processes.

---

[1] See Oksendal (2000) or Karatzas and Shreve (1991) for a complete treatment of continuous-time stochastic processes with financial applications.

[2] For more details about Lévy processes, see Sato (1999). Cont and Tankov (2004) provides details of Lévy processes with applications to finance.

4.1   SOME PRELIMINARIES

Before we continue with the discussion and the construction of processes, we briefly define terms that are used in this chapter:

- A *stochastic process* $X = (X_t)_{t \geq 0}$ is a family of $\mathbb{R}$-valued random variables X_t with parameter $t \geq 0$, defined on the sample space Ω. For every out come $\omega \in \Omega$, the function $t \mapsto X_t(\omega)$ is called a *sample path* of the process X.
- Let X be a stochastic process. Given $0 < t_1 < t_2 < \cdots < t_n$, if the random variables $X_{t_1} - X_0, X_{t_2} - X_{t_1}, \ldots, X_{t_n} - X_{t_{n-1}}$ are independent, we say that X has *independent increments*. Moreover, for $t \geq 0$, if the distribution of of $X_{t+h} - X_t$ does not depend on $t \geq 0$, we say that X has *stationary increments*. Loosely speaking, one could say that the distribution of the future changes does not depend on past realizations.
- A process X is said to be *nondecreasing*, if $Y_t \geq 0$ a.s. for $t \geq 0$, and $Y_t \geq Y_s$ a.s. for $0 \leq s \leq t$. Conversely, a process X is said to be *nonincreasing*, if $Y_t \leq 0$ a.s. for $t \geq 0$, and $Y_t \leq Y_s$ almost surely (a.s.) for $0 \leq s \leq t$.
- We say that a process X has *finite (infinite) variation* if its sample paths are of *finite (infinite) variation*, that is, the variation

$$V(X(\omega))_t = \lim_{n \to \infty} \sum_{k=1}^{n} |X_{tk/n}(\omega) - X_{t(k-1)/n}(\omega)|, \quad \forall t > 0$$

is finite (infinite) for almost every $\omega \in \Omega$.

4.2   POISSON PROCESS

Consider a process $N = (N_t)_{t \geq 0}$ derived by a Poisson distribution with parameter λ as follows:

1. $N_0 = 0$.
2. N has independent increments and stationary increments.
3. For any real numbers $t \geq 0$ and $h \geq 0$, the variable $(N_{t+h} - N_t)$ is a Poisson distributed random variable with parameter λh, that is,

$$\mathbb{P}(N_{t+h} - N_t = n) = e^{-\lambda h} \frac{(\lambda h)^n}{n!}, \quad n = 0, 1, 2, \ldots.$$

The process N is referred to as the *Poisson process* with intensity λ.

If $(\tau_j)_{j \in \mathbb{N}}$ are independent exponential random variables with parameter λ and the random variable N_t is given by

$$N_t = \inf \left\{ n \geq 1 : \sum_{j=1}^{n} \tau_j > t \right\},$$

then we can prove that the process $(N_t)_{t \geq 0}$ is the Poisson process with intensity λ.

The Poisson process is a fundamental example of a stochastic process with discontinuous trajectories, and a building block for constructing more complex jump processes.

4.2.1 Compounded Poisson Process

The process $X = (X_t)_{t \geq 0}$ is referred to as a *compounded Poisson process*, if X is defined by

$$X_t = \sum_{k=1}^{N_t} Y_k,$$

where

- $Y_1, Y_2, \ldots$ are independent and identically distributed (i.i.d.) random variables, and f is the probability density function of Y_1.
- $(N_t)_{t \geq 0}$ is a Poisson process with intensity λ.
- N_t and Y_k are independent for all $t \geq 0$ and $k = 1, 2, \ldots$.

The characteristic function of X_t is equal to

$$\phi_{X_t}(u) = \exp \left(\lambda t \int_{-\infty}^{\infty} (e^{iux} - 1) f(x) dx \right).$$

Moreover, if f is given by the probability density function of the normal distribution, then X is referred to as a *jump diffusion process*.

4.3 PURE JUMP PROCESS

Consider a process $X^x = (X_t^x)_{t \geq 0}$ for a given real number x such that

$$X_t^x = x N_t^{\lambda(x)},$$

where $(N_t^{\lambda(x)})_{t\geq 0}$ is the Poisson process with intensity $\lambda(x)$. The number x represents the jump size, and the intensity $\lambda(x)$ is the expected number of jumps with size x in the unit time.

Let $S = \{x_j \in \mathbb{R} : x_j \neq 0, j = 1, 2, \ldots\}$ be a discrete subset of jump sizes, $\lambda(x_j) > 0$ for all $x_j \in S$, and $Y = (Y_t)_{t\geq 0}$ be a process defined by

$$Y_t = \gamma t + \sum_{j=1}^{\infty} X_t^{x_j}.$$

If S consists of positive real numbers and $\gamma > 0$, then the process Y is non decreasing. Conversely, if S consists of negative real numbers and $\gamma < 0$, Y is non increasing.

Since the characteristic function of X_t^x is equal to

$$\phi_{X_t^x}(u) = \exp\left(\lambda(x)t(e^{iux} - 1)\right)$$

the characteristic function of Y_t is obtained by

$$\phi_{Y_t} = \exp\left(i\gamma ut + t\sum_{j=1}^{\infty} \lambda(x_j)(e^{iux_j} - 1)\right).$$

For the process Y, the function v defined by $v(A) = \sum_{x_j \in A} \lambda(x_j)$ represents the expected number of jumps with size $x \in A$ in the unit time interval, where A is a subset of S. For example, the expected number of jumps whose sizes are in $\{x_1, x_2, \ldots, x_n\}$ is equal to $v(\{x_1, x_2, \ldots, x_n\}) = \sum_{j=1}^{n} \lambda(x_j)$.

Now, we extend the set of jump size S to the real number $\mathbb{R}$. Then the expected number of jump is defined by a map v from a subset of $\mathbb{R}$ to a positive number, that is, a measure. For example, the expected number of jumps whose sizes are in a real interval $[a, b]$ is represented by $v([a, b])$. Using v, we can obtain an extended process Y such that the characteristic function of Y_t is given by

$$\phi_{Y_t} = \exp\left(i\gamma ut + t\int_{-\infty}^{\infty} (e^{iux} - 1)v(dx)\right), \qquad (4.1)$$

where $\gamma \in \mathbb{R}$. Jump sizes of process Y can be defined continuously. In this case, the measure v is referred to as a *Lévy measure*.[3]

---

[3]The exact definition of Lévy measure is a Borel measure v on $\mathbb{R}$ satisfying $v(0) = 0$ and $\int_{-\infty}^{\infty} \min\{1, x^2\}v(dx) < \infty$.

The class of jump processes satisfying equation (4.1) cannot contain infinite variation processes. To include infinite variation processes in the class of jump processes we will be using, we need a more general definition. Consider a process $Z = (Z_t)_{t \geq 0}$ such that the characteristic function of Z_t is given by

$$\phi_{Z_t} = \exp\left(i\gamma ut + t \int_{-\infty}^{\infty} (e^{iux} - 1 - iux 1_{|x| \leq 1}) v(dx) \right). \qquad (4.2)$$

The process Z is referred to as the *pure jump process*.[4] The path behavior of the pure jump process is determined by the Lévy measure v and real number γ:

- $\gamma > 0$ and $v(A) = 0$ for all $A \subset (-\infty, 0)$, then Z is nondecreasing.
- $\gamma < 0$ and $v(A) = 0$ for all $A \subset (0, \infty)$, then Z is nonincreasing.
- If $v(\mathbb{R}) < \infty$ (i.e., the expected number of jumps on the unit time is finite), then we say that Z has a *finite activity*.
- If $v(\mathbb{R}) = \infty$ (i.e., the expected number of jumps on the unit time is infinite), then we say that Z has an *infinite activity*.
- If $\int_{-1}^{1} |x| v(dx) < \infty$, the process Z has finite variation.
- If $\int_{-1}^{1} |x| v(dx) = \infty$, the process Z has infinite variation.

The building block of the pure jump process Z is the Poisson process. Hence, Z has the following properties:

- $Z_0 = 0$.
- Z has independent and stationary increments; that is, the random variable $(Z_t - Z_s)$ is independent to the random variable $(Z_v - Z_u)$ for all real number s, t, u, and v with $0 \leq s < t < u < v$.
- $Z_{s+t} - Z_s \stackrel{d}{=} Z_t$ for $s \geq 0$ and $t > 0$. Moreover, we have

$$\log \phi_{Z_t}(u) = t \log \phi_{Z_1}(u), \qquad (4.3)$$

where $\phi_{Z_t}(u)$ is the characteristic function of Z_t for $t > 0$.

---

[4]If $\int_{-1}^{1} |x| v(dx) = \infty$, then the characteristic function (4.1) is not defined, but the function (4.2) is well defined. The details can be found in Sato (1999) and Cont and Tankov (2004).

If $t = 1$, then we obtain the purely non-Gaussian infinitely divisible random variable. In fact, there is a one-to-one correspondence between a purely non-Gaussian infinitely divisible random variable and a pure jump process.

4.3.1   Gamma Process

Consider the gamma distribution with parameter (c, λ). Since the gamma distribution is a purely non-Gaussian infinitely divisible distribution, we can define a pure jump process $G = (G_t)_{t \geq 0}$ such that $G_1 \sim Gamma(c, \lambda)$. By equation (4.3) and Table 2.4 in Chapter 2, the characteristic function ϕ_{G_t} of G_t is given by

$$\phi_{G_t} = \left(\frac{\lambda}{\lambda - iu} \right)^{ct}. \tag{4.4}$$

In this case, the process G is referred to as the *gamma process* with parameter (λ, c). The sample path of the gamma process is a monotone increasing since the gamma distribution is supported only on the positive real line. When we take $c = 1$ of the gamma process, the process is referred to as an *exponential process*.

4.3.2   Inverse Gaussian Process

Consider the inverse Gaussian distribution with parameter (c, λ). Since the inverse Gaussian distribution is also a purely non-Gaussian infinitely divisible distribution, we can define a pure jump process $X = (X_t)_{t \geq 0}$ such that $X_1 \sim IG(c, \lambda)$. By equation (4.3) and Table 2.4 in Chapter 2, the characteristic function ϕ_{X_t} of X_t is given by

$$\phi_{X_t} = \exp \left(-ct(\sqrt{\lambda^2 - 2iu} - \lambda) \right). \tag{4.5}$$

In this case, the process X is referred to as the *inverse Gaussian (IG) process* with parameter (c, λ). The sample path of the gamma process is monotone increasing since the inverse Gaussian distribution is supported only on the positive real line.

4.3.3   Variance Gamma Process

The variance gamma are infinitely divisible distribution. Thus we can define pure jump processes $X = (X_t)_{t \geq 0}$ such that $X_1 \sim VG(C, \lambda_+, \lambda_-)$. By equation

(4.3) and Table 2.4 in Chapter 2, the characteristic function ϕ_{X_t} of X_t is given by

$$\phi_{X_t} = \left(\frac{\lambda_+ \lambda_-}{(\lambda_+ - iu)(\lambda_- + iu)} \right)^{Ct}. \tag{4.6}$$

In this case, the process X is referred to as the *variance gamma* (VG) *process* with parameter $(C, \lambda_+, \lambda_-)$.

4.3.4 α-Stable Process

The pure jump process $X = (X_t)_{t \geq 0}$ is referred to as the α-*stable process* with parameters $(\alpha, \sigma, \beta, \mu)$, if X_1 is the α-stable random variable, that is, $X_1 \sim S_\alpha(\sigma, \beta, \mu)$. By equations (4.3) and (3.1) in Chapter 3, the characteristic function ϕ_{X_t} of X_t is given by

$$\phi_{X_t}(u) = \begin{cases} \exp\left(i\mu u t - t|\sigma u|^\alpha \left(1 - i\beta(\text{sign } u) \tan \dfrac{\pi \alpha}{2} \right) \right), & \alpha \neq 1 \\[2mm] \exp\left(i\mu u t - t\sigma |u| \left(1 + i\beta \dfrac{2}{\pi}(\text{sign } u) \ln |u| \right) \right), & \alpha = 1 \end{cases}.$$

Recall the Lévy measure of the α-stable process:

$$v(dx) = \left(\frac{C_+}{x^{1+\alpha}} 1_{x>0} + \frac{C_-}{|x|^{1+\alpha}} 1_{x<0} \right) dx.$$

Then we can prove that

$$v(\mathbb{R}) = \int_{-\infty}^{\infty} v(dx) = \infty,$$

and hence the α-stable process is an infinite activity process. On the other hand, since we have

$$\int_{-1}^{1} |x| v(dx) = \begin{cases} \dfrac{C_+ + C_-}{1-\alpha}, & \alpha < 1 \\[2mm] \infty, & \alpha \geq 1 \end{cases},$$

we conclude that the α-stable process has finite variation if $\alpha < 1$ and the infinite variation if $\alpha \geq 1$.

4.3.5 Tempered Stable Process

The pure jump process $X = (X_t)_{t \geq 0}$ is referred to as the *tempered stable process*, if X_1 is the tempered stable random variable.

- The process X is referred to as the *classical tempered stable* (CTS) *process* with parameters $(\alpha, C, \lambda_+, \lambda_-, m)$, if $X_1 \sim \mathrm{CTS}(\alpha, C, \lambda_+, \lambda_-, m)$. The process X is referred to as the *standard CTS process* with parameters $(\alpha, \lambda_+, \lambda_-)$, if $X_1 \sim \mathrm{CTS}(\alpha, \lambda_+, \lambda_-)$.
- The process X is referred to as the *generalized tempered stable* (GTS) *process* with parameters $(\alpha_+, \alpha_-, C_+, C_-, \lambda_+, \lambda_-, m)$, if $X_1 \sim \mathrm{GTS}(\alpha_+, \alpha_-, C_+, C_-, \lambda_+, \lambda_-, m)$. The process X is referred to as the *standard GTS process* with parameters $(\alpha_+, \alpha_-, \lambda_+, \lambda_-, p)$, if $X_1 \sim \mathrm{stdGTS}(\alpha_+, \alpha_-, \lambda_+, \lambda_-, p)$.
- The process X is referred to as the *modified tempered stable* (MTS) *process* with parameters $(\alpha, C, \lambda_+, \lambda_-, m)$, if $X_1 \sim \mathrm{MTS}(\alpha, C, \lambda_+, \lambda_-, m)$. The process X is referred to as the *standard MTS process* with parameters $(\alpha, \lambda_+, \lambda_-)$, if $X_1 \sim \mathrm{stdMTS}(\alpha, \lambda_+, \lambda_-)$.
- The process X is referred to as the *normal tempered stable* (NTS) *process* with parameters $(\alpha, C, \lambda, \beta, m)$, if $X_1 \sim \mathrm{NTS}(\alpha, C, \lambda, \beta, m)$. The process X is referred to as the *standard NTS process* with parameters (α, λ, β), if $X_1 \sim \mathrm{stdNTS}(\alpha, \lambda, \beta)$.

  Moreover, the process X is referred to as the *normal inverse Gaussian* (NIG) *process* with parameters (c, λ, β, m), if $X_1 \sim \mathrm{NIG}(c, \lambda, \beta, m)$. The process X is referred to as the *standard NIG process* with parameters (λ, β), if $X_1 \sim \mathrm{stdNIG}(\lambda, \beta)$.
- The process X is referred to as the *Kim-Rachev tempered stable* (KRTS) *process* with parameters $(\alpha, k_+, k_-, r_+, r_-, p_+, p_-, m)$, if $X_1 \sim KRTS(\alpha, k_+, k_-, r_+, r_-, p_+, p_-, m)$. The process X is referred to as the *standard KRTS process* with parameters $(\alpha, r_+, r_-, p_+, p_-)$, if $X_1 \sim \mathrm{stdKRTS}(\alpha, r_+, r_-, p_+, p_-)$.
- The process X is referred to as the *rapidly decreasing tempered stable* (RDTS) *process* with parameters $(\alpha, C, \lambda_+, \lambda_-, m)$, if $X_1 \sim \mathrm{RDTS}(\alpha, C, \lambda_+, \lambda_-, m)$. The process X is referred to as the *standard RDTS process* with parameters $(\alpha, \lambda_+, \lambda_-)$, if $X_1 \sim \mathrm{stdRDTS}(\alpha, \lambda_+, \lambda_-)$.

The characteristic function ϕ_{X_t} of X_t is obtained by equation (4.3). For example, if X is the CTS process with parameters $(\alpha, C, \lambda_+, \lambda_-, m)$, then

$$\phi_{X_t}(u) = \exp\left(t \log\left(\phi_{CTS}(u; \alpha, C, \lambda_+, \lambda_-, m)\right)\right)$$

$$= \exp(iumt - iutC\Gamma(1 - \alpha)(\lambda_+^{\alpha-1} - \lambda_-^{\alpha-1})$$

$$+ tC\Gamma(-\alpha)((\lambda_+ - iu)^\alpha - \lambda_+^\alpha + (\lambda_- + iu)^\alpha - \lambda_-^\alpha)).$$

Characteristic exponents of tempered stable processes are presented in Table 4.1.

Let $\nu(dx)$ be the Lévy measure of the tempered stable process. Then we can prove that $\nu(\mathbb{R}) = \infty$, $\int_{-1}^{1} |x|\nu(dx) < \infty$ if $\alpha < 1$, and $\int_{-1}^{1} |x|\nu(dx) = \infty$ if $\alpha \geq 1$. Consequently, the tempered stable process has infinite activity, and has finite variation if $\alpha < 1$ and infinite variation if $\alpha \geq 1$.[5]

4.4 BROWNIAN MOTION

In this section, we discuss *Brownian motion* by means of an example. We begin with a short summary of the most important and defining properties of a standard Brownian motion $W = (W_t)_{t \geq 0}$:

TABLE 4.1 Characteristic Exponents of Tempered Stable Processes

Process	$\psi_{X_t}(u) = \log \phi_{X_t}(u)$
CTS	$iumt - iutC\Gamma(1-\alpha)(\lambda_+^{\alpha-1} - \lambda_-^{\alpha-1})$ $+ tC\Gamma(-\alpha)((\lambda_+ - iu)^\alpha - \lambda_+^\alpha + (\lambda_- + iu)^\alpha - \lambda_-^\alpha)$
GTS	$iumt - iut\Gamma(1-\alpha)(C_+\lambda_+^{\alpha_+-1} - C_-\lambda_-^{\alpha_--1})$ $+ tC_+\Gamma(-\alpha_+)((\lambda_+ - iu)^{\alpha_+} - \lambda_+^{\alpha_+}) + tC_-\Gamma(-\alpha_-)((\lambda_- + iu)^{\alpha_-} - \lambda_-^{\alpha_-}))$
MTS	$iumt + tC(G_R(u;\alpha,\lambda_+) + G_R(u;\alpha,\lambda_-))$ $+ iutC(G_I(u;\alpha,\lambda_+) - G_I(u;\alpha,\lambda_-))$ where $G_R(x;\alpha,\lambda) = 2^{-\frac{\alpha+3}{2}}\sqrt{\pi}\Gamma\left(-\frac{\alpha}{2}\right)\left((\lambda^2 + x^2)^{\frac{\alpha}{2}} - \lambda^\alpha\right)$ and $G_I(x;\alpha,\lambda) = 2^{-\frac{\alpha+1}{2}}\Gamma\left(\frac{1-\alpha}{2}\right)\lambda^{\alpha-1}\left[{}_2F_1\left(1,\frac{1-\alpha}{2};\frac{3}{2};-\frac{x^2}{\lambda^2}\right) - 1\right]$
NTS	$iumt - iut2^{-\frac{\alpha-1}{2}}C\sqrt{\pi}\Gamma\left(1-\frac{\alpha}{2}\right)\beta(\lambda^2-\beta^2)^{\frac{\alpha}{2}-1}$ $+ t2^{-\frac{\alpha+1}{2}}C\sqrt{\pi}\Gamma\left(-\frac{\alpha}{2}\right)\left((\lambda^2 - (\beta+iu)^2)^{\frac{\alpha}{2}} - (\lambda^2-\beta^2)^{\frac{\alpha}{2}}\right)$
NIG	$iumt - \frac{iutc\beta}{\sqrt{\lambda^2-\beta^2}} - tc\left(\sqrt{\lambda^2 - (\beta+iu)^2} - \sqrt{\lambda^2 - \beta^2}\right)$
KRTS	$iumt - iut\Gamma(1-\alpha)\left(\frac{k_+r_+}{p_++1} - \frac{k_-r_-}{p_-+1}\right)$ $+ tk_+H(iu;\alpha,r_+,p_+) + tk_-H(-iu;\alpha,r_-,p_-)$ where $H(x;\alpha,r,p) = \frac{\Gamma(-\alpha)}{p}({}_2F_1(p,-\alpha;1+p;rx) - 1)$
RDTS	$iumt + tC(G(iu;\alpha,\lambda_+) + G(-iu;\alpha,\lambda_-))$ where $G(x;\alpha,\lambda) = 2^{\frac{\alpha}{2}-1}\lambda^\alpha\Gamma\left(-\frac{\alpha}{2}\right)\left(M\left(-\frac{\alpha}{2},\frac{1}{2};\frac{x^2}{2\lambda^2}\right) - 1\right)$ $+ 2^{-\frac{\alpha}{2}-\frac{1}{2}}\lambda^{\alpha-1}x\Gamma\left(\frac{1-\alpha}{2}\right)\left(M\left(\frac{1-\alpha}{2},\frac{3}{2};\frac{x^2}{2\lambda^2}\right) - 1\right)$

---

[5]See Carr et al. (2002), Kim (2005), and Kim et al. (2007, 2010).

1. $W_0 = 0$.
2. W has independent increments and stationary increments.
3. For any real numbers $t \geq 0$ and $h \geq 0$, the variable $(W_{t+h} - W_t)$ is a normally distributed random variable with mean zero and variance h.
4. The paths of $W = (W_t)_{t \geq 0}$ are continuous.

Every process fulfilling the above four properties is referred to as the *standard Brownian motion*. From the second and third conditions it can be deduced that Brownian motion W_t at time t (which equals the increment from time 0 to time t) is normally distributed with mean zero and variance t.

The paths of Brownian motion are highly irregular and nowhere differentiable. In order to draw a true path, one would have to calculate the value of the process for every real number, which is clearly not feasible. Due to its characteristic path properties, it is impossible to draw a real path of Brownian motion. The process can only be evaluated for a discrete set of points. Figure 4.1 illustrates possible paths of Brownian motion. Strictly speaking, the plotted paths are only discrete approximations to the true paths.

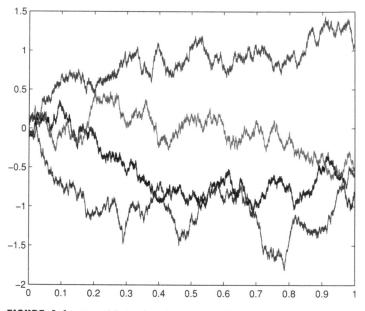

FIGURE 4.1   Possible Paths of a Standard Brownian Motion
Note: Every path consists of 10,000 equally spaced observations.

From the above definition of the process, it may not be clear how one can envision a Brownian motion or how one could construct it. Therefore, we will present a constructive method demonstrating how one can generate a Brownian motion as a limit of very simple processes. We restrict the presentation to the unit interval (i.e., we assume $0 \leq t \leq 1$) but the generalization to the abstract case should be obvious. The procedure is iterative, which means that on the kth step of the iteration we define a process $(X_t^{(k)})_{0 \leq t \leq 1}$, which will serve as an approximation for a standard Brownian motion.

Let random variables $I_1, I_2, I_3, \ldots$ be i.i.d. with

$$I_j = \begin{cases} 1 & \text{with probability } p = 0.5 \\ -1 & \text{with probability } 1 - p = 0.5 \end{cases}, \quad j = 1, 2, \ldots$$

Define $X_t^{(k)} = \frac{1}{\sqrt{k}} \sum_{j=1}^{n} I_j$ where $t = n/k$ and $n = 0, 1, \ldots, k$. If the value t is on the interval $(\frac{n}{k}, \frac{n+1}{k})$, then we take a value obtained by a linear interpolation as

$$X_t^{(k)} = (kt - n) X_{n/k}^{(k)} + (kt - n - 1) X_{(n+1)/k}^{(k)}.$$

By doing so, we get a stochastic process with continuous paths.

Let's start with $k = 1$. Then we have the following:

$$X_0^{(1)} = 0,$$

$$X_1^{(1)} = \begin{cases} 1 & \text{with probability } p = 0.5 \\ -1 & \text{with probability } 1 - p = 0.5 \end{cases}.$$

At any time t the random variable $X_1^{(1)}$ can take only two possible values, namely $-t$ and t. At any time, the process has zero mean and the variance at time $t = 1$ equals

$$\text{Var}\left(X_1^{(1)}\right) = 1^2 \cdot 0.5 + (-1)^2 \cdot 0.5 = 1.$$

That is not so bad for the first step, but obviously the distribution of $X_1^{(1)}$ is far from being normal.

What we do in the next step, $k = 2$, is allow for two different values until time $t = \frac{1}{2}$ and three different values for $\frac{1}{2} \le t \le 1$. We do so by defining:

$$X_0^{(2)} = 0,$$

$$X_{0.5}^{(2)} = \begin{cases} \frac{1}{\sqrt{2}} & \text{with probability } p = 0.5 \\ -\frac{1}{\sqrt{2}} & \text{with probability } 1 - p = 0.5 \end{cases}.$$

$$X_1^{(2)} = \begin{cases} \sqrt{2} & \text{with probability } p^2 = 0.25 \\ 0 & \text{with probability } p(1 - p) = 0.5 \\ -\sqrt{2} & \text{with probability } (1 - p)^2 = 0.25 \end{cases}.$$

The process $X_t^{(2)}$ now has four possible paths. The mean of $X_t^{(2)}$ is zero and the variance of $X_t^{(2)}$ equals

$$\text{Var}\left(X_{0.5}^{(2)}\right) = \left(\frac{1}{\sqrt{2}}\right)^2 \cdot 0.5 + \left(-\frac{1}{\sqrt{2}}\right)^2 \cdot 0.5 = 0.5,$$

$$\text{Var}\left(X_1^{(2)}\right) = \sqrt{2}^2 \cdot 0.25 + (-\sqrt{2})^2 \cdot 0.25 = 1.$$

but still the distribution of $X_t^{(2)}$ is far from being normal.

By iterating the stated procedure, the probability of $X_t^{(k)}$ is given by

$$\mathbf{P}\left(X_t^{(k)} = \frac{n - 2m}{\sqrt{k}}\right) = \binom{n}{m}\left(\frac{1}{2}\right)^n,$$

if $m \in \{0, 1, 2, \ldots, n\}$, $t = n/k$, $n \in \{0, 1, 2, \ldots, k\}$. The mean and variance can be obtained as follows:

$$E\left[X_t^{(k)}\right] = \frac{1}{\sqrt{k}}\sum_{j=1}^{n} E[I_j] = 0,$$

$$\text{Var}\left(X_t^{(k)}\right) = \frac{1}{k}\sum_{j=1}^{n} E[I_j^2] = \frac{n}{k},$$

where $t = n/k$, $n = 1, 2, \ldots, k$. Since $X_{n/k}^{(k)}$ is defined by the sum of i.i.d. random variables, it has:

- Independent increments: $X_{n_1/k}^{(k)}$ and $X_{n_2/k}^{(k)} - X_{n_1/k}^{(k)}$ are independent, for all $n_1, n_2 \in \{0, 1, \ldots, k\}$ with $n_1 < n_2$.
- Stationary increments: $X_{n_2/k}^{(k)} - X_{n_1/k}^{(k)} \stackrel{d}{=} X_{(n_2 - n_1)/k}^{(k)}$ for all $n_1, n_2 \in \{0, 1, \ldots, k\}$ with $n_1 < n_2$.

Moreover, the distribution of $X_t^{(k)}$ will approach the normal distribution due to the Central Limit Theorem. Consequently, we have found all the defining properties of a Brownian motion in this simple approximating process, that is, the process $(X_t^{(k)})_{0 \le t \le 1}$ converges in distribution to the standard Brownian motion $(W_t)_{0 \le t \le 1}$.

In the context of financial applications, there are two main variants of the standard Brownian motion that have to be mentioned: the arithmetic and the geometric Brownian motion. Both are obtained as a function of the standard Brownian motion.

4.4.1 Arithmetic Brownian Motion

Given a Brownian motion $(W_t)_{t \ge 0}$ and two real constants μ and σ, the *arithmetic Brownian motion* $(X_t)_{t \ge 0}$ is obtained as

$$X_t = \mu t + \sigma W_t.$$

The process $(X_t)_{t \ge 0}$ consists of a sum of a purely deterministic linear trend function μt and a rescaled Brownian motion σW_t. The latter has the property that at time t, σW_t is normally distributed with mean 0 and variance $\sigma^2 t$. The paths will therefore randomly jitter around the deterministic trend with a variance proportional to the point in time t under consideration. The arithmetic Brownian motion is a simple but popular model for financial returns.

4.4.2 Geometric Brownian Motion

Given a Brownian motion $(W_t)_{t \ge 0}$, two real constants μ and σ, and a starting value $S_0 > 0$, the geometric Brownian motion $(S_t)_{t \ge 0}$ is obtained as

$$S_t = S_0 e^{\mu t + \sigma W_t}.$$

The process $(S_t)_{t \geq 0}$ is just the exponential of an arithmetic Brownian motion multiplied by a factor. Therefore $\log(S_t/S_0)$ is normally distributed and

$$E[S_t/S_0] = e^{\mu t + \frac{1}{2}\sigma^2 t}.$$

4.5   TIME-CHANGED BROWNIAN MOTION

If a pure jump process process $T = (T_t)_{t \geq 0}$ is nondecreasing, that is, $T_t \geq 0$ a.s. for $t > 0$, and $T_t \geq T_s$ a.s. for $s \leq t$, then the process T is referred to as the *subordinator* or *intrinsic time process*. Intuitively, it can be thought of as the cumulative trading volume process that measures the cumulative volume of all the transition up to physical time t (Rachev and Mittnik 2000).

The Poisson, gamma, and inverse Gaussian processes are nondecreasing, and hence they are subordinators. Moreover, in case $0 < \alpha < 1$, the support of the α-stable distribution $S_\alpha(\sigma, 1, 0)$ is the positive real line. Hence, the α-stable process with parameters $(\frac{\alpha}{2}, \sigma, 1, 0)$ and $0 < \alpha < 2$ is a subordinator and referred to as α-*stable subordinator*. In some cases, we can consider an additional assumption, $E[T_t] = t$, which means the expected intrinsic time is the same as physical time.

If we take an arithmetic Brownian motion and change the physical time to a subordinator, then we obtain the *time-changed Brownian motion*. That is, take an arithmetic Brownian motion with drift μ and volatility σ as follows:

$$\mu t + \sigma W_t,$$

and consider a subordinator $T = (T_t)_{t \geq 0}$ independent to the standard Brownian motion $(W_t)_{t \geq 0}$. Then, substituting $t = T_t$ in the arithmetic Brownian motion, we have a new process $X = (X_t)_{t \geq 0}$ with

$$X_t = \mu T_t + \sigma W_{T_t},$$

which is the time-changed Brownian motion.

If T_t is fixed, then the conditional probability of X_t with a fixed variable T_t follows a normal distribution, that is

$$P(X_t < y | T_t) = P(\mu T_t + \sigma W_{T_t} < y | T_t) = \frac{1}{\sqrt{2\pi\sigma^2 T_t}} \int_{-\infty}^{y} e^{-\frac{(x-\mu T_t)^2}{2\sigma^2 T_t}} \, dx.$$

Using properties of the conditional probability and independentness between W_t and T_t, the distribution function F_{X_t} and the probability density function f_{X_t} of X_t of X_t are obtained by

$$F_{X_t}(y) = P(X_t < y) = \int_{-\infty}^{y} \int_{0}^{\infty} \frac{1}{\sqrt{2\pi\sigma^2 s}} e^{-\frac{(x-\mu s)^2}{2\sigma^2 s}} f_{T_t}(s) ds\, dx,$$

and

$$f_{X_t}(y) = \frac{d}{dy} F_{X_t}(y) = \int_{0}^{\infty} \frac{1}{\sqrt{2\pi\sigma^2 s}} e^{-\frac{(y-\mu s)^2}{2\sigma^2 s}} f_{T_t}(s) ds,$$

respectively, where f_{T_t} is the probability density function of T_t. Moreover, we can derive the characteristic function ϕ_{X_t} as follows:

$$\phi_{X_t}(u) = \phi_{T_t}\left(\mu u + \frac{iu^2\sigma^2}{2}\right), \tag{4.7}$$

where ϕ_{T_t} is the characteristic function of T_t. Using the time-changed Brownian motion, we can define various processes.[6]

4.5.1 Variance Gamma Process

By considering the gamma process as the subordinator of the Brownian motion, we obtain the VG process. That is, the VG process is defined by $X = (X_t)_{t\geq 0}$ with

$$X_t = \mu G_t + \sigma W_{G_t},$$

where $G = (G_t)_{t\geq 0}$ is the gamma process with parameter (c, λ). In order to reduce the number of parameters, we consider the assumption $E[G_t] = t$. Since we have $E[G_t] = \frac{c}{\lambda}$, the assumption satisfies if $c = \lambda$. Then the characteristic function of X_t is equal to

$$\phi_{X_t}(u) = \left(\frac{c}{c - i\mu u + \frac{u^2\sigma^2}{2}}\right)^{ct} = \left(\frac{\frac{2c}{\sigma^2}}{\frac{2c}{\sigma^2} - \frac{2\mu}{\sigma^2}ui + u^2}\right)^{ct} \tag{4.8}$$

---

[6]Theoretically, every Lévy process can be defined as the time-changed Brownian motion. See Clark (1973).

by equation (4.7) and the characteristic function of G_t given in equation (4.4) with $c = \lambda$. Inserting the parameterization

$$\lambda_- - \lambda_+ = \frac{2\mu}{\sigma^2},$$

$$\lambda_+ \lambda_- = \frac{2c}{\sigma^2},$$

$$C = c$$

into equation (4.8), we obtain the form (4.6).

4.5.2 Normal Inverse Gaussian Process

By considering the inverse Gaussian process as the subordinator of the Brownian motion, we obtain the NIG process.

Define a process $X = (X_t)_{t \geq 0}$ with

$$X_t = \mu T_t + \sigma W_{T_t},$$

where $T = (T_t)_{t \geq 0}$ is the inverse Gaussian process with parameter (c, λ), satisfying $E[T_t] = t$. The condition $E[T_t] = t$ holds if $c = \lambda$. Then the characteristic function of X_t is equal to

$$\phi_{X_t}(u) = \exp\left(-kt(\sqrt{k^2 - 2i\mu u + 2\sigma^2 u^2} - k)\right)$$

$$= \exp\left(-\sqrt{2}k\sigma t\left(\sqrt{\frac{k^2}{2\sigma^2} - \frac{\mu}{\sigma^2}iu + u^2} - \sqrt{\frac{k^2}{2\sigma^2}}\right)\right) \qquad (4.9)$$

by equation (4.7) and the characteristic function of T_t given in equation (4.5) with $k = c = \lambda$. Inserting the parameterization

$$\lambda^2 - \beta^2 = \frac{k^2}{2\sigma^2},$$

$$\beta = \frac{\mu}{2\sigma^2},$$

$$c = \sqrt{2}k\sigma$$

into equation (4.9), we obtain the NIG process with parameter $(c, \lambda, \beta, \frac{c\beta}{\sqrt{\lambda^2 - \beta^2}})$.

4.5.3 Normal Tempered Stable Process

Assume Lévy measure v is equal to

$$v(dx) = \frac{ce^{-\theta x}}{x^{\alpha/2+1}} 1_{x>0} dx, \tag{4.10}$$

where $\alpha \in (0, 2)$, $c > 0$, and $\theta > 0$, and consider the pure jump process $T = (T_t)_{t \geq 0}$ defined by v and γ, where

$$\gamma = \int_0^1 x v(dx).$$

Since $v(A) = 0$ for all $A \subset (-\infty, 0)$ and $\mu \geq 0$, the process T is a non-decreasing process. Hence it is a subordinator and referred to as the *tempered stable subordinator* with parameters (α, c, θ). Using equation (4.2), the characteristic function ϕ_{T_t} of T_t is equal to

$$\phi_{T_t}(u) = \exp\left(tc \int_0^\infty (e^{iux} - 1) \frac{e^{-\theta x}}{x^{\alpha/2+1}} dx \right).$$

Solving the integration in the last equation, we can obtain the following formula:

$$\phi_{T_t}(u) = \exp\left(tc\Gamma\left(-\frac{\alpha}{2}\right) \left((\theta - iu)^{\frac{\alpha}{2}} - \theta^{\frac{\alpha}{2}}\right) \right). \tag{4.11}$$

The mean of T_t is computed by the first cumulant, that is,

$$E[T_t] = \frac{1}{i} \frac{\partial}{\partial u} \log \phi_{T_t}(u)|_{u=0} = tc\Gamma\left(1 - \frac{\alpha}{2}\right) \theta^{\frac{\alpha}{2}-1}.$$

Hence, the condition $E[T_t] = t$ holds if $c = \left(\Gamma\left(1 - \frac{\alpha}{2}\right) \theta^{\frac{\alpha}{2}-1}\right)^{-1}$.

By considering the tempered stable subordinator as the subordinator of the Brownian motion, we obtain the NTS process. That is, define a process $X = (X_t)_{t \geq 0}$ with

$$X_t = \mu T_t + \sigma W_{T_t},$$

where $T = (T_t)_{t \geq 0}$ is the tempered stable subordinator with parameter $(\alpha, (\Gamma(1 - \frac{\alpha}{2})\theta^{\frac{\alpha}{2}-1})^{-1}, \theta)$. The characteristic function of X_t is equal to

$$\phi_{X_t}(u) = \exp\left(\frac{t\Gamma\left(-\frac{\alpha}{2}\right)}{\Gamma\left(1-\frac{\alpha}{2}\right)\theta^{\frac{\alpha}{2}-1}}\left(\left(\theta - i\left(\mu u + \frac{i\sigma^2 u^2}{2}\right)\right)^{\frac{\alpha}{2}} - \theta^{\frac{\alpha}{2}}\right)\right)$$

$$= \exp\left(\frac{-2t}{\alpha\theta^{\frac{\alpha}{2}-1}}\left(\left(\theta - i\left(\mu u + \frac{i\sigma^2 u^2}{2}\right)\right)^{\frac{\alpha}{2}} - \theta^{\frac{\alpha}{2}}\right)\right) \tag{4.12}$$

by equations (4.7) and equation (4.11) with $c = (\Gamma(1 - \frac{\alpha}{2})\theta^{\frac{\alpha}{2}-1})^{-1}$. The last equation can be changed to the following expression:

$$\phi_{X_t}(u) \tag{4.13}$$

$$= \exp\left(\frac{t\Gamma\left(-\frac{\alpha}{2}\right)\left(\frac{\sigma^2}{2}\right)^{\frac{\alpha}{2}}}{\Gamma\left(1-\frac{\alpha}{2}\right)\theta^{\frac{\alpha}{2}-1}}\left(\left(\frac{2\theta}{\sigma^2} + \left(\frac{\mu}{\sigma^2}\right)^2 - \left(\frac{\mu}{\sigma^2} + iu\right)^2\right)^{\frac{\alpha}{2}} - \left(\frac{2\theta}{\sigma^2}\right)^{\frac{\alpha}{2}}\right)\right)$$

Inserting the parameterization

$$\lambda = \sqrt{\frac{2\theta}{\sigma^2} + \left(\frac{\mu}{\sigma^2}\right)^2},$$

$$\beta = \frac{\mu}{\sigma^2}$$

$$C = \frac{\sqrt{2}\sigma^\alpha}{\sqrt{\pi}\Gamma\left(1-\frac{\alpha}{2}\right)\theta^{\frac{\alpha}{2}-1}}$$

into equation (4.13), we obtain the NTS process with parameter $(\alpha, C, \lambda, \beta, m)$ where $m = 2^{-\frac{\alpha-1}{2}}C\sqrt{\pi}\Gamma\left(1 - \frac{\alpha}{2}\right)\beta(\lambda^2 - \beta^2)^{\frac{\alpha}{2}-1}$.

4.6   LÉVY PROCESS

A stochastic process $X = (X_t)_{t \geq 0}$ is called a *Lévy process* if the following five conditions are satisfied:

1. $X_0 = 0$ a.s.
2. X has independent increments.
3. X has stationary increment.

4. X is stochastically continuous; that is, $\forall t \geq 0$ and $a > 0$,

$$\lim_{s \to t} \mathbf{P}[\,|X_s - X_t| > a\,] = 0.$$

5. X is right continuous and has left limits (*cadlag*).

The standard Brownian motion, arithmetic Brownian motions, and pure jump processes are all Lévy processes. Moreover, a Lévy process can be decomposed by a Brownian motion and a pure jump process $(Z_t)_{t \geq 0}$ independent to the Brownian motion, that is

$$X_t = \sigma W_t + Z_t.$$

Hence, we obtain the characteristic function of X_t as follows:

$$\phi_{X_t}(u) = \phi_{\sigma W_t}(u)\phi_{Z_t}(u)$$

$$= \exp\left(-\frac{t}{2}\sigma^2 u^2\right)\exp\left(i\gamma ut + t\int_{-\infty}^{\infty}(e^{iux} - 1 - iux1_{|x| \leq 1})v(dx)\right)$$

$$= \exp\left(i\gamma ut - \frac{t}{2}\sigma^2 u^2 + t\int_{-\infty}^{\infty}(e^{iux} - 1 - iux1_{|x| \leq 1})v(dx)\right),$$

where $\phi_{\sigma W_t}(u)$ is the characteristic function of $N(0, \sigma^2 t)$, and $\phi_{Z_t}(u)$ given by (4.2). Hence, if $X = (X_t)_{t \geq 0}$ is a Lévy process, then for any $t \geq 0$, X_t is an infinitely divisible random variable. Conversely, if Y is an infinitely divisible random variable, then there exists uniquely a Lévy process $(X_t)_{t \geq 0}$ such that $X_1 = Y$.[7]

4.7   SUMMARY

In this chapter, we discussed pure jump processes, Brownian motion, and Lévy processes. The purely non-Gaussian infinitely divisible random variables generate pure jump processes. Brownian motion is generated by the sum of i.i.d. random variables and Central Limit Theorem. Moreover, using subordinator instead of physical time for Brownian motion, we obtained various pure jump processes. Finally, all of these processes are included in the class of Lévy processes.

---

[7]See Sato (1999, p. 38).

REFERENCES

Bachelier, L. (1990). Théorie de la spéculation. *Annales d'Ecole Normale Superieure*, *3*, 21–86.

Carr, P., Geman, H., Madan, D., & Yor, M. (2002). The fine structure of asset returns: An empirical investigation. *Journal of Business*, *75*(2), 305–332.

Clark, P. (1973). A subordinated stochastic process model with finite variance for speculative prices. *Econometrica*, *41*(1), 135–155.

Cont, R. & Tankov, P. (2004). *Financial modelling with jump processes*. Boca Raton, FL: Chapman & Hall CRC.

Karatzas, I. & Shreve, S. (1991). *Brownian motion and stochastic calculus*. (2nd ed.) Berlin: Springer.

Kim, Y., Rachev, S., Bianchi, M., & Fabozzi, F. (2010). Tempered stable and tempered infinitely divisible GARCH models. *Journal of Banking and Finance*, *34*(9), 2096–2109.

Kim, Y. S. (2005). The modified tempered stable processes with application to finance. Ph.D. thesis, Sogang University.

Kim, Y. S., Rachev, S. T., Bianchi, M. L., & Fabozzi, F. J. (2007). A new tempered stable distribution and its application to finance. In G. Bol, S. T. Rachev, & R. Wuerth (Eds.), *Risk assessment: Decisions in banking and finance*, (pp. 77–110). Heidelberg: Physica-Verlag, Springer.

Oksendal, B. (2000). *Stochastic differential equations: An introduction with applications* (5th ed.). New York: Springer.

Rachev, S. T. & Mittnik, S. (2000). *Stable Paretian models in finance*. New York: John Wiley & Sons.

Sato, K. (1999). *Lévy processes and infinitely divisible distributions*. Cambridge: Cambridge University Press.

CHAPTER 5

Conditional Expectation and Change of Measure

In this chapter, we present some issues in stochastic processes. We begin by defining events of a probability space mathematically, and then discuss the concept of conditional expectation. We then explain two important notions for stochastic processes: *martingale properties* and *Markov properties*. The former relates to the fair price in a market and the latter describes the efficiency of a market. Finally, "change of measures" for processes are discussed. Change of measures for tempered stable processes are important for determining no-arbitrage pricing for assets, a topic that we cover in Chapters 7 and 13.

5.1   EVENTS, σ-FIELDS, AND FILTRATION

A set of possible outcomes in a given sample space Ω is called an *event*. An event is mathematically defined as a subset of Ω. If we have one event A, then the set of outcomes that are not included in A is also an event. For example, if we consider an event that the return of the stock of Disney tomorrow will be positive, then the set of outcomes that Disney's return tomorrow will be negative is also an event. Moreover, if we have two events A and B, then a set of outcomes included in both A and B is also an event. For instance, consider two events, the first event being that Disney's stock return of tomorrow will be positive, and the other event is that IBM's stock return of tomorrow will be positive. Then a set of outcomes that both stock returns will be positive tomorrow is an event.

The class of events is described mathematically by the σ-*field*. The σ-field, denoted by $\mathcal{F}$, is the class of the subsets of Ω that satisfy the following properties:

Property 1. $\emptyset \in \mathcal{F}$ and $\Omega \in \mathcal{F}$.

Property 2. If $A \in \mathcal{F}$, then $A^c = \{x \in \Omega | x \notin A\} \in \mathcal{F}$.

Property 3. If $A_1, A_2, A_3, \ldots \in \mathcal{F}$, then $\cup_{n=1}^{\infty} A_n \in \mathcal{F}$.

Let $\mathcal{G}$ denote a class of subsets contained in Ω. Then the smallest σ-field containing $\mathcal{G}$ is referred to as the σ-*field generated by* $\mathcal{G}$, and is denoted by $\sigma(\mathcal{G})$. For a given random variable X, consider the class $\mathcal{G} = \{A \subseteq \Omega : A = X^{-1}(I)$, for all open interval I in $\mathbb{R}\}$, where X^{-1} is the inverse image of X. Then the σ-field generated by $\mathcal{G}$ is referred to as the σ-*field generated by* X, and denoted by $\sigma(X)$. If there is a σ-field $\mathcal{F}$ such that $\sigma(X) \subseteq \mathcal{F}$, then we say that X is $\mathcal{F}$-measurable.

The probability $\mathbf{P}$ is a map from a given σ-field $\mathcal{F}$ to the unit interval $[0, 1]$. If $A \subseteq N \in \mathcal{F}$ and $P(N) = 0$, then the set A is referred to as a *null set* with respect to $(\Omega, \mathcal{F}, \mathbf{P})$. Let $\mathcal{N}$ be the class of all null sets with respect to $(\Omega, \mathcal{F}, \mathbf{P})$. The space $(\Omega, \tilde{\mathcal{F}}, \tilde{\mathbf{P}})$ is referred to as a *completion* of $(\Omega, \mathcal{F}, \mathbf{P})$ if $\tilde{\mathcal{F}} = \sigma(\mathcal{F} \cup \mathcal{N})$ and $\tilde{\mathbf{P}}(A \cup N) = \mathbf{P}(A)$ for all $A \in \mathcal{F}$ and $N \in \mathcal{N}$. All probability spaces in this book are assumed to be completions of spaces, that is, all null sets are contained in given σ-fields, and probabilities are defined on completed σ-fields.

Let $(\mathcal{F}_t)_{t \geq 0}$ be a sequence of σ-field with continuous index $t \geq 0$ (or discrete index $t = 0, 1, 2, \ldots$). If $\mathcal{F}_s \subseteq \mathcal{F}_t$ for all $0 \leq s \leq t$, then $(\mathcal{F}_t)_{t \geq 0}$ is referred to as a *filtration*. $\mathcal{F}_t$ can be interpreted as the "information" available to all market agents at time t. The filtration describes increasing information for time t.

Consider a stochastic process $X = (X_t)_{t \geq 0}$. If X_t is $\mathcal{F}_t$-measurable for all $t \geq 0$, then X is referred to as a $(\mathcal{F}_t)_{t \geq 0}$-*adapted process*. If X_t is $\mathcal{F}_{t-1}$-measurable for all discrete index $t = 0, 1, 2, \ldots$, then X is referred to as a $(\mathcal{F}_t)_{t \geq 0}$-*predictable process*.

For a given process $X = (X_t)_{t \geq 0}$, we can generate a filtration $(\mathcal{F}_t)_{t \geq 0}$ by

$$\mathcal{F}_t = \sigma(X_s; 0 \leq s \leq t),$$

where $\sigma(X_s; 0 \leq s \leq t)$ is the smallest σ-field containing all $\sigma(X_s)$ with $0 \leq s \leq t$. Then the process X is $(\mathcal{F}_t)_{t \geq 0}$-adapted and this filtration is referred to as a *filtration generated by* X.

5.2 CONDITIONAL EXPECTATION

The *conditional expectation* is a value of the expectation of a random variable under some restricted events. Let g be a Borel function, X be a random variable on a space $(\Omega, \mathbf{P})$ with $E[g(X)] < \infty$, and A be an event. The conditional expectation $E[g(X)|A]$ is defined by

$$E[g(X)|A] = \frac{E[g(X) \cdot 1_A],}{P(A)}$$

where

$$1_A(\omega) = \begin{cases} 0 & \text{if } \omega \notin A \\ 1 & \text{if } \omega \in A \end{cases}.$$

Consider a Borel function g, a stochastic process $X = (X_t)_{t \geq 0}$ adapted to a filtration $(\mathcal{F}_t)_{t \geq 0}$. We can define the conditional expectation on $\mathcal{F}_t$ as a random variable. That is, the conditional expectation $E[g(X_T)|\mathcal{F}_t]$ for $t \leq T$ is a random variable, such that

$$E[g(X_T)|\mathcal{F}_t](\omega) = E[g(X_T)|A_\omega], \quad \omega \in \Omega,$$

where A_ω is the smallest event in $\mathcal{F}_t$ with $\omega \in A_\omega$, or $A_\omega = \cap_{\omega \in B_\omega \in \mathcal{F}_t} B_\omega$. Moreover, if g and h are Borel functions, and $0 \leq s \leq t \leq T \leq T^*$, then we have the following properties:

- $E[g(X_t)|\mathcal{F}_0] = E[g(X_t)]$ where $\mathcal{F}_0 = \{\emptyset, \Omega\}$.
- $E[E[g(X_T)|\mathcal{F}_t]|\mathcal{F}_s] = E[g(X_T)|\mathcal{F}_s]$.
- $E[g(X_t)h(X_T)|\mathcal{F}_t] = g(X_t)E[h(X_T)|\mathcal{F}_t]$.
- $E[ag(X_T) + bh(X_{T^*})|\mathcal{F}_t] = a E[g(X_T)|\mathcal{F}_t] + bE[h(X_{T^*})|\mathcal{F}_t]$, for a, $b \in \mathbb{R}$.

We write $E[g(X_T)|X_t]$ instead of $E[g(X_T)|\mathcal{F}_t]$ when $\mathcal{F}_t = \sigma(X_t)$. Hence we have:

- $E[E[g(X_T)|X_t]|X_s] = E[g(X_T)|X_s]$.
- $E[g(X_t)h(X_T)|X_t] = g(X_t)E[h(X_T)|X_t]$.
- $E[ag(X_T) + bh(X_{T^*})|X_t] = a E[g(X_T)|X_t] + bE[h(X_{T^*})|X_t]$, for a, $b \in \mathbb{R}$.

If a $(\mathcal{F}_t)$-adapted process $X = (X_t)_{t\geq 0}$ satisfies the condition

$$E[g(X_T)|\mathcal{F}_t] = E[g(X_T)|X_t]$$

for all $0 \geq t \geq T$ and Borel function g, then the process X is referred to as a *Markov process*. In finance, a Markov process is used to explain the *efficient market hypothesis*. Suppose X is a price process of an asset, and consider a forward contract on the asset with maturity T. The σ-field $\mathcal{F}_t$ contains all market information until time t. Hence, $F_t = E[X_T|\mathcal{F}_t]$ is the expected price of the forward contract based on the information up to t. If the market is efficient, all information until t is impounded into the current price X_t. Hence, the expected price of the forward contract can be obtained by $F_t = E[X_T|X_t]$.

If a $(\mathcal{F}_t)$-adapted process $X = (X_t)_{t\geq 0}$ satisfies the condition

$$X_t = E[X_T|\mathcal{F}_t]$$

for all $0 \leq t \leq T$, then the process X is referred to as a *martingale process*. The process $X = (X_t)_{t\geq 0}$ with $X_t = \sigma W_t$ is a martingale process, where $\sigma > 0$ and $(W_t)_{t\geq 0}$ is the standard Brownian motion. Since X_t is $\mathcal{F}_t$-measurable, we have

$$E[X_T|\mathcal{F}_t] = E[X_T - X_t + X_t|\mathcal{F}_t] = E[X_T - X_t|\mathcal{F}_t] + X_t.$$

Since X has stationary and independent increments,

$$E[X_T - X_t|\mathcal{F}_t] = E[X_T - X_t] = E[X_{T-t}] = E[\sigma W_{T-t}] = 0.$$

Hence the process X is martingale. For the same reason, The classical tempered stable (CTS) process with parameter $(\alpha, C, \lambda_+, \lambda_-, 0)$ is martingale, and the other five tempered stable processes that we covered in Chapter 4—the generalized tempered stable (GTS), Kim-Rachev tempered stable (KRTS), modified tempered stable (MTS), normal tempered stable (NTS), and the rapidly decreasing tempered stable (RDTS) processes—are all martingale if the parameter m equals zero.

In finance, a martingale process describes the fair price or no-arbitrage price for an asset. For example, consider one share of a stock and a forward contract that required delivery of one share of that stock to the forward contract holder at the maturity date. Suppose $(S_t)_{t\geq 0}$ is a stock price process and $(F_t)_{0\leq t\leq T}$ is the price process for the forward contract with maturity T. The forward price at time $t < T$ is given by the conditional expectation of S_T based on the information until time t, that is, $F_t = E[S_T|\mathcal{F}_t]$. Moreover, we can see that $F_t = S_t$ for all t with $0 \leq t \leq T$ by the following argument.

Suppose $F_t > S_t$. Then we obtain the difference $F_t - S_t > 0$ at time t by purchasing one share of the stock at price S_t and selling the forward contract at price F_t. We invest the proceeds in a money market account with interest rate r. At time T, by delivering the stock to the holder of the forward contract, we then have $e^{r(T-t)}(F_t - S_t)$, which is an arbitrage profit. If $F_t > S_t$, then another arbitrage opportunity can be found by selling (i.e, shorting) one share of the stock and purchasing the forward contract. Therefore, to eliminate arbitrage opportunities, F_t should be equal to S_t; that is, the stock price process should be a martingale.

5.3   CHANGE OF MEASURES

In this section, we present *change of measure* for random variables and Lévy processes. Change of measure is an important method to determine no-arbitrage prices of assets and derivatives. Further details about no-arbitrage pricing with the change of measure will be discussed in Chapter 7.

5.3.1   Equivalent Probability Measure

Consider two probability measures **P** and **Q** on a sample space Ω and σ-field $\mathcal{F}$. If they satisfy the condition

$$\mathbf{Q}(A) = 0 \Rightarrow \mathbf{P}(A) = 0,$$

then we say that **P** is *absolutely continuous* with respect to **Q**, and denote **P** $\ll$ **Q**. Moreover, if **P** $\ll$ **Q** and **Q** $\ll$ **P**, that is,

$$\mathbf{Q}(A) = 0 \Leftrightarrow \mathbf{P}(A) = 0,$$

then we say that **P** and **Q** are *equivalent*.

If **Q** $\ll$ **P**, then there exists a positive random variable ξ with $\int_{\Omega} \xi \, d\mathbf{P} = 1$ and

$$\mathbf{Q}(A) = \int_A \xi \, d\mathbf{P} \tag{5.1}$$

for any $A \in \mathcal{F}$. In this case, ξ is referred to as *Radon-Nikodym derivative*, and denotes

$$\xi = \frac{d\mathbf{Q}}{d\mathbf{P}}.$$

Conversely, if there is a positive random variable ξ with $\int_{\Omega} \xi dP = 1$ and Q is defined by equation (5.1), then Q is also a probability measure and $Q \ll P$.

Let X be a random variable on a probability measure P, and $f(x) = \frac{\partial}{\partial x} P(X \le x)$ be the probability density function (p.d.f.) of X. Suppose Q is a probability measure and the probability density function of X on Q is given by $g(x) = \frac{\partial}{\partial x} Q(X \le x)$. If P and Q are equivalent, then the Radon-Nikodym derivative is equal to

$$\frac{dQ}{dP} = \frac{g(X)}{f(X)}.$$

For example, $X \sim N(0, 1)$ is normally distributed on P. If we take the Radon-Nikodym derivative by

$$\xi_1 = \frac{e^{-\frac{(X-\mu)^2}{2\sigma^2}} / \sqrt{2\pi\sigma^2}}{e^{-\frac{X^2}{2}} / \sqrt{2\pi}},$$

then the measure Q_1 defined by $Q_1(A) = \int_A \xi_1 dP$ for $A \in \mathcal{F}$ is equivalent to P and $X \sim N(\mu, \sigma^2)$ on the measure Q_1. On the other hand, if we take the Radon-Nikodym derivative by

$$\xi_2 = \frac{h(X)}{e^{-\frac{X^2}{2}} / \sqrt{2\pi}},$$

where

$$h(x) = \frac{\sigma}{\pi \left((x - \mu)^2 + \sigma^2\right)},$$

which is the probability density function of the Cauchy distribution, then the measure Q_2 defined by $Q_2(A) = \int_A \xi_2 dP$ for $A \in \mathcal{F}$ is equivalent to P and $X \sim S_1(\sigma, 0, \mu)$ on the measure Q_2.

Consider a finite discrete process $(X_t)_{t \in \{1,2,\dots,T\}}$ of independent and identically distributed (i.i.d.) real random variables on both probability measures P and Q, where T is a positive integer. By the independent property of the process on P, we have

$$P[X_1 \in \mathbb{R}, \dots, X_{t-1} \in \mathbb{R}, X_t < x, X_{t+1} \in \mathbb{R}, \dots, X_T \in \mathbb{R}]$$

$$= P[X_1 \in \mathbb{R}] \cdots P[X_{t-1} \in \mathbb{R}] \cdot P[X_t < x] \cdot P[X_{t+1} \in \mathbb{R}] \cdots P[X_T \in \mathbb{R}]$$

$$= P[X_t < x].$$

By the same argument, we have

$$Q[X_1 \in \mathbb{R}, \ldots, X_{t-1} \in \mathbb{R}, X_t < x, X_{t+1} \in \mathbb{R}, \ldots, X_T \in \mathbb{R}] = Q[X_t < x].$$

Since X_t's are identically distributed on **P** and **Q**, respectively, we have $P[X_t < x] = P[X_s < x]$ and $Q[X_t < x] = Q[X_s < x]$ for all $t, s \in \{1, 2, \ldots, T\}$. Suppose that for all $t \in \{1, 2, \ldots, T\}$ the probability density functions of X_t are given by $f(x)$ and $g(x)$ on probability measures **P** and **Q**, respectively. That is,

$$f(x) = \frac{\partial}{\partial x} P[X_t < x]$$

and

$$g(x) = \frac{\partial}{\partial x} Q[X_t < x].$$

If the domain of the function f is the same as the domain of the function g, then **P** and **Q** are equivalent and the Radon-Nikodym derivative is equal to

$$\frac{d\mathbf{Q}}{d\mathbf{P}} = \frac{g(X_1)g(X_2) \cdots g(X_T)}{f(X_1)f(X_2) \cdots f(X_T)}.$$

However, that method cannot be used for either continuous-time processes or infinite-discrete processes. In the next section, we discuss the change of measure for continuous-time processes using the Girsanov's theorem and extended Girsanov's theorem.

5.3.2 Change of Measure for Continuous-Time Processes

A continuous-time process is a function from the sample space to the set of appropriate functions. Hence, the change of measure for processes is more complex than the change of measure for a random variable.

Brownian motion is a function from the sample space to the set of continuous functions. For Brownian motion, we can find an equivalent measure using the following theorem, which is referred to as Girsanov's theorem:[1]

---

[1]The general form of the Girsanov's theorem is presented in many works including Karatzas and Shreve (1991), Oksendal (2000), and Klebaner (2005). Black-Scholes

Theorem 1. *Let* $W = (W_t)_{t \geq 0}$ *be a standard Brownian motion under measure* **P** *and* $(\mathcal{F}_t)_{t \geq 0}$ *be a filtration generated by* W. *Consider a process* $(\xi_t)_{t \geq 0}$ *defined by*

$$\xi_t = e^{-\theta W_t - \frac{\theta^2}{2} t}.$$

Then the probability measure **Q** *given by*

$$Q(A)|_{\mathcal{F}_t} = \int_A \xi_t d\mathbf{P}, \quad A \in \mathcal{F}_t$$

is equivalent to $\mathbf{P}|_{\mathcal{F}_t}$ *for all* $t \geq 0$, *and the process* $\tilde{W} = (\tilde{W}_t)_{t \geq 0}$ *with* $\tilde{W}_t = \theta t + W_t$ *is a standard Brownian motion under the measure* **Q**.

Girsanov's theorem shows how stochastic processes change under the change of measure. For example, let a process $X = (X_t)_{t \geq 0}$ be an arithmetic Brownian motion under measure **P** such that

$$X_t = \mu t + \sigma W_t,$$

where $(W_t)_{t \geq 0}$ is the standard Brownian motion. The process X is not martingale on the measure **P**, but we can obtain a measure where X is martingale by Girsanov's theorem. Indeed, we define a measure **Q** equivalent to **P** such that

$$Q(A)|_{\mathcal{F}_t} = \int_A e^{-\frac{\mu W_t}{\sigma} - \frac{\mu^2}{2\sigma^2} t} d\mathbf{P}, \quad A \in \mathcal{F}_t.$$

Then the process X becomes $X_t = \sigma \tilde{W}_t$ with $\tilde{W}_t = \frac{\mu t}{\sigma} + W_t$ and the process $(\tilde{W}_t)_{t \geq 0}$ is a standard Brownian motion on the measure **Q**. Therefore, the process X is martingale on the measure **Q**.

A Lévy process is a function from the sample space to the set of right continuous functions with left limits at any point of the domain.[2] Girsanov's theorem can be extended for Lévy processes by the following theorem:

Theorem 2. *Suppose a process* $X = (X_t)_{t \geq 0}$ *is a Lévy process with Lévy triplets* (σ^2, ν, γ) *under measure* **P**. *If there is a real number* θ *satisfying*

---

option pricing formula is derived by applying Girsanov's theorem in Harrison and Pliska (1981).

[2]We refer to such functions as *cadlag functions*.

$\int_{|x|\geq 1} e^{\theta x} \nu(dx) < \infty$, *then we can find the equivalent measure* **Q** *whose Radon-Nikodym derivative is given by*

$$\frac{d\mathbf{Q}}{d\mathbf{P}}\Big|_{\mathcal{F}_t} = \xi_t = \frac{e^{\theta X_t}}{E_\mathbf{P}[e^{\theta X_t}]} = e^{\theta X_t - l(\theta)t},$$

where $l(\theta) = \log E_\mathbf{P}[e^{\theta X_1}]$. *That is,*

$$\mathbf{Q}(A)|_{\mathcal{F}_t} = \int_A \xi_t d\mathbf{P}, \quad A \in \mathcal{F}_t$$

is equivalent to $\mathbf{P}|_{\mathcal{F}_t}$ *for all* $t \geq 0$. *Moreover, the process* X *is a Lévy process with Lévy triplets* $(\sigma^2, \tilde{\nu}, \tilde{\gamma})$ *under the measure* **Q**, *where* $\tilde{\nu}(dx) = e^{\theta x}\nu(dx)$ *and* $\tilde{\gamma} = \gamma + \int_{|x|\leq 1} x(e^{\theta x} - 1)\nu(dx)$.

The change of measure using Theorem 2 is referred to as the *Esscher transform*. The properties of pure-jump processes change under the change of measure using Esscher transform. For example, let a process $X = (X_t)_{t\geq 0}$ be a symmetric CTS process under measure **P**. Then the Lévy measure $\nu(dx)$ of X is given by

$$\nu(dx) = C\left(\frac{e^{-\lambda x}}{x^{1+\alpha}}1_{x>0} + \frac{e^{-\lambda|x|}}{|x|^{1+\alpha}}1_{x<0}\right)dx,$$

Since we have $\int_{|x|\geq 1} e^{\theta x}\nu(dx) < \infty$ for some real number θ with $-\lambda \leq \theta \leq \lambda$, we can define a measure **Q** equivalent to **P** such that

$$\mathbf{Q}(A)|_{\mathcal{F}_t} = \int_A e^{\theta X_t - l(\theta)t} d\mathbf{P}, \quad A \in \mathcal{F}_t,$$

where

$$l(\theta) = \log E_\mathbf{P}[e^{\theta X_1}] = C\Gamma(-\alpha)((\lambda - \theta)^\alpha + (\lambda + \theta)^\alpha - 2\lambda^\alpha).$$

Moreover, the Lévy measure $\tilde{\nu}(dx)$ of X under **Q** is given by

$$\tilde{\nu}(dx) = e^{\theta x}\nu(dx) = C\left(\frac{e^{-(\lambda-\theta)x}}{x^{1+\alpha}}1_{x>0} + \frac{e^{-(\lambda+\theta)|x|}}{|x|^{1+\alpha}}1_{x<0}\right)dx.$$

By the same argument, we discuss the relation between the symmetric MTS and NTS process. That is, let a process $X = (X_t)_{t\geq 0}$ be a symmetric

MTS process under measure **P**. Then the Lévy measure $v(dx)$ of X is given by

$$v(dx) = C(\lambda|x|)^{\frac{\alpha+1}{2}} K_{\frac{\alpha+1}{2}}(\lambda|x|)dx.$$

Since we have $\int_{|x|\geq 1} e^{-\beta x} v(dx) < \infty$ for some real number β with $-\lambda \leq \beta \leq \lambda$, we can define a measure **Q** equivalent to **P** such that

$$Q(A)|_{\mathcal{F}_t} = \int_A e^{-\beta X_t - l(-\beta)t} dP, \quad A \in \mathcal{F}_t,$$

where

$$l(x) = \log E_P[e^{xX_1}] = C2^{-\frac{\alpha+1}{2}} \sqrt{\pi} \Gamma\left(-\frac{\alpha}{2}\right) \left((\lambda^2 + x^2)^{\frac{\alpha}{2}} - \lambda^\alpha\right).$$

Moreover, the Lévy measure $\tilde{v}(dx)$ of X under **Q** is given by

$$\tilde{v}(dx) = e^{-\beta x} v(dx) = Ce^{-\beta x}(\lambda|x|)^{\frac{\alpha+1}{2}} K_{\frac{\alpha+1}{2}}(\lambda|x|)dx,$$

which is the Lévy measure for the NTS process.

The most general theorem of change of measure for Lévy processes is given by the following theorem (see Sato, 1999):

Theorem 3. *Suppose a process $X = (X_t)_{t\geq 0}$ has a Lévy triplets (σ^2, v, γ) and $(\tilde{\sigma}^2, \tilde{v}, \tilde{\gamma})$ under measures **P** and **Q**, respectively.*

1. *In the case where $\sigma^2 \neq 0$ and $\tilde{\sigma}^2 \neq 0$, $P|_{\mathcal{F}_t}$ and $Q|_{\mathcal{F}_t}$ are equivalent for all $t \geq 0$ if and only if the Lévy triplets satisfy*

$$\sigma^2 = \tilde{\sigma}^2 > 0, \tag{5.2}$$

and

$$\int_{-\infty}^{\infty} (e^{\psi(x)/2} - 1)^2 v(dx) < \infty, \tag{5.3}$$

where $\psi(x) = \ln\left(\frac{d\tilde{v}}{dv}\right)$.

2. *In the case where $\sigma^2 = \tilde{\sigma}^2 = 0$, $\mathbf{P}|_{\mathcal{F}_t}$ and $\mathbf{Q}|_{\mathcal{F}_t}$ are equivalent for all $t \geq 0$ if and only if the Lévy triplets satisfy (5.3) and*

$$\tilde{\gamma} - \gamma = \int_{|x| \leq 1} x(\tilde{\nu} - \nu)(dx). \tag{5.4}$$

When $\mathbf{P}$ and $\mathbf{Q}$ are equivalent, the Radon-Nikodym derivative is

$$\frac{d\mathbf{Q}}{d\mathbf{P}}\Big|_{\mathcal{F}_t} = e^{\xi_t}$$

where $\xi = (\xi_t)_{t \geq 0}$ is a Lévy process with Lévy triplet $(\sigma_\xi^2, \nu_\xi, \gamma_\xi)$ given by

$$\begin{cases} \sigma_\xi^2 = \sigma^2 \eta^2 \\ \nu_\xi = \nu \circ \psi^{-1} \\ \gamma_\xi = -\frac{\sigma^2 \eta^2}{2} - \int_{-\infty}^{\infty} (e^y - 1 - y 1_{|y| \leq 1}) \nu_\xi(dy) \end{cases} \tag{5.5}$$

and η is such that

$$\tilde{\gamma} - \gamma - \int_{|x| \leq 1} x(\tilde{\nu} - \nu)(dx) = \begin{cases} \sigma^2 \eta & \text{if } \sigma > 0 \\ 0 & \text{if } \sigma = 0 \end{cases}.$$

5.3.3 Change of Measure in Tempered Stable Processes

In this section, we present the change of measure for six tempered stable processes: the CTS, GTS, KRTS, MTS, NTS, and RDTS processes. Proofs can be obtained by Theorem 3, but we will not discuss the proofs here.

Let $(X_t)_{t \geq 0}$ be a CTS process with parameters $(\alpha, C, \lambda_+, \lambda_-, m)$ on measure $\mathbf{P}$ and a CTS process with parameters $(\tilde{\alpha}, \tilde{C}, \tilde{\lambda}_+, \tilde{\lambda}_-, \tilde{m})$ on measure $\mathbf{Q}$. Then $\mathbf{P}$ and $\mathbf{Q}$ are equivalent if and only if $C = \tilde{C}$, $\alpha = \tilde{\alpha}$, and

$$\tilde{m} - m = C\Gamma(1 - \alpha)(\tilde{\lambda}_+^{\alpha-1} - \tilde{\lambda}_-^{\alpha-1} - \lambda_+^{\alpha-1} + \lambda_-^{\alpha-1}). \tag{5.6}$$

When $\mathbf{P}$ and $\mathbf{Q}$ are equivalent, the Radon-Nikodym derivative is $\frac{d\mathbf{Q}}{d\mathbf{P}}\big|_{\mathcal{F}_t} = e^{U_t}$ where $U = (U_t)_{t \geq 0}$ is a Lévy process with Lévy triplet $(\sigma_U^2, \nu_U, \gamma_U)$ given by

$$\sigma_U^2 = 0, \quad \nu_U = \nu \circ \psi^{-1}, \quad \gamma_U = -\int_{-\infty}^{\infty} (e^y - 1 - y 1_{|y| \leq 1})(\nu \circ \psi^{-1})(dy). \tag{5.7}$$

In equation (5.7), ν is the CTS Lévy measure given by

$$\nu(dx) = C\left(\frac{e^{-\lambda_+ x}}{x^{1+\alpha}}1_{x>0} + \frac{e^{-\lambda_- |x|}}{|x|^{1+\alpha}}1_{x<0}\right)dx,$$

and $\psi(x) = (\lambda_+ - \tilde{\lambda}_+)x1_{x>0} - (\lambda_- - \tilde{\lambda}_-)x1_{x<0}$.[3]

We can apply the same argument to the GTS, MTS, NTS, KRTS, and RDTS processes.[4] The necessary and sufficient equivalent condition for change of measures for the six tempered stable distributions are presented in Table 5.1. Radon-Nikodym derivatives are omitted in the table.

By applying change of measures, we can obtain a martingale process from a CTS process. Let a process $X^0 = (X^0_t)_{t\geq 0}$ be a CTS process with parameters $(\alpha, C, \lambda_+, \lambda_-, 0)$ on measure **P** and let $X = (X_t)_{t\geq 0}$ be a process with $X_t = mt + X^0_t$. Then X becomes the CTS process with parameters $(\alpha, C, \lambda_+, \lambda_-, m)$ on the measure **P**. The process X is not martingale on the measure **P**, but we can obtain a measure where X is martingale by the change of measures for CTS processes. We assume that $\tilde{\lambda}_+$ and $\tilde{\lambda}_-$ are positive real numbers such that

$$0 - m = C\Gamma(1-\alpha)(\tilde{\lambda}_+^{\alpha-1} - \tilde{\lambda}_-^{\alpha-1} - \lambda_+^{\alpha-1} + \lambda_-^{\alpha-1}),$$

and we define a measure **Q** equivalent to **P** such that

$$Q(A)|_{\mathcal{F}_t} = \int_A e^{U_t}d\mathbf{P}, \quad A \in \mathcal{F}_t,$$

where $(U_t)_{t\geq 0}$ is the Lévy process with Lévy triplet $(\sigma_U^2, \nu_U, \gamma_U)$ given by equation (5.7). Then the process X becomes the CTS process with parameter $(\alpha, C, \tilde{\lambda}_+, \tilde{\lambda}_-, 0)$ on the measure **Q**. Therefore, the process X is martingale on measure **Q**.

Furthermore, by applying change of measures to the standard CTS process, we obtain the following result. Let $(X_t)_{t\geq 0}$ be a standard CTS process with parameters $(\alpha, \lambda_+, \lambda_-)$ under a measure **P**, and $\tilde{\lambda}_+, \tilde{\lambda}_+ > 0$ and real

---

[3]See Kim and Lee (2006) for more details.
[4]See Kim et al. (2008a, 2008b, 2010) and Kim et al. (2009), and Bianchi et al. (2010) for more details.

TABLE 5.1 Condition for Equivalent between P and Q

$(X_t)_{t\geq 0}$	Parameters under Measure P	Parameters under Measure Q	Equivalent Condition
CTS process	$(\alpha, C, \lambda_+, \lambda_-, m)$	$(\tilde{\alpha}, \tilde{C}, \tilde{\lambda}_+, \tilde{\lambda}_-, \tilde{m})$	$C = \tilde{C}, \alpha = \tilde{\alpha}$, and $\tilde{m} - m = C\Gamma(1-\alpha)(\tilde{\lambda}_+^{\alpha-1} - \tilde{\lambda}_-^{\alpha-1} - \lambda_+^{\alpha-1} + \lambda_-^{\alpha-1})$.
GTS process	$\begin{pmatrix} \alpha_+\, \alpha_-, C_+, C_-, \\ \lambda_+, \lambda_-, m \end{pmatrix}$	$\begin{pmatrix} \tilde{\alpha}_+\, \tilde{\alpha}_-, \tilde{C}_+, \tilde{C}_-, \\ \tilde{\lambda}_+, \tilde{\lambda}_-, m \end{pmatrix}$	$\alpha_+ = \tilde{\alpha}_+, \alpha_- = \tilde{\alpha}_-, C_+ = \tilde{C}_+, C_- = \tilde{C}_-$, and $\tilde{m} - m = C_+\Gamma(1-\alpha_+)(\tilde{\lambda}_+^{\alpha-1} - \tilde{\lambda}_-^{\alpha-1})$ $- C_-\Gamma(1-\alpha_-)(\lambda_+^{\alpha-1} + \lambda_-^{\alpha-1})$.
MTS process	$(\alpha, C, \lambda_+, \lambda_-, m)$	$(\tilde{\alpha}, \tilde{C}, \tilde{\lambda}_+, \tilde{\lambda}_-, \tilde{m})$	$C = \tilde{C}, \alpha = \tilde{\alpha}$, and $\tilde{m} - m = 2^{\frac{\alpha+1}{2}} C\Gamma\left(\frac{1-\alpha}{2}\right)(\tilde{\lambda}_+^{\alpha-1} - \tilde{\lambda}_-^{\alpha-1} - \lambda_+^{\alpha-1} + \lambda_-^{\alpha-1})$.
NTS process	$(\alpha, C, \lambda, \beta, m)$	$(\tilde{\alpha}, \tilde{C}, \tilde{\lambda}, \tilde{\beta}, \tilde{m})$	$C = \tilde{C}, \alpha = \tilde{\alpha}$, and $\tilde{m} - m = \kappa(\tilde{\beta}(\tilde{\lambda}^2 - \tilde{\beta}^2)^{\frac{\alpha}{2}-1} - \beta(\lambda^2 - \beta^2)^{\frac{\alpha}{2}-1})$, where $\kappa = 2^{-\frac{\alpha-1}{2}}\sqrt{\pi}C\Gamma\left(1 - \frac{\alpha}{2}\right)$.
KRTS process	$\begin{pmatrix} \alpha_1, k_{1,+}, k_{1,-}, r_{1,+}, \\ r_{1,-}, p_{1,+}, p_{1,-}, m_1 \end{pmatrix}$	$\begin{pmatrix} \alpha_2, k_{2,+}, k_{2,-}, r_{2,+}, \\ r_{2,-}, p_{2,+}, p_{2,-}, m_2 \end{pmatrix}$	$\begin{cases} p_{j,\pm} > 1/2 - \alpha_j \text{ and } p_{j,\pm} \neq 0, \alpha_j \in (0,1) \\ p_{j,\pm} > 1 - \alpha_j \text{ and } p_{j,\pm} \neq 0, \alpha_j \in (1,2) \end{cases}$, for $j = 1, 2$. $\alpha := \alpha_1 = \alpha_2$ $\frac{k_{1,+}r_{1,+}^\alpha}{\alpha + p_{1,+}} = \frac{k_{2,+}r_{2,+}^\alpha}{\alpha + p_{2,+}}$, $\frac{k_{1,-}r_{1,-}^\alpha}{\alpha + p_{1,-}} = \frac{k_{2,-}r_{2,-}^\alpha}{\alpha + p_{2,-}}$, and $m_2 - m_1 = \Gamma(1-\alpha)\sum_{j=1,2}(-1)^j\left(\frac{k_{j,+}r_{j,+}}{p_{j,+}+1} - \frac{k_{j,-}r_{j,-}}{p_{j,-}+1}\right)$
RDTS process	$(\alpha, C, \lambda_+, \lambda_-, m)$	$(\tilde{\alpha}, \tilde{C}, \tilde{\lambda}_+, \tilde{\lambda}_-, \tilde{m})$	$C = \tilde{C}, \alpha = \tilde{\alpha}$, and $\tilde{m} - m = 2^{-\frac{\alpha+1}{2}} C\Gamma\left(\frac{1-\alpha}{2}\right)(\tilde{\lambda}_+^{\alpha-1} - \tilde{\lambda}_-^{\alpha-1} - \lambda_+^{\alpha-1} + \lambda_-^{\alpha-1})$.

TABLE 5.2 Change of Measures for Standard TS Processes: $Y_t = \mu t + X_t$

$(X_t)_{t\geq 0}$ under measure **P**	Standard CTS process with parameters $(\alpha, \lambda_+, \lambda_-)$
$(Y_t)_{t\geq 0}$ under measure **Q**	Standard CTS process with parameters $(\alpha, \tilde{\lambda}_+, \tilde{\lambda}_-)$
Relations of parameters	$\lambda_+^{\alpha-2} + \lambda_-^{\alpha-2} = \tilde{\lambda}_+^{\alpha-2} + \tilde{\lambda}_-^{\alpha-2},$
	$\mu = \dfrac{\lambda_+^{\alpha-1} - \lambda_-^{\alpha-1} - \tilde{\lambda}_+^{\alpha-1} + \tilde{\lambda}_-^{\alpha-1}}{(1-\alpha)\left(\lambda_+^{\alpha-2} + \lambda_-^{\alpha-2}\right)}.$
$(X_t)_{t\geq 0}$ under measure **P**	Standard GTS process with parameters $(\alpha_+, \alpha_-, \lambda_+, \lambda_-, p)$
$(Y_t)_{t\geq 0}$ under measure **Q**	Standard GTS process with parameters $(\alpha_+, \alpha_-, \tilde{\lambda}_+, \tilde{\lambda}_-, \tilde{p})$
Relations of parameters	$p\lambda_+^{2-\alpha_+} = \tilde{p}\tilde{\lambda}_+^{2-\alpha_+}$
	$(1-p)\lambda_-^{\alpha_--2} = (1-\tilde{p})\tilde{\lambda}_-^{\alpha_--2}$
	$\mu = p\dfrac{\lambda_+^{\alpha_+-1} - \tilde{\lambda}_+^{\alpha_+-1}}{(1-\alpha_+)\lambda_+^{\alpha_+-1}} + (1-p)\dfrac{\tilde{\lambda}_-^{\alpha_--1} - \lambda_-^{\alpha_+-1}}{(1-\alpha_-)\lambda_+^{\alpha_+-1}}$
$(X_t)_{t\geq 0}$ under measure **P**	Standard MTS process with parameters $(\alpha, \lambda_+, \lambda_-)$
$(Y_t)_{t\geq 0}$ under measure **Q**	Standard MTS process with parameters $(\alpha, \tilde{\lambda}_+, \tilde{\lambda}_-)$
Relations of parameters	$\tilde{\lambda}_+^{\alpha-2} + \tilde{\lambda}_-^{\alpha-2} = \lambda_+^{\alpha-2} + \lambda_-^{\alpha-2}$
	$\mu = \dfrac{\Gamma\left(\dfrac{1-\alpha}{2}\right)\left(\lambda_+^{\alpha-1} - \lambda_-^{\alpha-1} - \tilde{\lambda}_+^{\alpha-1} + \tilde{\lambda}_-^{\alpha-1}\right)}{\sqrt{\pi}\,\Gamma\left(1 - \dfrac{\alpha}{2}\right)\left(\tilde{\lambda}_+^{\alpha-2} + \tilde{\lambda}_-^{\alpha-2}\right)}$
$(X_t)_{t\geq 0}$ under measure **P**	Standard NTS process with parameters (α, λ, β)
$(Y_t)_{t\geq 0}$ under measure **Q**	Standard NTS process with parameters $(\alpha, \tilde{\lambda}, \tilde{\beta})$
Relations of parameters	$\dfrac{\alpha\beta^2 - \lambda^2 - \beta^2}{(\lambda^2 - \beta^2)^{2-\frac{\alpha}{2}}} = \dfrac{\alpha\tilde{\beta}^2 - \tilde{\lambda}^2 - \tilde{\beta}^2}{(\tilde{\lambda}^2 - \tilde{\beta}^2)^{2-\frac{\alpha}{2}}}$
	$\mu = \dfrac{\beta(\lambda^2 - \beta^2)^{\frac{\alpha}{2}-1} - \tilde{\beta}(\tilde{\lambda}^2 - \tilde{\beta}^2)^{\frac{\alpha}{2}-1}}{(\lambda^2 - \beta^2)^{\frac{\alpha}{2}-2}(\alpha\beta^2 - \lambda^2 - \beta^2)}$
$(X_t)_{t\geq 0}$ under measure **P**	Standard KRTS process with parameters $(\alpha, r_{1,+}, r_{1,-}, p_{1,+}, p_{1,-})$
$(Y_t)_{t\geq 0}$ under measure **Q**	Standard KRTS process with parameters $(\alpha, r_{2,+}, r_{2,-}, p_{2,+}, p_{2,-})$
Relations of parameters	$\dfrac{\alpha + p_{1,+}}{2 + p_{1,+}}r_{1,+}^{2-\alpha} + \dfrac{\alpha + p_{1,-}}{2 + p_{1,-}}r_{1,-}^{2-\alpha} = \dfrac{\alpha + p_{2,+}}{2 + p_{2,+}}r_{2,+}^{2-\alpha} + \dfrac{\alpha + p_{2,-}}{2 + p_{2,-}}r_{2,-}^{2-\alpha}$
	$\mu = \sum_{j=1,2}(-1)^j c_j \left(\dfrac{p_{j,+} + \alpha}{p_{j,+} + 1}r_{j,+}^{1-\alpha} - \dfrac{p_{j,-} + \alpha}{p_{j,-} + 1}r_{j,-}^{1-\alpha}\right)$
	where $r_{2,+}, r_{2,-} > 0$ and
	$c_j = \dfrac{1}{\alpha - 1}\left(\dfrac{\alpha + p_{j,+}}{2 + p_{j,+}}r_{j,+}^{2-\alpha} + \dfrac{\alpha + p_{j,-}}{2 + p_{j,-}}r_{j,-}^{2-\alpha}\right)^{-1}.$
$(X_t)_{t\geq 0}$ under measure **P**	Standard RDTS process with parameters $(\alpha, \lambda_+, \lambda_-)$
$(Y_t)_{t\geq 0}$ under measure **Q**	Standard RDTS process with parameters $(\alpha, \tilde{\lambda}_+, \tilde{\lambda}_-)$
Relations of parameters	$\lambda_+^{\alpha-2} + \lambda_-^{\alpha-2} = \tilde{\lambda}_+^{\alpha-2} + \tilde{\lambda}_-^{\alpha-2},$
	$\mu = \dfrac{\Gamma\left(\dfrac{1-\alpha}{2}\right)\left(\lambda_+^{\alpha-1} - \lambda_-^{\alpha-1} - \tilde{\lambda}_+^{\alpha-1} + \tilde{\lambda}_-^{\alpha-1}\right)}{\sqrt{2}\,\Gamma\left(1 - \dfrac{\alpha}{2}\right)\left(\tilde{\lambda}_+^{\alpha-2} + \tilde{\lambda}_-^{\alpha-2}\right)}.$

number μ satisfy the following:

$$\begin{cases} \lambda_+^{\alpha-2} + \lambda_-^{\alpha-2} = \tilde{\lambda}_+^{\alpha-2} + \tilde{\lambda}_-^{\alpha-2}, \\ \mu = \dfrac{\lambda_+^{\alpha-1} - \lambda_-^{\alpha-1} - \tilde{\lambda}_+^{\alpha-1} + \tilde{\lambda}_-^{\alpha-1}}{(1-\alpha)\left(\lambda_+^{\alpha-2} + \lambda_-^{\alpha-2}\right)}. \end{cases} \tag{5.8}$$

Then we can find a measure $\mathbf{Q}$ equivalent to $\mathbf{P}$ such that a process $(Y_t)_{t\geq 0}$ with $Y_t = \mu t + X_t$ is a standard CTS process with parameters $(\alpha, \tilde{\lambda}_+, \tilde{\lambda}_-)$ under a measure $\mathbf{Q}$.

We apply the same argument to the standard GTS, standard MTS, standard NTS, standard KRTS, and standard RDTS processes. The relations of parameters between standard tempered stable process $(X_t)_{t\geq 0}$ under $\mathbf{P}$ and standard tempered stable process $(Y_t)_{t\geq 0}$ with $Y_t = \mu t + X_t$ under $\mathbf{Q}$ are presented in Table 5.2.

5.4 SUMMARY

In this chapter, we first defined some important concepts: σ-field, filtration, and conditional expectation. We next discussed the meaning of Markov processes and martingale processes in finance. We explain how the property of processes change by applying Girsanov's theorem and Esscher transform. Finally, the change of measure for the tempered stable processes discussed in Chapter 4 was presented.

REFERENCES

Bianchi, M. L., Rachev, S. T., Kim, Y. S., & Fabozzi, F. J. (2010). Tempered infinitely divisible distributions and processes. *Theory of Probability and Its Applications (TVP), Society for Industrial and Applied Mathematics (SIAM)*, 55(1), 59–89.

Harrison, J. M. & Pliska, S. R. (1981). Martingales and stochastic integrals in the theory of continuous trading. *Stochastic Processes and Their Applications*, 11(3), 215–260.

Karatzas, I. & Shreve, S. (1991). *Brownian motion and stochastic calculus* (2nd ed.). New York: Springer.

Kim, Y., Rachev, S., Bianchi, M., & Fabozzi, F. (2008a). Financial market models with Lévy processes and time-varying volatility. *Journal of Banking and Finance*, 32(7), 1363–1378.

Kim, Y., Rachev, S., Bianchi, M., & Fabozzi, F. (2008b). A new tempered stable distribution and its application to finance. In G. Bol, S. T. Rachev, & R. Wuerth

(Eds.), *Risk assessment: Decisions in banking and finance* (pp. 51–84). Heidelberg: Physica-Verlag, Springer.

Kim, Y., Rachev, S., Bianchi, M., & Fabozzi, F. (2010). Tempered stable and tempered infinitely divisible GARCH models. *Journal of Banking and Finance*, *34*(9), 2096–2109.

Kim, Y., Rachev, S., Chung, D., & Bianchi, M. (2009). The modified tempered stable distribution, GARCH-models and option pricing. *Probability and Mathematical Statistics*, *29*(1), 91–117.

Kim, Y. & Lee, J. (2006). The relative entropy in CGMY processes and its applications to finance. *Mathematical Methods of Operations Research*, *66*(2), 327–338.

Klebaner, F. C. (2005). *Introduction to stochastic calculus with applications* (2nd ed.). London: Imperial College Press.

Oksendal, B. (2000). *Stochastic differential equations: An introduction with applications* (5th ed.). New York: Springer.

Sato, K. (1999). *Lévy processes and infinitely divisible distributions*. Cambridge: Cambridge University Press.

CHAPTER 6

Exponential Lévy Models

In this chapter, we will discuss a continuous-market model referred to as the *exponential Lévy model* and discuss subclasses of the exponential Lévy model. We then discuss the parameter fitting for the market model and the goodness-of-fit test.

6.1 EXPONENTIAL LÉVY MODELS

Consider a Lévy process $(X_t)_{t\geq 0}$ on a sample space $(\Omega, \mathbb{P})$. If we assume that the stock price is given by the random variable $S_t = S_0 e^{X_t}$ at every time $t \geq 0$, where $S_0 > 0$ is the initial value of the stock price, then we say that the stock price follows an *exponential Lévy model*. The process $(S_t)_{t\geq 0}$ and the process $(X_t)_{t\geq 0}$ are referred to as the *stock price process* and the *driving process* of the stock price process, respectively.

If the driving process is Brownian motion, which is also a Lévy process, then the exponential Lévy model is referred to as the *exponential Brownian motion model* or the *geometric Brownian motion model*. More precisely, if the driving process $(X_t)_{t\geq 0}$ of the stock price process is given by

$$X_t = mt + \sigma W_t,$$

where $(W_t)_{t\geq 0}$ is the standard Brownian motion, $\sigma > 0$, and

$$m = \mu - \frac{\sigma^2}{2} \tag{6.1}$$

for some $\mu \in \mathbb{R}$, then we say that the stock price process follows the geometric Brownian motion model. By the condition (6.1), we have

$$E[S_t] = S_0 E[e^{X_t}] = S_0 e^{\mu t}.$$

If the driving process is the α-stable process, then the exponential Lévy model is referred to as the *exponential α-stable model*. If the driving process is the tempered stable process, the exponential Lévy model is referred to as the *exponential tempered stable model*. In Table 6.1, five exponential tempered stable models are presented.

- By the conditions in the table, we have

$$E[S_t] = S_0 E[e^{X_t}] = S_0 e^{\mu t}.$$

For example, let $(X_t)_{t \geq 0}$ is CTS process with parameter $(\alpha, C, \lambda_+, \lambda_-, m)$ and $m = \mu - \log \phi_{CTS}(-i; \alpha, C, \lambda_+, \lambda_-, 0)$. Then

$$
\begin{aligned}
E[S_t] &= S_0 E[e^{X_t}] \\
&= S_0 \exp\left(t \log \phi_{CTS}(-i; \alpha, C, \lambda_+, \lambda_-, m)\right) \\
&= S_0 \exp\left(tm + t \log \phi_{CTS}(-i; \alpha, C, \lambda_+, \lambda_-, 0)\right) \\
&= S_0 e^{\mu t}.
\end{aligned}
$$

- ϕ_{CTS}, ϕ_{MTS}, ϕ_{NTS}, ϕ_{KRTS}, and ϕ_{RDTS} are respectively given by (3.2), (3.6), (3.8), (3.12), and (3.14) in Chapter 3.
- We have the condition $\lambda_+ > 1$ for ϕ_{CTS} $(-i; \alpha, C, \lambda_+, \lambda_-, 0)$ and ϕ_{MTS} $(-i; \alpha, C, \lambda_+, \lambda_-, 0)$ to be well defined. Similarly, the conditions $\lambda - \beta > 1$ and $0 < r_+ < 1$, respectively, allow ϕ_{NTS} $(-i; \alpha, C, \lambda, \beta, 0)$ and ϕ_{KRTS} $(-i; \alpha, k_+, k_-, r_+, r_-, p_+, p_-, 0)$ to be well defined. However, ϕ_{RDTS} $(-i; \alpha, C, \lambda_+, \lambda_-, 0)$ is well defined without any condition (see section 3.3.1).
- By the condition

$$
\begin{cases}
p_+, p_- \in (1/2 - \alpha, \infty) \setminus \{0\}, & \text{if } \alpha \in (0, 1) \\
p_+, p_- \in (1 - \alpha, \infty) \setminus \{0\}, & \text{if } \alpha \in (1, 2)
\end{cases}
$$

in the exponential Kim-Rachev tempered stable (KRTS) model, we are able to use the change of measure for KRTS processes discussed in section 5.3.3 for finding an equivalent measure. This will be discussed in Chapter 7.

TABLE 6.1 Exponential Tempered Stable Model

Stock Price Process $S_t = S_0 e^{X_t}$	Driving Stock Price Process $(X_t)_{t\geq0}$	Condition
Exponential classical tempered stable (CTS) model	CTS process with parameter $(\alpha, C, \lambda_+, \lambda_-, m)$	$\lambda_+ > 1$ $m = \mu - \log\phi_{CTS}(-i; \alpha, C, \lambda_+, \lambda_-, 0)$
Exponential modified tempered stable (MTS) model	MTS process with parameter $(\alpha, C, \lambda_+, \lambda_-, m)$	$\lambda_+ > 1$ $m = \mu - \log\phi_{MTS}(-i; \alpha, C, \lambda_+, \lambda_-, 0)$
Exponential normal tempered stable (NTS) model	NTS process with parameter $(\alpha, C, \lambda, \beta, m)$	$\lambda - \beta > 1$ $m = \mu - \log\phi_{NTS}(-i; \alpha, C, \lambda, \beta, 0)$
Exponential Kim-Rachev tempered stable (KRTS) model	KRTS process with parameter $(\alpha, k_+, k_-, r_+, r_-, p_+, p_-, m)$	$0 < r_+ < 1$ $m = \mu - \log\phi_{KRTS}(-i; \alpha, k_+, k_-, r_+, r_-, p_+, p_-, 0)$ $\begin{cases} p_+, p_- \in (1/2 - \alpha, \infty) \setminus \{0\}, & \text{if } \alpha \in (0,1) \\ p_+, p_- \in (1 - \alpha, \infty) \setminus \{0\}, & \text{if } \alpha \in (1,2) \end{cases}$
Exponential rapidly decreasing tempered stable (RDTS) model	RDTS process with parameter $(\alpha, C, \lambda_+, \lambda_-, m)$	$m = \mu - \log\phi_{RDTS}(-i; \alpha, C, \lambda_+, \lambda_-, 0)$

6.2 FITTING α-STABLE AND TEMPERED STABLE DISTRIBUTIONS

There are two popular methods to estimate parameters of α-stable and tempered stable distributions. Although these distributions do not have a closed-form expression for the density function except a few special cases. However, they can characterized through their characteristic function.

The question is how can we use the distribution's characteristic function to estimate the parameters based on a sample of observations $S = \{x_1, x_2, \ldots, x_N\}$. The sample observations could be the daily log-returns of a bond, a stock index, or individual stock prices. The following two approaches can be used:

- Try to calculate the sample characteristic function and fit the unknown parameters of the theoretical characteristic function to the sample characteristic function.[1]
- Try to derive a numerical approximation of the density function of the stable distribution and estimate the unknown parameters by maximizing the numerical density.[2]

6.2.1 Fitting the Characteristic Function

To implement the first approach, we use the fact that the characteristic function is in fact nothing other than an expectation. It is the expected value of the random variable e^{iuX}, where X follows an α-stable distribution or a tempered stable distribution. Consequently, we can calculate a proxy for the characteristic function ϕ_X of X by computing the following arithmetic mean for different values of u:

$$\hat{\phi}_X(u) = \frac{1}{N} \sum_{j=1}^{n} e^{iux_j}$$

Using mathematical optimization software, it is easy to determine parameter estimates such that the theoretical function ϕ is as close as possible to its sample counterpart $\hat{\phi}$. This approach is referred to as *fitting the characteristic function*. For a detailed description of this approach, see Kogon and William (1998).

---

[1]This approach was suggested in Press (1972).
[2]This approach was first proposed and examined by Rachev and Mittnik (2000), Stoyanov and Racheva-Iotova (2004a, 2004b) and Rachev et al. (2007).

6.2.2 Maximum Likelihood Estimation with Numerical Approximation of the Density Function

The second approach requires a procedure to determine a numerical approximation of the density function of the α-stable law or the tempered stable law by using the so-called Fourier-inversion formula.

Let X be an α stable or a tempered stable random variable with a parameter vector $\theta = (\theta_1, \theta_2, \cdots, \theta_q)$. For example, if X is a CTS random variable with parameter $(\alpha, C, \lambda_+, \lambda_-, m)$, then $\theta = (\alpha, C, \lambda_+, \lambda_-, m)$. Let $\phi_X(u; \theta)$ and $f_X(x; \theta)$ be, respectively, the characteristic function and the density function of X. The following equation describes the relation between these two functions:

$$f_X(x; \theta) = \frac{1}{2\pi} \int_{-\infty}^{\infty} e^{-iux} \phi_X(u; \theta) \, du \qquad (6.2)$$

Given this relation and the characteristic function of an α-stable distribution and a tempered stable distribution as described in Chapter 3, we are able to calculate the value $f_X(x)$ of the density function at every given point x. This task can be performed in a very efficient way by using the so-called fast Fourier transform (FFT)—an algorithm that can be used for a simultaneous evaluation of the integral in equation (6.2) for different x-values. More details about this approach are presented in section 6.5.

We can estimate the parameter vector θ corresponding to the sample $S = \{x_1, x_2, \cdots, x_N\}$ by the *maximum likelihood estimation* (MLE). Using this estimation procedure, a parameter vector θ can be estimated by

$$\hat{\theta} = \arg\max \sum_{n=1}^{N} \log f_X(x_n; \theta).$$

6.2.3 Assessing the Goodness of Fit

To compare the goodness of fit for the estimated α-stable distribution or the estimated tempered stable distributions, we can employ the following criteria:

- Quantile-quantile plots
- Chi-square statistic
- Kolmogorov-Smirnov distance statistic
- Anderson-Darling statistic

Quantile-quantile plots (QQ-plots) provide a convenient technique to visually investigate a data set. QQ-plots show empirical quantiles versus the quantiles of a hypothesized distribution fitted to the data. In an ideal scenario, if the distribution is chosen correctly, then the QQ-plot would coincide with a 45° line.

The *Chi-square* statistic (χ^2-statistic) looks at the distances between the frequencies under the theoretical models and the actual frequencies. To obtain the χ^2-statistic, we need to divide the data into classes. For example, with discrete distributions, the classes can correspond to the specific values. The χ^2-statistic is calculated by finding the sum of the ratios of the squared differences between each observed and the corresponding theoretical frequencies:

$$\chi^2 = \sum_{k=1}^{K} \frac{n_k - \mathbb{E}n_k}{\mathbb{E}n_k}, \tag{6.3}$$

where n_k and $\mathbb{E}n_k$ are, respectively, the observed frequency and the expected frequency defined by the estimated theoretical distribution, for each of the classes $k = 1, 2, \cdots, K$. To obtain the p-value, the statistic must be compared with the percentile of the χ^2 distribution at the pre-specified confidence level, with degrees of freedom d equal to the number of classes minus 1. One disadvantage in calculating the p-value with the χ^2-statistic is that it is sensitive to the choice of classes. While it may be good for discrete distributions where each class corresponds to one value, one cannot avoid having to decide on the class size when working with continuous distributions. In addition, for the asymptotic χ^2 approximation to work, a sufficiently large sample size is required.

The *Kolmogorov-Smirnov distance statistic* (KS-statistic) is computed as follows:

$$KS = \sup_{x} |\hat{F}(x) - F_X(x)|, \tag{6.4}$$

where $\hat{F}(x)$ is the empirical sample distribution and $F_X(x)$ is the cumulative distribution function of the estimated theoretical distribution. The KS-statistic turns out to emphasize deviations around the median of the fitted distribution. It is a robust measure in the sense that it focuses only on the maximum deviation between empirical and estimated distributions. If F_X is continuous then $\sqrt{N} \cdot KS$ converges to the Kolmogorov distribution, where N is the number of samples. Hence, if N is large enough, the p-value of the KS-statistic is obtained by

$$p = P[K \leq \sqrt{N} \cdot KS],$$

where K is the Kolmogorov random variable.

Furthermore, to assess the goodness of fit, we consider another classical statistic. It might be of interest to test the ability to model extreme events. To this end, we also use the *Anderson-Darling statistic* (AD-statistic). We consider different versions of the AD-statistic. In its simplest version, it is a variance-weighted KS statistic

$$AD = \sup_x \frac{|\hat{F}(x) - F_X(x)|}{\sqrt{F_X(x)(1 - F_X(x))}} \quad (6.5)$$

As with the KS-statistic, the AD-statistic measures the distance between the empirical and theoretical distribution functions but is rescaled by dividing the distance through the "standard deviation" of this distance as given by the denominator in equation (6.5). By this definition, the AD-statistic accentuates more discrepancies in the tail. A more generally used version of the AD-statistic belongs to the quadratic class defined by

$$AD^2 = \int_{-\infty}^{\infty} \frac{(\hat{F}(x) - F_X(x))^2}{F_X(x)(1 - F_X(x))} dF_X(x). \quad (6.6)$$

Two modified versions of the AD-statistic are the *upper-tail AD-statistic* (AD_{up}) and the *lower-tail AD-statistic* (AD_{down}), which are defined as follows:[3]

$$AD_{up} = \sup_x \left| \frac{\hat{F}(x) - F_X(x)}{1 - F_X(x)} \right|, \quad (6.7)$$

$$AD_{down} = \sup_x \left| \frac{\hat{F}(x) - F_X(x)}{F_X(x)} \right|. \quad (6.8)$$

AD_{up} puts most of the weight on the upper tail and AD_{down} puts most of the weight on the lower tail. They are useful when one wants to test the goodness of fit of the distribution only in the upper quantiles or in the lower quantiles

---

[3]The upper-tail AD-statistic was proposed by Chernobai et al. (2005).

of the data sample. The corresponding quadratic classes of the upper-tail AD-statistic and the lower-tail AD-statistic are respectively expressed as

$$AD_{up}^2 = \int_{-\infty}^{\infty} \frac{(\hat{F}(x) - F_X(x))^2}{(1 - F_X(x))^2} dF_X(x), \tag{6.9}$$

$$AD_{down}^2 = \int_{-\infty}^{\infty} \frac{(\hat{F}(x) - F_X(x))^2}{(F_X(x))^2} dF_X(x). \tag{6.10}$$

By the Probability Integral Transformation formula of D'Agostino and Stephens (1986), we obtain the computing formulas for the KS and AD, AD_{up}, AD_{down} and their corresponding quadratic classes. Those computing formulas are presented in Table 6.2.

TABLE 6.2   Computing Formulas for the Goodness of Fit Test Statistic

---

$$KS = \max \left\{ \max_j \left\{ \frac{j}{n} - z_j \right\}, \max_j \left\{ z_j - \frac{j-1}{n} \right\} \right\}$$

$$AD = \max \left\{ \max_j \left\{ \frac{\frac{j}{n} - z_j}{\sqrt{z_j(1 - z_j)}} \right\}, \max_j \left\{ \frac{z_j - \frac{j-1}{n}}{\sqrt{z_j(1 - z_j)}} \right\} \right\}$$

$$AD^2 = \frac{1}{n^2} \left(\sum_{j=1}^{n} (1 - 2j) \log(z_j) - \sum_{j=1}^{n} (1 + 2(n - j)) \log(1 - z_j) \right) - 1$$

$$AD_{up} = \max \left\{ \max_j \left\{ \frac{\frac{j}{n} - z_j}{1 - z_j} \right\}, \max_j \left\{ \frac{z_j - \frac{j-1}{n}}{1 - z_j} \right\} \right\}$$

$$AD_{up}^2 = \frac{2}{n} \sum_{j=1}^{n} \log(1 - z_j) + \frac{1}{n^2} \sum_{j=1}^{n} \frac{1 + 2(n - j)}{1 - z_j}$$

$$AD_{down} = \max \left\{ \max_j \left\{ \frac{\frac{j}{n} - z_j}{z_j} \right\}, \max_j \left\{ \frac{z_j - \frac{j-1}{n}}{z_j} \right\} \right\}$$

$$AD_{down}^2 = \frac{2}{n} \sum_{j=1}^{n} \log(z_j) + \frac{1}{n^2} \sum_{j=1}^{n} \frac{2j - 1}{z_j}$$

Note: $z_j = F_X(x_j)$, $j = 1, 2, \cdots, n$ for the sample order statistics $x_1 \leq x_2 \leq \cdots \leq x_n$.

To obtain a QQ-plot, KS-statistic, and AD-statistic for a tempered stable distribution, we need cumulative distribution functions of the distribution. The numerical method for calculating the cumulative distribution function of tempered stable distributions is presented in section 6.5.

6.3 ILLUSTRATION: PARAMETER ESTIMATION FOR TEMPERED STABLE DISTRIBUTIONS

In this section, we illustrate the MLE of the exponential tempered stable models. We use historical prices of the Standard and Poor's (S&P) 500 index for our illustration and the Dow Jones Industrial Average (DJIA) index. The time series of the prices are from September 10, 1998 to September 10, 2008.

In the illustration, we used daily log-returns defined as

$$r_t = \log\left(\frac{s_{t+\Delta t}}{s_t}\right).$$

where $s_{t+\Delta t}$ is the closing price of each index at day $t + \Delta t$ and s_t is a closing price at day t, which is one day before day $t + \Delta t$. The value Δt is the year fraction of 1 day. We assume that number of days per year is 250. Thus, $\Delta t = 1/250$.

Since we have $S_t = S_0 e^{X_t}$ with a tempered stable driving process $(X_t)_{t\geq 0}$ in the exponential tempered stable models, we have

$$\log\left(\frac{S_{t+\Delta t}}{S_t}\right) = X_{t+\Delta t} - X_t.$$

By the property of the Lévy process, we have

$$X_{t+\Delta t} - X_t \stackrel{\mathrm{d}}{=} X_{\Delta t}.$$

Therefore, the tempered stable parameters of the driving process $(X_t)_{t\geq 0}$ can be estimated by fitting the distribution of $X_{\Delta t}$ to the sample $\mathcal{S}$, which is defined by

$$\mathcal{S} = \{r_t : r_t \text{ is a daily log-return of an index}\}.$$

We report the estimated parameters in Tables 6.3 and 6.4. For the assessment of the goodness of fit, we utilize the KS-statistic. The p-value of

TABLE 6.3 Parameter Fit for S&P 500 Index

Model	Parameters					KS (p-value)	AD	$n \cdot AD^2$	$n \cdot AD^2_{up}$	$n \cdot AD^2_{down}$
Normal	σ 0.1816	m 0.0493				0.4836 (0.0000)	0.9448	14.9718	3045.4098	2446.2596
CTS	α 0.0488	C 251.8642	λ_+ 143.8191	λ_- 131.6877	m 0.0488	0.0132 (0.7757)	0.0536	0.4548	9.0756	10.6188
MTS	α 0.0395	C 212.5446	λ_+ 145.8951	λ_- 133.6123	m 0.0491	0.0132 (0.7755)	0.0539	0.4547	9.3030	10.5052
NTS	α 0.1388	C 120.9876	λ 134.0942	β −5.8993	m 0.0491	0.0134 (0.7542)	0.0520	0.4668	8.3371	11.0336
KRTS	α 0.0490	k_+ 6010.2127 k_- 5996.7669	r_+ 0.0073 r_- 0.0076	$p_+ = p_-$ 18.5448	m 0.0604	0.0121 (0.9028)	0.0609	0.3606	12.7786	5.4997
RDTS	α 0.4484	C 14.8029	λ_+ 84.8728	λ_- 78.0741	m 0.0714	0.0161 (0.5288)	0.0498	0.9369	13.1196	5.4284

TABLE 6.4 Parameter Fit for DJIA

Model	Parameters		KS (p-value)	AD	$n \cdot AD^2$	$n \cdot AD^2_{up}$	$n \cdot AD^2_{down}$
Normal	σ 0.1740	m 0.0525	0.4829 (0.0000)	62.7046	15.3789	93609.0373	9867214.9568
CTS	α 0.1598, C 133.1319, λ_+ 139.1640	λ_- 131.1540, m 0.0525	0.0094 (0.9799)	0.0599	0.1968	7.0073	10.2644
MTS	α 0.2343, C 70.0296, λ_+ 139.2751	λ_- 131.6600, m 0.0555	0.0094 (0.9783)	0.0597	0.2118	6.4702	10.2126
NTS	α 0.2121, C 79.7948, λ 137.2245	β −4.0198, m 0.0525	0.0094 (0.9792)	0.0581	0.1966	7.3323	9.8125
KRTS	α 0.1563, k_+ 759.4179, k_- 756.2562, r_+ 0.0090, r_- 0.0092	$p_+ = p_-$ 2.1191, m 0.0710	0.0114 (0.9393)	0.0689	0.2115	10.4880	11.7264
RDTS	α 0.5652, C 7.6860, λ_+ 82.4432	λ_- 77.7278, m 0.0645	0.0123 (0.8410)	0.1605	0.3975	33.1927	65.4985

the KS-statistic is the probability of exceeding the observed statistic. The null hypothesis is rejected if the p-value is less than a significance level α. We also calculate the AD-statistic together with AD^2, AD_{up}^2, and AD_{down}^2 to better evaluate the tail fit. In the table, we present $n \cdot AD^2$, $n \cdot AD_{up}^2$, and $n \cdot AD_{down}^2$ instead of AD^2, AD_{up}^2, and AD_{down}^2, respectively, where n is sample size. The factor n allows standardization of the statistic to account for the difference in sample size.[4]

We define the null hypotheses as follows:

H_0(Normal): $(X_t)_{t \geq 0}$ follows the arithmetic Brownian motion with

$$X_t = mt + \sigma W_t.$$

H_0(CTS): $(X_t)_{t \geq 0}$ follows the CTS process, that is

$$X_{\Delta t} \sim \text{CTS}(\alpha, C\Delta t, \lambda_+, \lambda_-, m\Delta t).$$

H_0(MTS): $(X_t)_{t \geq 0}$ follows the MTS process, that is

$$X_{\Delta t} \sim \text{MTS}(\alpha, C\Delta t, \lambda_+, \lambda_-, m\Delta t).$$

H_0(NTS): $(X_t)_{t \geq 0}$ follows the NTS process, that is

$$X_{\Delta t} \sim \text{NTS}(\alpha, C\Delta t, \lambda, \beta, m\Delta t).$$

H_0(KRTS): $(X_t)_{t \geq 0}$ follows the KRTS process, that is

$$X_{\Delta t} \sim \text{KRTS}(\alpha, k_+\Delta t, k_-\Delta t, r_+, r_-, p, p, m\Delta t).[5]$$

H_0(RDTS): $(X_t)_{t \geq 0}$ follows the RDTS process, that is

$$X_{\Delta t} \sim \text{RDTS}(\alpha, C\Delta t, \lambda_+, \lambda_-, m\Delta t).$$

Tables 6.3 and 6.4 also provide the KS-statistic and their p-values. Based on the results in these tables, we conclude that:

1. Based on the KS test, H_0(Normal) is rejected but H_0(CTS), H_0(MTS), H_0(NTS), H_0(KRTS), and H_0(RDTS) are not rejected at the 1% significance level for both the S&P 500 index and the DJIA index.

---

[4]In this investigation, the sample size of the S&P 500 and DJIA indexes is the same, but the factor is still useful since AD^2, AD_{up}^2, and AD_{down}^2 values are so small.
[5]We assume that $p = p_+ = p_-$ for convenience.

2. The values of the AD-statistic for the normal distribution are considerably greater than those for the other distributions. That means the five tempered stable (CTS, MTS, NTS, KRTS, and RDTS) distributions explain the extreme events of the price processes for the two indexes better than the normal distribution does. The same conclusions hold for the AD^2, AD^2_{up}, and AD^2_{down} values.

Figure 6.1 shows the probability density fits of the normal and five tempered stable distributions that are fitted to the DJIA daily log-returns. We show QQ-plots in Figure 6.2. The empirical density deviates significantly from the normal density as can be seen from the first QQ-plots in Figure 6.2. This deviation almost completely disappears when we use the infinitely divisible distributions to fit the data.

6.4 SUMMARY

In this chapter, we first defined the geometric Brownian motion model and five tempered stable models. We discussed two methods of parameter fitting: fitting characteristic functions using the empirical characteristic function and MLE with numerical probability density function using the FFT method. The QQ-plot, KS-statistic, and AD-statistic were presented for assessing the goodness of fit for the estimated parameters. Finally, we provided a numerical illustration where we fitted parameters of the geometric Brownian motion model and five tempered stable models to the S&P 500 index and DJIA index.

6.5 APPENDIX: NUMERICAL APPROXIMATION OF PROBABILITY DENSITY AND CUMULATIVE DISTRIBUTION FUNCTIONS

Let f_X, ϕ_X, and F_X be the density function, the characteristic function, and the cumulative distribution function of a tempered stable random variable X, respectively.

The characteristic function of a given random variable X is defined by the *Fourier transform* of the probability density function; that is,

$$\phi_X(u) = E[e^{iuX}] = \int_{-\infty}^{\infty} e^{iux} f_X(x) dx.$$

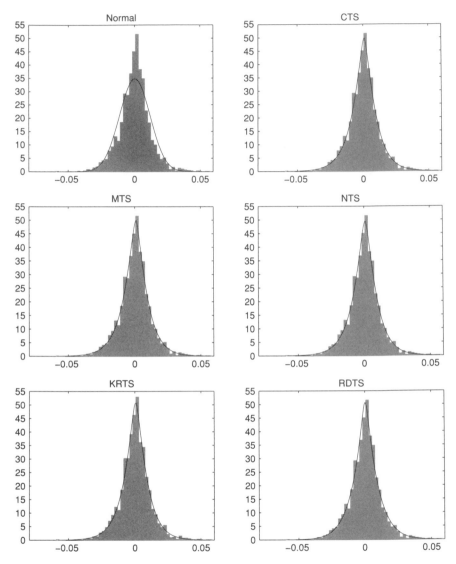

FIGURE 6.1   Bar Plots Showing the Empirical Density of the S&P 500 Returns
Note: The solid curves are density functions fitted by MLE.

Therefore, we can obtain the probability density function by the *inverse Fourier transform*:

$$f_X(x) = \frac{1}{2\pi} \int_{-\infty}^{\infty} e^{-uix} \phi_X(u) du.$$

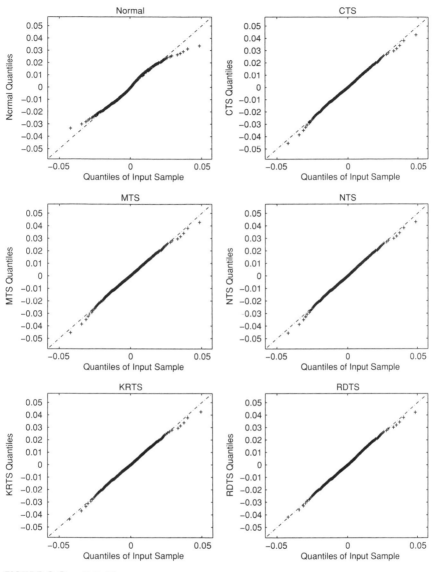

FIGURE 6.2 QQ-Plots

By the property $\phi_X(-u) = \overline{\phi_X(u)}$, we have

$$f_X(x) = \frac{1}{\pi}\mathrm{Re}\left(\int_0^\infty e^{-uix}\phi_X(u)du\right),\qquad (6.11)$$

where $Re(z)$ means taking only the real part of the complex number z. The numerical method for calculating the integral in equation (6.11) with the FFT method is presented in section 6.5.1.[6]

To obtain the cumulative distribution function of tempered stable distributions, we need the following proposition from Kim et al. (in print):

Proposition. *Suppose a random variable X is infinitely divisible. If there is a $\rho > 0$ such that $|\phi_X(u + i\rho)| < \infty$ for all $u \in \mathbb{R}$, then the cumulative distribution function F_X of X is given by*

$$F_X(x) = \frac{e^{x\rho}}{\pi} Re \left(\int_0^\infty e^{-ixu} \frac{\phi_X(u + i\rho)}{\rho - ui} du \right), \quad for \ x \in \mathbb{R}. \quad (6.12)$$

Note that we have

$$|\phi_X(u + i\rho)| = |E[e^{iuX - \rho X}]| \leq E[|e^{iuX - \rho X}|] = E[e^{-\rho X}],$$

and the existence region of the exponential moment for tempered stable distributions is explained in section 3.3.1. Therefore, the proposition can be applied to the tempered stable distribution as follows:

- For the CTS, GTS, and MTS distributions, $E[e^{-\rho X}] < \infty$ if and only if $-\rho \in [-\lambda_-, \lambda_+]$. Hence, $F_X(x)$ is obtained by (6.12) for $0 < \rho \leq \lambda_-$.
- For the KRTS distribution, $E[e^{-\rho X}] < \infty$ if and only if $-\rho \in [-1/r_-, 1/r_+]$. Hence, $F_X(x)$ is obtained by (6.12) for $0 < \rho \leq 1/r_-$.
- For the NTS and the NIG distributions, $E[e^{-\rho X}] < \infty$ for $-\rho \in [-\lambda - \beta, \lambda - \beta]$. Hence, $F_X(x)$ is obtained by (6.12) for $0 < \rho \leq \lambda + \beta$.
- For the RDTS distribution, $E[e^{-\rho X}] < \infty$ for the entire real number ρ. Hence, $F_X(x)$ is obtained by (6.12) for $\rho > 0$.

The numerical method for calculating the integral in equation (6.12) with the FFT method is presented in section 6.5.1.

---

[6]The methodology presented in Menn and Rachev (2006) provides a fast calculation of the desired approximate density while guaranteeing an acceptable level of accuracy.

6.5.1 Numerical Method for the Fourier Transform

Consider the following integration

$$f(x) = \frac{1}{2\pi} \int_0^\infty e^{-uix} g(u) du.$$

By the change of variable, we obtain

$$f(x) = \int_0^\infty e^{-2\pi uix} g(2\pi u) du,$$

and it can be approximated by

$$f(x) \approx \int_0^K e^{-2\pi uix} g(2\pi u) du$$

for some large real number K. We can approximate the value of $f(x)$ using the discrete numerical integration:

$$f(x) \approx \hat{f}(x) = \sum_{n=0}^{N-1} e^{-2\pi ix\left(\frac{nK}{N}\right)} g\left(\frac{2\pi nK}{N}\right) \frac{K}{N},$$

where N is a positive integer with $N > K$.
    If $x_k = \frac{k-N/2}{K}$, $k = 0, 1, 2, \cdots, N-1$, then we have

$$e^{-2\pi ix_k\left(\frac{nK}{N}\right)} = (-1)^n e^{-2\pi i\left(\frac{nk}{N}\right)}$$

and hence

$$\hat{f}(x_k) = \frac{K}{N} \sum_{n=0}^{N-1} w^{nk} g_n,$$

where $w = e^{-2\pi i/N}$ and $g_n = (-1)^n g\left(\frac{2\pi nK}{N}\right)$. To compute $\sum_{n=0}^{N-1} w^{nk} g_n$ we can use the FFT, which is implemented by many numerical software packages. If $x_k < x < x_{k+1}$, then $\hat{f}(x)$ can be obtained by the interpolation of $\hat{f}(x_k)$ and $\hat{f}(x_{k+1})$.

REFERENCES

Chernobai, A. S., Rachev, S. T., & Fabozzi, F. J. (2005). Composite goodness-of-fit tests for left-truncated loss samples. Technical report, University of California at Santa Barbara.

D'Agostino, R. & Stephens, M. (1986). *Goodness of fit techniques*. New York: Marcel Dekker, Inc.

Kim, Y., Rachev, S., Bianchi, M., & Fabozzi, F. (in print). Computing VaR and AVaR in infinitely divisible distributions. *Probability and Mathematical Statistics*.

Kogon, S. & William, B. (1998). Characteristic function based estimation of stable distribution parameters. In R. Adler, R. Feldman, and M. Taqqu (Eds.), *A practical guide to heavy tails* (pp. 311–335). Boston: Birkhäuser.

Menn, C. & Rachev, S. T. (2006). Calibrated FFT-based density approximations for alpha-stable distributions. *Computational Statistics and Data Analysis, 50,* 1891–1904.

Press, S. (1972). Estimation of univariate and multivariate stable distributions. *Journal of the American Statistical Association, 67,* 842–846.

Rachev, S. T. & Mittnik, S. (2000). *Stable Paretian models in finance*. New York: John Wiley & Sons.

Rachev, S., Mittnik, S., Fabozzi, F., Focardi, S., & Jašić, T. (2007). *Financial econometrics: From basics to advanced modeling techniques*. Hoboken, NJ: John Wiley & Sons.

Stoyanov, S. & Racheva-Iotova, B. (2004a). Univariate stable laws in the field of finance: Approximation of density and distribution functions. *Journal of Concrete and Applicable Mathematics, 2*(1), 37–58.

Stoyanov, S. & Racheva-Iotova, B. (2004b). Univariate stable laws in the field finance: Parameter estimation. *Journal of Concrete and Applicable Mathematics, 2*(4), 24–49.

CHAPTER 7

Option Pricing in Exponential Lévy Models

In this chapter, we present basic properties of the option contract and no-arbitrage pricing for the option. We then derive the option pricing formula under the exponential Lévy model. Finally, we discuss the subordinated stock price model and stochastic volatility Lévy process model, which are generalizations of exponential Lévy models.

7.1   OPTION CONTRACT

There are two parties to an option contract: the *buyer* and the *writer* (also called the *seller*). In an option contract, the writer of the option grants the buyer of the option the right, but not the obligation, to purchase from or sell to the writer the underlying asset at a specified price within a specified period of time (or at a specified date). The writer grants this right to the buyer in exchange for a certain sum of money, which is called the *option price* or *option premium*. The date after which an option is void is called the *expiration date* or *maturity date*.

When an option grants the buyer the right to purchase the underlying asset from the writer (seller), it is referred to as a *call option*. When the option buyer has the right to sell the underlying asset to the writer, the option is called a *put option*.

The timing of the possible exercise of an option is an important characteristic of the contract. There arc options that may be exercised at any time up to and including the expiration date. Such options are referred to as *American options*. Other options may be exercised only at the expiration date; these are called *European options*. An option can be created in which the option can be exercised at scveral specified dates as well as the expiration date of the option. Such options are referred to as *limited exercise options, Bermuda options*, and *Atlantic options*.

A cash flow when a option is exercised is referred to as *payoff*. We refer to a call option as a *vanilla call option* and a *vanilla put option* if the payoffs of two options are given by $\max\{S_t - K, 0\}$ and $\max\{K - S_t, 0\}$, respectively, where t is the time to exercise, S_t is the value of the underlying asset at time t, and K is a positive value referred to as the *exercise price* or the *strike price*. In the American option case, the time to exercise t can be any time up to and including the expiration date, but in the European option case, the payoff happens only at the expiration date. In this book, we refer to a vanilla call option and a vanilla put option as a *call option* (or simply *call*) and a *put option* (or simply *call*), respectively.

We can define various type of payoffs. If the payoff is given by the difference between the strike price and the average price of the underlying asset for some time interval, then we refer to the option as an *Asian option*. We also refer to an option as a *barrier option* if the payoff depends on the time for the underlying asset to hit some level.

7.2 BOUNDARY CONDITIONS FOR THE PRICE OF AN OPTION

Theoretical boundary conditions for the price of an option can be derived using arbitrage arguments. For example, assume the underlying asset is a stock. It can be shown that the minimum price for an American call option is its payoff; that is,

$$\text{Call option price} \geq (S_t - K)^+,$$

where t is the time to exercise, S_t is the stock price at time t, K is the strike price, and $(x)^+ = \max\{x, 0\}$. This expression says that the call option price will be greater than or equal to the difference between the price of the underlying stock and the strike price, or zero, whichever is higher.

The boundary conditions can be "tightened" by using arbitrage arguments. The idea is to build two portfolios that lead to the same payoff after one year. Assume the holdings of the two portfolios are as follows:

Portfolio A:
- One European call option that expires at time T with a strike price K.

- One money market account that will pay K amount of money at time T with an interest rate r. The present value of the account is $e^{-r(T-t)}K$ at time t.

Portfolio B:

- One share of the underlying stock.
- One short position in the European put option with the same underlying stock, strike, and expiration date.

Let us compare the payoffs of these two portfolios at the end of one year. The payoffs are summarized in Table 7.1. There are two possible scenarios for the price of the stock one year from now:

- *Scenario 1.* Terminal stock price is higher than the strike price for both options:
  - Portfolio A. The European call option will be exercised. The investment in the money market account matures and has a value equal to the strike price. The proceeds to exercise the call option are obtained from the matured investment. Therefore, the value of Portfolio A is equal to the price of the stock one year from now.
  - Portfolio B. The European put option is worthless because the price of the stock is greater than the strike price. The only asset of value in Portfolio B is the stock. Consequently, the value of Portfolio B is equal to the price of the stock one year from now.
  In summary, we can see that the value of the two portfolios is equal at the expiration date of the two European options.
- *Scenario 2.* Terminal stock price is less than or equal to the strike price of both options:
  - Portfolio A. The call option will be worthless. The investment in the money market account matures and will have a value equal to the strike price of the call option.

TABLE 7.1 Payoffs of Portfolio A and Portfolio B at Time T

		$S_T \geq K$	$S_T < K$
Portfolio A	Call (long position)	$S_T - K$	0
	Money market account	K	K
		S_T	K
Portfolio B	Underlying stock	S_T	S_T
	Put (short position)	0	$-(K - S_T)$
		S_T	K

■ Portfolio B. The put option will be exercised and therefore the one share of stock will be sold. Portfolio B receives the strike price when the put option is exercised and therefore the strike price is the value of Portfolio B.

Consequently, Portfolio A and Portfolio B have the same value.

Since in both scenarios the two portfolios have the same outcome, they must be priced the same. If not, market participants could realize riskless profits by buying the cheaper portfolio and selling the more expensive one. Thus, at time t, we know that

$$\text{Value of Portfolio A} = C_t + e^{r(T-t)}K$$

$$\text{Value of Portfolio B} = S_t - P_t,$$

where C_t and P_t are prices of the European call option and the European put option at time t, respectively. There is a minus sign before the European put price because it is a short position.

Since we have

$$\text{Value of Portfolio A} = \text{Value of Portfolio B}$$

we obtain

$$C_t + e^{r(T-t)}K = S_t - P_t$$

We then have the following boundary condition,

$$C_t = S_t - e^{r(T-t)}K - P_t \tag{7.1}$$

The relationship (7.1) is referred to as *put-call parity*.

The value of the call option cannot be negative. Therefore,

$$C_t = \max\{S_t - e^{r(T-t)}K - P_t, 0\}.$$

Since the European put price cannot be negative, we can rewrite the above as:

$$C_t \geq \max\{S_t - e^{r(T-t)}K, 0\}. \tag{7.2}$$

7.3   NO-ARBITRAGE PRICING AND EQUIVALENT MARTINGALE MEASURE

The price of the European call option today ($t = 0$) can be calculated by the expected value of the discounted value of its payoff. That is

$$C_0 = E[e^{-rT}(S_T - K)^+],$$

where T is the time to maturity, r is the risk-free rate of return, S_T is the underlying asset price at time T, and K is the strike price. The call price C_0 should allow no-arbitrage. In order to calculate the expectation, we need a probability **P** of S_T such that the expected value C_0 does not allow any arbitrage opportunity as the following example illustrates.

Suppose the price of underlying asset today is $S_0 = \$100$ and S_T is a random variable with only two outcomes such that

$$S_T = \begin{cases} \$120 \\ \$80 \end{cases}.$$

If the strike price is given by $K = \$110$, then we have the call price at time T as follows:

$$C_T = \begin{cases} \$10 & \text{if } S_T = \$120 \\ \$0 & \text{if } S_T = \$80 \end{cases}.$$

Consider a portfolio with $\frac{1}{4}$ share of the underlying asset. Now let's suppose that \$20 can be borrowed at the money market account rate. To simplify the problem, assume that the risk-free rate of return for the money market account is zero. Then the cash flow of the portfolio at time T is given by

$$\text{Cash flow of the portfolio at } T = \frac{1}{4}S_T - \$20 = \begin{cases} \$10 & \text{if } S_T = \$120 \\ \$0 & \text{if } S_I = \$80 \end{cases}$$

The portfolio has the same cash flow as the payoff of the call option. Hence, the call price C_0 at time 0 must be same as the price of the portfolio at time 0. Since the price of the portfolio at time 0 is $\frac{1}{4}S_0 - \$20 = \$5$, we have

$C_0 = 5$. On the other hand, the call price at time 0 can be obtained by

$$C_0 = E[e^{-rT}(S_T - K)^+] = \$10 \cdot P(S_T = \$120) + \$0 \cdot P(S_T = \$80)$$
$$= \$10 \cdot P(S_T = \$120),$$

where **P** is a probability of S_T. Therefore, we obtain

$$P(S_T = \$120) = \frac{1}{2}$$

and

$$P(S_T = \$80) = 1 - P(S_T = \$120) = \frac{1}{2}.$$

The probability **P** depends only on the no-arbitrage structure of the portfolio. Otherwise, there will be an arbitrage opportunity. For instance, suppose **P** is given by

$$\begin{cases} P(S_T = \$120) = \dfrac{2}{5} \\ P(S_T = \$80) = 1 - P(S_T = \$120) = \dfrac{3}{5}. \end{cases}$$

Then we have

$$C_0 = \$10 \cdot P(S_T = \$120) = \$4$$

In this case, we obtain an arbitrage opportunity by pursuing a strategy of taking a long position in the call option and a short position for the portfolio. At time 0, this strategy requires (1) a payment of $4 to purchase the call, (2) a cash outlay of $21 to invest in the money market account, and (3) a cash inflow of $25 from $\frac{1}{4}$ share of the short position in the underlying stock. Hence, this strategy results in $0 at time 0. Now let's look at what happens at time T. If the underlying stock price at time T is $120, then the strategy results in (1) a $10 cash flow from the exercise of the call option (since the strike price is $110), (2) a cash flow of $21 from the maturing money market account, and (3) a cash outlay equal to $30 ($\$\frac{120}{4}$) to cover the short position in $\frac{1}{4}$ share of the underlying stock. Therefore, the cash flow is $1 for this strategy at time T. Similarly, if the underlying stock price at time T is 80, then this strategy also generates $1 at time T. This is because (1) the value of the call option is zero, (2) $21 is received from the maturing investment, and (3) the cash outlay resulting from shorting the $\frac{1}{4}$ share is $20 ($\$\frac{80}{4}$). Consequently, this strategy produces no cash flow at time 0 and $1 at time T, which is an arbitrage. The cash flow of this strategy is summarized in Table 7.2.

The portfolio that has the same cash flow as the payoff of a given option is referred to as the *replicating portfolio* of the option. Generally, if there is a probability measure under which one cannot produce an arbitrage opportunity, then the probability measure is referred to as the *risk-neutral measure*.

If a probability measure $\mathbb{P}$ is estimated using historical return data for an underlying stock, the measure is referred to as the *market measure* or the *physical measure*. The risk-neutral measure can be found by the *equivalent martingale measure* (EMM) of the measure $\mathbb{P}$: A probability measure $\mathbb{Q}$ equivalent to $\mathbb{P}$ is called an EMM of $\mathbb{P}$ if the discounted price process $(\tilde{S}_t)_{t\in[0,T]}$ of an underlying asset is a $\mathbb{Q}$-martingale, where $\tilde{S}_t = e^{-rt}S_t$ and r is the risk-free rate of return. If the underlying asset is a stock that has a continuous dividend and dividend rate denoted by d, then the EMM $\mathbb{Q}$ of $\mathbb{P}$ is the equivalent measure such that the process $(\tilde{S}_t)_{t\in[0,T]}$ is a $\mathbb{Q}$-martingale, where $\tilde{S}_t = e^{-(r-d)t}S_t$.

The no-arbitrage price of a European option can be obtained by the expectation of the present value of the payoff for the options under the EMM $\mathbb{Q}$.[1] That is, at time $t < T$, the no-arbitrage price of a European option V_t with the payoff $\Pi(T)$ and the maturity T is obtained by

$$V_t = e^{-r(T-t)} E_{\mathbb{Q}}[\Pi(T)|\mathcal{F}_t]. \tag{7.3}$$

TABLE 7.2 Illustration of an Arbitrage Opportunity

	$t=0$	$t=T$	
	$S_0 = \$100$	$S_T = \$120$	$S_T = \$80$
Call (long position)	$-\$\ 4$	$\$10$	$\$\ 0$
Portfolio (short position)			
$\frac{1}{4}$ Underlying stock (short)	$\$25$	$-\$30$	$-\$20$
Money market account (long)	$-\$21$	$\$21$	$\$21$
	$\$\ 0$	1	1

Note: If one consider $P(S_T = 120) = \frac{2}{5}$ and $P(S_T = 120) = \frac{3}{5}$, then $C_0 = \$4$.

---

[1]See Harrison and Pliska (1981).

7.4 OPTION PRICING UNDER THE BLACK-SCHOLES MODEL

In the Black-Scholes model, the stock price process is modeled by a geometric Brownian motion process. That is, the stock price process $(S_t)_{t \geq 0}$ is given by

$$S_t = S_0 e^{\mu t - \frac{\sigma^2}{2} t + \sigma W_t}$$

under the measure $\mathbb{P}$, where $(W_t)_{t \geq 0}$ is the standard Brownian motion. The parameters μ and σ can be estimated from historical data.

For calculating options using equation (7.3), we have to find an EMM $\mathbb{Q}$ of $\mathbb{P}$. The EMM $\mathbb{Q}$ can be founded by the Girsanov theorem (see Chapter 5). We have

$$S_t = S_0 e^{(r-d)t - \frac{\sigma^2}{2} t + \sigma \left(\frac{\mu - r + d}{\sigma} + W_t \right)},$$

where as defined earlier r and d are the risk-free rate of return and the dividend rate, respectively. Let

$$\tilde{W}_t = \lambda + W_t.$$

where $\lambda = \frac{\mu - r + d}{\sigma}$, which is referred to as the *market price of risk*. Then we have

$$S_t = S_0 e^{(r-d)t - \frac{\sigma^2}{2} t + \sigma \tilde{W}_t}.$$

By the Girsanov theorem, there is a measure $\mathbb{Q}$ such that $\mathbb{Q}$ is equivalent to $\mathbb{P}$ and the process $(\tilde{W}_t)_{t \geq 0}$ becomes a standard Brownian motion under $\mathbb{Q}$.

By substituting $\Pi(T) = (S_T - K)^+$ and $\Pi(T) = (K - S_T)^+$ into equation (7.3) with the EMM $\mathbb{Q}$, we obtain the Black-Scholes call option price (C_t) and the put option price (P_t) at time t, respectively:[2]

$$C_t = S_t e^{-d(T-t)} N(x) - X e^{-r(T-t)} N(x - \sigma \sqrt{T-t}), \tag{7.4}$$

$$P_t = X e^{-r(T-t)} N(-x + \sigma \sqrt{T-t}) - S_t e^{-d(T-t)} N(-x), \tag{7.5}$$

---

[2]See Black and Scholes (1973).

where

$$x = \frac{\ln(S_t/K) + (r - d + \sigma^2/2)(T - t)}{\sigma\sqrt{T - t}},$$

and $N(x)$ is the cumulative distribution function of the standard normal distribution.

7.5 EUROPEAN OPTION PRICING UNDER EXPONENTIAL TEMPERED STABLE MODELS

In this section, we derive the pricing formula for European options based on exponential Lévy models by means of the Fourier transform method. The derivation was provided in Carr and Madan (1999) and Lewis (2001).

Let $\mathbb{P}$ be a market measure and $\mathbb{Q}$ be a risk-neutral measure. We assume that the stock price process under a market measure $\mathbb{P}$ is given by the exponential tempered stable model introduced in Chapter 6. That is, we assume that

$$S_t = S_0 e^{X_t}, \tag{7.6}$$

where $X = (X_t)_{t\in[0,T]}$ is one tempered stable process defined in Table 6.1. Moreover, X is assumed to be a tempered stable process under $\mathbb{Q}$.

The parameters of a tempered stable process under $\mathbb{P}$ and $\mathbb{Q}$ are referred to as *market parameters* and *risk-neutral parameters*, respectively. If the underlying asset has a continuous dividend rate d, then $\tilde{S}_t = e^{-(r-d)t}S_t$ and the martingale property of $(\tilde{S}_t)_{t\geq 0}$ is satisfied if $e^{(r-d)t}E[S_t] = S_0$. Since we have $S_0 = E_{\mathbb{Q}}[\tilde{S}_t] = e^{-(r-d)t}S_0 E_{\mathbb{Q}}[e^{X_t}]$, the driving process $(X_t)_{t\geq 0}$ must satisfy

$$\phi_{X_t}(-i) = E_{\mathbb{Q}}[e^{X_t}] = e^{(r-d)t}, \tag{7.7}$$

where ϕ_{X_t} is the characteristic function of X_t under $\mathbb{Q}$. Therefore, by the condition (7.7) and change of measure for tempered stable processes discussed in Chapter 5, we can find the condition for the market and risk-neutral parameters for which $\mathbb{Q}$ corresponds to $\mathbb{P}$.

For example, suppose X is the CTS process under both the market measure $\mathbb{P}$ and the risk-neutral measure $\mathbb{Q}$, having market parameters $(\alpha, C, \lambda_+, \lambda_-, m)$ and risk-neutral parameters $(\tilde{\alpha}, \tilde{C}, \tilde{\lambda}_+, \tilde{\lambda}_-, \tilde{m})$. The condition (7.7) is satisfied if

$$\tilde{m} = (r - d) - \log \phi_{CTS}(-i;\; \tilde{\alpha}, \tilde{C}, \tilde{\lambda}_+, \tilde{\lambda}_-, 0),$$

and $\tilde{\lambda}_+ > 1$. The measures $\mathbb{P}$ and $\mathbb{Q}$ are equivalent if and only if $\alpha = \tilde{\alpha}$, $C = \tilde{C}$, and

$$\tilde{m} - m = C\Gamma(1 - \alpha)(\tilde{\lambda}_+^{\alpha-1} - \tilde{\lambda}_-^{\alpha-1} - \lambda_+^{\alpha-1} + \lambda_-^{\alpha-1}).$$

In order to find the EMM, we have to find λ_+ and λ_- satisfying

$$(r - d) - \log \phi_{CTS}(-i; \alpha, C, \tilde{\lambda}_+, \tilde{\lambda}_-, 0)$$
$$= m + C\Gamma(1 - \alpha)(\tilde{\lambda}_+^{\alpha-1} - \tilde{\lambda}_-^{\alpha-1} - \lambda_+^{\alpha-1} + \lambda_-^{\alpha-1}).$$

We can use the same arguments for all the tempered stable models described in Chapter 6: CTS, modified tempered stable (MTS), normal tempered stable (NTS), rapidly decreasing tempered stable (RDTS), and Kim-Rachev tempered stable (KRTS).

In Table 7.3, the distribution of the driving process under market and risk-neutral measures is presented for the five tempered stable models. In the table, the parameterized condition for the risk-neutral measure $\mathbb{Q}$ to be the EMM of $\mathbb{P}$ is also presented. If the driving processes for the market measure and the risk-neutral measure are both the same tempered stable process, the option pricing model is referred as a tempered stable process (e.g., CTS option pricing model) or simply process followed by model's name (e.g., CTS model).

Using equation (7.3), we can calculate the call and put option prices. Let ϕ_{X_1} be the characteristic function of X_1 under an EMM $\mathbb{Q}$. The call option price C_t at time t under the tempered stable model is given by

$$C_t = \frac{K^{1+\rho} e^{-r(T-t)}}{\pi S_t^\rho} \mathrm{Re} \int_0^\infty e^{-iu \log(K/S_t)} \frac{e^{(T-t)\log \phi_{X_1}(u+i\rho)}}{(\rho - iu)(1 + \rho - iu)} du, \qquad (7.8)$$

where ρ is a real number such that $\rho < -1$ and $\phi_{X_1}(u + i\rho) < \infty$ for all $u \in \mathbb{R}$. The put option price P_t at time t can be obtained by the same formula, but the condition of ρ is different; that is

$$P_t = \frac{K^{1+\rho} e^{-r(T-t)}}{\pi S_t^\rho} \mathrm{Re} \int_0^\infty e^{-iu \log(K/S_t)} \frac{e^{(T-t)\log \phi_{X_1}(u+i\rho)}}{(\rho - iu)(1 + \rho - iu)} du \qquad (7.9)$$

TABLE 7.3 Tempered Stable Option Pricing Models

Model	Measure	Parameters
CTS	$\mathbb{P}$	$(\alpha, C, \lambda_+, \lambda_-, m)$
	$\mathbb{Q}$	$(\tilde{\alpha}, \tilde{C}, \tilde{\lambda}_+, \tilde{\lambda}_-, \tilde{m})$
		with $\tilde{m} = r - d - \log \phi_{CTS}(-i; \tilde{\alpha}, \tilde{C}, \tilde{\lambda}_+, \tilde{\lambda}_-, 0)$
	EMM condition	$\alpha = \tilde{\alpha}, C = \tilde{C}, \tilde{\lambda}_+ > 1,$
		$r - d - \log \phi_{CTS}(-i; \alpha, C, \tilde{\lambda}_+, \tilde{\lambda}_-, 0)$
		$= m + C\Gamma(1-\alpha)(\tilde{\lambda}_+^{\alpha-1} - \tilde{\lambda}_-^{\alpha-1} - \lambda_+^{\alpha-1} + \lambda_-^{\alpha-1})$
MTS	$\mathbb{P}$	$(\alpha, C, \lambda_+, \lambda_-, m)$
	$\mathbb{Q}$	$(\tilde{\alpha}, \tilde{C}, \tilde{\lambda}_+, \tilde{\lambda}_-, \tilde{m})$
		with $\tilde{m} = r - d - \log \phi_{MTS}(-i; \tilde{\alpha}, \tilde{C}, \tilde{\lambda}_+, \tilde{\lambda}_-, 0)$
	EMM condition	$\alpha = \tilde{\alpha}, C = \tilde{C}, \tilde{\lambda}_+ > 1,$
		$r - d - \log \phi_{MTS}(-i; \alpha, C, \tilde{\lambda}_+, \tilde{\lambda}_-, 0)$
		$= m + 2^{-\frac{\alpha+1}{2}} C\Gamma\left(\frac{1-\alpha}{2}\right)(\tilde{\lambda}_+^{\alpha-1} - \tilde{\lambda}_-^{\alpha-1} - \lambda_+^{\alpha-1} + \lambda_-^{\alpha-1})$
NTS	$\mathbb{P}$	$(\alpha, C, \lambda, \beta, m)$
	$\mathbb{Q}$	$(\tilde{\alpha}, \tilde{C}, \tilde{\lambda}, \tilde{\beta}, \tilde{m})$
		with $\tilde{m} = r - d - \log \phi_{NTS}(-i; \tilde{\alpha}, \tilde{C}, \tilde{\lambda}, \tilde{\beta}, 0)$
	EMM condition	$\alpha = \tilde{\alpha}, C = \tilde{C}, \tilde{\lambda} - \tilde{\beta} > 1,$
		$r - d - \log \phi_{NTS}(-i; \alpha, C, \tilde{\lambda}, \tilde{\beta}, 0)$
		$= m + \kappa(\tilde{\beta}(\tilde{\lambda}^2 - \tilde{\beta}^2)^{\frac{\alpha}{2}-1} - \beta(\lambda^2 - \beta^2)^{\frac{\alpha}{2}-1})$
		where $\kappa = 2^{-\frac{\alpha-1}{2}}\sqrt{\pi} C\Gamma\left(1 - \frac{\alpha}{2}\right)$
RDTS	$\mathbb{P}$	$(\alpha, C, \lambda_+, \lambda_-, m)$
	$\mathbb{Q}$	$(\tilde{\alpha}, \tilde{C}, \tilde{\lambda}_+, \tilde{\lambda}_-, \tilde{m})$
		with $\tilde{m} = r - d - \log \phi_{RDTS}(-i; \tilde{\alpha}, \tilde{C}, \tilde{\lambda}_+, \tilde{\lambda}_-, 0)$
	EMM condition	$\alpha = \tilde{\alpha}, C = \tilde{C},$
		$r - d - \log \phi_{RDTS}(-i; \alpha, C, \tilde{\lambda}_+, \tilde{\lambda}_-, 0)$
		$= m + 2^{-\frac{\alpha+1}{2}} C\Gamma\left(\frac{1-\alpha}{2}\right)\left(\tilde{\lambda}_+^{\alpha-1} - \tilde{\lambda}_-^{\alpha-1} - \lambda_+^{\alpha-1} + \lambda_-^{\alpha-1}\right)$
KRTS	$\mathbb{P}$	$(\alpha, k_+, k_-, r_+, r_-, p_+, p_-, m)$
	$\mathbb{Q}$	$(\tilde{\alpha}, \tilde{k}_+, \tilde{k}_-, \tilde{r}_+, \tilde{r}_-, \tilde{p}_+, \tilde{p}_-, \tilde{m})$
		with $\tilde{m} = r - d - \log \phi_{KRTS}(-i; \tilde{\alpha}, \tilde{k}_+, \tilde{k}_-, \tilde{r}_+, \tilde{r}_-, \tilde{p}_+, \tilde{p}_-, 0)$
	EMM condition	$\alpha = \tilde{\alpha}, k_+ = \tilde{k}_+, k_- = \tilde{k}_-, 0 < \tilde{r}_+ < 1,$
		$r - d - \log \phi_{KRTS}(-i; \tilde{\alpha}, \tilde{k}_+, \tilde{k}_-, \tilde{r}_+, \tilde{r}_-, \tilde{p}_+, \tilde{p}_-, 0)$
		$= m + \Gamma(1-\alpha)\left(\dfrac{\tilde{k}_+\tilde{r}_+}{\tilde{p}_+ + 1} - \dfrac{\tilde{k}_-\tilde{r}_-}{\tilde{p}_- + 1} - \dfrac{k_+ r_+}{p_+ + 1} + \dfrac{k_- r_-}{p_- + 1}\right)$
		$\begin{cases} p_+, p_-, \tilde{p}_+, \tilde{p}_- \in (1/2 - \alpha, \infty) \setminus \{0\}, & \text{if } \alpha \in (0, 1) \\ p_+, p_-, \tilde{p}_+, \tilde{p}_- \in (1 - \alpha, \infty) \setminus \{0\}, & \text{if } \alpha \in (1, 2) \end{cases}$

Note: CTS = classical tempered stable; MTS = modified tempered stable; NTS = normal tempered stable; RDTS = rapidly decreasing tempered stable; KRTS = Kim-Rachev tempered stable.

TABLE 7.4 Condition of ρ for Call and Put Option Prices

Model	Existence Condition of $\phi_{X_1}(u + i\rho)$ for all $u \in \mathbb{R}$	Condition of ρ Call	Put
CTS	$-\lambda_+ \leq \rho \leq \lambda_-$	$-\lambda_+ \leq \rho < -1$	$0 < \rho \leq \lambda_-$
MTS	$-\lambda_+ \leq \rho \leq \lambda_-$	$-\lambda_+ \leq \rho < -1$	$0 < \rho \leq \lambda_-$
NTS	$-\lambda + \beta \leq \rho \leq \lambda + \beta$	$-\lambda + \beta \leq \rho < -1$	$0 < \rho \leq \lambda + \beta$
RDTS	$-\infty < \rho < \infty$	$\rho < -1$	$0 < \rho$
KRTS	$-1/r_+ \leq \rho \leq 1/r_-$	$-1/r_+ \leq \rho < -1$	$0 < \rho \leq 1/r_-$

where ρ is real number such that $\rho > 0$ and $\phi_{X_1}(u + i\rho) < \infty$ for all $u \in \mathbb{R}$. The condition of ρ for call and put option prices for each tempered stable models is presented in Table 7.4.

The general formula for pricing European options is given by Lewis (2001). Let $h(x)$ be a payoff function with $x = \log S_T$ and $\hat{h}(\xi) = \int_{-\infty}^{\infty} e^{-i\xi x} h(x) dx$. Suppose $\hat{h}(\xi)$ is defined for all $\xi \in R_h$ where $R_h = \{z \in \mathbb{C} : \text{Im}(z) \in I_h\}$ for some open interval I_h. The driving process $(X_t)_{t \geq 0}$ is a Lévy process such that a characteristic function $\phi_{X_{T-t}}(\xi)$ of X_{T-t} is defined for all $\xi \in R_\phi$ where $R_\phi = \{z \in \mathbb{C} : \text{Im}(z) \in I_\phi\}$ for some open interval I_ϕ. Then a European option price V_t at time t can be calculated by

$$V_t = \frac{e^{-r(T-t)}}{2\pi} \int_{-\infty}^{\infty} e^{i(u+i\rho)Y} \phi_{X_{T-t}}(u + i\rho) \hat{h}(u + i\rho) du, \qquad (7.10)$$

where $Y = \log S_t$ and $\rho \in I_h \cap I_\phi$.

7.5.1 Illustration: Implied Volatility

The implied volatility of a European call option (or put option) is the volatility implied from option prices using the Black-Scholes formula. If the stock price process follows the Black-Scholes model, then the implied volatility would be constant for all maturities and strike prices at a specific point in time. However, this is not what is observed in real-world option markets. Typically, deep in-the-money and deep out-of-the-money options have higher volatilities than at-the-money options. This phenomenon is referred to as the *volatility smile*.

Suppose we observe call prices in the market. The call prices are described by the strike price and the time to maturity. Hence the market call prices can be denoted by $\hat{C}(K, \tau)$, where K is the strike price and τ is the time to maturity. Given strike prices and times to maturity, the implied volatility is the value σ that satisfies the following equation:

$$\hat{C}(K, \tau) = C_{BS}(S_0, K, \tau, \sigma_{imp}, r).$$

where $C_{BS}(S_0, K, \tau, \sigma_{imp}, r) = C_t$ is Black-Scholes call option pricing formula that is given by equation (7.4). Since S_0 and r are fixed in today's market data, the value σ_{imp} depends on strike prices and times to maturities. Hence σ_{imp} becomes a function from a strike price and a time to maturity to a positive real number. We denote the function by $\sigma_{imp}(K, \tau)$. If we plot the graph of $\sigma_{imp}(K, \tau)$ in 3-dimensional space, we obtain a surface. The surface is referred to as the *implied volatility surface.*

By calculating implied volatilities for theoretical option prices of tempered stable models, we can verify whether models can capture the volatility smile effect. For example, we consider the MTS option pricing model and assume that the current stock price is \$100 and the risk-free interest rate is 5%. To get the implied volatilities from the option prices based on the MTS option pricing model, we find σ_{BS} satisfying

$$C_{MTS}(K, \tau) = C_{BS}(S_0, K, \tau, \sigma_{imp}, r)$$

by the bisection method, where $C_{MTS}(K, \tau)$ is a call option price computed from equation (7.8) based on the MTS option pricing model. The implied volatilities for the MTS option pricing model are displayed in Figure 7.1. We choose two sets of parameters for the MTS option pricing model. One is symmetric and the other is nonsymmetric. For the symmetric parameter case, we assume that $(\alpha, C, \lambda_+, \lambda_-) = (0.88, 0.08, 1.4, 1.4)$ and for the nonsymmetric parameter case, we assume that $(\alpha, C, \lambda_+, \lambda_-) = (0.88, 0.08, 2.0, 1.2)$. The three left plots in the figure are for the symmetric case and the three right plots are for the nonsymmetric case. The plots in Figure 7.1 show that the MTS option pricing model captures the volatility smile.

7.5.2 Illustration: Calibrating Risk-Neutral Parameters

We now calibrate risk-neutral parameters of the Black-Scholes model and five tempered stable option pricing models (CTS, MTS, NTS, RDTS, and KRTS option pricing models) from one day's option prices by minimizing the root-mean-square error between market prices and the model prices. In this calibration, we do not consider the market measure, but only consider the risk-neutral measure reflected in option prices.

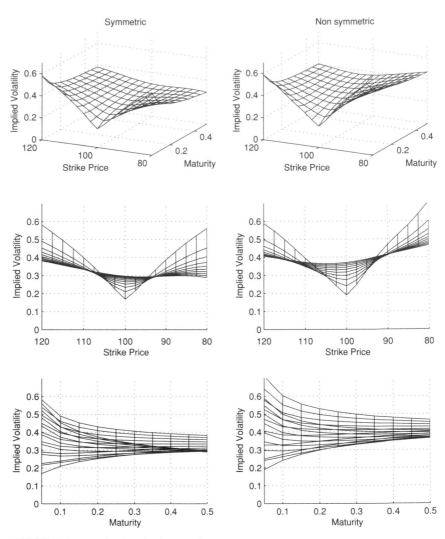

FIGURE 7.1 Implied Volatility Surface

Note:

Parameters for the plots on the left plot: $r = 5\%$, $\alpha = 0.88$, $C = 0.08$, $\lambda_+ = 1.4$, $\lambda_- = 1.4$.

Parameters for the plots on the right plot: $r = 5\%$, $\alpha = 0.88$, $C = 0.08$, $\lambda_+ = 2.0$, $\lambda_- = 1.2$.

Maturity is expressed in terms of fraction of a year.

Let us consider a given market model and observed prices $\hat{C}_i$ of call options with strikes K_i and maturities T_i, $i \in \{1, \ldots, N\}$, where N is the number of options on a fixed day. The risk-neutral process is fitted by matching model prices to market prices using nonlinear least squares. Hence, to obtain a practical solution to the calibration problem, our purpose is to find a parameter set $\tilde{\theta}$, such that the optimization problem

$$\min_{\tilde{\theta}} \sum_{i=1}^{N} (\hat{C}_i - C^{\tilde{\theta}}(K_i, T_i))^2 \qquad (7.11)$$

is solved, where by $\hat{C}_i$ we denote the price of an option as observed in the market and by $C_i^{\tilde{\theta}}$ the price computed according to a pricing formula in a chosen model with a parameter set $\tilde{\theta}$.

We use the set of call option prices on the S&P 500 index at the close of market on August 6, 2008. We consider call options with prices between $5 and $180, and $0.8 \leq M \leq 1.2$, where M is *moneyness* defined by $M = K/S_0$. Days to maturity are given by 10, 45, 73, 108, 136, 227, 318, and 500 days. The S&P 500 index on that day and dividend rate were 1289.19 and 2.035013%, respectively. The 13-week Treasury bill index (IRX) is used for risk-free rate of return and it was 1.6% on that day.

In Table 7.5, we give parameters computed from the calibration procedure. In Table 7.6, the relevant values of four error estimators are given. The four error estimators are the *average prediction error* (APE), *average absolute error* (AAE), *root mean-square error* (RMSE), and *average relative pricing error* (ARPE).[3] Implied volatility curves of five tempered stable option pricing model prices and market prices are presented in Figure 7.2 for each days to maturity.

---

[3]Let N be the number of observation, $\hat{P}_n$ be the nth price determined by the option price formula for Black-Scholes model or tempered stable option pricing models, and P_n be the nth observed price. Then the four error estimators are defined as follows:

$$\text{AAE} = \sum_{n=1}^{N} \frac{|P_n - \hat{P}_n|}{N}, \qquad \text{APE} = \text{AAE} \left(\sum_{n=1}^{N} \frac{P_n}{N} \right)^{-1},$$

$$\text{ARPE} = \frac{1}{N} \sum_{n=1}^{N} \frac{|P_n - \hat{P}_n|}{P_n}, \qquad \text{RMSE} = \sqrt{\sum_{n=1}^{N} \frac{(P_n - \hat{P}_n)^2}{N}}.$$

TABLE 7.5 Results for the Calibration of the Risk-Neutral Parameters

τ	N	Model	Parameters				
10	15	Black-Scholes	$\sigma = 0.1681$				
		CTS	$\alpha = 0.90$	$C = 0.69$	$\lambda_+ = 88.3$	$\lambda_- = 14.3$	
		MTS	$\alpha = 0.81$	$C = 1.00$	$\lambda_+ = 47.3$	$\lambda_- = 42.6$	
		NTS	$\alpha = 0.89$	$C = 0.82$	$\lambda_+ = 51.9$	$\beta = -8.8$	
		KRTS	$\alpha = 0.88$	$k_+ = 58.3$	$k_- = 12.2$	$r_+ = 0.0143$	$r_- = 0.0841$
		RDTS	$\alpha = 0.93$	$C = 0.59$	$\lambda_+ = 48.1$	$\lambda_- = 37.7$	$p_+ = p_- = 0.3$
45	25	Black-Scholes	$\sigma = 0.1749$				
		CTS	$\alpha = 0.85$	$C = 0.67$	$\lambda_+ = 90.6$	$\lambda_- = 12.9$	
		MTS	$\alpha = 0.82$	$C = 1.08$	$\lambda_+ = 74.9$	$\lambda_- = 34.9$	
		NTS	$\alpha = 0.86$	$C = 0.83$	$\lambda_+ = 50.5$	$\beta = -13.6$	
		KRTS	$\alpha = 0.86$	$k_+ = 40.9$	$k_- = 9.80$	$r_+ = 0.0176$	$r_- = 0.0924$
		RDTS	$\alpha = 0.94$	$C = 0.66$	$\lambda_+ = 53.4$	$\lambda_- = 43.9$	$p_+ = p_- = 0.3$
73	7	Black-Scholes	$\sigma = 0.1832$				
		CTS	$\alpha = 0.84$	$C = 0.71$	$\lambda_+ = 93.9$	$\lambda_- = 12.7$	
		MTS	$\alpha = 0.73$	$C = 1.05$	$\lambda_+ = 52.0$	$\lambda_- = 20.3$	
		NTS	$\alpha = 0.81$	$C = 0.90$	$\lambda_+ = 52.6$	$\beta = -24.2$	
		KRTS	$\alpha = 0.86$	$k_+ = 79.8$	$k_- = 15.6$	$r_+ = 0.0136$	$r_- = 0.0914$
		RDTS	$\alpha = 1.16$	$C = 0.25$	$\lambda_+ = 94.3$	$\lambda_- = 77.6$	$p_+ = p_- = 1.1$
108	7	Black-Scholes	$\sigma = 0.1844$				
		CTS	$\alpha = 0.78$	$C = 0.66$	$\lambda_+ = 94.7$	$\lambda_- = 9.7$	
		MTS	$\alpha = 0.54$	$C = 1.05$	$\lambda_+ = 59.3$	$\lambda_- = 10.0$	
		NTS	$\alpha = 0.69$	$C = 0.80$	$\lambda_+ = 40.3$	$\beta = -23.6$	
		KRTS	$\alpha = 0.71$	$k_+ = 43.5$	$k_- = 8.20$	$r_+ = 0.0128$	$r_- = 0.1326$
		RDTS	$\alpha = 1.15$	$C = 0.29$	$\lambda_+ = 85.9$	$\lambda_- = 72.3$	$p_+ = p_- = 0.9$

τ	N	Model						
136	8	Black-Scholes	$\sigma = 0.1838$					$p_+ = p_- = 0.8$
		CTS	$\alpha = 0.70$	$C = 0.65$	$\lambda_+ = 95.5$	$\lambda_- = 7.7$		
		MTS	$\alpha = 0.45$	$C = 0.86$	$\lambda_+ = 39.0$	$\lambda_- = 7.1$		
		NTS	$\alpha = 0.58$	$C = 0.76$	$\lambda_+ = 38.5$	$\beta = -26.4$		
		KRTS	$\alpha = 0.62$	$k_+ = 31.1$	$k_- = 6.21$	$r_+ = 0.0114$	$r_- = 0.1559$	
		RDTS	$\alpha = 1.13$	$C = 0.31$	$\lambda_+ = 84.4$	$\lambda_- = 70.6$		
227	7	Black-Scholes	$\sigma = 0.1796$					$p_+ = p_- = 0.2$
		CTS	$\alpha = 0.94$	$C = 0.16$	$\lambda_+ = 26.9$	$\lambda_- = 3.4$		
		MTS	$\alpha = 0.86$	$C = 0.15$	$\lambda_+ = 62.5$	$\lambda_- = 2.6$		
		NTS	$\alpha = 0.71$	$C = 0.25$	$\lambda_+ = 38.8$	$\beta = -31.4$		
		KRTS	$\alpha = 0.44$	$k_+ = 3.75$	$k_- = 0.793$	$r_+ = 0.0146$	$r_- = 0.4813$	
		RDTS	$\alpha = 1.06$	$C = 0.38$	$\lambda_+ = 76.0$	$\lambda_- = 62.6$		
318	5	Black-Scholes	$\sigma = 0.1889$					$p_+ = p_- = 1.0$
		CTS	$\alpha = 0.92$	$C = 0.20$	$\lambda_+ = 99.8$	$\lambda_- = 4.2$		
		MTS	$\alpha = 0.69$	$C = 0.23$	$\lambda_+ = 49.4$	$\lambda_- = 3.0$		
		NTS	$\alpha = 0.59$	$C = 0.21$	$\lambda_+ = 36.0$	$\beta = -32.1$		
		KRTS	$\alpha = 0.74$	$k_+ = 2.87$	$k_- = 0.434$	$r_+ = 0.0615$	$r_- = 0.7943$	
		RDTS	$\alpha = 0.96$	$C = 0.50$	$\lambda_+ = 63.2$	$\lambda_- = 50.3$		
500	5	Black-Scholes	$\sigma = 0.1904$					$p_+ = p_- = 1.4$
		CTS	$\alpha = 0.90$	$C = 0.20$	$\lambda_+ = 100.0$	$\lambda_- = 4.1$		
		MTS	$\alpha = 0.53$	$C = 0.26$	$\lambda_+ = 53.1$	$\lambda_- = 2.6$		
		NTS	$\alpha = 0.34$	$C = 0.32$	$\lambda_+ = 34.9$	$\beta = -31.6$		
		KRTS	$\alpha = 0.30$	$k_+ = 3.88$	$k_- = 1.42$	$r_+ = 0.0164$	$r_- = 0.4642$	
		RDTS	$\alpha = 0.40$	$C = 0.40$	$\lambda_+ = 50.9$	$\lambda_- = 40.9$		

Note: τ = days to maturity; N = number of options.

TABLE 7.6 Error Estimators

τ	N	Model	APE	AAE	RMSE	ARPE
10	15	Black-Scholes	0.0196	0.5323	0.6152	0.0357
		CTS	0.0160	0.4335	0.5437	0.0340
		MTS	0.0149	0.4057	0.5024	0.0320
		NTS	0.0163	0.4427	0.5603	0.0358
		KRTS	0.0161	0.4380	0.5655	0.0380
		RDTS	0.0166	0.4502	0.5409	0.0307
45	25	Black-Scholes	0.0427	1.6423	1.8635	0.1115
		CTS	0.0433	1.6657	1.9128	0.1276
		MTS	0.0380	1.4610	1.6712	0.1071
		NTS	0.0379	1.4575	1.6753	0.1078
		KRTS	0.0464	1.7864	2.0142	0.1244
		RDTS	0.0310	1.1934	1.3576	0.0794
73	7	Black-Scholes	0.0587	2.1940	2.4789	0.1538
		CTS	0.0470	1.7585	2.0571	0.1360
		MTS	0.0587	2.1938	2.5094	0.1563
		NTS	0.0472	1.7647	2.0163	0.1288
		KRTS	0.0568	2.1233	2.4455	0.1538
		RDTS	0.0209	0.7795	0.8362	0.0486
108	7	Black-Scholes	0.0646	2.6679	3.0482	0.1382
		CTS	0.0394	1.6265	1.8658	0.0913
		MTS	0.0557	2.3010	2.6088	0.1256
		NTS	0.0416	1.7174	1.9532	0.0932
		KRTS	0.0556	2.2970	2.5910	0.1207
		RDTS	0.0134	0.5529	0.6145	0.0258
136	8	Black-Scholes	0.0742	3.2071	3.5794	0.1584
		CTS	0.0337	1.4550	1.5958	0.0751
		MTS	0.0509	2.1984	2.4476	0.1131
		NTS	0.0373	1.6105	1.7513	0.0795
		KRTS	0.0549	2.3708	2.6468	0.1155
		RDTS	0.0143	0.6165	0.6900	0.0276
227	7	Black-Scholes	0.0797	3.5912	3.9623	0.1297
		CTS	0.0025	0.1143	0.1222	0.0036
		MTS	0.0084	0.3793	0.4662	0.0165
		NTS	0.0056	0.2511	0.3127	0.0116
		KRTS	0.0111	0.4990	0.5982	0.0215
		RDTS	0.0118	0.5297	0.5882	0.0197

TABLE 7.6 (*Continued*)

τ	N	Model	APE	AAE	RMSE	ARPE
318	5	Black-Scholes	0.0383	3.1002	3.9130	0.0572
		CTS	0.0018	0.1487	0.1625	0.0022
		MTS	0.0014	0.1141	0.1255	0.0016
		NTS	0.0021	0.1730	0.1928	0.0024
		KRTS	0.0006	0.0468	0.0521	0.0005
		RDTS	0.0058	0.4697	0.5252	0.0074
500	5	Black-Scholes	0.0378	4.0096	4.6719	0.0436
		CTS	0.0019	0.2060	0.2166	0.0021
		MTS	0.0027	0.2887	0.3110	0.0029
		NTS	0.0037	0.3883	0.4156	0.0039
		KRTS	0.0031	0.3289	0.3790	0.0030
		RDTS	0.0041	0.4349	0.4627	0.0046

Note: τ = days to maturity; N = number of options.

Based on Table 7.6, we conclude the following:

- In the case of 10 days to maturity, the MTS option pricing model has the smallest APE, AAE, and RMSE, and the RDTS model has the smallest ARPE.
- In the case of 45, 73, 108, and 136 days to maturity, the RDTS option pricing model performs the best; that is, it is the model that produced the smallest values for all the error estimators.
- In the case of 227 and 500 days to maturity, the CTS option pricing model has the best performance. In the case of 318 days to maturity, the KRTS option pricing model has the best performance.

From Figure 7.2, we observe the following:

- In Figure 7.2(A) and (B) (i.e., 10 and 45 days to maturity), both the volatility curve of the five tempered stable option pricing models and the market volatility curve are skewed left. However, the volatility curves of the five tempered stable option pricing models do not exactly match the market volatility curve.
- Figure 7.2(C) to (E) (i.e., 73, 108, and 136 days to maturity) show that the RDTS option pricing model's volatility curve comes closer to matching the market volatility curve than the volatility curves for the other four tempered stable option pricing models.

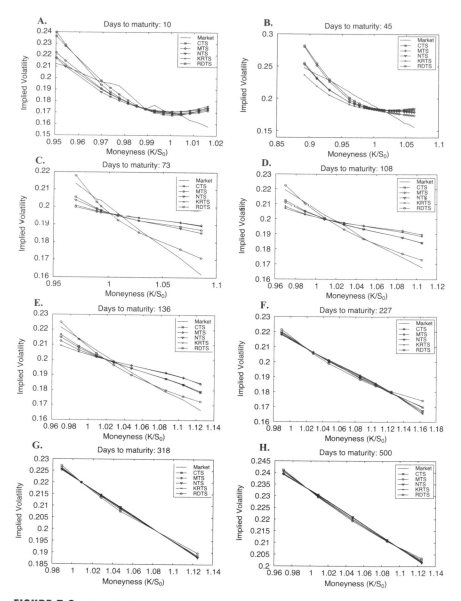

FIGURE 7.2 Implied Volatilities for Market Option Prices and for Tempered Stable Model Prices

- In Figure 7.2(F) to (H) (i.e., 227, 318, and 500 days to maturity), the volatility curves of the five tempered stable option pricing models match the market volatility curves.

7.5.3 Illustration: Calibrating Market Parameters and Risk-Neutral Parameters Together

In this section, we will discuss a parametric approach to risk-neutral density extraction from option prices based on knowledge of the estimated historical density.

To find the risk-neutral parameters for an EMM of a given market measure with market parameters, we begin by estimating market parameters using historical returns of an underlying asset, and then finding a solution to the minimization problem (7.11), which satisfies conditions in Table 7.3.

In our illustration, time-series data for the period September 10, 1998, to September 10, 2008, are used, while the option data are for September 10, 2008. The market parameters for the S&P 500 index are estimated in Table 6.3 of Chapter 6. To estimate risk-neutral parameters, we use the set of call option prices on the S&P 500 index at the close of market on September 10, 2008. We consider call options with prices between \$5 and \$180, and $0.8 \leq M \leq 1.2$, where $M = K/S_0$. Days to maturity we use in this illustration are 10, 38, 73, 101, and 192 days. The S&P 500 index and dividend rate on that day are observed by 1232.04 and 2.2190%, respectively. The 13-week Treasury bill index (IRX) is 1.62% on that day.

For the CTS, MTS, NTS, and RDTS we have only two free parameters,[4] but in the KRTS case there are four free parameters[5] to fit model prices to market prices; therefore, the KRTS distribution is more flexible for finding an equivalent change of measure and, at the same time, takes into account historical estimates.

Each maturity is calibrated separately. The results reported in Table 7.7 also show the four error estimators. The Black-Scholes model does not have a parameter that needs to be estimated in order to calculate option prices. In the process, the parameter σ is estimated from market volatility. The flexibility of the KRTS distribution produces smaller error estimators than the CTS, NTS, MTS, and RDTS option pricing models do.

---

[4] The free parameters for the CTS, MTS, and RDTS are λ_+ and λ_-, and for NTS are λ and β.
[5] They are $r_+, r_-, p_+,$ and p_-.

TABLE 7.7 Risk-Neutral Parameters and Error Estimators

τ	N	Model	Parameters	APE	AAE	RMSE	ARPE
10	16	Black-Scholes	$\sigma = 0.1823$	0.1022	2.6717	2.7558	0.1568
		CTS	$\tilde{\lambda}_+ = 113.6$ $\tilde{\lambda}_- = 103.0$	0.0242	0.6322	0.6990	0.0445
		MTS	$\tilde{\lambda}_+ = 115.4$ $\tilde{\lambda}_- = 104.6$	0.0242	0.6328	0.6996	0.0445
		NTS	$\tilde{\lambda} = 104.3$ $\tilde{\beta} = -5.2$	0.0241	0.6311	0.6976	0.0444
		KRTS	$\tilde{r}_+ = 0.00792$ $\tilde{r}_- = 0.01068$ $\bar{p}_+ = 16.1$ $\bar{p}_- = 20.6$	0.0200	0.5219	0.5957	0.0402
		RDTS	$\tilde{\lambda}_+ = 57.7$ $\tilde{\lambda}_- = 58.5$	0.0298	0.7786	0.8695	0.0510
38	20	Black-Scholes	$\sigma = 0.1823$	0.1605	4.1189	4.6210	0.1736
		CTS	$\tilde{\lambda}_+ = 116.8$ $\tilde{\lambda}_- = 103.0$	0.0734	1.8826	2.1158	0.1512
		MTS	$\tilde{\lambda}_+ = 120.0$ $\tilde{\lambda}_- = 108.4$	0.0677	1.7377	1.9798	0.1213
		NTS	$\tilde{\lambda} = 108.5$ $\tilde{\beta} = -5.6$	0.0677	1.7376	1.9795	0.1213
		KRTS	$\tilde{r}_+ = 0.00770$ $\tilde{r}_- = 0.01067$ $\bar{p}_+ = 17.5$ $\bar{p}_- = 22.8$	0.0530	1.3608	1.5190	0.0970
		RDTS	$\tilde{\lambda}_+ = 59.9$ $\tilde{\lambda}_- = 60.7$	0.0798	2.0480	2.3586	0.1402
73	8	Black-Scholes	$\sigma = 0.1823$	0.1276	4.4610	5.5217	0.1215
		CTS	$\tilde{\lambda}_+ = 119.0$ $\tilde{\lambda}_- = 107.5$	0.0892	3.1191	3.6155	0.2124
		MTS	$\tilde{\lambda}_+ = 120.0$ $\tilde{\lambda}_- = 108.4$	0.0906	3.1656	3.6263	0.2238
		NTS	$\tilde{\lambda} = 108.5$ $\tilde{\beta} = -5.6$	0.0906	3.1655	3.6256	0.2239
		KRTS	$\tilde{r}_+ = 0.00756$ $\tilde{r}_- = 0.01023$ $\bar{p}_+ = 17.4$ $\bar{p}_- = 22.1$	0.0608	2.1234	2.3630	0.1547
		RDTS	$\tilde{\lambda}_+ = 59.7$ $\tilde{\lambda}_- = 60.4$	0.1066	3.7255	4.4222	0.2445

	τ	Model									
101	16	Black-Scholes	$\sigma = 0.1823$				0.1276	4.9723	6.0472	0.1221
		CTS	$\tilde{\lambda}_+ = 119.0$	$\tilde{\lambda}_- = 107.5$			0.0892	3.4781	4.0567	0.1857
		MTS	$\tilde{\lambda}_+ = 121.6$	$\tilde{\lambda}_- = 109.8$			0.0882	3.4376	4.0459	0.1774
		NTS	$\tilde{\lambda} = 108.5$	$\tilde{\beta} = -5.6$			0.0908	3.5380	4.0954	0.1957
		KRTS	$\tilde{r}_+ = 0.00756$	$\tilde{r}_- = 0.01023$	$\bar{p}_+ = 18.0$	$\bar{p}_- = 22.8$	0.0600	2.3375	2.6103	0.1285
		RDTS	$\tilde{\lambda}_+ = 59.7$	$\tilde{\lambda}_- = 60.5$			0.1052	4.1013	4.9482	0.2044
192	9	Black-Scholes	$\sigma = 0.1823$				0.1118	3.4225	4.6553	0.1171
		CTS	$\tilde{\lambda}_+ = 126.6$	$\tilde{\lambda}_- = 113.8$			0.1263	3.8659	4.3673	0.2322
		MTS	$\tilde{\lambda}_+ = 128.5$	$\tilde{\lambda}_- = 115.5$			0.1263	3.8658	4.3672	0.2322
		NTS	$\tilde{\lambda} = 116.3$	$\tilde{\beta} = -6.3$			0.1263	3.8658	4.3671	0.2322
		KRTS	$\tilde{r}_+ = 0.00711$	$\tilde{r}_- = 0.00967$	$\bar{p}_+ = 17.9$	$\bar{p}_- = 22.8$	0.0933	2.8561	3.1987	0.1757
		RDTS	$\tilde{\lambda}_+ = 63.8$	$\tilde{\lambda}_- = 64.4$			0.1442	4.4135	5.0247	0.2612

Note: τ = days to maturity; N = number of options.

163

7.6   SUBORDINATED STOCK PRICE MODEL

In this section, we discuss a generalization of time-changed Brownian motion that was covered in Chapter 4. In addition, we present an option pricing formula based on various time-changed Brownian motions and generalized models of them.

The *subordinated stock price model* is given by

$$S_t = S_0 e^{\mu t - \frac{\sigma}{2} \tau_t + \sigma W_{\tau_t}},$$

where $W = (W_t)_{t \geq 0}$ is the standard Brownian motion and $\tau = (\tau_t)_{t \geq 0}$ is the subordinator or intrinsic time process (see section 4.5). For the convenience, let $X = (X_t)_{t \geq 0}$ be a process with $X_t = \sigma W_{\tau_t}$. For this model, the value of a European call option at time t with strike price K and time to maturity T is given by

$$C_t = S_t e^{-d(T-t)} F_- \left(\log \left(\frac{S_0 e^{(r-d)(T-t)}}{K} \right) \right) - K e^{-r(T-t)} F_+ \left(\log \left(\frac{S_0 e^{(r-d)(T-t)}}{K} \right) \right),$$

where

$$F_{\pm}(x) = \int_0^{\infty} N \left(\frac{x \mp \frac{1}{2} y}{\sqrt{y}} \right) dF_{\sigma \tau_t}(y),$$

and $F_{\sigma \tau_t}$ is the cumulative distribution function of the random variable $\sigma \tau_t$, N denotes the standard normal cumulative distribution function, r is the risk-free rate of return, and d is the dividend rate.

The subordinated stock price model is defined by the process $\tau = (\tau_t)_{t \geq 0}$ as follows.[6]

- If $\tau_t = t$, then we obtain the Black-Scholes model.
- If τ is an α-stable process with

$$\tau_t \sim S_\alpha(c t^{\frac{2}{\alpha}}, 1, 0), \quad 0 < \alpha < 2, \quad c > 0,$$

---

[6]See Hurst et al. (1999) and Rachev and Mittnik (2000).

then X becomes a symmetric α-stable process with $X_t \sim S_\alpha(\tilde{c}t^{\frac{1}{\alpha}}, 0, 0)$ where

$$\tilde{c} = \frac{\sigma\sqrt{c/2}}{\cos\left(\frac{\pi\alpha}{4}\right)^{1/\alpha}},$$

and we obtain the log-stable model.[7]

- If τ is the inverse Gaussian process, we obtain the Barndorff-Nielsen model or the normal inverse Gaussian (NIG) model.[8]
- If τ is the *Cox-Ingersoll-Ross* (CIR) *process*,[9] then we obtain the Heston model.[10]

When we consider discrete-time steps $t = 0, 1, 2, \ldots$, then we obtain the discrete version of the subordinated stock price model. In this case, a stock price process is given by

$$S_{t+1} = S_t \exp\left(\mu t - \frac{\sigma}{2}(\tau_{t+1} - \tau_t) + \sigma\, W_{\tau_{t+1}-\tau_t}\right).$$

- If the unit increments of τ have the exponential distribution, that is, $(\tau_{t+1} - \tau_t) \sim Exp(\lambda)$ for some $\lambda > 0$, then the log-Laplace model is obtained.[11]
- The Clark model[12] is driven when the unit increments of τ have the log-normal distribution, that is,

$$\log(\tau_{t+1} - \tau_t) \sim N(\mu, \varphi^2), \quad \mu \in \mathbb{R}, \varphi > 0.$$

---

[7]See Mandelbrot (1963, 1967) and Fama (1963).
[8]See Barndorff-Nielsen (1995) and Eberlein and Keller (1995).
[9]The CIR process is defined by the stochastic differential equation

$$d\tau_t = a(b - \tau_t)dt + c\sqrt{\tau_t}dW_t, \quad Z_0 = z$$

This equation does not have a closed-form solution. Instead, it has the analytic form of the characteristic function as

$$\phi_{\tau_t}(u) = \frac{e^{a^2 bt/c^2 + 2ziu/(a+\gamma\cosh(\gamma t/2))}}{(\cosh(\gamma t/2) + a\sinh(\gamma t/2)/\gamma)^{2ab/c^2}}$$

where $\gamma = \sqrt{a^2 - 2c^2iu}$.
[10]See Heston (1993).
[11]See Mittnik and Rachev (1993a, 1993b).
[12]See Clark (1973).

- In the log-Student-t model,[13] the unit increments of τ have an inverse χ^2-distribution, that is,

$$\frac{\nu}{\tau_{t+1} - \tau_t} \sim \chi^2(\nu), \quad \nu > 0,$$

where $\chi^2(\nu)$ denote a χ^2-distribution with ν degrees of freedom.[14]

7.6.1 Stochastic Volatility Lévy Process Model

In this section, we discuss the *stochastic volatility Lévy process model* by Carr et al. (2003). This model also use the subordination method, but the intrinsic time process is subordinated in the Lévy process instead of the standard Brownian motion. That is, we first take the Lévy process $(Z_t)_{t \geq 0}$ and then change the physical time t to the subordinator process $\tau = (\tau_t)_{t \geq 0}$. Hence, the price process $(S_t)_{t \geq 0}$ for an underlying stock of the stochastic volatility Lévy process model is given by $S_t = S_0^{X_t}$ with $X_t = Z_{\tau_t}$ in market measure. The risk-neutral process of the stochastic volatility Lévy process model is given by

$$S_t = S_0 \frac{e^{(r-d)t + X_t}}{E[e^{X_t}]}$$

in the EMM, which is found by the Esscher transform, where r is the risk-free rate of return and d is the dividend rate. For this model, European option prices can be computed by (7.10).

The CIR process is a good choice for the subordinator process τ. Stochastic volatility Lévy process models such that Z is given by the normal inverse Gaussian, variance gamma, and CTS process and the subordinator T is given by the CIR process are presented in Carr et al. (2003). Other stochastic volatility Lévy process models can be found in Schoutens (2003).

---

[13]See Praetz (1972) and Blattberg and Gonedes (1974).
[14]Consider ν independent standard normal random variable $X_1, \ldots, X_\nu$ and define a random variable Y such as $Y = X_1 + \cdots + X_\nu$. Then the distribution of Y is referred to as χ^2-*distribution with ν degrees of freedom*. The probability density function of Y has the following form:

$$f(x) = \frac{e^{-\frac{x}{2}} x^{\frac{\nu}{2} - 1}}{2^{\frac{\nu}{2}} \Gamma\left(\frac{\nu}{2}\right)}, \quad x > 0.$$

7.7 SUMMARY

In this chapter, we discussed the option pricing formula for tempered stable models and subordinated stock price models including stochastic volatility Lévy process model. The formula can be calculated efficiently by using the fast Fourier transform method.

The empirical illustrations were also given for the S&P 500 call option prices. Two methods to calibrate risk-neutral parameters for using market prices of option were presented. The first involves calibrating risk-neutral parameters without any information about market measures. The other method considers market parameters and then estimates risk-neutral parameters satisfying conditions of the EMM.

REFERENCES

Barndorff-Nielsen, O. E. (1995). Normal inverse Gaussian distributions and the modeling of stock returns. Research Report no. 300, Department of Theoretical Statistics, Aarhus University.

Black, F. & Scholes, M. (1973). The pricing of options and corporate liabilities. *The Journal of Political Economy*, 81(3), 637–654.

Blattberg, R. C. & Gonedes, N. J. (1974). A comparison of the stable and Student distribution as statistical models for stock prices. *Journal of Business*, 47, 244–280.

Carr, P., Geman, H., Madan, D., & Yor, M. (2003). Stochastic volatility for Lévy processes. *Mathematical Finance*, 13, 345–382.

Carr, P. & Madan, D. (1999). Option valuation using the fast Fourier transform. *Journal of Computational Finance*, 2(4).

Clark, P. (1973). A subordinated stochastic process model with finite variance for speculative prices. *Econometrica*, 41(1), 135–155.

Eberlein, E. & Keller, U. (1995). Hyperbolic distributions in finance. *Bernoulli, 1*, 281–299.

Fama, E. (1963). Mandelbrot and the stable Paretian hypothesis. *Journal of Business*, 36(4), 420–429.

Harrison, J. M. & Pliska, S. R. (1981). Martingales and stochastic integrals in the theory of continuous trading. *Stochastic Processes and Their Applications*, 11(3), 215–260.

Heston, S. L. (1993). A closed form solution for options with stochastic volatility with applications to bond and currency options. *Review of Financial Studies*, 6, 327–343.

Hurst, S., Platen, E., & Rachev, S. (1999). Option pricing for a logstable asset price model. *Mathematical and Computer Modelling*, 29(10), 105–119.

Lewis, A. L. (2001). A simple option formula for general jump-diffusion and other exponential Lévy processes. Working paper, Envision Financial Systems. Available from www.optioncity.net.

Mandelbrot, B. (1963). The variation of certain speculative prices. *Journal of Business*, *36*, 394–419.

Mandelbrot, B. (1967). The variation of some other speculative prices. *Journal of Business*, *40*(4), 393–413.

Mittnik, S. & Rachev, S. T. (1993a). Modeling asset returns with alternative stable distributions. *Econometric Reviews*, *12*, 347–389.

Mittnik, S. & Rachev, S. T. (1993b). Reply to comments on 'modeling asset returns with alternative stable models' and some extensions. *Econometric Reviews*, *12*, 347–389.

Praetz, P. (1972). The distribution of share price changes. *Journal of Business*, *45*, 49–55.

Rachev, S. T. & Mittnik, S. (2000). *Stable Paretian models in finance*. New York: John Wiley & Sons.

Schoutens, W. (2003). *Lévy processes in finance*. Hoboken, NJ: John Wiley & Sons.

CHAPTER 8

Simulation

One of the classical problems in mathematical finance is option pricing. Even if we consider the price process of stocks modeled by a geometric Brownian motion, there are no closed formulas to find the fair value of complex path-dependent options. The so-called *trader approach* to price a complex exotic option involves first finding risk-neutral parameters by matching model prices to market prices of European call options using nonlinear least squares, and then simulating the dynamic of the risk-neutral process to find the price via Monte Carlo methods.

As explained earlier in this book, there is ample evidence that many financial return series are heavy-tailed and have variances that change through time. The exponential Lévy model does not completely describe the statistical properties of financial time series. Continuous-time stochastic volatility and discrete-time generalized autoregressive conditional heteroskedastic (GARCH) models have been widely investigated to overcome these drawbacks. Recent empirical studies have shown that GARCH models can be successfully used to describe option prices. However, because they are discrete-time models, generally it is not possible to have closed formulas to calculate option prices. Also in the continuous-time case, option pricing by means of simulation could be an alternative. In the discrete-time case, Monte Carlo integration seems to be the better choice in order to obtain good statistical properties of time series and a more accurate approach to pricing options.

Unfortunately, analytical solutions for pricing options utilizing GARCH processes, as well as pricing derivatives with complex structures in continuous-time models, are not generally available and hence numerical procedures have to be considered. The use of GARCH models combined with Monte Carlo simulation methods allows one to obtain suitable results. Closed formulas are faster than numerical procedures and hence an ideal outcome for finance professionals who need to calculate values quickly such as traders. Unfortunately, a closed-formula solution is not always easy to derive. For this reason, in this chapter we show how to simulate infinitely divisible distributions and Lévy processes in one dimension, focusing on tempered stable (TS) and tempered infinitely divisible (TID) distributions and processes, how to price an option by combining GARCH models with TS and TID innovations, and how to compute derivative prices in continuous-time models by simulation.

8.1 RANDOM NUMBER GENERATORS

The generation of random numbers is the first step to many standard statistical applications and the fundamental tool for using the Monte Carlo integration method. The practical implementation is not so simple because it involves transforming a random event into a number. Ever since the introduction of computer simulation, there were some attempts to use physical devices to generate randomness. In some situations, *real random* numbers are preferable with respect to deterministic methods commonly used today in finance applications. Deterministic methods, usually used and implemented via commercial software as well as in open-source software, only mimic randomness. Some researchers use the term *pseudorandom* to highlight the fact that a computer cannot generate random numbers.[1] Fortunately, there are algorithms to generate good random numbers and statistical tests to assess the quality of the output. In this section, we explain several methods for generating uniform and nonuniform random variables. We draw paths of Poisson processes, Brownian motions, and more complex Lévy processes such as α-stable motions, TS, and TID motions.

8.1.1 Uniform Distributions

Consider the simplest distribution: the uniform distribution in the open interval $(0, 1)$. We want a mechanism for producing a sequence $U_1, \ldots, U_n$ such that for each $j = 1, \ldots, n$:

- U_j are uniform random variable on $(0, 1)$.
- U_j are independent.

The generation of a sequence of independent and identically distributed (i.i.d.) uniform distributions is a complex problem. Algorithms dealing with

---

[1]See Gentle (2003).

this problem are now largely considered a specialized topic, beyond the scope of this book.[2]

A visual inspection can help one to assess how good (or bad) a generator is. Let $U_1, \ldots, U_n$ be a sequence of uniform variables, then consider two different vectors

$$X = (U_1, \ldots, U_{n-1})$$

and

$$Y = (U_2, \ldots, U_n)$$

and draw points (x_i, y_i) for each $i = 1, \ldots, n-1$ and see the visual assessment. If the points seem to be distributed along particular lines or to have some particular structure that appears in a different part of the picture, then there is some clustering in the generator and hence the generator is not a good one. In Figure 8.1, the MATLAB function *rand* is used to simulate uniform random numbers. An examination of the figure suggests that no

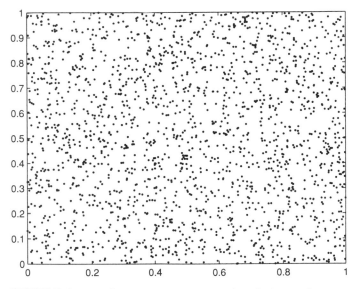

FIGURE 8.1 Uniform Variates Generated with the *rand* Function of MATLAB

---

[2] Modular arithmetics is commonly applied to mimic uniform random variables. See Gentle (2003) and Glasserman (2004) for further details.

patterns appear. Therefore, the correlation between X and Y is small and this means that they appear to be distributionally independent. We will always work with good sequences of uniform variables. Unless indicated otherwise, we will denote by $U_1, \ldots, U_n$ a sequence of a uniform random variable.

8.1.2   Discrete Distributions

Now we propose an efficient method to simulate a discrete distribution. Let X be a point random variable on $x_1, \ldots, x_n$ with weight p_k for $k = 1, \ldots, n$ and define $s_k = p_1 + \cdots p_k$. To generate random numbers from X, we follow the algorithm below.

Discrete distributions

1. Generate a uniform random variable U.
2. Find the index k, such that $s_{k-1} \leq U \leq s_k$.
3. Set $X = x_k$ and return to step 1.

If the set of points $x_1, \ldots, x_n$ is large, typically the procedure for searching for the index k becomes slow. Consequently, it is preferable to use more efficient methods. One such method is the *alias method*.[3]

8.1.3   Continuous Nonuniform Distributions

Assume that we have a sequence of uniform random variables. Now we are in the position to use it to generate a given distribution F. We will begin by analyzing two general methods that can be used for each continuous distribution.

Inverse Transform Algorithm   By considering the inversion of the cumulative distribution function (c.d.f.) F, we can construct an algorithm to generate a sequence of random variables with distribution F. The general inverse of a function F is defined as follows: For each $0 < u < 1$

$$F^{\leftarrow}(u) := \inf\{x : F(x) \geq u\} = \min\{x : F(x) \geq u\}. \tag{8.1}$$

---

[3]For more details, readers are referred to Gentle (2003).

In the particular case in which F is strictly increasing and continuous, then the function $F^{\leftarrow}(u)$ coincides with $F^{-1}(u)$; that is,

$$x = F^{\leftarrow}(u) = F^{-1}(u).$$

The procedure is based on a simple result from probability theory.

Proposition 1. *Let F be a probability distribution, $F^{\leftarrow}$ the function defined in equation (8.1), and U a uniform random variable on $(0, 1)$. Then the random variable*

$$X = F^{\leftarrow}(U)$$

has c.d.f. F.

Proof. By definition of a uniform random variable we can write the following equalities:

$$P(X \leq x) = P(F^{\leftarrow}(U) \leq x) = P(U \leq F(x)) = F(x),$$

thus X has c.d.f. F.

Now we can construct our first algorithm to obtain a sequence of i.i.d. random numbers with distribution F.

Inverse transform algorithm

1. Generate a sequence $U_1, \ldots, U_n$ of i.i.d. uniform variables.
2. Find a root of the equation $F(X_i) - U_i = 0$ for each $i = 1, \ldots, n$.
3. Return the sequence $X_1, \ldots, X_n$.

The computational tractability of this method comes at a potential cost in terms of computational time. Despite this, it can be efficiently employed in some cases if a closed form for the inverse function exists. If the inverse function cannot be found by an analytical method, we need to find in each trial of the above algorithm a root $\hat{x}$ of the equation

$$F(\hat{x}) - U_i = 0$$

with the help of numerical procedure, such as bisection method or the more efficient Newton-Raphson method.[4]

In choosing an algorithm to solve a problem, one must of course consider its speed. Suppose F is a TS distribution, for example a CTS distribution, introduced in Chapter 3. It easy to see that the function F is not available in closed form. To find values of F, first we have to invert the characteristic function[5] and then find the root of the equation above, and the computational time increases remarkably. We now propose a simple example.

Example 1. *Let X be an exponential random variable with parameter λ, that is a random variable with density*

$$f(x) = \lambda e^{-\lambda x}.$$

Then the function can be easily calculated

$$F^{\leftarrow}(u) = -\frac{\log(1-u)}{\lambda},$$

and we find that

$$X_i = -\frac{\log(1-U_i)}{\lambda}.$$

Acceptance/Rejection Method   The problem of generating random numbers from a given distribution X can be solved by using another random variable Y possessing a probability density g similar to the probability density of X, f. One can generate a value for Y and accept (reject) this value, if a given condition is satisfied (not satisfied).[6] We want to find a constant C such that $f(x) \leq Cg(x)$ and we define the acceptance event A as

$$A = \{U \leq f(Y)/Cg(Y)\}.$$

By conditioning with respect to the random variable Y, we can calculate the probability of the acceptance event

$$P(U \leq f(Y)/Cg(Y)) = \frac{1}{C},$$

---

[4]See Bartholomew-Biggs (2005).
[5]Here the term inversion means Fourier inversion.
[6]The acceptance/rejection method is usually attributed to Von Neumann (1951).

and in order to maximize the probability of the acceptance event, we look for the optimal C, that is, $C = \sup_x [f(x)/g(x)]$. This is done by using the following algorithm:

Acceptance/rejection method

1. Generate Y from the distribution with density g.
2. Generate a uniform variable U.
3. If

$$U \le \frac{f(Y)}{Cg(Y)},$$

return Y, otherwise return to step 1.

To obtain good results, the constant C has to be as close as possible to 1. A numerical method can be used to find an approximation of the optimal C. With the aid of nonuniform random numbers that are easier to generate, we can obtain complex ones. We illustrate this method, using a classical example by Fishmann (1996).[7]

Example 2. *Consider a half normal random variable X with density*

$$f(x) = \sqrt{\frac{2}{\pi}} e^{-x^2/2}$$

and the natural choice for g is the density of the exponential random variable Y with parameter 1

$$g(x) = e^{-x},$$

which can be easily calculated by inverting the c.d.f. Therefore, we obtain

$$\frac{f(x)}{g(x)} = \sqrt{\frac{2}{\pi}} e^{x - x^2/2},$$

which has maximum $C = \sqrt{2e/\pi}$. Then the acceptance probability is $1/C \approx 0.76$.

---

[7]See also Asmussen and Glynn (2007).

Using the Characteristic Function   In many financial applications, the density f of the random variable X is not given by a closed formula. Instead, we only have the characteristic function ϕ. A general method to obtain an approximation of random numbers from such distributions is to use the Fourier inversion in the following way.

Characteristic function method

1. Evaluate the function f on a increasing sorted vector $x_1, \ldots, x_n$ with the inverse Fourier transform

$$f(x) = \frac{1}{2\pi} \int_{-\infty}^{\infty} \phi(s) e^{-isx} ds.$$

2. Consider the discrete distribution $\tilde{F}$ with point mass in x_i defined as

$$p_i := \frac{f(x_i)}{f(x_1) + \ldots + f(x_n)}.$$

3. Generate random numbers from the discrete distribution $\tilde{F}$ and use them as an approximation of F.

By using the discrete Fourier transform, we can increase the speed of the procedure.[8]

Let's look at a more sophisticated method where we assume that F has the second moment. In models for option pricing, we will consider distributions with exponential moments; therefore, assuming the existence of the second moment is not restrictive for the purpose of option pricing.

We consider an example that combines the acceptance/rejection method and Fourier inversion.[9] Given the assumption of the existence of the second moment, the second derivative of the characteristic function ϕ exists and the density function $f(x)$ is of order at most $O(x^{-2})$. In particular, the following inequalities hold for all $x \in \mathbb{R}$

$$f(x) \leq \frac{1}{2\pi} \int_{-\infty}^{\infty} |\phi(s)| ds,$$

$$f(x) \leq \frac{1}{2\pi x^2} \int_{-\infty}^{\infty} |\phi''(s)| ds$$

---

[8]See Asmussen and Glynn (2007), Example 2.21.
[9]The example is adapted from Devroye (1986a).

Thus we can set

$$c := \frac{1}{2\pi} \int_{-\infty}^{\infty} |\phi(s)| ds,$$

$$k := \frac{1}{2\pi} \int_{-\infty}^{\infty} |\phi''(s)| ds,$$

Characteristic function method modified

1. Generate uniform variable U and V on $(-1, 1)$.
2. If $U < 0$, then set

$$Y = \frac{\sqrt{k}V}{\sqrt{c}} \qquad t = c|U|;$$

if otherwise, set

$$Y = \frac{\sqrt{k}}{V\sqrt{c}} \qquad t = cV^2|U|.$$

3. Evaluate the function f in Y.
4. If $f(Y) \geq t$ return Y; otherwise return to step 1.

Each step requires evaluation of the density f. If the characteristic function is real, convex on $(0, \infty)$, and absolutely integrable,[10] an approximate method for the density f can be constructed.[11] This more efficient algorithm can be applied in the symmetric α-stable case, for example.

8.1.4 Simulation of Particular Distributions

In this section, we explain the simulation of the normal distribution, the gamma distribution, and the stable distribution.

Normal Distribution One of the most popular distributions used in finance is the normal distribution, despite the empirical evidence that asset returns

---

[10]A characteristic function satisfying these properties is symmetric, non-negative, and nonincreasing on $(0, \infty)$.
[11]See Devroye (1986a).

do not follow a geometric Brownian motion. Since most of the models in quantitative finance are based on the normal distribution, we show in this section how one can simulate it. If we consider the sum of finite variance random variables, by the Central Limit Theorem (CLT) we have that the series converges to a normal random variable. It is a fact that this convergence is too slow to be considered in practical applications. If one seeks a random walk approximation of a Brownian motion, it is necessary to know how to simulate normally distributed increments. The method we present here is a faster variant of the Box-Muller algorithm that is well known in the literature. It does not involve evaluation of a trigonometric function.

Fast Box-Muller algorithm

1. Generate uniform variables U and V on $(-1, 1)$.
2. Set $R^2 = U^2 + V^2$.
3. If $R^2 \geq 1$ return to step 1.
4. If $R^2 < 1$ set

$$X_1 = U\sqrt{\frac{-2\log R^2}{R^2}}$$

$$X_2 = V\sqrt{\frac{-2\log R^2}{R^2}}$$

With this algorithm, we generate a pair of normal variates.[12] For generating a random variable for a given decreasing density, one of the faster methods is the *ziggurat method* introduced by Marsaglia and Tsang (2000), and widely used in scientific C++ libraries and MATLAB. As far as we can discern, the fastest algorithm for generating normal random numbers seems to be the ziggurat method. The method involves forming a decomposition of a density into horizontal slices that have equal areas. Marsaglia and Tsang developed the *Monty Python method* in which the density (or a part of the density) is divided into three regions. An extended explanation of these methods is beyond the scope of this chapter.[13] We will be using these algorithms for option pricing based on normal random variables.

---

[12]The proof is based on a polar representation. See Letta (1993) and Asmussen and Glynn (2007).

[13]The details are provided in Marsaglia and Tsang (1998, 2000).

Gamma Distribution   The gamma is one of the most important distribution in probability and statistics. Since simple functions of such gamma variates can easily provide many of the important variates for simulations—such as the χ^2, Student-t, F, beta, and Dirichlet distribution—a fast and simple method for generating gamma variates is useful for Monte Carlo simulation. For our purpose, it is sufficient to be able to simulate gamma random variables $\gamma(a, 1)$ with a density of the form

$$f(x) = \frac{x^{a-1}}{\Gamma(a)} e^{-x}.$$

A well-known generator is the following.

Jöhnk's method

1. Generate uniform variables U and V on $(0, 1)$.
2. Set $X = U^{1/a}$ and $Y = V^{1/(1-a)}$.
3. If $X + Y \leq 1$, generate an exponential variate E.
4. Return $\frac{XE}{X+Y}$.

This algorithm, known as the Jöhnk's generator,[14] works only for $a \leq 1$. Two other gamma generators are the Best[15] and Berman[16] generators. If a very fast normal generator is available, we should get a gamma variate without much more difficulty than that for the normal variate itself. Furthermore, Marsaglia[17] developed the following algorithm:

Marsaglia method

1. Set $d = a - 1/3$ and $c = 1/\sqrt{9d}$.
2. Generate a normal random variable X.
3. Set $V = (1 + cX)^3$ and return to step 2 if $V \leq 1$.
4. Generate a uniform U on $(0, 1)$.
5. If $U < 1 - 0.0331 X^4$, return dV.
6. If $\log U < 0.5 X^2 + d(1 - V + \log V)$, return dV.
7. Go to step 2.

---

[14]See Jöhnk (1964).
[15]See Devroye (1986b), Cont and Tankov (2004).
[16]See Berman (1971).
[17]For a proof of this method, see Marsaglia and Tsang (2000).

This algorithm works if $a \geq 1$. If $a < 1$, one can use $\gamma(a, 1) = \gamma(1 + a, 1)U^{1/a}$ with U uniform $(0,1)$ and still have a fast algorithm.

Stable Distribution   Random number generation from an α-stable distribution is an important tool to obtain the TS and the TID distributions. A density transformation allow one to simulate the TS or the TID distributions starting from the simulation of the stable distribution. The problems associated with the simulation for stable distributions and processes has been widely studied in the literature.[18] Let us consider the following result by Samorodnitsky and Taqqu (1994).

Proposition 2. *Let U be uniform on* $(-\pi/2, \pi/2)$ *and let E be an exponential with mean 1. Assume U and E are independent. Then*

$$X = \frac{\sin \alpha U}{(\cos U)^{1/\alpha}} \left(\frac{\cos((1 - \alpha)U)}{E} \right)^{\frac{1-\alpha}{\alpha}} \tag{8.2}$$

is $S_\alpha(1, 0, 0)$.

The above method allows one to simulate symmetric α-stable random variables. In order to find an algorithm to generate α-stable with skewness random numbers, we are going to explain the algorithm of Weron (1996).

Theorem 4. *Let* γ_0 *be defined as in equation* (A.2) *in the Appendix to this chapter. Let U be uniformly distributed on* $(-\frac{\pi}{2}, \frac{\pi}{2})$ *and E be an independent exponential random variable with mean 1. Then*

for $\alpha \neq 1$,

$$X = \frac{\sin(\alpha(U - \gamma_0))}{(\cos U)^{1/\alpha}} \left(\frac{\cos(\alpha\gamma_0 + (1 - \alpha)U)}{E} \right)^{\frac{1-\alpha}{\alpha}}$$

is $S_\alpha(1, \beta_2, 0)$ *and*
for $\alpha = 1$,

$$X = \left(\frac{\pi}{2} + \beta_2 U \right) \tan U - \beta_2 \log \left(\frac{E \cos U}{\frac{\pi}{2} + \beta_2 U} \right)$$

is $S_1(1, \beta_2, 0)$ *for the representation* (A.1).

---

[18]See Nolan (2007) and references therein.

Finally, to generate a skewed α-stable random number from $S_\alpha(1, \beta, 0)$ we will use the following procedure:

Weron's algorithm

1. Generate U uniform on $(-\pi/2, \pi/2)$ and E exponential with mean 1.
2. Compute

$$B_{\alpha,\beta} = \arctan\left(\beta \tan \frac{\pi\alpha}{2}\right)\alpha$$

and

$$S_{\alpha,\beta} = \left(1 + \beta^2 \tan^2 \frac{\pi\alpha}{2}\right)^{1/(2\alpha)}.$$

3. If $\alpha \neq 1$, compute

$$X = S_{\alpha,\beta} \frac{\sin(\alpha(U + B_{\alpha,\beta}))}{(\cos(U))^{1/\alpha}} \left(\frac{\cos(U - \alpha(U + B_{\alpha,\beta}))}{E}\right)^{(1-\alpha)/\alpha}.$$

4. If $\alpha = 1$, compute

$$X = \frac{2}{\pi}\left(\frac{\pi}{2} + \beta U\right)\tan U - \beta \log\left(\frac{E \cos U}{\frac{\pi}{2} + \beta U}\right)$$

Weron's algorithm is enough to simulate a general α-stable distribution. In fact, if $X \sim S_\alpha(1, \beta, 0)$ then

$$Y = \begin{cases} \sigma X + \mu, & \alpha \neq 1 \\ \sigma X + \frac{2}{\pi}\beta\sigma \log \sigma + \mu, & \alpha = 1, \end{cases}$$

is $S_\alpha(\sigma, \beta, \mu)$.

Figure 8.2 shows stable processes with different values of $\alpha = 0.5$, 1, 1.5, 2 based on the Weron's algorithm. Random sequences U and E have been kept fixed.

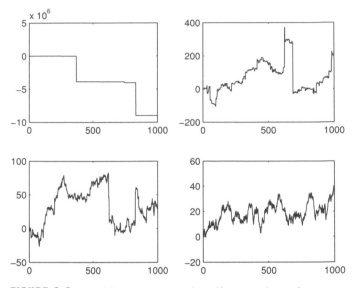

FIGURE 8.2   Stable Processes with Different Values of
$\alpha = 0.5, 1, 1.5, 2$
Note: Random sequences U and E have been kept fixed.

8.2   SIMULATION TECHNIQUES FOR LÉVY PROCESSES

Computer methods for the construction of stochastic processes involve at least two kinds of discretization techniques. First, we have to consider the discretization of the time parameter and then an approximate representation of random variates with the aid of artificially produced finite time-series data sets.[19] A Lévy process has stationary and independent increments; therefore, the easiest approach to solve this problem is equivalent to the problem of generating random numbers from an infinitely divisible distribution.

Let us consider a Lévy process $(X_t)_{t\geq 0}$. If the density f_t has a simple form, then the random numbers generator can be implemented in a rather easy way since one may consider algorithms described in section 8.1.3. If the evaluation of the function f_t involves special functions, then the algorithm implementing the simulation becomes slow yet easy to implement. In the literature, there are so many cases in which the density function f_t is not known in analytic form and thereby requires that one work with the

[19]See Janicki and Weron (1994).

characteristic function. In some cases that we are interested in, although an analytic form for the characteristic function exists, the Lévy measure v contains complicated special functions or does not have a closed-form solution. By the inverse transform algorithm, we can obtain random variates. This method involves three numerical procedures. First, the characteristic function must be inverted[20] in order to obtain the density function. Second, the density function must be integrated, and finally the solution of a nonlinear equation must be found. However, this method does not to be seem a fast way to proceed. Moreover, with this method, extreme events are not simulated. This is due to computer algebra. The support of the distribution function is bounded to the interval $[-M, M]$ since a computer cannot deal with the interval $(-\infty, \infty)$. In general, alternative methods that involve the inversion of the Lévy measure do not seem to be easily implementable. Consequently, we need to show the general framework for simulating Lévy processes. Because we know that the exact simulation of such processes is impossible, a process that is close to the original one is generated instead. We now show some general results from Rosiński (2001). Two methods are considered in the next sections: random walk approximation and shot noise representation.

8.2.1 Taking Care of Small Jumps

Series representation of Lévy processes involves at least one discretization error, due to the impossibility of dealing with infinite summations. Furthermore, we also have to take into account the approximation of small jumps. In the infinite activity case, this truncation of small jumps involves an approximation error. This is because for a noncompound Lévy process with a nonzero Lévy measure, the set of jumps is dense in $[0, \infty)$. Without loss of generality, we can consider a Lévy process without a Gaussian part.[21] Suppose we want to simulate a Lévy process $(X_t)_{t \geq 0}$ with Lévy measure v. Let $(X_t^\varepsilon)_{t \geq 0}$ be a compound Poisson process with a drift and distribution of jumps proportional to $v^\varepsilon = v_{|\{|x|>\varepsilon\}}$, and $(R_t^\varepsilon)_{t \geq 0}$ a process with no Gaussian part, zero mean, and Lévy measure $v_\varepsilon = v_{|\{|x|\leq\varepsilon\}}$. Then we have

$$X_t = X_t^\varepsilon + R_t^\varepsilon.$$

---

[20]This is accomplished using a Fourier inversion.
[21]This discussion is based on Asmussen and Rosiński (2001), Asmussen and Glynn (2007), and Rosiński (2007a).

Now we will consider an approximation of X_t. First, in the compensated case, the Lévy measure satisfies the condition

$$\int_{|x|<1} |x|\nu(dx) = \infty$$

and one can consider an approximation of the process X_t, given by a compound Poisson process with a drift. This approximation is obtained by removing small jumps

$$X_t \approx \sum_{s<t} \Delta X_s I_{|\Delta X_s|\geq 1} + \left(\sum_{s\leq t} \Delta X_s I_{\varepsilon<|\Delta X_s|<1} - t\mu_\varepsilon \right)$$

where we set

$$\mu_\varepsilon := \int_{\varepsilon\leq|x|\leq 1} x\nu(dx).$$

If one approximates X_t with only a compound Poisson process with a drift, without considering small jumps, a poor approximation is obtained. In the finite variation case, the Lévy measure satisfies the condition

$$\int_{|x|<1} |x|\nu(dx) < \infty \tag{8.3}$$

and one can use the zero truncation function[22] in the Lévy-Khinchin representation. It is possible to discard small jumps, replacing them with their mean value. Thus, also in this case, the resulting process is a compound Poisson process with a drift. In both methods a Lévy process is approximated by a Poisson process, and large jumps are precisely simulated. If condition 8.3 is fulfilled, we can write

$$X_t \approx + \sum_{s\leq t} \Delta X_s I_{|\Delta X_s|\geq\varepsilon} + ta_\varepsilon$$

where we define

$$a_\varepsilon := \int_{|x|\leq\varepsilon} x\nu(dx)$$

---

[22]The truncation function is defined in Chapter 3.

that is, rather then just removing small jumps, we replace them with their expected value.

When the intensity of small jumps is high, discarding them may produce a substantial error. In such case, one can approximate the small jump part by a Brownian motion with small variance. This means that we can write

$$X_t \approx X_t^\varepsilon + A_t \qquad (8.4)$$

where the process A_t is defined as

$$A_t = a_\varepsilon t + \sigma_\varepsilon W_t$$

where we define

$$\sigma_\varepsilon^2 := \int_{|x|<\varepsilon} x^2 \nu(dx)^{23}$$

and

$$a_\varepsilon = \begin{cases} 0, & \int_{|x|<1} |x|\nu(dx) = \infty, \\ \int_{|x|\le\varepsilon} x\nu(dx), & \int_{|x|<1} |x|\nu(dx) < \infty, \end{cases}$$

where W_t is a standard Brownian motion. Also if a series representation is available, under some additional conditions, we can apply the method above. More precisely, we will show under which conditions the Brownian approximation of small jumps can be used. Let R_t^ε be the Lévy process previously defined, whose characteristic function is

$$E[e^{iuR_t^\varepsilon}] = \exp\left\{ t \int_{|x|<\varepsilon} (e^{iux} - 1 - iux)\nu(dx) \right\}.$$

Then we have[24]

$$R^\varepsilon/\sigma_\varepsilon \xrightarrow{d} W \quad \text{as} \quad \varepsilon \to 0$$

---

[23]Here we are considering σ as a function of epsilon; indeed, the notation σ_ε means $\sigma(\varepsilon)$.

[24]See Theorem 2.1. of Asmussen and Rosiński (2001). Furthermore, error-bound conditions can be found in Cont and Tankov (2004) and Asmussen and Rosiński (2003).

if and only if for each $k > 0$

$$\sigma_{k\sigma_\varepsilon \wedge \varepsilon} \sim \sigma_\varepsilon. \tag{8.5}$$

If we assume that ν has a density of the form $L(x)/|x|^{\alpha+1}$ for all small x, where $L(x)$ is slowly varying as $x \to 0$ and $0 < \alpha < 2$, then equation (8.5) is equivalent to

$$\frac{R_t^\varepsilon - a^\varepsilon t}{\sigma_\varepsilon} \xrightarrow{d} W_t.$$

Sometimes it seems to be easy to check[25] if the limit

$$\lim_{\varepsilon \to 0} \frac{\sigma_\varepsilon}{\varepsilon} = +\infty. \tag{8.6}$$

is fulfilled. If it is satisfied, one can approximate such small jumps with a Brownian motion. Thus, we obtain a useful result for TS processes.

Proposition 3. *In the TS case we can always consider the Brownian approximation of small jumps.*

Figure 8.3 shows a simulation of a CTS process with and without the approximation of small jumps.

8.2.2 Series Representation: A General Framework

The series representation plays an important role also in the construction of a stochastic integral of a deterministic function with respect to a random measure, that is, the integral

$$I(f) = \int_E f(x)M(dx),$$

where $(E, \mathcal{E}, m)$ is a finite measure space and M is a random measure with finite control measure m.[26] First, we show a general result from Rosiński (2001).

---

[25]See Proposition 2.1 in Asmussen and Rosiński (2001).
[26]See the Appendix to this chapter, Samorodnitsky and Taqqu (1994), and Janicki and Weron (1994) for more details about random measures.

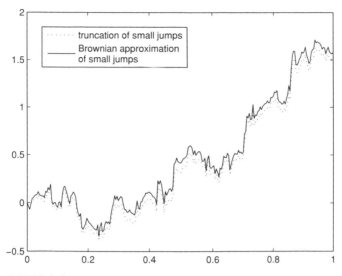

FIGURE 8.3 Simulation of a CTS Process with $C = 2$, $\lambda_- = 3$, $\lambda_+ = 10$, and $\alpha = 1.5$, with and without Brownian Approximation of Small Jumps, $\epsilon = 1e - 5$.

Let us consider the process of jumps N_* of a Lévy process X_t. This process of jumps has the form

$$N_* = \sum_{i=1}^{\infty} \delta_{(U_i, J_i)}, \tag{8.7}$$

where $\{J_i\}$ is an i.i.d. sequence of random variables in $\mathbb{R}$, independent of the i.i.d. sequence $\{U_i\}$ of uniformly distributed random variables on $(0, T)$. As explained earlier, a Lévy process can be approximated by a compound Poisson process. The basic idea is to consider a Lévy process with zero Lévy measure in a neighborhood $(-\varepsilon, \varepsilon)$, with $\varepsilon > 0$. If it is possible, jumps less than ε can be approximated by a Brownian motion, as described in equation (8.4), otherwise by their mean. Let X_t with $t \in [0, T]\}$ be a Lévy process. We can remove small jumps of magnitude less than ε_n and write

$$X_{\varepsilon_n}(t) = ta + \int_{\varepsilon_n \leq x \leq 1} x(N_*([0, T], dx)) - tv(dx)) + \int_{|x| > 1} (N_*([0, T], dx)),$$

then by equation (8.7) we obtain

$$X_{\varepsilon_n}(t) = \sum_{\{i \geq 1: |J_i(\omega)| \geq \varepsilon_n\}} J_i I_{\{U_i \leq t\}} - tb_n,$$

where

$$b_n = \int_{\varepsilon_n \leq x \leq 1} x\nu(dx) - a$$

and by the Lévy-Itô decomposition,[27] we have the following convergence result

$$\sum_{\{i \geq 1: |J_i(\omega)| \geq \varepsilon_n\}} J_i I_{\{U_i \leq t\}} - tb_n \rightarrow X(t) \quad a.s.$$

as ε_n goes to zero. Therefore, we get a series representation of the following form:

$$X(t) = \sum_{i=0}^{\infty} (J_i I_{\{U_i \leq t\}} - tc_i) \quad a.s.$$

where the term c_i depends on the choice on J_i. In order to simulate Lévy processes, we need to find a suitable representation on J_i and calculate the value of c_i. In computer simulation, we cannot deal with infinite summation, and therefore we have to truncate the series and calculate the summation only for a finite number of addends. Some small jumps are inevitably truncated. We consider J_i defined as

$$J_i = H(\Gamma_i, V_i)$$

for some i.i.d. sequence $\{V_i\}$, where $\{\Gamma_i\}$ are arrival times of a unit rate Poisson process on $[0, \infty)$, and H is a measurable function

$$H : (0, \infty) \times S \rightarrow \mathbb{R},$$

nonincreasing with respect to the first variable and where S is a measurable space. Furthermore, $\{U_i\}$ is an i.i.d. sequence of uniformly distributed random variable in $[0, T]$. Let $\{U_i\}$ be independent of $\{V_i\}$ and $\{\Gamma_i\}$. Thus, it is

---

[27]Theorem A.2 in the Appendix to this chapter.

possible to prove that the Lévy measure associated with the process X_t can be written as

$$v(A) = \int_0^\infty P(H(r, V_i) \in A)dr \qquad A \in \mathcal{B}(\mathbb{R}).$$

By Corollary 1 of the Appendix to this chapter, if we consider the Poisson point process

$$N = \sum_{i=1}^\infty \delta_{(U_i, \Gamma_i, V_i)},$$

then by taking a function h defined as

$$h(u, \gamma, v) = (u, H(\gamma, v))$$

we obtain

$$\tilde{N} = \sum_{i=1}^\infty \delta_{(U_i, H(\Gamma_i, V_i))}$$

where the sequences $\{U_i, \Gamma_i, V_i\}$ can be defined on the same probability space as $\tilde{N}$. The different choice of the function H gives us different algorithms to simulate infinitely divisible distributions and Lévy processes as well.[28] First define two measures on $\mathbb{R}$ by

$$\sigma(r; \cdot) = P(H(r, V_i) \in \cdot), \qquad r > 0$$

and

$$v(\cdot) = \int_0^\infty \sigma(r; \cdot)dr$$

and let

$$A(s) = \int_0^s \int_{|x| \leq 1} x\sigma(r; dx)dr \qquad s \geq 0$$

Furthermore, let us consider the increment of the process X_t defined as $X = X_1 - X_0$. Then, it can be proven that X is an infinitely divisible random variable. We now show a converge result by Rosiński (2001).

---

[28] See Rosiński (2001) for all details.

Theorem 5. (A) *The series* $X = \sum_{i=1}^{\infty} H(\Gamma_i, V_i)$ *converges a.s. if and only if:*

(i) v *is a Lévy measure on* $\mathbb{R}_0$.
(ii) $a := \lim_{s \to \infty} A(s)$ *exists in* $\mathbb{R}$.

If (i) *and* (ii) *are satisfied, then* X *is infinitely divisible with characteristic triplet* $(a, 0, v)$.
(B) *If only* (i) *holds, then* $X = \sum_{i=1}^{\infty} |H(\Gamma_i, V_i) - c_i|$ *converges a.s. for* $c_i = A(i) - A(i-1)$. *In this case, the characteristic triplet is* $(0, 0, v)$.

Furthermore, if we want to simulate a Lévy process, the following convergence result:[29]

$$X(t) = at + \sum_{i=1}^{\infty} (H(\Gamma_i, V_i) I_{\{U_i \le t\}} - tc_i) \qquad a.s.$$

for each $t \in [0, T]$. The speed of convergence is determined by the choice of the function H.

Now, we consider a well-known example. If the Lévy measure is written in spherical coordinates

$$v(A) = \int_{S^0} \int_0^{\infty} I_{\{rs \in B\}} \rho(dr, s) \sigma(ds),$$

where $\rho(\cdot, s)$ is a family of Lévy measures on $(0, \infty)$ and σ a measure on S^0, then a function

$$\rho^{\leftarrow}(u, v) := \inf\{x > 0 : \rho([x, \infty), v) < u\}$$

can be defined. By changing variable, the Lévy measure v can be written as

$$
\begin{aligned}
v(A) &= \int_0^{\infty} P(H(r, V) \in A) dr \\
&= \int_0^{\infty} \int_{S^0} I_{\{H(r, V) \in A\}} \sigma(ds) dr \\
&= \int_{S^0} \int_0^{\infty} I_{\{s\rho^{\leftarrow}(r, s) \in A\}} \sigma(ds) dr
\end{aligned}
$$

---

[29]The proof is given in Theorem 5.1 of Rosiński (2001).

If we set H as

$$H(\gamma, v) = \rho^{\leftarrow}(\gamma, v)v,$$

then we can apply the construction above and obtain the so called LePage's series representation.[30] In the α-stable case this series converges slowly.[31]

8.2.3 Rosiński Rejection Method

In this section, we describe the rejection method of Rosiński (2001). Suppose that one want to simulate a Lévy process $(X_t)_{t \geq 0}$, by considering a similar Lévy process $(X_t^0)_{t \geq 0}$. If we can find an easy way to generate $(X_t^0)_{t \geq 0}$ and if the ratio

$$\frac{dv}{dv^0} \leq 1,$$

then we can construct the following algorithm. Additionally, J_i^0 is an approximation of the ith jump of X_i^0, and we assume that it is easy to generate. Let $\{W_i\}$ be a i.i.d. sequence of uniform random variables on $(0,1)$ independent of $\{U_i, J_i^0\}$. The algorithm follows:

Rosiński rejection method

1. Generate a uniform variable W_i on $(0,1)$.
2. Generate a variable J_i^0 independent from W_i.
3. Define

$$J_i = \begin{cases} J_i^0, & \frac{dv}{dv^0}(J_i^0) \geq W_i, \\ 0, & \text{otherwise.} \end{cases}$$

4. Take J_i as an approximation of the ith jump of X_i.

The key to this method is to find an easy way to generate the Lévy process X^0 from which only a small finite number of jumps must be removed to get the jumps of X. In practical applications of this method, one only needs to consider nonzero jumps. The proof of this result is a direct consequence of

---

[30]See LePage (1981).
[31]This fact has been noted in Janicki and Weron (1994).

Corollary 1 in the Appendix to this chapter, based on the fact that given the Poisson point process

$$N = \sum_{i=1}^{\infty} \delta_{(U_i, W_i, J_i^0)},$$

and a function h so defined

$$h(u, w, j) = (u, j \, I_{\{\frac{v}{v_0}(j) \geq w\}}),$$

we obtain

$$\tilde{N} = \sum_{i=1}^{\infty} \delta_{(U_i, J_i)},$$

where the sequences $\{U_i, W_i, J_i^0\}$ can be defined on the same probability space as $\tilde{N}$.

8.2.4 α-Stable Processes

We can consider a random walk approximation of a stable process by using Weron's algorithm. Another approach is a shot noise representation, by following the general result of section 8.2.2. The stochastic integral of a deterministic function[32] with respect to an α-stable random measure is the integral

$$I(f) = \int_E f(x) M(dx)$$

where $(E, \mathcal{E}, m)$ is a finite measure space and M is a random measure with finite control measure m. This integral can be defined also by a series representation. Indeed, an α-stable Lévy motion $S_\alpha(1, \beta, 0)$ can be viewed as

$$X_t \stackrel{d}{=} \int_0^T I_{[0,t]} M(dx) \qquad 0 \leq t \leq T,$$

---

[32]The function is measurable in the sense of Rajput and Rosiński (1989).

where M is an α-stable random measure on $([0, T], \mathcal{B}([0, T]))$ with Lebesgue control measure m and skewness intensity $\beta(x) \equiv \beta$.[33] Therefore, we have that if $0 < \alpha < 1$, then

$$X_t = C_\alpha^{1/\alpha} T^{1/\alpha} \sum_{i=1}^{\infty} V_i \Gamma^{-1/\alpha} I_{\{U_i \leq t\}} \qquad 0 \leq t \leq T, \qquad (8.8)$$

for $\alpha = 1$,

$$X_t = \frac{2}{\pi} T^{1/\alpha} \sum_{i=1}^{\infty} (V_i \Gamma^{-1/\alpha} I_{\{U_i \leq t\}} - \beta \frac{t}{T} b_i^{(1)}) + \beta t \frac{2}{\pi} \log \frac{2}{\pi} \qquad 0 \leq t \leq T \qquad (8.9)$$

and $1 < \alpha < 2$,

$$X_t = C_\alpha^{1/\alpha} T^{1/\alpha} \sum_{i=1}^{\infty} (V_i \Gamma^{-1/\alpha} I_{\{U_i \leq t\}} - \beta \frac{t}{T} b_i^{(\alpha)}) \qquad 0 \leq t \leq T, \qquad (8.10)$$

where we define three independent sequences. That is, $\{V_i\}$ is a sequence of i.i.d. random variables satisfying

$$P(V_i = 1) = 1 - P(V_i = -1) = \frac{1 + \beta}{2},$$

$\{\Gamma_i\}$ is a sequence of arrival times of a standard Poisson process with unit arrival rate, and $\{U_i\}$ a sequence of i.i.d. random variables uniformly distributed on $[0, T]$. Furthermore $b_i^{(\alpha)}$ is given by

$$b_i^{(\alpha)} = \begin{cases} 0, & 0 < \alpha < 1, \\ \int_{1/i}^{1/(i-1)} x^{-2} \sin x \, dx, & \alpha = 1, \\ \frac{\alpha}{\alpha-1}(i^{\frac{\alpha-1}{\alpha}} - (i-1)^{\frac{\alpha-1}{\alpha}}), & 1 < \alpha < 2. \end{cases} \qquad (8.11)$$

and $C_\alpha = (1 - \alpha)/(\Gamma(2 - \alpha)\cos(\pi\alpha/2))$.

8.3 TEMPERED STABLE PROCESSES

In this section, we will describe a method for simulating TS distributions, as well as TS processes. There are different methods to simulate Lévy processes,

---

[33]See Theorem 3.10.1 in Samorodnitsky and Taqqu (1994).

but most of these methods are not suitable for the simulation of TS processes due to the complicated structure of their Lévy measure. The usual method of the inverse of Lévy measure is hard to implement,[34] even if the spectral measure R has a simple form. To overcome this problem, we will find a shot noise representation for proper TS distributions, and consequently also TS processes, without constructing any inverse. This representation holds for every TS process, and in particular we obtain the well-known procedure for simulating CTS process.[35] Let ν be the Lévy measure of a proper TS distribution on $\mathbb{R}$, and Q and R corresponding measures.[36] Let us define $\|\sigma\|$ as

$$\|\sigma\| := \sigma(S^0), \tag{8.12}$$

and

$$Q(\mathbb{R}) = \int_{\mathbb{R}} |x|^\alpha R(dx),$$

we obtain

$$\|\sigma\| = Q(\mathbb{R}) = \int_{\mathbb{R}} |x|^\alpha R(dx) < \infty.$$

Let $\{V_j\}$ be an i.i.d. sequence of random variables in $\mathbb{R}$ with distribution $Q/\|\sigma\|$. Let $\{U_j\}$ and $\{T_j\}$ be i.i.d. sequences of uniform random variables in $(0, 1)$ and $(0, T)$ respectively, and let $\{E_j\}$ and $\{E'_j\}$ be i.i.d. sequences of exponential random variables with parameters 1. Furthermore, we assume that $\{V_j\}, \{U_j\}, \{E_j\}$, and $\{E'_j\}$ are independent. We consider $\Gamma_j = E'_1 + \ldots + E'_j$ and, by definition of $\{E'_j\}$, $\{\Gamma_j\}$ is a Poisson point process on $(0, \infty)$ with Lebesgue intensity measure; that is, the distribution of Γ_j is $\Gamma(j, 1)$.[37] First, we consider a simple case. If $\alpha \in (0, 1)$, or if $\alpha \in [1, 2)$ and Q is symmetric, the series

$$X_t = \sum_{j=1}^{\infty} I_{\{T_j \le t\}} \left(\left(\frac{\alpha \Gamma_j}{T\|\sigma\|} \right)^{-1/\alpha} \wedge E_j U_j^{1/\alpha} |V_j|^{-1} \right) \frac{V_j}{|V_j|} \tag{8.13}$$

---

[34]This fact has been already pointed out in Rosiński (2007b).
[35]See Example 4.5 in Asmussen and Glynn (2007). Our presentation is based on results in Rosiński (2001) and Theorem 5.1 in Rosiński (2007b).
[36]The definition of the measures R and Q, as well as of σ, are given in Rosiński (2007b) and Bianchi et al. (2010b).
[37]A Poisson point process describes the arrival times of a standard Poisson process.

converges a.s. and uniformly in $t \in [0, T]$ to a TS Lévy process. Then in the general case if $\alpha \in [1, 2)$ and Q is a nonsymmetric, assume additionally that

$$\int_{\mathbb{R}} |x| \log |x| R(dx) < \infty \tag{8.14}$$

when $\alpha = 1$ and that

$$\int_{\mathbb{R}} |x| R(dx) < \infty \tag{8.15}$$

when $\alpha \in (1, 2)$. The series

$$X_t = \sum_{j=1}^{\infty} \left[I_{\{T_j \leq t\}} \left(\left(\frac{\alpha \Gamma_j}{T \|\sigma\|} \right)^{-1/\alpha} \wedge E_j U_j^{1/\alpha} |V_j|^{-1} \right) \frac{V_j}{|V_j|} \right.$$
$$\left. - \frac{t}{T} \left(\frac{\alpha j}{T \|\sigma\|} \right)^{-1/\alpha} x_0 \right] + t b_T, \tag{8.16}$$

converges a.s. uniformly in $t \in [0, T]$ to a TS Lévy process, with[38]

$$b_T = \begin{cases} \alpha^{-1/\alpha} \zeta \left(\frac{1}{\alpha} \right) T^{-1} (T \|\sigma\|)^{1/\alpha} x_0 - \Gamma(1 - \alpha) x_1, & 1 < \alpha < 2 \\ (2\gamma + \log(T \|\sigma\|)) x_1 - \int_{\mathbb{R}} x \log |x| R(dx), & \alpha = 1, \end{cases} \tag{8.17}$$

and

$$x_0 = E \left[\frac{V_j}{\|V_j\|} \right] = \|\sigma\|^{-1} \int_{S^0} u \sigma(du),$$
$$x_1 = \int_{\mathbb{R}} x R(dx). \tag{8.18}$$

This method allows one to simulate a stable process as well, by considering all jumps of the form

$$\left(\frac{\alpha \Gamma_j}{T \|\sigma\|} \right)^{-1/\alpha} \frac{V_j}{|V_j|}$$

---

[38] ζ is the Riemann zeta function, as defined in equation (23.2) in Abramowitz and Stegun (1974), and γ is the Euler constant as defined in equation (6.1.3) in Abramowitz and Stegun (1974).

without tempering big jumps throughout the minimum function. Therefore, if big jumps are not tempered, we obtain a procedure equivalent to the one described in section 8.2.4.

Remark 1 It can be proven that if one removes the indicator function $I_{\{T_j \leq t\}}$, instead of a process the corresponding distribution can be simulated.

8.3.1 Kim-Rachev Tempered Stable Case

Now we will show a method based on the previous algorithm to simulate Kim-Rachev tempered stable (KRTS) processes. Consider a KRTS process X_t with parameters $(\alpha, k_+, k_-, r_+, r_-, p_+, p_-, 0)$. The i.i.d. sequence $\{V_j\}$ of random variables in $\mathbb{R}$ with distribution $Q/\|\sigma\|$ has density

$$f_V(r) = \frac{1}{\|\sigma\|} \left(k_+ r_+^{-p_+} I_{\{r > \frac{1}{r_+}\}} r^{-\alpha - p_+ - 1} + k_- r_-^{-p_+} I_{\{r < -\frac{1}{r_-}\}} |r|^{-\alpha - p_- - 1} \right),$$

where by the definition of KRTS distribution,

$$\|\sigma\| = \frac{k_+ r_+^\alpha}{\alpha + p_+} + \frac{k_- r_-^\alpha}{\alpha + p_-}.$$

If $\alpha \in (0, 1)$, or if $\alpha \in [1, 2)$ with $k_+ = k_-$, $r_+ = r_-$ and $p_+ = p_-$, then the series

$$X_t = \sum_{j=1}^{\infty} I_{\{T_j \leq t\}} \left(\left(\frac{\alpha \Gamma_j}{T \|\sigma\|} \right)^{-1/\alpha} \wedge E_j U_j^{1/\alpha} |V_j|^{-1} \right) \frac{V_j}{|V_j|} + tb \qquad (8.19)$$

converges a.s. and uniformly in $t \in [0, T]$ to a KRTS process with parameters $(\alpha, k_+, k_-, r_+, r_-, p_+, p_-, m)$ where we set

$$b = -\Gamma(1 - \alpha) \left(\frac{k_+ r_+}{p_+ + 1} - \frac{k_- r_-}{p_- + 1} \right).$$

If instead $\alpha \in [1, 2)$ and $k_+ \neq k_-$ (or $r_+ \neq r_-$ or alternatively $p_+ \neq p_-$), then

$$X_t = \sum_{j=1}^{\infty} \left[I_{\{T_j \leq t\}} \left(\left(\frac{\alpha \Gamma_j}{T \|\sigma\|} \right)^{-1/\alpha} \wedge E_j U_j^{1/\alpha} |V_j|^{-1} \right) \frac{V_j}{|V_j|} \right.$$
$$\left. - \frac{t}{T} \left(\frac{\alpha j}{T \|\sigma\|} \right)^{-1/\alpha} x_0 \right] + t b_T, \qquad (8.20)$$

converges a.s. and uniformly in $t \in [0, T]$ to a KRTS process with parameters $(\alpha, k_+, k_-, r_+, r_-, p_+, p_-, m)$, where we set[39]

$$
b_T = \begin{cases}
\alpha^{-1/\alpha} \zeta\left(\tfrac{1}{\alpha}\right) T^{-1}(T\|\sigma\|)^{1/\alpha} x_0 - \Gamma(1-\alpha)x_1, & 1 < \alpha < 2 \\
(2\gamma + \log(T\|\sigma\|))x_1 - \left(\frac{k_+ r_+}{p_+ + 1}\left(\log r_+ - \frac{1}{p_+ + 1}\right)\right. \\
\left. \quad - \frac{k_- r_-}{p_- + 1}\left(\log r_- - \frac{1}{p_- + 1}\right)\right), & \alpha = 1.
\end{cases}
$$

with

$$
x_0 = \|\sigma\|^{-1}\left(\frac{k_+ r_+^{\alpha}}{\alpha + p_+} - \frac{k_- r_-^{\alpha}}{\alpha + p_-}\right),
$$

$$
x_1 = \frac{k_+ r_+}{p_+ + 1} - \frac{k_- r_-}{p_- + 1},
$$

Finally, we can write a procedure to simulate a KRTS process with parameters $(\alpha, k_+, k_-, r_+, r_-, p_+, p_-, m)$ for discrete values of time t_i, where $\{t_i\}_{0 \le i \le K}$ is a partition of the interval $[0, T]$ with equal length subinterval and mesh

$$
\Delta t = \frac{T}{K}
$$

with $K \in \mathbb{N}$.

KRTS process

1. Fix a time T and consider a partition of the interval $[0, T]$ in K parts of equal length.
2. Fix a number K' ($\sim 10^5, 10^6$).
3. Simulate independent sequences $\{V_j\}, \{\Gamma_j\}, \{U_j\}, \{T_j\},$ and $\{E_j\}$ of length K'.
4. Calculate the vector $\{X_{t_i}\}$ by equality (8.20) or (8.19).

Figure 8.4 shows the goodness of fit of a simulated sample from a symmetric KRTS distribution. The theoretical and the simulated density are plotted together.

---

[39]The Riemann zeta function ζ is explained in footnote 38.

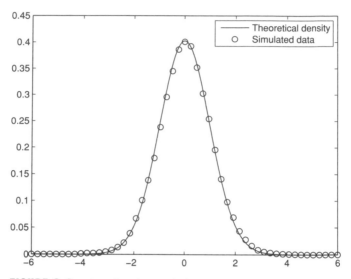

FIGURE 8.4 Simulated Sample for a Symmetric KRTS Distribution with Parameters $k_+ = k_- = 8.0225, r_+ = r_- = 0.5,$ $p_+ = p_- = 10, \alpha = 1.7000,$ and $m = 0$

8.3.2 Classical Tempered Stable Case

By similar arguments, a series representation of a CTS process also can be obtained. In this case, $\{V_j\}$ is an i.i.d. sequence of discrete random variables with distribution

$$P(V_j = -\lambda_-) = P(V_j = \lambda_+) = \frac{1}{2},$$

a positive constant $0 < \alpha < 2$ and $\|\sigma\| = \sigma(S^{d-1}) = 2C.$ Then

$$X_t \stackrel{d}{=} \sum_{j=1}^{\infty} \left[\left(\frac{\alpha \Gamma_j}{2C} \right)^{-1/\alpha} \wedge E_j U_j^{1/\alpha} |V_j|^{-1} \right] \frac{V_j}{|V_j|} I_{\{T_j \le t\}} + t b_T \qquad t \in [0, T],$$

$$(8.21)$$

where

$$b_T = \begin{cases} -\Gamma(1-\alpha)C(\lambda_+^{\alpha-1} - \lambda_-^{\alpha-1}), & 0 < \alpha < 2 \text{ and } \alpha \ne 1 \\ (2\gamma + \log(2TC))C(\lambda_+^{\alpha-1} - \lambda_-^{\alpha-1}) \\ \quad -C(\lambda_-^{\alpha-1} \log \lambda_- - \lambda_+^{\alpha-1} \log \lambda_+), & \alpha = 1, \end{cases} \qquad (8.22)$$

converges a.s. and uniformly in $t \in [0, T]$ to a CTS process with parameters $(C, \lambda_-, \lambda_+, \alpha, 0)$. Finally, we can write a procedure to simulate a CTS process with parameters $(C, \lambda_-, \lambda_+, \alpha, m)$ for discrete values of time t_i, where $\{t_i\}_{0 \leq i \leq K}$ is a partition of the interval $[0, T]$ with equal length subinterval and mesh

$$\Delta t = \frac{T}{K}$$

with $K \in \mathbb{N}$.

CTS process

1. Fix a time T and consider a partition of the interval $[0, T]$ in K parts of equal length.
2. Fix a number K' ($\sim 10^5, 10^6$).
3. Simulate independent sequences $\{V_j\}, \{\Gamma_j\}, \{U_j\}, \{T_j\},$ and $\{E_j\}$ of length K'.
4. Calculate the vector $\{X_{t_i}\}$ by equality (8.21).

By the algorithm above, we can simulate the entire trajectory of a TS process.[40] Figure 8.5 shows different paths of TS processes in comparison with the stable process:[41] Big jumps of stable process are tempered in the CTS and KRTS case. Figure 8.6 shows the goodness of fit of a simulated sample from a CTS distribution. The theoretical and the simulated density are plotted together.

8.4 TEMPERED INFINITELY DIVISIBLE PROCESSES

With similar arguments, TID distributions and processes can be simulated by a shot noise representation.[42]

---

[40]This method is particularly useful for path-dependent options, such as barrier options or Asian options, as described in Kawai (2006).

[41]Here the same i.i.d. sequences $\{U_j\}, \{T_j\}, \{E_j\}, \{E'_j\},$ and $\{V_j\}$ are considered for the three different processes.

[42]See Bianchi et al. (2010a) for the theoretical results about simulation algorithms.

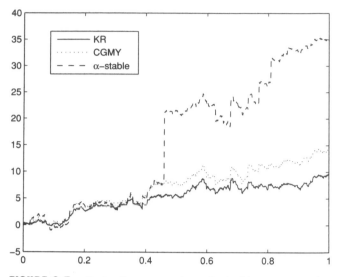

FIGURE 8.5 Series Representation of a Stable Process and Two Different TS Processes with Truncation of Small Jumps

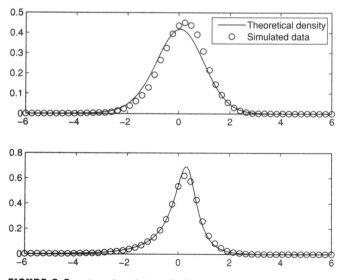

FIGURE 8.6 Simulated Sample for a CTS Distribution with Parameters $C = 0.1579$, $\lambda_- = 0.5$, $\lambda_+ = 1.5$, $\alpha = 1.7$, and $m = 0$ (above), and with Parameters $C = 0.3650$, $\lambda_- = 0.5$, $\lambda_+ = 1.5$, $\alpha = 0.7$, and $m = 0$ (below)

8.4.1 Rapidly Decreasing Tempered Stable Case

By taking into consideration the series representation of a CTS process, a rapidly decreasing tempered stable (RDTS) process can also be simulated. In this case, $\{V_j\}$ is an i.i.d. sequence of discrete random variables with distribution

$$P(V_j = -\lambda_-) = P(V_j = \lambda_+) = \frac{1}{2},$$

a positive constant $0 < \alpha < 2$ and $\|\sigma\| = \sigma(S^{d-1}) = 2C$. Then the series

$$X_t \overset{d}{=} \sum_{j=1}^{\infty} \left[\left(\frac{\alpha \Gamma_j}{2C} \right)^{-1/\alpha} \wedge \sqrt{2} E_j^{1/2} U_j^{1/\alpha} |V_j|^{-1} \right] \frac{V_j}{|V_j|} I_{\{T_j \le t\}} + t b_T, \quad (8.23)$$

where

$$b_T = -2^{-\frac{1+\alpha}{2}} C\Gamma \left(\frac{1-\alpha}{2} \right) C(\lambda_+^{\alpha-1} - \lambda_-^{\alpha-1}), \ 0 < \alpha < 2 \text{ and } \alpha \ne 1$$

converges a.s. and uniformly in $t \in [0, T]$ to a RDTS process with parameters $(\alpha, C, \lambda_+, \lambda_-, 0)$. Finally, we can write a procedure to simulate a RDTS process with parameters $(\alpha, C, \lambda_+, \lambda_-, 0)$ for discrete values of time t_i, where $\{t_i\}_{0 \le i \le K}$ is a partition of the interval $[0, T]$ with equal length subinterval and mesh

$$\Delta t = \frac{T}{K}$$

with $K \in \mathbb{N}$.

RDTS process

1. Fix a time T and consider a partition of the interval $[0, T]$ in K parts of equal length.
2. Fix a number K' ($\sim 10^5, 10^6$).
3. Simulate independent sequences $\{V_j\}$, $\{\Gamma_j\}$, $\{U_j\}$, $\{T_j\}$, and $\{E_j\}$ of length K'.
4. Calculate the vector $\{X_{t_i}\}$ by equality (8.23).

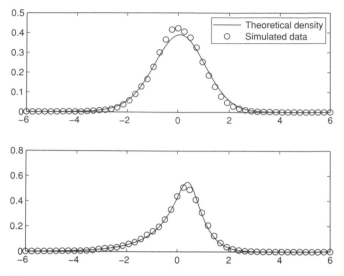

FIGURE 8.7   Simulated Sample for a RDTS Distribution with Parameters $C = 0.1579$, $\lambda_+ = 1.5$, $\lambda_- = 0.5$, $\alpha = 1.7$, and $m = 0$ (above), and with Parameters $C = 0.3650$, $\lambda_+ = 1.5$, $\lambda_- = 0.5$, $\alpha = 0.7$, and $m = 0$ (below)

Figure 8.7 shows the goodness of fit of a simulated sample from a RDTS distribution. The theoretical and the simulated density are plotted together.

8.4.2 Modified Tempered Stable Case

Now, we will show a method to simulate modified tempered stable (MTS) processes. Consider a MTS process X_t with parameters $(\alpha, C, \lambda_+, \lambda_-, 0)$ and an i.i.d. sequence $\{V_j\}$ of random variables in $\mathbb{R}$ with distribution $Q/\|\sigma\|$ with density

$$f_V(x) = \frac{2^{-\frac{\alpha+11}{2}}}{\Gamma\left(\frac{\alpha}{2} - \frac{1}{2}\right)} \left(\lambda_+^{\alpha+1} e^{-\frac{\lambda_+^2 x^2}{2}} I_{x>0} + \lambda_-^{\alpha+1} e^{-\frac{\lambda_-^2 x^2}{2}} I_{x<0} \right),$$

where by the definition of the MTS distribution

$$\|\sigma\| = 2^{\frac{\alpha+1}{2}} C \Gamma\left(\frac{\alpha}{2} - \frac{1}{2}\right).$$

Then the series

$$X_t = \sum_{j=1}^{\infty} I_{\{T_j \le t\}} \left(\left(\frac{\alpha \Gamma_j}{T \|\sigma\|} \right)^{-1/\alpha} \wedge \sqrt{2} E_j^{1/2} U_j^{1/\alpha} |V_j|^{-1} \right) \frac{V_j}{|V_j|} + tb \quad (8.24)$$

converges a.s. and uniformly in $t \in [0, T]$ to a MTS process with parameters $(\alpha, C, \lambda_+, \lambda_+, m)$ where we set

$$b = -2^{-\frac{\alpha+1}{2}} C\Gamma \left(\frac{1-\alpha}{2} \right) (\lambda_+^{\alpha-1} - \lambda_-^{\alpha-1}).$$

Finally, we can write a procedure to simulate a MTS process with parameters $(\alpha, C, \lambda_+, \lambda_-, m)$ for discrete values of time t_i, where $\{t_i\}_{0 \le i \le K}$ is a partition of the interval $[0, T]$ with equal length subinterval and mesh

$$\Delta t = \frac{T}{K}$$

with $K \in \mathbb{N}$.

MTS process

1. Fix a time T and consider a partition of the interval $[0, T]$ in K parts of same length.
2. Fix a number K' ($\sim 10^5, 10^6$).
3. Simulate independent sequences $\{V_j\}, \{\Gamma_j\}, \{U_j\}, \{T_j\}$, and $\{E_j\}$ of length K'.
4. Calculate the vector $\{X_{t_i}\}$ by equality (8.24).

8.5 TIME-CHANGED BROWNIAN MOTION

The time-changed Brownian motion construction we use is well known from the theory of stochastic processes and is known as the *Skorokhod embedding problem*.[43] A process can be embedded in a Brownian motion if and only if it is a local semimartingale.[44] In particular, every semimartingale can be written as a time-changed Brownian motion, where the random time G_t is a subordinator. As already observed in Chapter 4, a *subordinator* is a

---

[43]For a review of this problem, see Obloj (2004) and the references therein.
[44]See the seminal work of Monroe (1978).

nondecreasing process that can be used as the stochastic time of a Brownian motion. As a consequence of the Lévy-Itô decomposition, every Lévy process Y_t is a semimartingale,[45] thus there exists a subordinator G_t such that Y_t and $\tilde{W}_{G_t}$ coincide, where $\tilde{W}_t$ is a Brownian motion.

A large part of modern finance has been concerned with modeling the evolution of return processes over time. By subordination, it is possible to capture empirically observed anomalies that contradict the classical log-normality assumption for asset prices.[46] In periods of high volatility, time runs faster than in periods of low volatility. The subordinator models operational time and provides the so-called fat-tail effects, often observed in financial markets. The Skorokhod embedding problem is also related to the subordination of Lévy processes. If the subordinated Lévy process is of the form

$$Y_t = \theta G_t + W_{G_t} \qquad (8.25)$$

then the Lévy measure[47] of the process Y_t is given by

$$\nu^\sharp(dx) = \int_0^\infty \frac{e^{-\frac{(x-\theta y)^2}{2y}}}{\sqrt{2\pi y}} \nu(dy), \qquad (8.26)$$

where ν is the Lévy measure of the subordinator.

The knowledge of the time process, the so-called *business time*, is very convenient for the simulation. First, we can generate the subordinator and then the Brownian motion. Since normal random variables are the building blocks of many simulation algorithms, it is then clear that all the difficulty comes from the generation of increments of the new time scale, represented by the subordinator.

Although the representation via Brownian subordination is a nice property, we do not know a general constructive method to find the process G_t such that $Y_t = \tilde{W}_{G_t(\omega)}$. This means that given a semimartingale Y_t, the time process G_t is not always known. Thus, this approach can be applied only

---

[45]In the following we will not use the concept of semimartingale and will not deal with the theory of stochastic integration. However, it is important to know that a Lévy process is a semimartingale.

[46]The subordination problem has been widely studied in the literature by Hurst et al. (1997, 1999), Marinelli et al. (2000), Geman et al. (2001, 2002), Carr and Wu (2004), and De Giovanni et al. (2008).

[47]In order to obtain the generating triplet of the subordinated process, we refer to the general result proved in Theorem 30.1 of Sato (1999).

for some particular Lévy processes.[48] If one knows how to simulate the increments of the subordinator, the increments of G_t can be simulated using a random walk approximation with a fixed time grid and a Brownian motion with volatility σ and mean μ.

Time-changed Brownian motion

1. Fix a time grid $t_1, \ldots, t_n$ and $G_0 = 0$.
2. Simulate increments of the subordinator $\Delta G_i = G_{t_i} - G_{t_i-1}$.
3. Simulate n independent standard normal random variables $N_1, \ldots, N_n$.
4. Calculate increments $\Delta Y_i = \sigma N_i \sqrt{\Delta G_i} - \mu \Delta G_i$.
5. Set $Y_{t_i} = \sum_{k=1}^{i} \Delta Y_i$.

8.5.1 Classical Tempered Stable Processes

A CTS process can be described as time-changed Brownian motion.[49] The time-changed Brownian motion framework and the Rosińsky rejection method can be combined to obtain CTS random numbers. The subordinator G_t is absolutely continuous with respect to the one-sided $\alpha/2$-stable subordinator with Lévy measure

$$\nu^0(dx) = \frac{K}{x^{\frac{\alpha}{2}+1}}.$$

The Lévy measure of the subordinator G_t is

$$\nu(dx) = s(x)\nu^0(dx),$$

where the function s is defined as

$$s(x) = \frac{2^{\frac{\alpha}{2}} \Gamma\left(\frac{\alpha}{2} + \frac{1}{2}\right) e^{\frac{x}{2}A^2 - \frac{x}{4}B^2}}{\sqrt{\pi}} D_{-\alpha}(B\sqrt{x})$$

---

[48]See, for example, Cont and Tankov (2004), De Giovanni et al. (2008), and Madan and Yor (2006).
[49]The explicit time change is known from a result proved in Madan and Yor (2006), and a procedure based on this result has been developed by Poirot and Tankov (2006).

with

$$A = \frac{\lambda_- - \lambda_+}{2} \qquad B = \frac{\lambda_- + \lambda_+}{2},$$

where C, λ_-, λ_+ and α are parameters of the process and $D_\alpha(x)$ is a parabolic cylinder function of parameter α.[50] Stable distributions and processes are relatively easy to simulate. Thus, the Rosiński rejection method explained in section 8.2.3 can be applied in order to obtain a feasible simulation of the subordinator process. We take

$$\frac{dv}{dv^0} = f(x),$$

which can be shown to be strictly less that one.

Furthermore, a density transformation can be applied to approximate the jumps of a CTS process. By a suitable change of measure, a CTS process becomes an α-stable process, which can be easily simulated. This approach seems to be particularly useful for Monte Carlo methods.[51]

The theory of TS processes allows us to consider CTS processes as an example of the more general class of proper TS processes. Furthermore, the particular structure of this process provides an easily implementable shot noise representation, as already noted in section 8.3.2. Figure 8.8 shows the different behavior of a CTS process simulated by time-changing Brownian motion and by series representation.

8.5.2 Variance Gamma and Skewed Variance Gamma Processes

If one is able to simulate a gamma process, there is a very simple way to generate the path of a variance gamma (VG) or a skewed variance gamma (SVG) process. We have that the SVG or bilateral gamma (BΓ) distribution,[52] of parameters $(c_+, c_-, \lambda_+, \lambda_-, 0)$, is defined as the convolution of two gamma random variables $\Gamma^+(c_+, \lambda_+)$ and $\Gamma^-(c_-, \lambda_-)$,

$$X_t^{SVG} = \Gamma_t^+ - \Gamma_t^-.$$

---

[50]A special function of this kind is defined in Tricomi (1954) and Abramowitz and Stegun (1974).
[51]See the work of Poirot and Tankov (2006).
[52]This distribution was introduced by Küchler and Tappe (2008).

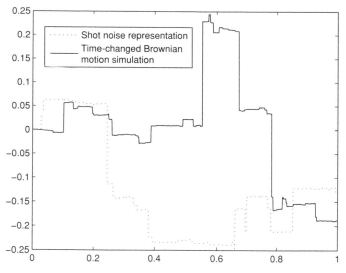

FIGURE 8.8 Simulation of a CTS Process with $C = 0.5$, $\lambda_- = 2$, $\lambda_+ = 3$, and $\alpha = 0.5$ by Time-Changing Brownian Motion Described in Poirot and Tankov (2006) and by Series Representation
Note: Simulations are not comparable, due to differences of the generating algorithms.

Figure 8.9 shows the goodness of fit of a simulated sample from a SVG distribution. The theoretical and the simulated density are plotted together. When $c_+ = c_-$, we have the VG case. Furthermore, the VG process[53] with parameters (σ, θ, v) can be simulated also by considering a time-changed Brownian motion,

$$X_t^{VG} = \theta\, G_t + \sigma\, W_{G_t},$$

where G_t is a gamma process with parameters $(1/v, 1/v, 0)$.

8.5.3 Normal Tempered Stable Processes

The normal tempered stable (NTS) process can be obtained as a time-changed Brownian motion with a tempered stable subordinator. Furthermore, a NTS distribution can be obtained via the exponential tilting[54] of a

---

[53]This distribution is described in Chapter 4.
[54]This change of measure is described in Chapter 3.

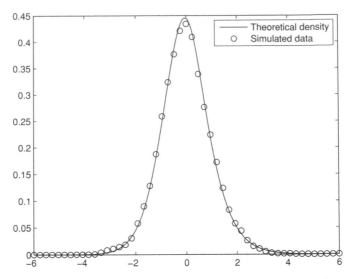

FIGURE 8.9   Simulated Sample for a SVG Distribution with Parameters $c_+ = 2$, $c_- = 8$, $\lambda_+ = 2$, $\lambda_- = 4$, and $m = 0$

symmetric MTS distribution. This second approach also may be considered since one can approximate the trajectory of the NTS process by simulating first a symmetric MTS process and then by using the Rosiński rejection method. In this setting, this amounts to accepting every jump J_i^0 of the MTS process for which

$$\frac{d\nu}{d\nu_0}(y_i) = e^{\beta y_i}$$

is greater than an independent uniform random variable on $[0, 1]$. Even this approach is also possible; it seems to be easier to consider the time-changed Brownian motion since one can use the series representation or the Rosiński rejection method applied to an α-stable subordinator to generate a TS subordinator.[55]

8.5.4   Normal Inverse Gaussian Processes

Since the normal inverse Gaussian (NIG) process is a special case of the NTS process, one may use all previous techniques. As in the VG case, we can also

---

[55]This approach is similar to the one described in Poirot and Tankov (2006).

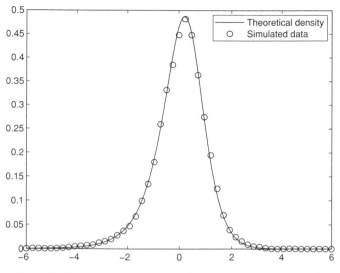

FIGURE 8.10 Simulated Sample for a NIG Distribution with Parameters $\alpha = 1.5$, $\beta = -0.5$, $\delta = 1.2571$, and $m = 0$

simulate an NIG process as a time-changed Brownian motion,

$$X_t^{NIG} = \beta \delta^2 I_t + \delta W_{I_t},$$

where I_t is an inverse Gaussian process with parameters $(1, \delta(\alpha^2 - \beta^2), 0)$. Figure 8.10 shows the goodness of fit of a simulated sample from a NIG distribution. The theoretical and the simulated density are plotted together.

8.6   MONTE CARLO METHODS

Monte Carlo methods[56] are stochastic techniques based on the use of random numbers to evaluate mathematical expressions. Monte Carlo is used to solve problems that are strictly deterministic as well as problems that involve randomness.[57] The core of Monte Carlo methods is simulation; therefore, a

---

[56]These methods will be used in Chapter 13.
[57]For a comprehensive review of Monte Carlo methods applied to financial engineering, see Gentle (2003) and Glasserman (2004).

fast random number generator is needed to obtain estimates in a reasonable period of time. A large number of simulations (i.e., $10,000$) generally is required to achieve a high degree of accuracy. However, its efficiency can be improved using control variates and quasi-random numbers.

In this chapter, we discuss Monte Carlo simulation in order to solve the problem of pricing European options when closed-form analytical solutions are not available, in particular in the case in which the dynamic of the volatility has a GARCH structure. For our purpose, we will focus on the evaluation of the integral

$$\theta = e^{-rT} E_Q[f(X_t; t \in [0, T])]$$

where X_T is the value of the stochastic process $\{X_t\}_{t \geq 0}$ at time T and Q is a given equivalent martingale measure. Since we take the expected value of the discounted payoff under an equivalent martingale measure, it is easy to understand that θ is exactly the price at time 0 of a European option with payoff $f(X_T)$. The method can be easily extended to complex path-dependent options like Asian options or Russian options, just to say a few.

In Chapters 11, 12, 13, and 14 we consider GARCH models. Unfortunately, when computing option prices under GARCH processes, analytical solutions for prices of options are not generally available and hence numerical procedures have to be invoked. In the work of Heston and Nandi (2000), a closed-form solution for European options under a very specific GARCH structure has been developed, but the dynamic of the GARCH process seems not to be realistic. In order to obtain a more realistic GARCH model, we have to use the recursive procedure and consider Monte Carlo simulations for option pricing. In order to obtain a faster converge and smaller variance, we will see some procedures that provide a smaller variance than the crude Monte Carlo method.

8.6.1   Variance Reduction Techniques

Variance reduction techniques allow one to obtain a faster convergence speed. Though these methods are theoretically acceptable, we always have to take into account the computational effort and the computational time. If a small gain is obtained by variance reduction, but the computational time is largely increased, then one has to prefer crude Monte Carlo methods. It is beyond the scope of this chapter to delve into the details of variance-reduction techniques. Instead, we describe only some basic algorithms.

Antithetic Sampling   Suppose we want to simulate a sample from the random variable X.[58] In a Monte Carlo procedure with antithetic sampling, first we generate n i.i.d. copies of X,

$$X_1, \ldots, X_n$$

and then we consider also a sample

$$X'_1, \ldots, X'_n$$

such that X_i and X'_i have the same distribution but are not independent with covariance

$$Cov(X_i, X'_i) < 0.$$

Our Monte Carlo estimate will be

$$\hat{\theta} = \frac{1}{2n} \sum_{i=1}^{n} (X_i + X'_i).$$

It is not difficult to evaluate the variance of

$$Var(\hat{\theta}) = \frac{1}{n} Var \left(\frac{X_1 + X'_1}{2} \right) = \frac{1}{4n} (Var(X_1) + Var(X'_1) + 2Cov(X_1, X'_1))$$

$$= \frac{1}{2n} (Var(X_1) + Cov(X_1, X'_1)).$$

Therefore, there is a variance reduction. If X is a uniform random variable, one can take

$$X_i = U_i \qquad X'_i = 1 - U_i$$

and in general if X is a random variable with a given distribution function F, one can take

$$X_i = F^{-1}(U_i) \qquad X'_i = F^{-1}(1 - U_i),$$

---

[58]For example, $X = e^{-rT} E_Q[f(X_T)]$, where f is some payoff function.

due to the monotonicity of the function F^{-1}. In particular, if the distribution is symmetric, it is possible to consider the sample generated by

$$X_i = F^{-1}(U_i) \qquad X_i' = -X_i.$$

Importance Sampling In order to compute an expectation under a given probability measure Q of a random variable X, we can find another measure $\tilde{Q}$ equivalent to Q such that the following equation is satisfied

$$E_Q[X] = E_{\tilde{Q}}\left[X\frac{dQ}{d\tilde{Q}}\right].$$

We define the Radon-Nikodym derivative as $L = dQ/d\tilde{Q}$. The measure $\tilde{Q}$ is called an *importance measure* because the change of measure tries to give more weight to important outcomes. We have to find a suitable change of measure that gives us the optimal importance sampling.[59]

Theorem 6. *Let Q^* be defined by*

$$\frac{dQ^*}{dQ} = \frac{|X|}{E|X|},$$

then the importance sampling estimator ZL^* under Q^* has a smaller variance than the estimator ZL under any other $\tilde{Q}$.

Proof. See Chapter V, Theorem 1.2, in Asmussen and Glynn (2007).

The importance sampling method is aimed at reducing the variance by appropriately transforming the underlying probability measure so as to place more weight on important events and less on unimportant ones. Roughly speaking, the change of measure in the mathematical finance literature means that, given a market measure $\mathbb{P}$, we want to find an equivalent measure $\mathbb{Q}$ under which our process is a martingale. Now, taking into account financial derivatives pricing with Monte Carlo methods, a density transformation can be considered to also accelerate the convergence through variance reduction.[60] Therefore, the solution of the change of measure problem in models

---

[59]An importance sampling method based on density transformations of Lévy processes has been studied in Kawai (2006) and Asmussen and Glynn (2007).
[60]This approach has been proposed by Kawai (2006).

with jumps and, in particular, in models involving TS processes[61] allows one to obtain a feasible probability measure transformation. It can be used to find an equivalent martingale measure as well as a variance reduction method for Monte Carlo simulations. Now we can consider similar density transformations and apply them to Monte Carlo simulation.

A widely applied density transformation is the *exponential tilting*, that is given a probability density function f on $\mathbb{R}_+$, for every $\lambda > 0$ we can consider the tilted density f_λ so defined

$$f_\lambda(x) = \frac{e^{-\lambda x} f(x)}{\int_0^\infty e^{-\lambda x} f(x) dx}$$

if the integral in the denominator is finite. The procedure of tilting is also related to the *Esscher transform*.[62] It can be viewed as tilting but on the level of stochastic processes.

Empirical Martingale Simulation   In this section, we describe the empirical martingale simulation[63] for pricing European claims. The simulated asset price paths arc opportunely modified to ensure that the risk-neutral expectation of the underlying asset equals its forward price. This method to reduce the Monte Carlo variance has been widely used for GARCH models.[64] Suppose we simulate the process $f(X_t)$, where f is some payoff function under a risk-neutral probability measure. In a Monte Carlo procedure, we generate n copies of the process and define the sample mean as

$$\overline{f(X_t)} = \frac{1}{n} \sum_{i=1}^n f(X_t^i).$$

Theoretically, we know that the discounted process has to be a martingale under the risk-neutral probability measure; that is, the following relation holds

$$e^{-rt} E[f(X_t)] = f(X_0).$$

---

[61]The change of measure problem for TS processes has been studied in Kim et al. (2008) to obtain a risk-neutral probability measure to find a fair price for European options.

[62]The Esscher transform can be viewed as a particular density transformation of Lévy processes; see Theorem 33.1 in Sato (1999) for the general result and Rosiński (2007b) for the TS case.

[63]This method has been proposed by Duan and Simonato (1998).

[64]See Menn and Rachev (2005) and Barone-Adesi et al. (2008).

Unfortunately, this relation is not satisfied in real-world applications. It is a matter of fact that

$$e^{-rt}\overline{f(X_t)} \neq f(X_0)$$

in general appears. With a crude Monte Carlo method, the discounted simulated process is not a martingale. To avoid this inexact simulation, an additive[65] or a multiplicative[66] adjustment can be considered to transform generated paths

$$\widetilde{f(X_t^i)} = f(X_t^i) + E[f(X_t)] - \overline{f(X_t)}$$

$$\widehat{f(X_t)} = f(X_t^i)\frac{E[f(X_t)]}{\overline{f(X_t)}}.$$

If the multiplicative adjustment is applied to the exponent of an exponential martingale, no mispricing is obtained even if the equality

$$E[\widetilde{f(X)_t}] = E[f(X_t)]$$

holds only by considering the additive one. An additional drawback of the additive transformation is that it also allows a negative value for the trajectory. Both approaches change the law of the simulated process, and this introduces some bias in the estimated price. This effect is almost negligible for large values of n. We will consider this method to price options based on the infinitely divisible GARCH model.

8.6.2   A Nonparametric Monte Carlo Method

A possible alternative to classical Monte Carlo methods, where a distributional assumption is always considered, can be the *filtering historical probability* (FHS) approach[67] to compute portfolio risk measures. It has been recently applied to the study of option pricing in the GARCH framework.[68] Permutations of the historical series are considered as the source of the randomness, without any distributional assumption. The idea comes from the observation that Monte Carlo simulations drawn from a particular distribution impose the risk structure that one was supposed to investigate.

---

[65]The method was introduced by Barraquand (1995).
[66]The method was introduced by Duan and Simonato (1998).
[67] The algorithm was proposed by Barone-Adesi et al. (1999).
[68]See Barone-Adesi et al. (2008).

In particular, with the normal distribution hypothesis we cannot incorporate excess skewness and kurtosis, and cannot capture extreme events. Empirical studies show that residuals are not normally distributed; therefore, one possibility to overcome this drawback is not to impose any theoretical distribution. Historical simulations usually sample from past data assuming that returns are i.i.d. Thus, one needs to remove any serial correlation and volatility clusters present in the historical series.

A standard way to remove volatility clusters is by modeling returns with a GARCH(1,1) specification.[69] A modified version of the GARCH model can be considered for modeling returns, that is

$$
\begin{aligned}
r_t &= \mu + \eta_t \quad \eta_t \sim N(0, \sigma_t^2) \\
\sigma_t^2 &= \alpha_0 + \alpha_1 \eta_{t-1}^2 + \gamma\, I_{t-1} \eta_{t-1}^2 + \beta \sigma_{t-1}^2
\end{aligned}
\tag{8.27}
$$

where η_t is the residual and $I_{t-1} = 1$ for positive residual; otherwise, it is zero. The empirical innovation density captures potential non-normalities in the true innovation density. In order to use estimated residual for historical simulations, one needs to scale them with respect to the volatility, that is

$$
z_t = \frac{\eta_t}{\sigma_t}
$$

It is clear that the first step is the estimation of the model's parameters and then the extraction of estimated residuals. The historical simulation is provided by a random choice within the set of estimated residuals, after an opportune scaling by σ_t as above. For each step i, the value of the innovation z_i is chosen and the conditional variance is updated until the entire path is generated. Repeating this procedure 10,000 times, we obtain convergence to the option price. To ensure the convergence of the calibration algorithm, the FHS innovations used to simulate the GARCH sample paths are kept fixed across all the iterations of the algorithm.[70]

We note that innovations are the same under the market measure, even in the risk-neutral one. Parameters of the volatility dynamics under the risk-neutral measure are estimated by matching market option prices to model prices. Furthermore, the variance of the historical simulation can be reduced by the empirical martingale simulation method. We analyze the pricing performance of this approach in Chapter 14.

---

[69]See Bollerslev (1987), Bollerslev (1995), and Rachev et al. (2007) for more details.
[70]This algorithm is shown in Barone-Adesi et al. (2008).

8.6.3 A Monte Carlo Example

In this section, we assess the goodness of fit of random number generators proposed in the previous section. A brief Monte Carlo study is performed and prices of European put options with different strikes are calculated.[71] We consider a CTS process[72] with parameters $C = 0.5$, $\lambda_- = 2$, $\lambda_+ = 3.5$, $\alpha = 0.5$, constant interest rate $r = 0.04$, initial stock price $S_0 = 100$, and annualized maturity $T = 0.25$. We also consider a GTS process[73] with parameters $c_+ = 0.5$, $c_- = 1$, $\lambda_+ = 3.5$, $\lambda_- = 2$, and $\alpha = 0.5$, and the same interest rate r, initial stock price S_0, and maturity T as in the CTS case.

Monte Carlo prices are obtained through 50,000 simulations. The Esscher transform with parameter $\theta = -1.5$ is considered to reduce the variance.[74] We want to emphasize that the Esscher transform is an exponential tilting and therefore if applied to a CTS or a GTS process, it modifies only the parameters, not the form of the characteristic function.

In Table 8.1, simulated prices and prices obtained by using the Fourier transform method[75] are compared. Even if there is a competitive CTS random number generator where a time-changed Brownian motion is

TABLE 8.1 European Put Option Prices Computed Using the Fourier Transform Method (Price) and by Monte Carlo Simulation (Monte Carlo)

	CTS			GTS	
Strike	Price	Monte Carlo	Strike	Price	Monte Carlo
80	1.7444	1.7472	80	3.2170	3.2144
85	2.3926	2.3955	85	4.2132	4.2179
90	3.2835	3.2844	90	5.4653	5.4766
95	4.5366	4.5383	95	7.0318	7.0444
100	6.3711	6.3724	100	8.9827	8.9968
105	9.1430	9.1532	105	11.3984	11.4175
110	12.7632	12.7737	110	14.3580	14.3895
115	16.8430	16.8551	115	17.8952	17.9394
120	21.1856	21.2064	120	21.9109	21.9688

---

[71]This example is drawn from Bianchi et al. (2010b).

[72] We consider the same artificial parameters as in the work of Poirot and Tankov (2006).

[73]This process is defined in Chapter 4.

[74]See Kawai (2006).

[75]See Carr and Madan (1999).

considered,[76] we prefer to use an algorithm based on series representation. Contrary to the CTS case, in general there is no constructive method to find the subordinator process that changes the time of the Brownian motion; that is, we do not know the process T_t such that the TS process X_t can be rewritten as $W_{T(t)}$. The shot noise representation allows one to generate any TS process.

APPENDIX

Alternative Representation of Stable Distributions

The canonical representation of stable distributions presented by equation (3.1) in Chapter 3 has a disadvantage. The characteristic function is not a continuous function of the parameters; therefore, if we want to look at the simulation problem, we prefer to consider the alternative representation.[77]

Definition 1. *A random variable X is α-stable if and only if its characteristic function is given by*

$$E[e^{iuX}] = \begin{cases} \exp\{-\sigma_2^\alpha |u|^\alpha \exp\{-i\beta_2(\text{sign}(u)\frac{\pi}{2}K(\alpha))\} + i\mu u\}, & \text{if } \alpha \neq 1, \\ \exp\{-\sigma_2 |u|(\frac{\pi}{2} + i\beta_2\text{sign}(u)\ln|u|) + i\mu u\}, & \text{if } \alpha = 1, \end{cases}$$

$$(A.1)$$

where

$$K(\alpha) = \alpha - 1 + \text{sign}(1 - \alpha)\begin{cases} \alpha, & \alpha < 1, \\ \alpha - 2, & \alpha > 1. \end{cases}$$

The parameters σ_2 and β_2 are related to σ and β, from the representation (3.1), as follows. For $\alpha \neq 1$, β_2 is such that

$$\tan\beta_2 \frac{\pi K(\alpha)}{2} = \beta \tan\frac{\pi\alpha}{2},$$

and the new scale parameter is

$$\sigma_2 = \sigma\left(1 + \beta^2 \tan^2\frac{\pi\alpha}{2}\right)^{1/(2\alpha)}.$$

---

[76]As proposed in Cont and Tankov (2004) and Poirot and Tankov (2006).
[77]See Zolotarev (1986) and Weron (1996).

For $\alpha = 1$, $\beta_2 = \beta$ and $\sigma_2 = \frac{2}{\pi}\sigma$. Furthermore, we define γ_0 as

$$\gamma_0 = -\frac{\pi}{2}\beta_2 \frac{K(\alpha)}{\alpha}. \tag{A.2}$$

Poisson Random Measure and Lévy-Itô Decomposition

Next we briefly turn our attention to the analysis of the Lévy measure and its connection with jumps of a Lévy process.

Definition 2. *Let $(E, \mathcal{E})$ be a measurable space and m a σ-finite measure on this space. Then $(M(A), A \in \mathcal{E})$ a Poisson random measure satisfies the following conditions.*

(i) For any $A \in \mathcal{E}_0$, where

$$\mathcal{E}_0 = \{A \in \mathcal{E} : m(A) < \infty\},$$

then $M(A) = M(\omega, A)$ is a Poisson random variable on $(\Omega, \mathbb{F}, P)$ such that

$$M(A) \sim Poisson(m(A)).$$

(ii) For any $A \in \mathcal{E}/\mathcal{E}_0$ we have

$$M(A) = \infty \quad a.s.$$

(iii) If $A_1, \ldots, A_k$ are disjoint sets in $\mathcal{E}_0$, then $M(A_1), \ldots, M(A_k)$ are independent.
(iv) There is an event $\Omega_0 \in \mathbb{F}$ with $P(\Omega_0) = 1$ such that for every $\omega \in \Omega_0$, $(M(A), A \in \mathcal{E})$ is a measure.

Let C be a set in $(0, \infty) \times \mathbb{R}^d$. For a Lévy process $\{X(t), t \geq 0\}$, we define the counting process

$$N_*(C) = \#\{t > 0 : (t, \Delta X(t)) \in C\}.$$

Theorem A.1. *For any Lévy process $\{X(t), t \geq 0\}$, the jump counting measure N_* is a Poisson random measure on $(0, \infty) \times \mathbb{R}^d$ with mean measure $Leb \times v = n$, where v is the Lévy measure of $X(1)$.*

We can also write[78]

$$N_* = \sum_{\{t : \Delta X_t \neq 0\}} \delta_{(t, \Delta X_t)}. \tag{A.3}$$

Think of a Poisson random measure N_* as a point process on E: for each $A \in \mathcal{E}_0$, $N_*(A)$ can be regarded as the random number of points belonging to A, which is why N_* is also called a *counting measure*. That is, there are random elements $\{T_i\}_{i \geq 1}$ on $(\Omega, \mathbb{F}, P)$ with value on E such that

$$N_*(A) = \sum_{i=1}^{\infty} I_A(T_i).$$

Now we want to underline some properties of this random measure.

Proposition 1. *Let N be a Poisson random measure on $(E, \mathcal{E})$ with mean measure n. Let $(\tilde{E}, \tilde{\mathcal{E}})$ be another measurable space and $h : E \to \tilde{E}$ a measurable function. Then $(\tilde{N}(A), A \in \tilde{\mathcal{E}})$ is a Poisson random measure on $(\tilde{E}, \tilde{\mathcal{E}})$ with σ-finite mean measure*

$$\tilde{n} = n \circ h^{-1}$$

Corollary 1. *We assume additionally that $\tilde{N}$ is defined on a probability space rich enough to support a uniform random variable U on $(0, 1)$ independent of $\tilde{N}$, and N can be written as*

$$N = \sum_{i=1}^{\infty} I_A(T_i)$$

for random elements $\{T_i\}_{i \geq 1}$ defined on $(\Omega, \mathbb{F}, P)$ with values in $(E, \mathcal{E})$. Then there exists a sequence of random elements $\{\tilde{T}_i\}_{i \geq 1}$ defined on the same probability space as $\tilde{N}$ such that

$$\{\tilde{T}_i\}_{i \geq 1} \overset{d}{=} \{T_i\}_{i \geq 1}$$

and

$$\tilde{N} = \sum_{i=1}^{\infty} I_{\tilde{A}}(H(\tilde{T}_i)) \quad a.s.$$

---

[78]We follow the notation of Kallenberg (1997) and Rosiński (2001).

Proof. See Corollary 5.11 in Kallenberg (1997).

Theorem A.2 (Lévy-Itô decomposition). *Let X be a Lévy process and ν the Lévy measure of X. Then X has a decomposition*

$$X_t = W_t + at + \int_{|x|<1} x(N_t(\cdot, dx) - t\nu(dx)) + \sum_{0<s\leq t} \Delta X_s I_{\{|\Delta X_s| \geq 1\}},$$

where $(W_t)_{t\geq 0}$ is Brownian motion; for any set Λ, $0 \notin \bar{\Lambda}$, $N_t^\Lambda = \int_\Lambda N_t(\cdot, dx)$ is a Poisson process independent of $(W_t)_{t\geq 0}$; N_t^Λ is independent of N_t^Γ if Λ and Γ are independent and N_t^Λ has parameter $\nu(\Lambda)$.

From Theorem A.2 it follows that a Lévy process X can be write as a sum:

$$X = X(1) + X(2) + X(3),$$

where $X(1)$ is a scaled Brownian motion with drift, $X(2)$ is a square integrable martingale with an almost surely countable number of jumps on each finite time interval, which are of magnitude less than unity, and $X(3)$ is a compound Poisson process.

REFERENCES

Abramowitz, M. & Stegun, I. (1974). *Handbook of mathematical functions, with formulas, graphs, and mathematical tables.* New York: Dover.

Asmussen, S. & Glynn, P. (2007). *Stochastic simulation: Algorithms and analysis.* Berlin: Springer.

Asmussen, S. & Rosiński, J. (2001). Approximations of small jumps of Lévy processes with a view towards simulation. *Journal of Applied Probability*, 38(2), 482–493.

Asmussen, S. & Rosiński, J. (2003). On error rates in normal approximations and simulation schemes for Lévy processes. *Stochastic Models*, 19(3), 287–298.

Barone-Adesi, G., Engle, R., & Mancini, L. (2008). A GARCH option pricing model with filtered historical simulation. *Review of Financial Studies*, 21(3), 1223–1258.

Barone-Adesi, G., Giannopoulos, K., & Vosper, L. (1999). VaR without correlations for portfolios of derivative securities. *Journal of Futures Markets*, 19(5), 583–602.

Barraquand, J. (1995). Numerical valuation of high dimensional multivariate European securities. *Management Science*, 41(12), 1882–1891.

Bartholomew-Biggs, M. (2005). *Nonlinear optimization with financial applications.* Dordrecht: Kluwer.

Berman, M. (1971). Generating gamma distributed variates for computer simulation models. Technical report r-641-pr, Rand Corporation.

Bianchi, M. L., Rachev, S. T., Kim, Y. S., & Fabozzi, F. J. (2010a). Tempered infinitely divisible distributions and processes. *Theory of Probability and Its Applications (TVP), Society for Industrial and Applied Mathematics (SIAM),* 55(1), 59–86.

Bianchi, M. L., Rachev, S. T., Kim, Y. S., & Fabozzi, F. J. (2010b). Tempered stable distributions and processes in finance: Numerical analysis. In M. Corazza and C. Pizzi (Eds.), *Mathematical and statistical methods for actuarial sciences and finance.* New York: Springer, 2010b.

Bollerslev, T. (1987). A conditionally heteroskedastic time series model for speculative prices and rates of return. *Review of Economics and Statistics,* 69(3), 542–547.

Bollerslev, T. (1995). Generalized autoregressive conditional heteroskedasticity. In R. Engle (Ed.), *ARCH: Selected readings.* Oxford: Oxford University Press.

Carr, P. & Madan, D. (1999). Option valuation using the fast Fourier transform. *Journal of Computational Finance,* 2(4), 61–73.

Carr, P. & Wu, L. (2004). Time-changed Lévy processes and option pricing. *Journal of Financial Economics,* 71(1), 113–141.

Cont, R. & Tankov, P. (2004). *Financial modelling with jump processes.* Boca Raton, FL.: CRC Press.

De Giovanni, D., Ortobelli, S., & Rachev, S. (2008). Delta hedging strategies comparison. *European Journal of Operational Research,* 185(3), 1615–1631.

Devroye, L. (1986a). An automatic method for generating random variates with a given characteristic function. *SIAM Journal on Applied Mathematics,* 46(4), 698–719.

Devroye, L. (1986b). *Non-uniform random variate generation.* New York: Springer.

Duan, J. & Simonato, J. (1998). Empirical martingale simulation for asset prices. *Management Science,* 44(9), 1218–1233.

Fishman, G. (1996). *Monte Carlo: Concepts, algorithms, and applications.* New York: Springer.

Geman, H., Madan, D., & Yor, M. (2001). Time changes for Lévy processes. *Mathematical Finance,* 11(1), 79–96.

Geman, H., Madan, D., & Yor, M. (2002). Stochastic volatility, jumps and hidden time changes. *Finance and Stochastics,* 6(1), 63–90.

Gentle, J. (2003). *Random number generation and Monte Carlo methods.* Berlin: Springer.

Glasserman, P. (2004). *Monte Carlo methods in financial engineering.* Berlin: Springer.

Heston, S. & Nandi, S. (2000). A closed-form GARCH option valuation model. *Review of Financial Studies,* 13(3), 585–625.

Hurst, S., Platen, E., & Rachev, S. (1997). Subordinated market index models: A comparison. *Asia-Pacific Financial Markets,* 4(2), 97–124.

Hurst, S., Platen, E., & Rachev, S. (1999). Option pricing for a logstable asset price model. *Mathematical and Computer Modelling, 29*(10), 105–119.

Janicki, A. & Weron, A. (1994). *Simulation and chaotic behavior of α-stable stochastic processes.* New York: Marcel Dekker.

Jöhnk, M. (1964). Erzeugung von betaverteilten und gammaverteilten Zufallszahlen. *Metrika, 8*(1), 5–15.

Kallenberg, O. (1997). *Foundations of modern probability.* Berlin: Springer.

Kawai, R. (2006). An importance sampling method based on the density transformation of Lévy processes. *Monte Carlo Methods and Applications, 12*(2), 171–186.

Kim, Y., Rachev, S., Bianchi, M., & Fabozzi, F. (2008). A new tempered stable distribution and its application to finance. In G. Bol, S. T. Rachev, & R. Wuerth (Eds.), *Risk assessment: Decisions in banking and finance* (pp. 51–84). Heidelberg: Springer.

Küchler, U. & Tappe, S. (2008). Bilateral gamma distributions and processes in financial mathematics. *Stochastic Processes and their Applications, 118*(2), 261–283.

LePage, R. (1981). Multidimensional infinitely divisible variables and processes: Part II. *Lecture Notes in Mathematics, 860,* 279–284.

Letta, G. (1993). *Probabilitá elementare.* Bologna: Zanichelli.

Madan, D. & Yor, M. (2006). CGMY and Meixner subordinators are absolutely continuous with respect to one sided stable subordinators. Retrieved from http://arxiv.org/abs/math/0601173.

Marinelli, C., Rachev, S., Roll, R., & Goppl, H. (2000). Subordinated stock price models: Heavy tails and long range dependence in the high frequency Deutsche Bank price record. In G. Bol, G. Nakhaeizadeh, & K. Vollmer (Eds.), *Datamining and computational finance.* Heidelberg: Physica-Verlag, Springer.

Marsaglia, G. & Tsang, W. (1998). The Monty Python method for generating random variables. *ACM Transactions on Mathematical Software, 24*(3), 341–350.

Marsaglia, G. & Tsang, W. (2000). The ziggurat method for generating random variables. *Journal of Statistical Software, 5*(8), 1–7.

Menn, C. & Rachev, S. (2005). A GARCH option pricing model with α-stable innovations. *European Journal of Operational Research, 163*(1), 201–209.

Monroe, I. (1978). Processes that can be embedded in Brownian motion. *Annals of Probability, 6*(1), 42–56.

Nolan, J. (2007). Bibliography on stable distributions, processes and related topics. Retrieved from http://academic2.american.edu/~jpnolan/stable/Stable Bibliography.pdf.

Obloj, J. (2004). The Skorokhod embedding problem and its offspring. *Probability Surveys, 1,* 321–392.

Poirot, J. & Tankov, P. (2006). Monte Carlo option pricing for tempered stable (CGMY) processes. *Asia-Pacific Financial Markets, 13*(4), 327–344.

Rachev, S., Mittnik, S., Fabozzi, F., Focardi, S., & Jašić, T. (2007). *Financial econometrics: From basics to advanced modeling techniques.* Hoboken, NJ: John Wiley & Sons.

Rajput, B. & Rosiński, J. (1989). Spectral representations of infinitely divisible processes. *Probability Theory and Related Fields*, 82(3), 451–487.

Rosiński, J. (2001). Series representations of Lévy processes from the perspective of point processes. In O. Barndorff-Nielsen, T. Mikosch, & S. Resnick (Eds.), *Lévy processes: Theory and applications* (pp. 401–415). Boston: Birkhäuser.

Rosiński, J. (2007a). Simulation of Lévy processes. In F. Ruggeri, R. Kenett, & F. Faltin (Eds.), *Encyclopedia of statistics in quality and reliability: Computationally intensive methods and simulation*. Hoboken NJ: John Wiley & Sons.

Rosiński, J. (2007b). Tempering stable processes. *Stochastic Processes and Their Applications*, 117(6), 677–707.

Samorodnitsky, G. & Taqqu, M. (1994). *Stable non-Gaussian random processes: Stochastic models with infinite variance*. Boca Raton, FL: CRC Press.

Sato, K. (1999). *Lévy processes and infinitely divisible distributions*. Cambridge: Cambridge University Press.

Tricomi, F. (1954). *Funzioni ipergeometriche confluenti*. Rome: Edizioni Cremonese.

Von Neumann, J. (1951). *Various techniques used in connection with random digits*. NBS Applied Mathematics Series 12. Washington, DC: National Bureau of Standards.

Weron, R. (1996). On the Chambers-Mallows-Stuck method for simulating skewed stable random variables. *Statistics and Probability Letters*, 28(2), 165–171.

Zolotarev, V. (1986). *One-dimensional stable distributions*. Transl. from the Russian by H. H. McFaden, ed. by B. Silver. Translations of Mathematical Monographs, 65. Providence, RI: American Mathematical Society.

CHAPTER 9

Multi-Tail *t*-Distribution

9.1 INTRODUCTION

As explained in Chapter 1, the preponderance of empirical evidence finds that return distributions are not normally distributed. Despite this evidence, non-normal multivariate modeling of asset returns does not appear to play an important role in asset management or risk management because of the complexity of estimating multivariate non-normal distributions from market return data.

In this chapter, we consider a multivariate distribution capable of explaining the tail dependence among assets traded in financial markets. In particular, we describe a subclass of generalized elliptical distributions for stock returns that is sufficiently user friendly so that it can be utilized by asset managers and risk managers for modeling multivariate non-normal distributions of asset returns.[1] For the distribution we present, which we refer to as the *multi-tail generalized elliptical distribution*, we derive its densities using results from the theory of generalized elliptical distributions and introduce a function that we label the tail function to describe its tail behavior. We test the model on German stock returns included in the DAX 30 index and find that (1) the multi-tail model significantly outperforms the classical elliptical model and (2) the hypothesis of homogeneous tail behavior can be rejected.

Several models have been proposed to model multivariate heavy-tailed return data. Rachev and Mittnik (2000) suggest multivariate α-stable distributions to model multivariate asset returns because such distributions (1) are a natural extension of the normal distribution in terms of the generalized Central Limit Theorem and (2) allow the modeling of the rich dependence

---

[1]This chapter is drawn from Kring et al. (2009) and uses more recent data for the empirical analysis.

structure of asset returns. In addition, they proposed the generalized hyperbolic distribution[2] and the multivariate t-distributions[3] for modeling asset returns in order to explain these empirical findings of stock market returns.

A stylized fact that has been observed in equity prices is that extreme price declines are often joint extremes, in the sense that a large price decline for the stock of one company is accompanied by a simultaneously large price drop for the stock of other companies.[4] This stylized fact can be captured by choosing distributions in multivariate models that allow for so-called tail dependence. While with the covariance one can only capture a linear dependence structure, tail dependence can be assessed by considering particular multivariate distributions that enhance the widely used multivariate normal distribution. Heavy-tailed elliptical distributions exhibit tail dependence and, in the case of elliptical distributions, this property has been extensively studied.[5] Elliptical distributions, such as t-distributions, symmetric generalized hyperbolic distributions, and α-stable sub-Gaussian distributions, are radial symmetric.[6] Empirical studies report that the lower tail dependence is often much stronger than the upper tail dependence. This property, however, cannot be captured by elliptical distributions because of their radial symmetry. Skew-elliptical distributions are a generalization of elliptical distributions that might be capable of capturing this behavior observed for asset returns in financial markets. Frahm (2004) introduces generalized elliptical distributions by assuming that the radial and spherical component of an elliptical distribution are not independent. Frahm's approach simplifies the modeling of stylized facts of multivariate financial time series.

These well-documented findings reported for asset returns are not mere academic conclusions that hold little interest for practitioners. Rather they have important implications for asset managers and risk managers. Not properly accounting for these stylized facts can result in models that produce inferior investment performance by asset managers and disastrous financial consequences for financial institutions that rely upon them for risk management. Discussions with practitioners as to why models that can deal with these stylized facts are not used in practice suggest that it is due to the complexity of estimating the non-normal multivariate models proposed in the literature.

---

[2]See Eberlein and Keller (1995) and Eberlein et al. (1998).
[3]See Kotz and Nadarajah (2004).
[4]This empirical finding is analyzed in McNeil et al. (2005).
[5]See Schmidt (2002) and Hult and Lindskog (2002).
[6]See Fang et al. (1990).

Accordingly, our purpose in this chapter is to introduce a flexible model for dealing with these stylized facts, but, at the same time, a model that is relatively easy for a practitioner to estimate. This is accomplished by introducing a subclass of generalized elliptical distributions characterized by a tail parameter that depends on the direction. The particular form for the function of the tail parameter is motivated by the fact that we want to use information given by the principal component analysis applied to asset returns. The way in which we construct the tail function provides (1) an economic justification for our model and (2) a feasible estimation algorithm. Furthermore, the stochastic representation allows a practitioner to easily simulate random variates from the distribution and to consider it in models for risk management.

The focus of this chapter is that tail dependence among stock returns is modeled through a tail function whose value depends on the direction. Furthermore, from a practical perspective, we derive a flexible model that is simple to estimate and simulate, and competitive with the generalized hyperbolic framework.

This chapter is organized as follows. In section 9.2, we describe the well-known principal component analysis. Then we introduce the multi-tail t-distribution and derive its basic properties. In section 9.3, we develop a three-step procedure to estimate the parameters of a multi-tail t–random vector. Application of a multi-tail generalized elliptical model to return data is provided in section 9.4, followed by a summary of our findings in section 9.5.

9.2 PRINCIPAL COMPONENT ANALYSIS

The principal component analysis (PCA) is a statistical procedure to implement a dimensionality reduction in linear factors models.[7] Assume that we have N different stock returns: A portfolio can be viewed as a linear combination of different stocks. Suppose now that only k portfolios have a significant variance, while the remaining $N - k$ have very small variances. We can then implement a dimensionality reduction by choosing only those portfolios whose variance is significantly different from zero. By doing so, each stock return can be approximated by a linear combination of these k high variance portfolios plus a random error. These maximum variance portfolios can be found by diagonalizing either the variance-covariance

---

[7]See Chapter 13 in Rachev et al. (2007) for a review of principal component analysis.

matrix or the correlation matrix. It can be proved that the kth eigenvectors with greater eigenvalues represent portfolios with greatest variance. In the following we will explain an application of this algorithm to find the tail parameter of a multi-tail t-distribution.

9.2.1 Principal Component Tail Functions

We begin by reviewing the definition of a multi-tail generalized elliptical random vector.[8] Let $S \in \mathbb{R}^d$ be a uniformly distributed random vector on the unit hypersphere $\mathcal{S}^{d-1}$, I an interval of tail parameters, and $(R_\alpha)_{\alpha \in I}$ a family of positive random variables with tail parameter $\alpha > 0$. The random vector

$$X = (X_1, X_2, \ldots, X_d)' \in \mathbb{R}^d$$

has a multi-tail generalized elliptical distribution, if X satisfies

$$X \stackrel{d}{=} \mu + R_{\alpha(s(AS))} AS, \tag{9.1}$$

where $A \in \mathbb{R}^{d \times d}$ is an invertible matrix, μ a location parameter, and $\alpha : \mathcal{S}^{d-1} \to I$ a function.

We call the function $\alpha : \mathcal{S}^{d-1} \to I$ the *tail function of a multi-tail generalized elliptical distribution*. In the following we introduce tail functions based on the principal components of the dispersion matrix $\Sigma = AA'$ of the multi-tail generalized elliptical random vector given by equation (9.1). By taking into consideration the approach of Frahm (2004), we will construct a tail index of a multivariate random variable that depends on directionality. We denote eigenvector-eigenvalue pairs of the dispersion matrix $\Sigma = AA'$ of a multi-tail t random vector with[9]

$$(v_1, \lambda_1), (v_2, \lambda_2), \ldots, (v_d, \lambda_d),$$

where

$$\lambda_1 \geq \lambda_2 \ldots \geq \lambda_d > 0$$

---

[8]See Kring et al. (2009).
[9]We indicate with $\langle \cdot, \cdot \rangle$ the scalar product and with $\| \cdot \|$ the norm; A' indicates the transpose of the matrix A.

and

$$||v_1|| = \ldots = ||v_d|| = 1.$$

We see in section 9.3 that we can estimate Σ without knowing the tail function. This is, of course, important in applications.

Let $X \in \mathbb{R}^d$ be a multi-tail t random vector with dispersion matrix $\Sigma \in \mathbb{R}^{d \times d}$, and $\mathcal{S}^{d-1}$ be a d-dimensional unit sphere in $\mathbb{R}^d$. We call the tail function $\alpha : \mathcal{S}^{d-1} \to I$ of X a *principal component tail function* (pc-tail function) if it is of the form

$$\alpha(s) = \sum_{i=1}^{d} \left(w_i^+(\langle s, v_i \rangle) \alpha_i^+ + w_i^-(\langle s, v_i \rangle) \alpha_i^- \right),$$

where $s \in \mathcal{S}^{d-1}$, $w_i^+, w_i^- : [-1, 1] \to [0, 1]$, $i = 1, \ldots, d$, with weighting functions satisfying

$$\sum_{i=1}^{d} \left(w_i^+(\langle s, v_i \rangle) + w_i^-(\langle s, v_i \rangle) \right) = 1$$

and $w_i^+(0) = w_i^-(0) = 0$. Note that for all pc-tail functions α we have $\alpha(s) \in I$, $s \in \mathcal{S}^{d-1}$ since I is an interval and $\alpha(s)$ can be interpreted as a convex combination of $\alpha_i^-, \alpha_i^+ \in I$, $i = 1, \ldots, d$.

The tail parameter of X in direction $s(X - \mu)$ is $\alpha(s(X - \mu))$.[10] This means that the tail parameters for the direction v_i are

$$\alpha(v_i) = w_i^+(1) \alpha_i^+ + w_i^-(1) \alpha_i^-, \quad i = 1, \ldots, d,$$

and for the direction $-v_i$

$$\alpha(-v_i) = w_i^+(-1) \alpha_i^+ + w_i^-(-1) \alpha_i^-, \quad i = 1, \ldots, d.$$

For any other direction $s \in \mathcal{S}^{d-1}$, we have the tail parameter

$$\alpha(s) = \sum_{i=1}^{d} \left(w_i^+(\langle s, v_i \rangle) \alpha_i^+ + w_i^-(\langle s, v_i \rangle) \alpha_i^- \right).$$

---

[10]The function $s : \mathbb{R}^d \to \mathcal{S}^{d-1}$ projects a vector x on the unit sphere, that is $s(x) = x/||x|| \in \mathcal{S}^{d-1}$.

The general idea behind the pc-tail function is that the tail parameter of a direction s is a weighted sum of the tail parameters α_i^+ and α_i^-. The weights are determined by the scalar product $\langle s, v_i \rangle$ and weighting functions w_i^- and w_i^+, $i = 1, \ldots, d$. We capture the phenomenon that in different areas, in particular cones around the principal components, the distribution of the asset returns has different tail parameters according to the discussion in section 9.1.

In the following, we give two examples of the pc-tail functions. The first pc-tail function $\alpha_1 : \mathcal{S}^{d-1} \to I$ is given by

$$\alpha_1(s) = \sum_{i=1}^{d} \langle s, v_i \rangle^2 \alpha_i$$

with weighting functions $w_i^+(\langle s, v_i \rangle) = w_i^-(\langle s, v_i \rangle) = \frac{1}{2}\langle s, v_i \rangle^2$ for all $i = 1, \ldots, d$. This tail function assigns to every principal component a tail parameter α_i, $i = 1, \ldots, d$. In particular, we have $\alpha(v_i) = \alpha(-v_i) = \alpha_i$ for $i = 1, \ldots, d$. In any other direction $s \in \mathcal{S}^{d-1}$ $\alpha(s)$ is a convex combination of the tail parameters α_i. In fact, $\alpha_1(.)$ is a pc-tail function since we have for all $s \in \mathcal{S}^{d-1}$

$$\sum_{i=1}^{d} \frac{1}{2}\langle s, v_i \rangle^2 + \frac{1}{2}\langle s, v_i \rangle^2 = \sum_{i=1}^{d}\langle s, v_i \rangle^2 = \langle s, \sum_{i=1}^{d}\langle s, v_i \rangle v_i \rangle$$

$$= \langle s, s \rangle = 1.$$

A refinement of the pc-tail function $\alpha_1(.)$ is the pc-tail function given by

$$\alpha_2(s) = \sum_{i=1}^{d} \langle u, v_i \rangle^2 I_{(0,\infty)}(\langle u, v_i \rangle)\alpha_i^+$$

$$+ \sum_{i=1}^{d} \langle u, v_i \rangle^2 I_{(-\infty,0)}(\langle u, v_i \rangle)\alpha_i^-,$$

which allows for different tail parameters for each direction and thus for asymmetry. It is a tail function since we have

$$\sum_{i=1}^{d} \left(\langle s, v_i \rangle^2 I_{(0,\infty)}(\langle s, v_i \rangle) + \langle s, v_i \rangle^2 I_{(-\infty,0)}(\langle s, v_i \rangle) \right) = 1. \tag{9.2}$$

9.2.2 Density of Multi-Tail *t* Random Variable

We can take into consideration a specific parametric example in the class of multi-tail generalized elliptical random vectors by slightly modifying a t random vector. A tail parameter which, depending on the direction, is considered and the random vector so constructed is called *multi-tail t random vector*.

Starting from the density of a t-distribution, one can derive the corresponding density of a multi-tail t-distribution. The density of a t distributed random vector Y is given by

$$
f_Y(x) = \frac{\Gamma(\frac{1}{2}(\nu + d))}{\Gamma(\frac{1}{2}\nu)(\pi\nu)^{d/2} \det(c\Sigma_0)^{1/2}} \left(1 + \frac{(x - \mu)'(c\Sigma_0)^{-1}(x - \mu)}{\nu}\right)^{-(\nu+d)/2},
$$

where $\nu > 0$ is the tail parameter, $c > 0$ is a scaling parameter, and Σ_0 is the normalized dispersion matrix. We discuss this issue more thoroughly and introduce normalization criteria for a dispersion matrix Σ in section 9.3.

As in the classical elliptical case, the dispersion matrix of a multi-tail generalized elliptical distribution is only determined up to a scaling constant, hence we have to normalize it. We denote the normalized dispersion matrix by Σ_0. The corresponding density of a multi-tail t-distribution is

$$
f_X(x) = \frac{\Gamma(\frac{1}{2}(\nu(s(x - \mu)) + d))}{\Gamma(\frac{1}{2}\nu(s(x - \mu)))(\pi\nu(s(x - \mu)))^{d/2} \det(c\Sigma_0)^{1/2}}
$$

$$
\cdot \left(1 + \frac{(x - \mu)'(c\Sigma_0)^{-1}(x - \mu)}{\nu(s(x - \mu))}\right)^{-(\nu(s(x-\mu))+d)/2}, \tag{9.3}
$$

where $\nu : \mathcal{S}^{d-1} \to (0, \infty)$ is a tail function, Σ_0 is the normalized dispersion matrix, $c > 0$ is a scaling parameter, and $\mu \in \mathbb{R}^d$ is a location parameter.[11]

Summing up, the matrix Σ determines the elliptical shape of the distribution around the mean while the influence of the tail functions increases in the tails of a multi-tail t-distribution.

---

[11] A similar extension of the multivariate t-distribution can be found in Frahm (2004), p. 54.

9.3   ESTIMATING PARAMETERS

In this section, we present a three-step procedure to estimate the parameters of a multi-tail t random vector X.

In the first step, we estimate the location vector $\mu \in \mathbb{R}^d$ with some robust method.[12] In the second step, we estimate the dispersion matrix $\Sigma \in \mathbb{R}^{d \times d}$ up to a scaling constant $c > 0$. In the third step, we estimate the scaling constant c and the tail function $\alpha(.)$, applying the maximum likelihood method. Since we have an analytic expression for the density of a multi-tail t-distribution, we could in principle estimate all parameters in a single optimization step. But this approach is not recommended, at least in higher dimensions, because it leads to an extremely complex optimization problem since one has to estimate in one run the dispersion matrix, and pc-tail function parameter, together with the location and scale parameters.

As in the classical elliptical case,[13] a dispersion matrix of a multi-tail t random vector is only determined up to a scaling constant $c > 0$. Hence we have to normalize it. If second moments exist, one can normalize the dispersion matrix by the covariance matrix. In general, the following normalization schemes are always applicable:

$$\text{(i)} \ \Sigma_{11} = 1 \quad \text{(ii)} \ \det(\Sigma) = 1 \quad \text{(iii)} \ \text{tr}(\Sigma) = 1, \quad (9.4)$$

even though second moments do not exist. For the remainder of this section, we denote a normalized dispersion matrix by Σ_0.

In the third step, we have to estimate the scale parameter c and the tail function $\alpha(.)$. Since we assume a pc-tail function, we have to evaluate the tail parameters $(\alpha_1, \ldots, \alpha_k) \in I^k$, $k \in \mathbb{N}$, of the pc-tail function. In Step 3 we also determine the parameters from the set $\Theta = \mathbb{R}_+ \times I^k$, where I is the interval of tail parameters.

We summarize the three-step estimation procedure for multi-tail distribution estimation as follows:

Step 1. Estimate the location vector $\mu \in \mathbb{R}^d$.

Step 2. Select a normalization of the dispersion matrix according to one of the schemes in (9.4) and then estimate it as described next in section 9.3.1.

Step 3. Estimate the tail function and the scale parameter c by using a maximum likelihood approach as described below in section 9.3.2.

---

[12] See Frahm (2004) for more details.
[13] See McNeil et al. (2005).

9.3.1 Estimation of the Dispersion Matrix

In order to estimate the dispersion matrix of a generalized elliptical distribution, we use the so-called spectral estimator based on the work of Tyler.[14] Furthermore, we assume the location parameter to be known. The next algorithm shows how to apply the spectral estimator to the multi-tail *t*-distribution.

Let $X_1, \ldots, X_n$ be a sample of identically distributed multi-tail *t* data vectors with $n \rangle d$. Then a fix point $\hat{\Sigma}$ of the equation

$$\hat{\Sigma} = \frac{d}{n} \sum_{i=1}^{n} \frac{(X_i - \mu)(X_i - \mu)'}{(X_i - \mu)' \hat{\Sigma}^{-1}(X_i - \mu)}$$

exists and it is unique up to a scale parameter. In particular, the sequence $(\tilde{\Sigma}^{(i)})_{i \in \mathbb{N}}$ defined by

$$\tilde{\Sigma}^{(0)} = \mathrm{Id}$$

$$\tilde{\Sigma}^{(i+1)} = \frac{d}{n} \sum_{i-1}^{n} \frac{(X_i - \mu)'(X_i - \mu)}{(X_i - \mu)'(\tilde{\Sigma}^{(i)})^{-1}(X_i - \mu)} \tag{9.5}$$

converges almost surely to the maximum likelihood (ML) estimator $\hat{\Sigma}$.

In order to estimate a normalized version of the dispersion matrix of a multi-tail generalized elliptical random vector, we apply this iterative scheme *k*-times (*k* sufficiently large) and normalize $\tilde{\Sigma}^{(k)}$ through one of the schemes given in equation (9.4).

9.3.2 Estimation of the Parameter Set Θ

We assume that we have already estimated the location parameter μ and the normalized dispersion matrix Σ_0. Note that we cannot estimate *c* in the second step because in that step the dispersion matrix Σ can only be determined up to this scale parameter. Since we assume $\alpha(.)$ to be a pc-tail function (see section 9.2.1), it can be determined by the tail parameters $(\alpha_1, \ldots, \alpha_k) \in I^k$, $k \in \mathbb{N}$. Hence, we have to estimate $(c, \alpha_1, \alpha_2, \ldots, \alpha_k) \in \mathbb{R}_+ \times I^k = \Theta$. In the following, we present a method to estimate the parameters $(c, \alpha_1, \ldots, \alpha_k) \in \Theta$.

The density generator ML-approach uses directly the density f_X of a multi-tail *t* random vector. Denoting by *g* the density of a *t* random variable

---

[14]See Frahm (2004).

with tail parameter α, we know that the density satisfies

$$f_X(x) = |\det(c^2\Sigma_0)|^{-1/2} g_{\alpha(s(x-\mu))}((x-\mu)'(c^2\Sigma_0)^{-1}(x-\mu)).$$

Since we assume Σ_0 and μ are known, we obtain the following log-likelihood function

$$\log\left(\prod_{i=1}^{n} f_X(X_i)\right) = \sum_{i=1}^{n} \log f_X(X_i) = -dn\log(c) - \frac{n}{2}\log(\det(\Sigma_0))$$

$$+ \sum_{i=1}^{n} \log\left(g_{\alpha(s(X_i-\mu))}\left(\frac{(X_i-\mu)'\Sigma_0^{-1}(X_i-\mu)}{c^2}\right)\right)$$

Since the term $-\frac{n}{2}\log(\det(\Sigma_0))$ is a constant subject to Θ, we can neglect this term in the optimization problem. Thus, we obtain the following log-likelihood optimization problem

$$\hat{\theta} = \text{argmax}_{\theta\in\Theta} -dn\log(c) + \sum_{i=1}^{n} \log\left(g_{\alpha(s(X_i-\mu))}\left(\frac{(X_i-\mu)\Sigma_0^{-1}(X_i-\mu)}{c^2}\right)\right).$$

$$(9.6)$$

Statistical Analysis   For an empirical assessment of the estimation algorithm described above, we simulate samples from a multi-tail t-distribution. Random samples from a multi-tail t-distribution can be easily drawn from the stochastic representation in equation (9.1). In particular, we choose the location parameter μ to be $(0, 0)'$ and the dispersion matrix Σ to be

$$\Sigma = \begin{pmatrix} 2 & 1 \\ 1 & 2 \end{pmatrix}.$$

We choose a tail function $\alpha(.)$ of the following structure

$$\alpha(s) = \langle s, F_1\rangle^2 \cdot 3 + \langle s, F_2\rangle^2 \cdot 6,$$

where $F_1 = s((1, 1)')$ and $F_2 = s((1, -1)')$ are the first two principal components of Σ. We assume that the scaling parameter $c^2 = 2$, the first tail parameter $v_1 = 3$, and the second tail parameter $v_2 = 6$. Thus we have that

TABLE 9.1 Quantiles of the Estimators c^2, $\hat{v}_1$, and $\hat{v}_2$ for Different Sample Sizes per Estimate and the Corresponding Relative Errors

Size	$q_{0.05}$	$q_{0.1}$	$q_{0.25}$	$q_{0.5}$	$q_{0.75}$	$q_{0.9}$	$q_{0.95}$	$e_{rel}^{0.5}$	$e_{rel}^{0.9}$
				$\hat{c}^2$					
100	1.564	1.660	1.838	2.030	2.297	2.550	2.701	14%	35%
250	1.665	1.734	1.868	2.011	2.164	2.313	2.413	8.2%	20%
500	1.774	1.819	1.904	2.008	2.117	2.231	2.301	5.8%	15%
1,000	1.820	1.862	1.930	2.000	2.074	2.137	2.173	3.7%	8.6%
3,000	1.896	1.917	1.959	2.001	2.046	2.086	2.112	2.3%	5.6%
6,000	1.928	1.943	1.972	2.000	2.031	2.058	2.077	1.5%	3.8%
				$\hat{v}_1$					
100	1.784	1.997	2.431	3.133	4.165	5.975	7.932	38%	164%
250	2.081	2.252	2.584	2.976	3.594	4.318	4.896	19%	63%
500	2.372	2.477	2.699	3.039	3.412	3.815	4.140	13%	38%
1,000	2.494	2.604	2.790	3.008	3.264	3.490	3.607	8.8%	20%
3,000	2.704	2.769	2.877	3.012	3.164	3.290	3.393	5.4%	13%
6,000	2.783	2.825	2.899	3.000	3.101	3.197	3.256	3.3%	8.5%
				$\hat{v}_2$					
100	2.880	3.404	4.493	6.650	11.00	19.69	20.00	83%	233%
250	3.547	4.009	4.889	6.256	8.391	11.09	13.37	39%	122%
500	4.182	4.555	5.178	6.155	7.498	9.056	10.65	24%	77%
1,000	4.615	4.845	5.294	6.005	6.820	7.744	8.234	13%	37%
3,000	5.099	5.267	5.585	6.001	6.436	6.875	7.181	7.2%	19%
6,000	5.293	5.461	5.713	6.000	6.327	6.614	6.815	5.4%	13%

the dispersion matrix up to a scaling constant is

$$\Sigma_0 = \begin{pmatrix} 1 & 0.5 \\ 0.5 & 1 \end{pmatrix}.$$

Since we know the density of multi-tail t-distribution, we apply the density generator ML-approach to estimate these parameters from simulated data.

In Table 9.1 we report the quantiles of the empirical distributions and the relative error of the estimators $\hat{c}^2$, $\hat{v}_1$, and $\hat{v}_2$ and in Figure 9.1 we show the boxplots of their empirical distribution. The relative error is defined by

$$e_{rel}^{1-\alpha} = \max\left\{ \left| \frac{q_{\alpha/2} - c}{c} \right|, \left| \frac{q_{1-\alpha/2} - c}{c} \right| \right\}. \tag{9.7}$$

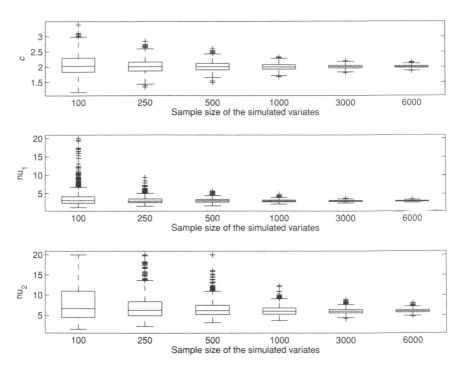

FIGURE 9.1 Boxplots of the Estimate of $\hat{c}^2$, $\hat{v}_1$ and $\hat{v}_2$ (Each boxplot consists of 1,000 estimates.)

and it means the relative error of the estimator is smaller than $e_{rel}^{1-\alpha}$ with probability $1 - \alpha$ measured by the empirical distribution of the estimator.

We observe that medians are close to the corresponding true values. The empirical distributions of $\hat{c}^2$, $\hat{v}_1$, and $\hat{v}_2$ are skewed to the left for small sample sizes and become more symmetric for large sample size per estimate. The accuracy of the estimator $\hat{c}^2$ is higher than the one of $\hat{v}_1$ and the one of $\hat{v}_1$ is higher than the one of $\hat{v}_2$ compared to the relative errors of Table 9.1 and Figure 9.1. It is not surprising that $\hat{c}^2$ performs better than both $\hat{v}_1$ and $\hat{v}_2$ since the parameters v_1 and v_2 determine the tail behavior of the distribution, and naturally we do not have many observations in the tails. In particular, the accuracy of $\hat{v}_1$ and especially $\hat{v}_2$ is very poor for small sample sizes per estimate (i.e., sample size less than 1,000). For reliable estimates, we need at least a sample size of 3,000 because of the relative error $e_{rel}^{0.9}$ reported in Table 9.1.

9.4 EMPIRICAL RESULTS

To empirically investigate the multi-tail generalized elliptical distribution, we used the daily logarithmic return series for all German stocks included in the DAX on June 30, 2009. The period covered is February 5, 2001[15] through June 30, 2009 (2,135 daily observations for each stock). In particular, the main focus of our analysis is to empirically assess whether a multi-tail model is superior to a classical elliptical one in the analysis of asset-return behavior. In the statistical analysis, we assume that the return series are stationary. Our intention is to estimate the unconditional multivariate distribution of the asset returns. We assume an unconditional model, thus a ML estimation is performed. It is a well-known result that ML-estimators are consistent for the parameters of a stationary distribution but statistical inference cannot be applied when the data are serially dependent. The model does not capture the serial dependence of the data since we consider stationary time series.[16]

9.4.1 Comparison to Other Models

We compare the multi-tail generalized elliptical model to the multivariate normal distribution, and to the multivariate generalized hyperbolic (GH) distribution.[17] We select these multivariate distributions for two reasons: (1) They are simple to estimate and (2) they are simple to simulate since there exists a suitable stochastic representation. The normal distribution is widely used in the industry, while the GH distribution is a well-known example of a non-normal distribution applied to model stock returns (see Prause, 1999).

The density of a multivariate normal distribution with mean $\mu \in \mathbb{R}^d$ and covariance matrix $\Sigma \in \mathbb{R}^{d \times d}$ is given by

$$f(x) = \frac{1}{(2\pi)^{d/2}|\Sigma|^{1/2}} e^{(x-\mu)'\Sigma^{-1}(x-\mu)} \quad x \in \mathbb{R}^d, \tag{9.8}$$

and a ML estimation can be easily computed because the following holds

$$\mu = E(X) \quad \text{and} \quad \Sigma = cov(X),$$

where we refer to cov as the covariance matrix.

---

[15]On February 2, 2001, the Deutsche Boerse (with ticker DB1) stock was listed on the DAX, while all other 29 stocks were already listed on the index.

[16]For a discussion of conditional and unconditional financial time-series modeling, see McNeil et al. (2005).

[17]For more information about these two examples of multivariate distributions, see McNeil et al. (2005).

The generalized hyperbolic density is given by

$$f(x) = c \frac{K_{\lambda-(d/2)}\left(\sqrt{(\chi + (x-\mu)'\Sigma^{-1}(x-\mu))(\phi + \gamma'\Sigma^{-1}\gamma)}\right) e^{(x-\mu)'\Sigma^{-1}\gamma}}{\left(\sqrt{(\chi + (x-\mu)'\Sigma^{-1}(x-\mu))(\phi + \gamma'\Sigma^{-1}\gamma)}\right)^{(d/2)-\lambda}},$$

where the normalizing constant is

$$c = \frac{(\sqrt{\chi\psi})^{-\lambda}\psi^{\lambda}(\psi + \gamma'\Sigma^{-1}\gamma)^{(d/2)-\lambda}}{(2\pi)^{d/2} \det \Sigma^{1/2} K_{\lambda}(\sqrt{\chi\psi})}$$

and $K_.(.)$ is a modified Bessel function of the third kind. The parameters satisfy $\chi > 0, \psi \geq 0$ if $\lambda < 0$; $\chi > 0, \psi > 0$ if $\lambda = 0$; and $\chi \geq 0, \psi > 0$ if $\lambda > 0$. We choose the GH distribution since it covers many special cases, such as the generalized hyperbolic, generalized Laplace, and skew t-distribution.

In order to calculate the ML-estimates for the generalized hyperbolic distribution, we apply the stepwise expectation maximization (EM) algorithm[18] described in McNeil et al. (2005).

9.4.2   Two-Dimensional Analysis

We selected daily log-returns from February 5, 2001, through June 30, 2009, for four selected companies included in the DAX30: BMW (ticker BMW) and DaimlerChrysler (ticker DAI), representing companies with high market capitalization in the German automobile sector; and Deutsche Bank (ticker DBK) and Commerzbank (ticker CBK), representing companies with high market capitalization in the German bank sector. Figure 9.2A depicts the two-dimensional scatter plots of BMW versus DAI; Figure 9.2B depicts the scatter plots of CBK versus DBK. In all figures we can see that there are more outliers in the directions around the first principal component F_1, motivating a multi-tail model. A stylized fact of short-term log-returns of financial time series is that one can assume a negligible median.

The location parameter of a generalized elliptical random vector is computed by means of the component-wise median, and not with the mean.[19] Applying the spectral estimator for both samples, we obtain the normalized

---

[18]The actual MATLAB code was provided by Saket Sathe, and it is available at the MATLAB Central web site www.mathworks.se/matlabcentral/index.html.
[19]See Frahm (2004).

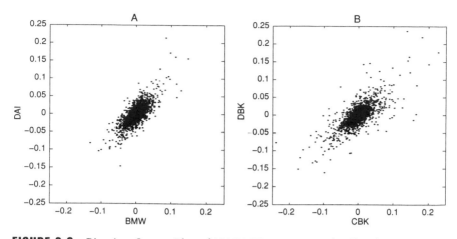

FIGURE 9.2 Bivariate Scatter Plot of (A) BMW versus DaimlerChrysler, (B) Commerzbank versus Deutsche Bank (daily log-returns from February 5, 2001, through June 30, 2009)

dispersion matrix ($\hat{\sigma}_{11} = 1$)

$$\hat{\Sigma}_0(X_1, \ldots, X_{1,000}) = \begin{pmatrix} 1.0000 & 0.7519 \\ 0.7519 & 1.1450 \end{pmatrix}$$

for BMW versus DAI,

$$\hat{\Sigma}_0(Y_1, \ldots, Y_{1,000}) = \begin{pmatrix} 1.0000 & 0.6112 \\ 0.6112 & 0.8172 \end{pmatrix}$$

for CBK versus DBK, representing the first step of the estimation procedure described in section 9.3. Note that due to the properties of the spectral estimator, these normalized dispersion matrices are valid for the elliptical, as well as for the multi-tail t, model and eventually for other multi-tail generalized elliptical models.

In our analysis, we choose the t, the multi-tail t, the normal, and the generalized hyperbolic distribution. Note that the t-distribution has a constant tail function $v : \mathcal{S}^1 \rightarrow I = R^+$, $v(s) = v_0$, whereas for the multi-tail model two different tail functions are specified, satisfying

$$v(s) = \langle s, F_1 \rangle^2 v_1 + \langle s, F_2 \rangle^2 v_2, \tag{9.9}$$

and

$$v_{\pm}(s) = \langle s, F_{1_+} \rangle^2 v_{1_+} + \langle s, F_{1_-} \rangle^2 v_{1_-}$$
$$+ \langle s, F_{2_+} \rangle^2 v_{2_+} + \langle s, F_{2_-} \rangle^2 v_{2_-}, \tag{9.10}$$

respectively, where F_1 and F_2 are the first and second principal components of $\hat{\Sigma}_0$.

Besides estimating the scale parameter c and the tail parameters, we apply the *Akaike information criterion* (AIC) and likelihood ratio test to identify the superior model. The AIC is defined as

$$AIC = 2k - 2\ln(L), \tag{9.11}$$

where k is the number of parameters of the statistical model, and L is the maximized value of the likelihood function for the estimated model. The likelihood ratio test statistic satisfies

$$\lambda(X) = \frac{\sup_{\theta \in \Theta_0} L(\theta, X)}{\sup_{\theta \in \Theta} L(\theta, X)}.$$

Under the null hypothesis, it can be shown that $-2\ln\lambda(X) \sim \chi_q^2$, where q is the difference between the free parameters in Θ and Θ_0.

Table 9.2(A) and (B) shows the estimates for the scale parameter and tail parameters in both models. In both t and multi-tail t models, the scale parameters are close to each other while the tail parameters differ. This result is to be expected because the scaling properties expressed by Σ_0 and c, and the tail behavior captured by the tail parameters and the specified tail function, are fairly independent for larger sample sizes.

According to the AIC, the multi-tail model given by the tail function $v_{\pm}$ is better because we observe a smaller value for that model.

We consider two different ML-ratio tests. We compare the t model to the multi-tail t model with tail function defined by tail function (9.9), by considering the following hypothesis test:

$$H_0 : \theta \in \Theta_0 = \{(v_1, v_2) \in \mathbb{R}^+ : 0 < v_1 = v_2\}$$
$$H_1 : \theta \in \Theta_0 = \{(v_1, v_2) \in \mathbb{R}^+ : 0 < v_1 < v_2\}. \tag{9.12}$$

According to Table 9.2, the *p*-value for this test is less than 5%, so it is reasonable to reject the elliptical model. Then, we compare the two

TABLE 9.2 Two-Dimensional ML Estimates (February 5, 2001, through June 30, 2009)

(A) BMW-DAI returns.

	#par					ln L	AIC	p-value
t	6	$\hat{c}^2$ 2.1449e-4	$\hat{v}_1$ 3.2329			1.12319e+4	−2.1534e+4	0.0016
multi-t	7	$\hat{c}^2$ 2.1582e-4	$\hat{v}_1$ 2.8264	$\hat{v}_2$ 4.7426		1.12369e+4	−2.1542e+4	0.7059
multi-t	9	$\hat{c}^2$ 2.1602e-4	$\hat{v}_{1_+}$ 2.6852 $\hat{v}_{1_-}$ 2.9823	$\hat{v}_{2_+}$ 4.7562 $\hat{v}_{2_-}$ 4.7426		1.12373e+4	−2.2457e+4	
normal	6					1.08306e+4	−2.1649e+4	
GH	9	ψ 0.7555	λ −0.4	χ 0.6150		1.12432e+4	−2.2469e+4	

(B) CB-DB returns.

	#par					ln L	AIC	p-value
t	6	$\hat{c}^2$ 2.5801e-4	$\hat{v}_1$ 2.3101			1.05957e+4	−2.0262e+4	3.8627e-04
multi-t	7	$\hat{c}^2$ 2.5880e-4	$\hat{v}_1$ 2.0264	$\hat{v}_2$ 3.2042		1.06020e+4	−2.0272e+4	0.6796
multi-t	9	$\hat{c}^2$ 2.5902e-4	$\hat{v}_{1_+}$ 2.1227 $\hat{v}_{1_-}$ 1.9323	$\hat{v}_{2_+}$ 3.2113 $\hat{v}_{2_-}$ 3.2042		1.06024e+4	−2.1187e+4	
normal	6					9.75676e+3	−1.9502e+4	
GH	9	ψ 0.2150	λ −0.7	χ 0.4206		1.06068e+4	−2.1196e+4	

Note: The scale parameter and tail parameters for both models are estimated through MLE. The table shows the number of parameters (#par), the value of the log-likelihood at the maximum (ln$L$), the value of the Akaike information criterion (AIC), and the p-value for the likelihood ratio tests.

models defined by tail functions (9.9) and (9.10), by considering the following hypothesis test:

$$H_0 : \theta \in \Theta_0 = \{(v_1, v_2) \in \mathbb{R}^+ : 0 < v_{1_+} = v_{1_-}, 0 < v_{2_+} = v_{2_-}\}$$
$$H_1 : \theta \in \Theta_0 = \{(v_1, v_2) \in \mathbb{R}^+ : 0 < v_{1_+} \neq v_{1_-}, 0 < v_{2_+} \neq v_{2_-}\}. \quad (9.13)$$

According to Table 9.2, the p-value for this test is greater than 5%, so it is reasonable to accept the multi-tail model with tail function (9.9).

Table 9.2 shows that we obtain basically the same results as in the previous case. The returns for CBK and DBK demand even more of a multi-tail model. The spread in the first and second tail parameters is larger than before. The difference between the log-likelihood values and AIC is also greater. Finally, the p-value of the ML-ratio test (9.12) is practically equal to zero. Again, the scaling parameters are close and the tail parameters differ, indicating that the ML estimator $\hat{c}^2$ for the scale parameter is fairly independent of the ML estimates for v_1 and v_2.

In particular, the results reported in Table 9.2(A) and (B) coincide with scatter plots in Figure 9.2(A) and (B) since in (B) we observe more pronounced outliers along the first principal component than in (A).

In Table 9.2 we also report the estimation results of the normal model. It is clearly outperformed by the more sophisticated model that takes into account tail dependence.

In addition, Table 9.2 shows the estimates for χ, ψ, and λ in the GH model. The parameter vectors γ and μ are not reported since they are close to zero ($< 10^{-4}$). The EM-algorithm works extremely well for the two-dimensional data set. Comparing the GH model with the multi-tail generalized elliptical model, we observe that based on the AIC, the GH model for both BMW-DC returns and CB-DB returns is preferred.

In order to have a visual assessment of the estimation, we run a simulation of the normal, the multi-t, and the GH model with the parameters reported in Table 9.2. In Figures 9.3 and 9.4 we show the simulated returns from the selected bivariate distributions and compare them to real market data. By looking at the scatter plots, we can assert that the normal model cannot capture tail dependence, while both the multi-t and the generalized hyperbolic do.

9.4.3   Multi-Tail t Model Check for the DAX

The investigated return data $X_1, X_2, \ldots, X_{2,135} \in \mathbb{R}^{30}$ are all German stocks included in the DAX index. The period covered is February 5, 2001, to June 30, 2009. We start our analysis by estimating the normalized dispersion

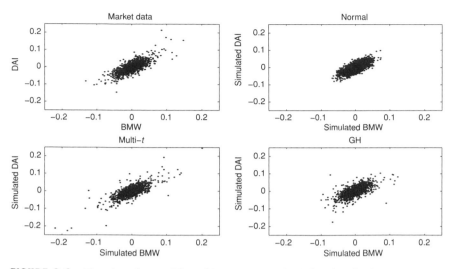

FIGURE 9.3 Bivariate Scatter Plot of BMW versus DaimlerChrysler by Considering Market Data and Simulated Sample from the Multivariate Normal, Multi-*t*, and Generalized Hyperbolic Distribution (market data are daily log-returns from February 5, 2001, through June 30, 2009)

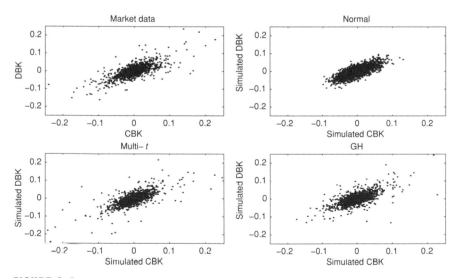

FIGURE 9.4 Bivariate Scatter Plot of CBK versus DBK by Considering Market Data and Simulated Sample from the Multivariate Normal, Multi-*t*, and Generalized Hyperbolic Distribution (market data are daily log-returns from February 5, 2001, through June 30, 2009)

matrix $\hat{\Sigma}_0(X_1, \ldots, X_{1,000})$ using the spectral estimator given by equation (9.5).

We conduct the same statistical analysis as in section 9.4.2. In particular, we fit a t and multi-tail t-distribution to the data and then compare the estimated with the normal and the GH model. The results are reported in Table 9.3. The elliptical model has 30 location parameters, $30 \cdot 15 = 450$ dispersion parameters, and one tail parameter; the multi-tail model has two (ν_1 and ν_2) and four ($\nu_{1_+}, \nu_{1_-}, \nu_{2_+}$, and ν_{2_-}) tail parameters, according to the tail functions defined in tail functions (9.9) and (9.10), respectively. Thus, we have 481 parameters in the elliptical and 482 and 484 in the multi-tail models.

In the first step, we estimate the dispersion parameter with the spectral estimator up to a scaling constant. The scale parameter $\hat{c}^2$ and tail parameters are estimated in the second step.

Table 9.3 shows that for both models the scale parameter $\hat{c}^2$ is almost the same, whereas the tail parameters differ significantly. The AIC as well as the ML-ratio test favor the multi-tail model. A p-value of less than 0.05% for this test indicates that we can reject the null hypothesis of an elliptical model at a very high confidence level. Furthermore, the multi-tail model with tail function (9.9) is preferred to the model with tail function (9.10).

While the multivariate normal and the multi-tail t-distribution can be easily estimated, in the case of the DAX returns, we had problems in applying the EM-algorithm to estimate the GH model since the algorithm converges very slowly. Thus, some uncertainty remains concerning the true maximum since we bounded the maximum number of iterations to assure that a solution is obtained in finite time. For example, in the GH model the value of the log-likelihood is $1.77328e + 5$, while in the t model the log-likelihood is $1.77353e + 5$ (see Table 9.3) when applying the three-step estimation procedure. In particular, the empirical findings show that a multi-tail generalized elliptical model is a suitable model to apply with high-dimensional data. This makes it even more attractive, especially for practitioners.

9.5 SUMMARY

In this chapter, we described the subclass of generalized elliptical distributions that is flexible enough to capture a varying-tail behavior for multivariate stock return data. This new type of distribution is motivated by the typical behavior of returns observed in real-world financial markets. By introducing the notion of tail function, we show how to capture varying tail behavior and present examples for tail functions. A three-step estimation

TABLE 9.3 DAX ML Estimates (February 5, 2001, through June 30, 2009)

DAX returns.

	#par						$\ln L$	AIC	p-value
t	481	$\hat{c}^2$ 2.0127e-4	$\hat{\nu}_1$ 3.7012				1.77346e+5	−3.53731+5	3.0391e-4
multi-t	482	$\hat{c}^2$ 2.0065e-4	$\hat{\nu}_1$ 2.6047	$\hat{\nu}_2$ 4.2105			1.77353e+5	−3.53742e+5	0.5676
multi-t	484	$\hat{c}^2$ 2.0041e-4	$\hat{\nu}_{1+}$ 2.5223	$\hat{\nu}_{1-}$ 2.6505	$\hat{\nu}_{2+}$ 4.6054	$\hat{\nu}_{2-}$ 3.4178	1.77353e+5	−3.53739e+5	
normal	480						1.67393e+5	−3.33827e+5	
GH	513	ψ 0.4745	λ −1	χ 1.2461			1.77328e+5	−3.53630e+5	

Note: The scale parameter and tail parameters for both models are estimated using MLE. The table shows the number of parameters (#par), the value of the log-likelihood at the maximum ($\ln L$), the value of the Akaike information criterion (AIC), and the p-value for the likelihood ratio tests.

procedure is presented to fit the multi-tail t-distributions to data. By applying the Akaike information criterion and likelihood ratio test, we find empirical evidence that a simple multi-tail t-model outperforms common elliptical models. Moreover, for the sample of stocks investigated, the hypothesis of homogeneous tail behavior is rejected.

REFERENCES

Eberlein, E. & Keller, U. (1995). Hyperbolic distributions in finance. *Bernoulli, 1*, 281–299.

Eberlein, E., Keller, U., & Prause, K. (1998). New insights into smile, mispricing, and value at risk: The hyperbolic model. *Journal of Business, 71*(3), 371–405.

Fang, K., Kotz, S., & Ng, K. (1990). *Symmetric multivariate and related distributions.* New York: Chapman and Hall.

Frahm, G. (2004). *Generalized elliptical distributions: Theory and applications.* Ph.D. thesis, University of Cologne.

Hult, H. & Lindskog, F. (2002). Multivariate extremes, aggregation and dependence in elliptical distributions. *Advances in Applied Probability, 587–608.*

Kotz, S. & Nadarajah, S. (2004). *Multivariate t distributions and their applications.* Cambridge: Cambridge University Press.

Kring, S., Rachev, S., Höchstötter, M., Fabozzi, F., & Bianchi, M. (2009). Multi-tail generalized elliptical distributions for asset returns. *Econometrics Journal, 12*(2), 272–291.

McNeil, A., Frey, R., & Embrechts, P. (2005). *Quantitative risk management.* Princeton, NJ: Princeton University Press.

Prause, K. (1999). *The generalized hyperbolic model: Estimation, financial derivatives, and risk measures.* Ph.D. thesis, Freiburg i. Br. Universität.

Rachev, S. & Mittnik, S. (2000). *Stable Paretian models in finance.* New York: John Wiley & Sons.

Rachev, S., Mittnik, S., Fabozzi, F., Focardi, S., & Jašić, T. (2007). *Financial econometrics: From basics to advanced modeling techniques.* Hoboken, NJ: John Wiley & Sons.

Schmidt, R. (2002). Tail dependence for elliptically contoured distributions. *Mathematical Methods of Operations Research (ZOR), 55*(2), 301–327.

CHAPTER 10

Non-Gaussian Portfolio Allocation

10.1   INTRODUCTION

We are now in a position to discuss a general framework to perform a proper calibration of risk factors, to measure risk, and to construct optimal portfolios. The economic ideas behind the model come from three stylized facts about real-world financial markets.[1] First, financial return series are asymmetric and heavy tailed, where the tails are important because bad news constitute tail events. The normal distribution is symmetric and has tails that are too light to match market data. Second, there is volatility clustering in time series (i.e., calm periods followed by highly volatile periods and vice versa).

Finally, a dependence structure of multivariate distribution is needed beyond simple linear correlation. The dependence model has to be flexible enough to account for several empirical phenomena observed in the data, in particular asymmetry of dependence during severe market disruptions and dependence of the tail events. Bad events occur in clusters; that is, a bad event for a company can result in unfavorable outcomes for other companies. The dependence model implied by the multivariate normal distribution fails to describe both phenomena, since the covariance is a symmetric dependence concept and the tail events that we are interested in are asymptotically independent.

While in Chapter 9, we analyzed a multivariate random vector allowing for tail dependence, in this chapter, we consider copula functions to model. As described in Chapter 2, a copula is a function that represents the dependency structure of a multivariate random variable. The use of copula functions allows one to take into account phenomena such as clustering of the volatility effect, heavy tails, and skewness, and then one can separately model the dependence structure among them. Furthermore, from a practical

---

[1]See Cont and Tankov (2004), Rachev et al. (2005), and Rachev et al. (2007).

point of view, the problem of fitting the model to market data can be dealt with in two steps: marginals and copula can be estimated separately.

In searching for an acceptable model to describe these three stylized facts, we are going to employ the following four main ingredients:

1. A preliminary dimension reduction performed by multifactor linear models.
2. A general one-dimensional time series process belonging to the ARMA-GARCH family.[2]
3. An innovation process where the marginals of the probability distribution follow a tempered stable distribution.
4. A copula approach to model the dependence structure.

We want to develop a model that takes into account the stylized facts that have been observed in real-world financial markets and avoid extremely cumbersome problems that would be encountered in estimating models in a highly dimensional setting. The chapter is organized as follows. In section 10.2 we review the well-known multifactor linear model. Multivariate models using copula are presented in section 10.3. The average value-at-risk measure together with optimal portfolio allocation are presented in sections 10.4 and 10.5. The implemented algorithm is summarized in section 10.6. Finally, section 10.7 contains an empirical using stocks that make up the DAX 30 index.

10.2   MULTIFACTOR LINEAR MODEL

Multifactor models are usually adopted to reduce the dimension of portfolio allocation problems.[3] Our focus will be on equity models. The log-return of each stock i is written as a linear combination of some fundamental portfolios, commonly referred to as *factors*, plus a random term. In classical models, we have that stock return i is modeled by

$$r_i = \alpha_i + \sum_{j=1}^{K} \beta_{i,j} f_j + \varepsilon_i,$$

---

[2]For a detailed description of time-series ARMA-GARCH models, see Rachev et al. (2007).
[3]See Zenios (2008).

where α_i and $\beta_{i,j}$ are constants, f_j are the factors, and ε_i is a a random error, assumed to be normally distributed with zero mean and variance $\sigma_{\varepsilon_i}^2$. Furthermore, the following assumptions are made

$$
\begin{aligned}
cov(\varepsilon_i, f_j) &= 0, &&\text{for all} \quad i, \; j, \\
cov(\varepsilon_i, \varepsilon_k) &= 0, &&\text{for all} \quad i, \; k, &&(10.1) \\
cov(f_i, f_j) &= 0, &&\text{for all} \quad i \neq j.
\end{aligned}
$$

Factors are supposed to be uncorrelated to each other, meaning that stock returns are correlated only through the factors.

Under the above assumptions, we are able to compute the mean, variance, and covariance to be used in the mean-variance optimization problem. More specifically, by construction, we obtain the mean of the ith stock's log-return

$$
E(r_i) = \mu_i = \alpha_i + \sum_{j=1}^{K} \beta_{i,j} E(f_j) \tag{10.2}
$$

and with simple calculation, we can write both the variance

$$
var(r_i) = \sigma_i^2 = \sum_{j=1}^{K} \beta_{i,j}^2 \sigma_j^2 + \sigma_{\varepsilon_i}^2 \tag{10.3}
$$

and the covariance between ith and kth stock log-returns

$$
cov(r_i, r_k) = \sigma_{i,k} = \sum_{j=1}^{K} \beta_{i,j} \beta_{k,j}^2 \sigma_j^2 \tag{10.4}
$$

Now, in order to write the mean-variance portfolio problem in the multifactor setting, as we will see in section 10.4, we define the random variable r_p representing the portfolio; that is,

$$
r_p = \sum_{i=1}^{N} w_i r_i,
$$

where $w = (w_1, \ldots, w_N)$ is the vector of weights for the portfolio, under the assumption $\sum_{i=1}^{N} w_i = 1$. The portfolio return can be rewritten as

$$r_p = \sum_{i=1}^{N} \alpha_i w_i + \sum_{i=1}^{N} \left(\sum_{j=1}^{K} \beta_{i,j} f_j \right) w_i + \sum_{i=1}^{N} \varepsilon_i w_i$$

In order to provide more simple calculation, we define

$$\beta_{p,j} = \sum_{i=1}^{N} \beta_{i,j} w_i \tag{10.5}$$

that can be considered as the sensitivity of the portfolio to factor j.[4] Therefore, we can write

$$r_p = \sum_{i=1}^{N} \alpha_i w_i + \sum_{j=1}^{K} \beta_{p,j} f_j + \sum_{i=1}^{N} \varepsilon_i w_i$$

from which we derive the portfolio expected return

$$E(r_p) = \mu_{r_p} = \sum_{i=1}^{N} \alpha_i w_i + \sum_{j=1}^{K} \beta_{p,j} E(f_j) \tag{10.6}$$

and with simple calculation, the portfolio variance

$$var(r_p) = \sigma_{r_p}^2 = \sum_{j=1}^{K} \beta_{p,j}^2 \sigma_j^2 + \sum_{i=1}^{N} \sigma_{\varepsilon_i}^2 w_i. \tag{10.7}$$

Note that in this framework we have considered only linear dependencies and for this reason we will introduce in section 10.3 a more complex structure for the dependencies that also allows for nonlinear dependencies among factors.

---

[4]Detailed explanations are proposed in Zenios (2008).

10.3 MODELING DEPENDENCIES

Understanding and quantifying dependence is the core of portfolio risk analysis. The classical way to model dependencies is by hypothesizing a multivariate distribution directly. Such an approach does not always offer a good means for estimating the true dependence structure and, as a consequence, it leads to an unsatisfactory measure of risk. A multivariate normal distribution is a classical example of a distribution that does not possess the ability to explain major adverse events such as market crashes.

In the last decade, a second approach has become popular. One can specify separately the behavior of each single portfolio component and the dependence structure through a function called a copula.[5] The major advantages of the copula framework are the possibility of specifying marginals and the dependence structure separately, and the capability of modeling extreme events is largely improved. Through the copula, we just define this dependence structure.

From a mathematical viewpoint, a copula function C is nothing more than a probability distribution function on the d-dimensional hypercube

$$I_d = [0, 1] \times [0, 1] \times \cdots \times [0, 1]$$

$$\begin{aligned} C : I_d &\to [0, 1] \\ (u_1, \ldots, u_d) &\to C(u_1, \ldots, u_d) \end{aligned}$$

(10.8)

It is well known that for any multivariate cumulative distribution function F one can uniquely define its copula function, and, conversely, given a copula function C, a unique multivariate distribution F is obtained. Let F be a multivariate distribution function on $\mathbb{R}^d$ with margins $f_1, \ldots, f_d$. Then F has a unique representation

$$F(x_1, \ldots, x_d) = C(F_1(x_1), \ldots, F_d(x_d)).$$

By using the flexibility of this structure, one can define a marginal distribution to model the risk factors, and then specify a copula function C to capture the multivariate dependency structure in the best-suited manner. It is common to represent a copula by its distribution function, with the choice based on a consideration of multivariate distribution of known random variables or by specifying the copula distribution in a simple parametric form.

---

[5]See Embrechts et al. (2003).

The copulas that belong to the first family are called *implicit copulas*, while the latter are call *explicit copulas*.

The Gaussian copula, defined in Chapter 2, is an example of an implicit copula. Although this form of copula is easy to work with, it has one major drawback: it implies that extreme events are asymptotically independent. Thus, the probability of the joint occurrence of large negative returns of two stocks is significantly underestimated. To overcome this drawback, we will consider a skewed t-copula[6] because it allows more heterogeneity in modeling dependencies. The skewed t copula of the multivariate skewed Student's t-distribution X with degrees of freedom v is defined by means of the following stochastic representation[7]

$$X = \mu + \gamma W + Z\sqrt{W}, \tag{10.9}$$

where $\mu \in \mathbb{R}^d$ is a location vector, $\gamma \in \mathbb{R}^d$ is a vector accounting for the skewness, $W \sim IG(v/2, v/2)$ is an inverse gamma distributed, and $Z \sim N(0, \Sigma)$ is a multivariate normal distribution independent of W. Most importantly, the multivariate skewed t-distribution allows for a closed-form expression of its density given by the following expression:

$$f(x) = \frac{c \, K_{\frac{v+d}{2}}(a) \exp\left((x-\mu)'\Sigma^{-1}\gamma\right)}{a^{-\frac{v+d}{2}} \left(1 + \frac{(x-\mu)'\Sigma^{-1}(x-\mu)}{v}\right)^{\frac{v+d}{d}}} \tag{10.10}$$

with

$$a = \sqrt{(v + (x-\mu)'\Sigma^{-1}(x-\mu))\gamma'\Sigma^{-1}\gamma}$$

$$c = \frac{2^{\frac{2-(v+d)}{2}}}{\Gamma(\frac{v}{2})(\pi v)^{\frac{d}{2}}|\Sigma|^{\frac{1}{2}}}$$

where K_λ and Γ are the modified Bessel function of the third kind and the gamma function, respectively.[8] Then, the derived implicit skewed t-copula

---

[6]As defined in Demarta and McNeil (2005).

[7]See Rachev and Mittnik (2000).

[8] See Abramowitz and Stegun (1974) for the definition of this special function and Gil et al. (2007) for numerical issues regarding these functions.

distribution function has the form

$$C(u_1, \ldots, u_d) = \int_{\infty}^{t_{v,\gamma_1}(u_1)} \cdots \int_{\infty}^{t_{v,\gamma_d}(u_d)} f(x)dx \qquad (10.11)$$

The stochastic representation (10.9) facilitates scenario generation from the copula and gives a parametric form that makes the copula an attractive model in higher dimensions. Furthermore, this copula function may describe both tail and asymmetric dependence.

10.4 AVERAGE VALUE-AT-RISK

The value-at-risk (VaR) measure has been adopted as a standard risk measure in the banking and financial industry.[9] Nonetheless, it has a number of deficiencies recognized by financial professionals.[10] An important property does not hold for VaR: This is the sub-additivity property that ensures that the VaR measure cannot always account for diversification. There are cases in which the portfolio VaR is larger than the sum of the VaRs of the portfolio constituents. This is why VaR cannot be used as a true risk measure.

The average value-at-risk (AVaR) is a risk measure that is a superior alternative to VaR. Not only does it lack the deficiencies of VaR, but it also has an intuitive interpretation. There are convenient ways for computing and estimating AVaR that allows its application in optimal portfolio selection problems. Moreover, it satisfies all axioms of coherent risk measures and is consistent with the preference relations of risk-averse investors.[11] Furthermore, not only does AVaR provide information about losses beyond VaR, it is a convex, smooth function of portfolio weights and is therefore attractive as a risk measure for optimizing portfolios. The AVaR at tail probability δ is defined as the average of the VaRs that are larger than the VaR at tail probability δ. Therefore, by construction, AVaR is focused on the losses in the tail that are larger than the corresponding VaR level.

Let X be a real random variable in L^1, that is $E|X| < \infty$.[12] Then we define the risk measure AVaR as the following convergent integral

$$AVaR_\delta(X) := \frac{1}{\delta} \int_0^\delta VaR_p(X)dp, \qquad (10.12)$$

---

[9]See Basel Committee on Banking Supervision (2009).
[10]See Kim et al. (2010).
[11]See Rachev et al. (2008) and references therein.
[12]This condition is always satisfied by a random variable commonly used in applications in finance.

where VaR is defined as follows:

$$Va\,R_p(X) = -\inf_x\{x|P(X \le x) \ge p\} = -F_X^{-1}(p)$$

Unfortunately, due to the definition of AVaR, a closed-form formula for the valuation of equation (10.12) is available only for a few distributions.[13] Moreover, for our purposes we do not need a closed form for the AVaR calculation, since portfolio returns combine both infinitely divisible (ID) distributions and the GARCH behavior in a multivariate setting. In general, it is not possible to obtain a closed-form formula to this kind of model, and one has to adopt simulation methods. We define the AVaR estimation from a sample that is sufficiently large so as to allow to calculate the value of the AVaR. This method is particularly useful for more complex multivariate models in which one must generate scenarios when it is not possible to compute a closed-form formula for AVaR.

Suppose that we have a sample of observations of length N of the random variable X and we do not know its distribution. Provided that we do not impose any distributional model, AVaR can be estimated from a sample of observations. Denote the observations by

$$(x_1, x_2, \ldots, x_n)$$

at time instants

$$(0 = t_1 < t_2 < \cdots < t_n = T).$$

Denote the sorted observations vector by

$$(x_1' \le x_2' \le \cdots \le x_n'),$$

thus, x_1' equals the smallest observation and x_n' is the largest. By a simple consequence of the definition of AVaR for discrete distributions, the AVaR from a sample for X at tail probability δ is estimated according to the formula

$$\widehat{AVa\,R_\delta}(X) = -\frac{1}{\delta}\left(\frac{1}{N}\sum_{k=1}^{\lceil N\delta\rceil-1} x_k' + \left(\delta - \frac{\lceil N\delta\rceil - 1}{N}x_{\lceil N\delta\rceil}'\right)\right), \qquad (10.13)$$

---

[13] See Kim et al. (in press).

where the notation $\lceil x \rceil$ stands for the smallest integer larger than x. Equation (10.13) is a very convenient form for use in scenario-based portfolio optimization.

Now let's see how to apply equation (10.13) in our setting, where X will be the random variable representing the portfolio return r_p. We proceed in the following way

- We select a statistical model capable of explaining a number of observed phenomena in stock returns, such as heavy tails and volatility clustering, which we think influence the portfolio risk.
- We estimate the model parameters by taking into account a sample of observed stocks returns from a predetermined time window.
- We generate scenarios from the fitted model using Monte Carlo methods.
- On the basis of the scenarios from the previous step, we calculate the portfolio risk and the optimal portfolio allocation.

10.5 OPTIMAL PORTFOLIOS

Now, let $\{r_i\}_{1 \leq i \leq N}$ be the universe of stock returns that are candidates for inclusion in the portfolio, and $w = (w_1, \ldots, w_N)$ the column vector of weights of the portfolio under the assumption $\sum_{i=1}^{N} w_i = 1$. Let r_p be the random variable representing the portfolio returns; that is,

$$r_p = \sum_{i=1}^{N} w_i r_i.$$

In the spirit of mean-variance analysis,[14] we want to solve a more general reward-to-risk problem,[15] that is,

$$\max_{w} \frac{E(r_p - r_b)}{\rho(r_p - r_b)}$$
$$\text{subject to } w'e = 1$$
$$w \geq 0,$$

$$(10.14)$$

---

[14]See Markowitz (1952).
[15]See Rachev et al. (2008).

where ρ is a risk measure and $e \in \mathbb{R}^N$ is the column vector with all elements equal to 1. Here we assume r_b is constant and $E(r_p)$ follows by equation (10.6). Thus, we have

$$E(r_p - r_b) = \sum_{i=1}^{N} \alpha_i w_i + \sum_{j=1}^{K} \beta_{p,j} E(f_j) - r_b.$$

The implication of the last inequality in the optimization problem means that we are restricting portfolio selection to consider long-only portfolios. However, this constraint can be modified to allow for long/short portfolios.

   If one selects the variance as the risk measure ρ, we obtain the classical (Markowitz) mean-variance problem given by

$$\max_{w} \frac{E(r_p - r_b)}{\sigma_{r_p}}$$
$$\text{subject to} \ \ w'e = 1$$
$$w \geq 0.$$
(10.15)

For different risk measures, the portfolio selection criteria may be more complex. The principal difference between mean-risk and mean-variance optimization problems is that the risk measure may capture completely different characteristics of the portfolio return distribution. In particular, the use of AVaR as a risk measure allows one to focus attention on tail events because the risk is given by a measure of losses beyond the VaR; that is, AVaR seeks to explain and forecast bad events represented by the expected value of losses beyond VaR. Even if the structure of the problem (10.14) is close to the mean-variance problem, the idea behind it is quite different.

   After defining the statistical model and estimating its parameters from historical data, a scenario matrix that is based on Monte Carlo simulations can be generated. Denoting the possible scenarios for the stock returns by $r_1, \ldots, r_N$, the scenario matrix H is defined as

$$\begin{pmatrix} r_1^1 & r_2^1 & \cdots & r_N^1 \\ r_1^2 & r_2^2 & \cdots & r_N^2 \\ \vdots & \vdots & \ddots & \vdots \\ r_1^K & r_2^K & \cdots & r_N^K \end{pmatrix},$$
(10.16)

where K is the number of scenarios and N the number of stocks. By equation (10.13), the optimization problem given by (10.14) can be rewritten as

$$\max_{w} \frac{E(r_p - r_b)}{\widehat{AVaR}_\delta(Hw) + r_b}$$
$$\text{subject to } w'e = 1$$
$$w \geq 0.$$

(10.17)

The concavity property of the function to maximize in the optimization problem above together with equation (10.13) offer an easy procedure to find an optimal portfolio. From a computational perspective, the optimization procedure takes only a few minutes. Most of the computing time is spent on the Monte Carlo simulation. The computing time for the scenario generation may become time consuming if a large number of scenarios are desired under some more sophisticated statistical model. However, if the computing speed can be improved, for instance, through parallel computing, this will be of minor concern. Even though parallel computing is a well-known algorithm, today software companies are moving to extend the use of such types of procedures. For example the recent releases of MATLAB can run a parallel computing algorithm by using a cluster or even a multi-core processor by a user-friendly interface.[16]

Note that the AVaR evaluation can be converted in a linear programming problem.[17] However, as the number of scenario increases, the dimension of the linear programming problem increases as well and it is no longer possible to find a solution utilizing MATLAB's standard optimization package; for this reason, we have selected formula (10.13). An alternative is writing a MATLAB code for linear programming problem or using well-known optimization software (such as GAMS), which can deal with these problems in very large dimensions.

10.6 THE ALGORITHM

The first step of the implementation of a portfolio optimization problem requires a reduction of the dimensionality. This first step is necessary because the number of parameters may become quite large even for problems of reasonable size. There is a general consensus that a multifactor linear

---

[16]See the MATLAB toolbox *parallel computing*.
[17]See Rachev et al. (2008).

model of returns should be employed to solve this dimensionality problem. The reasons for the use of factor models are twofold: (1) in financial econometrics, multifactor models make estimation feasible and (2) multifactor models try to identify the causes that drive financial data. Since random variables we consider have finite second moment, factors can be found by means of *principal component analysis* (PCA).[18] PCA is a statistical method that can be employed to reduce the dimension of the portfolio allocation problem: among all possible market portfolios, a few portfolios are selected to be used as explanatory factors of the model. In particular, PCA selects portfolios with maximum variance and a single stock market behavior is approximated through a linear combination of these maximum variance portfolios.

From a practical point of view, we use PCA to determine principal components and take into consideration only those principal components that have a large variance as explicative variables of the multilinear model. Let us consider the multifactor model

$$r_i = \alpha_i + \sum_{j=1}^{K} \beta_{ij} f_j + \varepsilon_i \qquad (10.18)$$

where r_i is a random variable representing the ith stock log-return. Thus the algorithm given the portfolio optimal allocation in our statistical model can be summarized as follows:

Step 1. Reduce the dimensionality of the problem by modeling stock returns using the multifactor linear model

$$r_i = \alpha_i + \sum_{j=1}^{K} \beta_{i,j} f_j + \varepsilon_i$$

where factors are given by the PCA. Furthermore, we estimate parameters α_i and $\beta_{i,j}$ by the ordinary least squares (OLS) method.

Step 2. Model separately the univariate time series

$$\hat{\varepsilon}_{i,t} = r_{i,t} - \hat{\alpha}^i - \sum_{j=1}^{K} \hat{\beta}_{i,j} f_{j,t}$$

---

[18]See Rachev et al. (2007) and Chapter 15.

with $\hat{\alpha}^i$, $\hat{\beta}_{i,j}$, and $\hat{\varepsilon}_{i,t}$ as estimated in Step 1. We assume that the time series $\varepsilon_{i,t}$, $1 \le t \le T$ follow an ARMA(1,1)-GARCH(1,1) dynamic with a standard CTS (stdCTS)[19] noise and calibrate the model.

Step 3. Assume that the marginals of the multivariate time-series of factor returns

$$(f_{j,t})_{1 \le j \le K, 1 \le t \le T}$$

follow an ARMA(1,1)-GARCH(1,1) dynamic with a stdCTS noise and calibrate each individual one-dimensional factor. Moreover, model the dependence structure by a skewed *t*-copula and calibrate as well by employing maximum likelihood estimation (MLE).[20]

Step 4. Generate the scenarios matrix H using Monte Carlo simulations and then solve the optimization problem given by equation (10.17).

Step 5. Rebalance the portfolio by extending the time window by five days and repeat Step 1 to Step 4 for a sufficient number of times until the last period is reached.

Step 6. Compare the performance of the optimal portfolio with the benchmark index and with the mean-variance portfolio.

10.7   AN EMPIRICAL TEST

We provide a back-testing example of optimal portfolio strategies using the DAX universe. The analysis is based on all 30 German companies included in the DAX index. The back-testing time period is the highly volatile period from June 2008 to June 2009. Daily data are considered with weekly portfolio rebalancing. We considered the data from February 7, 2001, to June 30, 2009, for a total of 2,134 daily observations for each of the 30 companies listed in the DAX index in order to calibrate the model. Although it would have been better to use a longer time series, we start on February 5, 2001, because the Deutsche Böerse (ticker DB1) stock was listed on that date. In any case, eight years of daily data are suitable for the purpose at hand.

---

[19]The CTS distribution is the classical tempered stable distribution described in Chapter 3.

[20]The authors are grateful to Stoyan Stoyanov of Edhec School of Business for providing the MATLAB code for the skewed *t*-copula.

TABLE 10.1 DAX Index Composition on June 30, 2009, with Corresponding *International Securities Identification Number* (ISIN)

Trading Symbol	Company	ISIN
ADS	Adidas-Salomon	DE0005003404
ALV	Allianz	DE0008404005
BAS	Basf	DE0005151005
BMW	Bay.Motoren Werke	DE0005190003
BAY	Bayer	DE0005752000
BEI	Beiersdorf	DE0005200000
CBK	Commerzbank	DE0008032004
DAI	Daimlerchrysler	DE0007100000
DBK	Deutsche Bank	DE0005140008
DB1	Deutsche Börse	DE0005810055
DPW	Deutsche Post	DE0005552004
DTE	Deutsche Telekom	DE0005557508
EOAN	E.ON	DE000ENAG999
FME	Fresenius Medical Care	DE0005785802
FRE3	Fresenius	DE0005785638
HNR1	Hannover Rückversicherungs	DE0008402215
HEN3	Henkel	DE0006048432
SDF	K+S	DE0007162000
LIN	Linde	DE0006483001
LHA	Lufthansa	DE0008232125
MAN	Man	DE0005937007
MRK	Merck	DE0006599905
MEO	Metro	DE0007257503
MUV2	Münchener Rückversicherungs	DE0008430026
RWE	Rwe	DE0007037129
SZG	Salzgitter	DE0006202005
SAP	SAP	DE0007164600
SIE	Siemes	DE0007236101
TKA	Thyssenkrupp	DE0007500001
VOW	Volkswagen	DE0007664005

In the study, we consider only long positions. That is, we do not have to consider the short selling ban imposed by Germany's Bafin, which prohibited uncovered short transactions during the period September 20, 2008, to May 31, 2009. On June 30, 2009, the DAX 30 index was composed of the companies shown in Table 10.1.

In the empirical analysis, we rebalance the portfolio on any trading Wednesday between June 30, 2008, and June 30, 2009. We consider 49 different time series with daily observations for each stock component of

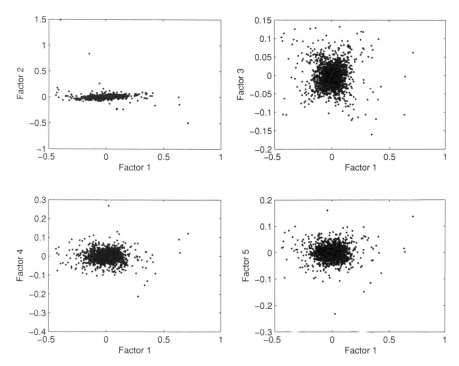

FIGURE 10.1 Scatter Plots of the First Principal Factor against All Others Factors between February 7, 2001, and June 24, 2009

the DAX starting on February 7, 2001 and ending on any Wednesday in the time window considered above.

Transaction costs are not considered in the analysis and we assume that portfolio rebalancing is done based on each Wednesday's closing prices without taking into consideration intraday trades, bid and ask quotes, or volumes. This is a simplification. Moreover, we assume that the portfolio trades occur in a liquid market at a narrow bid-ask spread.

In Step 1 of the AVaR model, we run the PCA and find the statistical factors. In our model, we assume ARMA-GARCH dynamics and a dependence structure among factors in order to capture tail dependencies. In Figure 10.1 we show the scatter plots between some of the considered principal factors. The scatter plots suggest that the factors are not independent. The time series analyzed contains the Volkswagen (ticker VOW) major price movement of 146% on October 27, 2008.

Then, using OLS we estimate α_i and $\beta_{i,j}$ and calculate the residuals $\hat{\varepsilon}_{i,t}$. In Figure 10.2 we report the estimation of $\beta_{i,j}$ and the corresponding R^2.

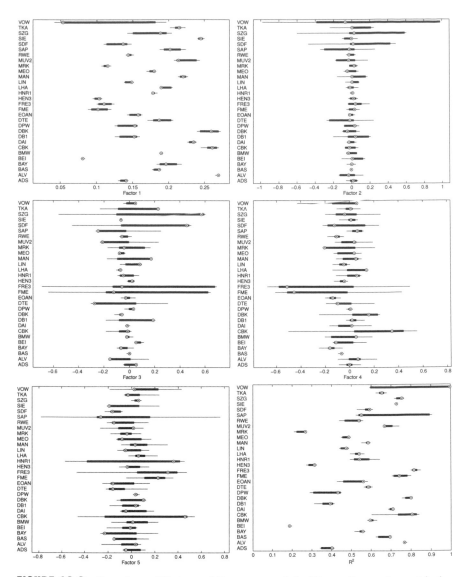

FIGURE 10.2 Boxplots of Estimated Parameters of the Linear Regression with the Corresponding R^2 for all Log-Returns of the 30 Stocks Included in the DAX Index

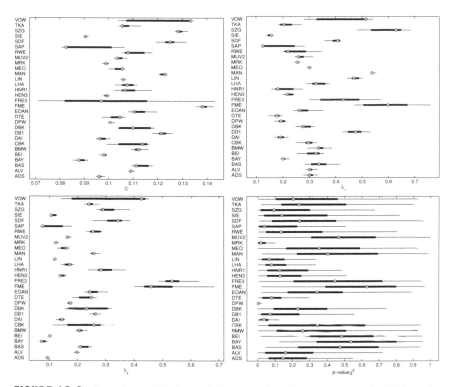

FIGURE 10.3 Boxplots of Estimated C, λ_+, and λ_- Parameters, and p-Value of the χ^2 Test of Fitted stdCTS Residuals for all 30 Stocks Included in the DAX Index

In Step 2 these residuals are calibrated assuming that they follow an ARMA(1,1)-GARCH(1,1) dynamic with stdCTS noise with parameter $\alpha = 1.7$. In Figure 10.3 we show the estimates of C, λ_+, and λ_- for all 49 time series of 30 residuals considered in the model for each rebalancing day.[21] On each box, the central mark is the median, the edges of the box are the 25th and 75th percentiles, the whiskers extend to the most extreme data points not considered outliers, and outliers are plotted individually.[22] Furthermore, in Figure 10.3 we report the p-value of the χ^2 test for the stdCTS assumption for each stock and for each of the 49 estimated time series. On average, the tempered stable assumption for residuals is largely satisfied.

---

[21]For each stock there is a corresponding residual time series that we model with an ARMA-GARCH process with stdCTS innovation.
[22]This is obtained from the MATLAB *boxplot* reference guide.

In Step 3, the ARMA-GARCH parameters, C, λ_+, and λ_- are also estimated for the five factors. These estimations are not reported, but the stdCTS hypothesis is always satisfied. The dependence structure is also calibrated by MLE.

In Step 4, scenarios one week ahead are simulated and the AVaR optimization problem is solved with $\delta = 0.001$. In the simulation we consider the AVaR five days ahead. For each day, we generate $10,000$ possible scenarios for each factor and for each stock. This means that we generate $35,000 \times 5$ stdCTS random numbers for each rebalancing day. Then, the optimization problem given by equation (10.17) is solved.

We consider the same portfolio allocation for the entire week and at the end of week, the portfolio's current value is calculated. The process is repeated; that is, we recalibrate the model by moving the end date of the time series, then scenarios one week ahead are simulated again and the optimal portfolio is calculated. This procedure is repeated each week in the back-testing time period for a total of 49 times. In the optimization problem given by equation (10.17), the value of the lower bound r_b is equal to the historical expected return of the DAX index, calculated on the time series ending on the rebalancing Wednesday.[23] Then, we solve a second optimization problem where the value of the lower bound r_b is constant and equal to the market value of the three-month German Treasury bill rate on the given rebalancing date.

As an alternative model we propose the multifactor model based on the Markowitz mean-variance approach.[24] Factors and residuals are calculated in the same way we have seen in Step 1, but they are assumed to follow a normal distribution and to be independent. Furthermore, the mean-variance portfolio is found by means of equations (10.6) and (10.7). In this alternative model based on the Markowitz mean-variance analysis, the Sharpe ratio is selected as the reward-to-risk measure and, therefore, the optimization problem is

$$\max_{w} \frac{E(r_p - r_b)}{\sigma_{r_p}}$$

subject to $w'e = 1$

$$w \geq 0$$

(10.19)

---

[23]As an alternative, the benchmark dynamic could also be modeled by an ARMA-GARCH process with a tempered stable innovation.
[24]See Zenios (2008).

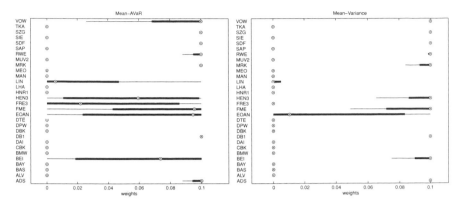

FIGURE 10.4   Boxplots of the Weights of the Mean-AVaR and Mean-Variance Portfolios

Each week the covariance matrix as well as the expected return are estimated through the factor model, and the mean-variance optimization problem is solved. In the first optimization, the constant r_b is the mean return of the DAX index between February 7, 2001, and the rebalancing day, while in the second optimization it is constant and equal to the market value of the three-month German Treasury bill rate. Figure 10.4 displays the boxplots of weights for all 30 stocks and different rebalancing times for the first optimization in which we take the expected return of the DAX index as the lower bound. Even though the portfolio allocation is similar for some stocks, we observe some different weights for BEI, EOAN, FRE3, HEN3, and LIN. Note that only DB1 has a weight different from zero among companies included in the list of banned shorted companies.[25] Figures 10.5 and 10.6 show the evolution of the portfolio's actual values. In Figures 10.5 and 10.6, we report the behavior of the portfolio solving the optimization problem with the lower bound being the expected value of the DAX index and the three-month German Treasury bill rate, respectively. In order to compare the behavior of portfolios and the DAX index, the actual value of the AVaR and the Markowitz mean-variance portfolio is scaled to start with the same capital.

Then an ex-post analysis is considered, and two performance measures are calculated.[26] The two performance measures, examined are the

---

[25]Also ALV, DBK, CBK, DB1, DPB, HNR, and MUV had this short-selling restriction.
[26]See Rachev et al. (2008).

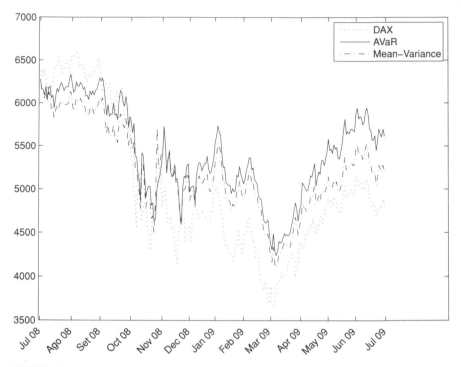

FIGURE 10.5 Behavior of the Mean-AVaR Portfolio, Mean-Variance Portfolio, and DAX 30 Index
Note: The expected value of the DAX index is taken as the lower bound in the optimization procedure.

well-known Sharpe ratio and the stable tail-adjusted return ratio. The Sharpe ratio (SR) is given by

$$S R(r_p) = \frac{E(r_p - r_f)}{\sigma(r_p - r_f)},$$

where r_p is the random variable representing the portfolio, $\sigma(r_p)$ is the standard deviation, and r_f is the risk-free rate. We select the three-month German Treasury bill time series between June 30, 2008, and June 30, 2009, as the risk-free asset. The expected value $E(r_p - r_f)$ is the sample mean of the selected portfolios minus the risk-free rate.

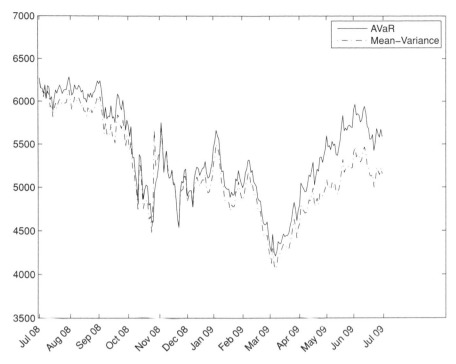

FIGURE 10.6   Behavior of the Mean-AVaR Portfolio, and Mean-Variance
Portfolio
Note: The market value of the three-month German Treasury bill rate is taken as
the lower bound in the optimization procedure.

The other performance measure evaluated is the stable tail-adjusted
return ratio (STARR)[27] given by

$$STARR_\delta(r_p) = \frac{E(r_p - r_f)}{AVaR_\delta(r_p - r_f)}$$

with $\delta = 0.1$. A greater value for ε is selected since we have only one year
of daily data to compute the sample AVaR; otherwise, we cannot compute
it with precision with such a short time series.

---

[27]See Rachev et al. (2008).

TABLE 10.2   Annualized Value of Sharpe Ratio and STARR

	DAX 30	Mean-Variance	Mean-AVaR
		Benchmark	
SR	−0.4834	−0.3141	−0.1713
STARR	−0.0166	−0.0120	−0.0060
		Risk-Free Asset	
SR		−0.3376	−0.1735
STARR		−0.0129	−0.0062

Note: In the first optimization problem, we consider the expected return of the DAX index as lower bound; in the second, we take the three-month German Treasury bill rate.

In Table 10.2, we report the performance measures of portfolios between June 30, 2008, and June 30, 2009. The table shows that both the Sharpe ratio and STARR for the portfolio based on AVaR with nonlinear dependence among factors and ARMA-GARCH process with tempered stable innovations are greater than the ratios computed for the portfolio based on the Markowitz model.

The final value of the portfolio constructed by minimizing AVaR is greater than the mean-variance final value and greater than the DAX level. Furthermore, the performance measures indicate that the AVaR optimal portfolio performs better in the crisis period.

The model can be easily extended to a larger universe such as the S&P 500, the MSCI, or the Russell global indexes because the use of the PCA analysis allows one to reduce the dimension of the problem. Then a more complex optimization procedure can be applied to perform a more realistic portfolio allocation in order to consider transaction costs and even the inclusion of a minimum quantity constraint on stocks that can be bought or sold. Furthermore, this setting could be extended to a 130/30 strategy or more speculative long/short strategies allowing for short selling.

10.8   SUMMARY

In this chapter, we investigate different stylized facts observed for the German stock market: (1) volatility varying over time in order to allow for stock price log-returns that are not independently distributed; (2) the CTS distribution to allow skewness and kurtosis of the distribution for the residuals; (3) tail dependencies that allow for extreme events whereby one stock can result in unfavorable outcomes for other stocks; (4) factors models that reduce the dimensionality of the portfolio optimization problem and thereby decrease the computational effort required to find an optimal solution; and (5) use of AVaR (a coherent risk measure) to take into account the extreme events beyond VaR and provide a more reliable view of extreme events.

REFERENCES

Abramowitz, M. & Stegun, I. (1974). *Handbook of mathematical functions, with formulas, graphs, and mathematical tables*. New York: Dover.

Basel Committee on Banking Supervision (2009). Revisions to the Basel II market risk framework. Bank of International Settlements.

Cont, R. & Tankov, P. (2004). *Financial modelling with jump processes*. Boca Raton, FL: CRC Press.

Demarta, S. & McNeil, A. (2005). The t copula and related copulas. *International Statistical Review, 73*(1), 111–129.

Embrechts, P., Lindskog, F., & McNeil, A. (2003). Modelling dependence with copulas and applications to risk management. In S. Rachev (Ed.), *Handbook of heavy-tailed distributions in finance* (pp. 329–384). Amsterdam: Elsevier.

Gil, A., Segura, J., & Temme, N. (2007). *Numerical methods for special functions*. Philadelphia: SIAM.

Kim, Y., Rachev, S., Bianchi, M., & Fabozzi, F. (2010). Time series analysis for financial market meltdowns. Technical report, University of Karlsruhe and KIT.

Kim, Y. S., Rachev, S. T., Bianchi, M. L., & Fabozzi, F. J. (in press). Computing VaR and AVaR in infinitely divisible distributions. *Probability and mathematical statistics*.

Markowitz, H. (1952). Portfolio selection. *Journal of Finance, 7*(1), 77–91.

Rachev, S., Menn, C., & Fabozzi, F. (2005). *Fat-tailed and skewed asset return distributions: Implications for risk management, portfolio selection, and option pricing*. Hoboken, NJ: John Wiley & Sons.

Rachev, S. & Mittnik, S. (2000). *Stable Paretian models in finance*. New York: Wiley.

Rachev, S., Mittnik, S., Fabozzi, F., Focardi, S., & Jašić, T. (2007). *Financial econometrics: From basics to advanced modeling techniques*. Hoboken, NJ: Wiley.

Rachev, S., Stoyan, S., & Fabozzi, F. (2008). *Advanced stochastic models, risk assessment, and portfolio optimization: The ideal risk, uncertainty, and performance measures*. Hoboken, NJ: John Wiley & Sons.

Zenios, S. (2008). *Practical financial optimization: Decision making for financial engineers*. Hoboken, NJ: Wiley-Blackwell.

CHAPTER 11

Normal GARCH Models

11.1   INTRODUCTION

In this chapter, we review some classical models for asset log-returns with time-dependent volatility with a view toward option pricing. The classical Black-Scholes model assumes that volatility is constant thorough time. Yet, one may consider a volatility whose evolution is not deterministic but depends on random events, that is a stochastic volatility or time-dependent volatility. A simplistic model of financial markets that departs too far from reality may give an incorrect view of future scenarios, resulting in mispricing. A practitioner has to take into consideration in pricing financial instruments that variances and covariances[1] vary over time.

Most of the recent empirical studies show that the amplitude of the daily returns varies across time. Moreover, there is ample empirical evidence that if the volatility is high, it remains high, and if it is low, it remains low. This means that volatility moves in clusters; for this reason it is important to find a way to explain such observed patterns.

Our focus in this chapter is principally oriented to the valuation of derivatives. Econometric research on inflation and business cycle motivated Engle's studies and only recently were applied to finance. Today, these models have become a standard financial econometric tool used by practitioners due to their simplicity in comparison with stochastic volatility models and to the discrete nature of financial data.

Even though the theory of GARCH models with normal innovation has been widely studied and a large number of research papers have dealt with empirical analysis focused on these models, there have been only a few papers focusing on option pricing with GARCH. The first paper applying GARCH

---

[1] The ARCH and GARCH technologies discussed in this chapter for dealing with time-dependent volatilities are not restricted to univariate processes but can be extended to multivariate processes.

to option pricing was by Duan (1995). Subsequent papers focused on empirically testing different discrete-time models with volatility clustering.[2] In comparison to stochastic volatility models, option pricing with GARCH allows a simple parameter estimation in both stock and option markets. In general, for discrete-time models a closed-form solution for pricing plain vanilla derivatives does not exist; however, using Monte Carlo simulations risk-neutral scenarios can be easily generated. Simulating one million of normal variates is no longer an obstacle with a modern computer. Furthermore, GARCH models allow one to develop an integrated stock and option market framework. It is possible to assess the risk of the equity position while at the same time calculate the day-by-day derivatives' position. This framework allows one to evaluate risk measures with the goal of risk minimization, to determine portfolio allocation or to calculate capital charge requirements. Furthermore, with the same market model one can trade and hedge derivatives.

In this chapter, we review some classical GARCH models with normal innovation and their application to explaining stock market returns and fitting option prices. We assess the GARCH model performance in stock price returns fitting (market estimation) and compare them with the classical log-normal model. Then we also assess their option pricing performance in fitting prices of traded option (risk-neutral estimation) in order to demonstrate that a model that permits volatility to change over time can improve both market and risk-neutral estimation.

In particular, we estimate risk-neutral parameters by minimizing the error between model prices and market prices of options. Even though we will focus on derivatives written on stock indexes, these models can be applied to a wide spectrum of financial instruments traded in the market. We compare these models with the standard Black-Scholes model in order to show that a time-dependent variance model provides a better fit for option pricing.

11.2 GARCH DYNAMICS WITH NORMAL INNOVATION

In this section, we review the well-known GARCH dynamics based on the normal distribution assumption. We refer to this model as the *normal GARCH model*. We then define different dynamics for the conditional variance process. Our objective here is not to delve deeply into the statistical

---

[2]See Hsieh and Ritchken (2005).

properties of the model, but rather to explain how the model we are principally interested in can be used in the valuation of derivatives written on stocks and stock indexes. The normal GARCH framework cannot explain all stylized facts observed in financial time series, as leptokurtic and fat-tailed distributions do. For this reason, this model based on the normal distribution has to be viewed as the starting point to understand the non-normal models that will be developed in Chapters 12 and 13.

We assume that the stock price log returns has the form

$$\log \left(\frac{S_t}{S_{t-1}} \right) = g(r_t, d_t, \lambda_t, \sigma_t) + \sigma_t \varepsilon_t, \quad 1 \leq t \leq T$$

and the conditional variance process is defined as

$$\sigma_t^2 = h(\sigma_{t-1}, \varepsilon_{t-1}; \theta), \quad 1 \leq t \leq T, \quad \varepsilon_0 = 0.$$

The function g explains the behavior of the log-returns, while the function h provides the conditional variance dynamic depending on parameters θ. This second function h defines the behavior of the conditional variance varying over time. The process r_t represents the interest rate, and it can be directly inferred by the three-month Treasury bill. The process d_t represents the dividend yield process. The process λ_t may be viewed as the market price of risk, and in general it can be considered constant. In fact, a market price of risk varying over time is difficult to estimate. The product $\sigma_t \varepsilon_t$ represents the error term with zero mean and variance σ_t. In the normal case, it is simple to prove that for each t it is normally distributed with zero mean and conditional variance σ_t.

In general, in the normal GARCH framework, stock log-returns are defined as

$$\log \left(\frac{S_t}{S_{t-1}} \right) = r_t - d_t + \lambda_t \sigma_t - \frac{\sigma_t^2}{2} + \sigma_t \varepsilon_t, \quad 1 \leq t \leq T \tag{11.1}$$

and the conditional variance process can have different dynamics depending on the choice of the function h. In the normal GARCH model proposed by Duan (1995), the volatility dynamic has a GARCH(1,1) form, that is

$$\sigma_t^2 = \alpha_0 + \alpha_1 \sigma_{t-1}^2 \varepsilon_{t-1}^2 + \beta_1 \sigma_{t-1}^2, \quad 1 \leq t \leq T, \quad \varepsilon_0 = 0. \tag{11.2}$$

The process $\lambda_t \equiv \lambda$ is considered constant. The set of constant parameters is $\theta = \{\alpha_0, \alpha_1, \beta_1, \lambda\}$ and the residual ε_t is assumed to be normally distributed with zero mean and unit variance. An assumption needed to obtain a strong stationary solution is $\alpha_1 + \beta_1 < 1$.

The GARCH specification described in equation (11.2) is not unique. In particular, it is possible to define different specifications and assess their performances in explaining stock market behavior and matching option prices. In particular, one may consider a modified version of the GARCH(1,1) model: the asymmetric Glosten-Jagannathan-Runkle (GJR). This model is defined as follows

$$\sigma_t^2 = \alpha_0 + \alpha_1 \eta_{t-1}^2 + \gamma I_{t-1} \eta_{t-1}^2 + \beta \sigma_{t-1}^2 \tag{11.3}$$

where $I_{t-1} = 1$ for negative residuals, otherwise it is zero. It is clear that the volatility definition differs from the GARCH(1,1) model given by equation (11.2). The set of constant parameters is $\theta = \{\alpha_0, \alpha_1, \beta_1, \lambda, \gamma\}$. If $\gamma > 0$, then the model considers the *leverage effect*, that is, bad news raises the future volatility more than good news. This information is captured by the indicator function I_t since the volatility increases when a negative event occurs. In order to obtain a strong stationary solution, it is necessary to assume that $(\alpha_1 + \gamma/2) + \beta_1 < 1$. Furthermore, the model requires the condition $\alpha_1 + \gamma \geq 0$.

An alternative is to assume a conditional variance σ_t^2, which follows a process defined as follows

$$\sigma_t^2 = \alpha_0 + \alpha_1 \sigma_{t-1}^2 (\varepsilon_{t-1} - \gamma)^2 + \beta_1 \sigma_{t-1}^2, \quad t \in \mathbb{N}, \tag{11.4}$$

where we assume $\alpha_1(1 + \gamma^2) + \beta_1 < 1$ in order to guarantee the existence of a strong stationary solution with finite unconditional mean. If the conditional variance is of the form described in equation (11.4), we refer to this normal GARCH model as the NGARCH model.[3] The set of constant parameters is $\theta = \{\alpha_0, \alpha_1, \beta_1, \lambda, \gamma\}$. The choice of this particular GARCH specification is motivated by empirical studies on option pricing models. The NGARCH model seems to have minor option pricing errors in comparison with the competitors previously defined.

One of the most well-known models for option pricing with GARCH was proposed by Heston and Nandi (2000), where the stock price log-returns are as follows:

$$\log\left(\frac{S_t}{S_{t-1}}\right) = r_t - d_t + \lambda \sigma_t + \frac{\sigma_t}{2} - \frac{\sigma_t^2}{2} + \sigma_t \varepsilon_t, \quad 1 \leq t \leq T \tag{11.5}$$

---

[3]This model was introduced by Engle and Ng (1993).

and the conditional variance is defined as

$$\sigma_t^2 = \alpha_0 + \alpha_1(\varepsilon_{t-1} - \gamma\sigma_t)^2 + \beta_1\sigma_{t-1}^2, \quad t \in \mathbb{N}. \tag{11.6}$$

We assume $\beta_1 + \alpha_1\gamma^2 < 1$ in order to guarantee the existence of a strong stationary solution with finite mean and variance. The set of constant parameters is $\theta = \{\alpha_0, \alpha_1, \beta_1, \lambda, \gamma\}$. The particular conditional volatility structure allows one to obtain a recursive formula to calculate the price of a European option. Anyway, the benefit of this model comes at the cost of imposing a too restrictive volatility dynamic.[4]

As an alternative to modifying the conditional volatility one may change the distributional assumption of the model so as to obtain a skewed and fat-tailed GARCH model. This approach is used in Chapters 12 and 13.

11.3 MARKET ESTIMATION

In this section, we analyze all models using stock index returns. In our study, we use the adjusted closing index values of the S&P 500 index from Thursday, September 10, 1998, to Wednesday September 10, 2008, obtained from OptionMetrics. The daily S&P 500 index log-return is calculated.[5] The size of this data set, 2,506 observations, is large enough for GARCH model fitting. The dividend yield will not be used since adjusted closing index values are taken into account; that is, $d_t = 0$ for each t in our sample. For the daily interest rate, we take the time series of the above time window of the three-month Treasury bill rate.

We estimate parameters using the classical *maximum likelihood estimation* (MLE) procedure. The log-likelihood function to be maximized is of the form

$$\log l(\theta) = \sum_{t=1}^{T} \log f\left(y_t - \frac{g(r_t, d_t, \lambda_t, \sigma_t)}{\sigma_t}\right), \tag{11.7}$$

where f is the density function of the innovation. Such function can be easily written in the normal case, but in general it has a complex structure

---

[4]See Hsieh and Ritchken (2005).
[5]We have already analyzed this historical time series in Chapter 7, and we will study it further in Chapters 12 and 14.

or cannot be written in analytic form.[6] Note that because the conditional volatility σ_t strictly depends on parameters θ, the likelihood function to be maximized is viewed as a function of this set of parameters.

In the classical normal GARCH and in the NGARCH case, we consider the market model defined in (11.1); in the Heston-Nandi (HN) case we consider the model defined in (11.5), while in the GJR case we consider the following[7]

$$
\log\left(\frac{S_t}{S_{t-1}}\right) = \mu + \sigma_t\varepsilon_t, \quad 1 \leq t \leq T
$$

$$
\sigma_t^2 = \alpha_0 + \alpha_1\eta_{t-1}^2 + \gamma I_{t-1}\eta_{t-1}^2 + \beta\sigma_{t-1}^2.
$$

(11.8)

Under the normal hypothesis the log-likelihood can be easily written in analytic form as

$$
\log l(\theta) = -\sum_{t=1}^{T}\left(\frac{1}{2}\log(2\pi) + \log(\sigma_t) + \frac{(y_t - g(r_t, d_t, \lambda_t, \sigma_t))^2}{2\sigma_t^2}\right), \quad (11.9)
$$

where we define

$$
y_t = \frac{S_t}{S_{t-1}}.
$$

Starting values for the parameters θ of the two series ε_t and σ_t need to be specified for this iterative MLE. On each time step, the conditional variance is updated by the following scheme:

1. Set a starting point for parameters θ_0. Let us consider $t = 1$.
2. Calculate $\sigma_0 = \frac{\alpha_0}{1-\alpha_1-\beta_1}$ and set $\varepsilon_0 = 0$.
3. Calculate $\varepsilon_t = \frac{g(r_t,d_t,\lambda_t,\sigma_t)^2}{\sigma_{t-1}}$.
4. Calculate $\sigma_t^2 = h(\sigma_{t-1}, \varepsilon_{t-1}; \theta)$ and the sum in equation (11.9) until t.
5. If $t = T$, return $\log L(\theta)$; otherwise, go to the next step.
6. Set $t = t + 1$ and return to step 3.

The optimization procedure will move the starting point θ in a suitable direction until it reaches the problem's optimal solution. The MATLAB `fmincon`

---

[6]Non-normal random variables for modeling the innovation will be widely described in more detail in Chapters 12 and 13.

[7]This approach has been used in Barone-Adesi et al. (2008).

TABLE 11.1 S&P 500 Market Parameters Estimated Using the MLE Approach on the Time Series from September 10, 1998, to September 10, 2008

	μ	σ			
Lognormal	8.0802e-05	0.0115			
	β	α_1	α_0	γ	μ
GJR-GARCH	0.9376	0.0000	1.0176e-6	0.1098	-4.1376e-5
	β	α_1	α_0	λ	γ
Normal GARCH	0.9482	0.0500	5.0740e-7	0.0307	
NGARCH	0.8866	0.0733	1.8852e-6	1.0000e-6	0.6415
HN-GARCH	0.9009	7.629e-6	2.425e-6	-0.5000	50

function together with a suitable selection for the starting value and of the constraints have been used to minimize the objective function. The choice of the initial value σ_0 is of minor concern as soon as the dimension of the time series increases. The estimated parameters are reported in Table 11.1.

After the parameter estimation, one can extract both the volatility and the innovation process. Then, based on the observations of the innovation process, some particular goodness-of-fit statistics can be calculated in order to see how the innovation closely fits the standard normal distribution.

The Kolmogorov-Smirnov (KS), the Anderson-Darling (AD, AD^2, and AD_{up}^2), and the χ^2 statistics are given in Table 11.2. These tests are described in Chapter 6. The values of the KS statistic show the better fit performances of all GARCH models in comparison to the model, which assumes a constant volatility. The AD family of statistics captures the improvement on the tail approximation with respect to the constant volatility model. An examination of the values of all the goodness-of-fit statistics indicates that allowing for nonconstant volatility improves the model fitting, at least for this time series we investigate, even though the p-value of the χ^2 statistic is less than 5% for all models.

TABLE 11.2 Goodness-of-Fit Statistics on the Time Series from September 10, 1998, to September 10, 2008

	KS	AD	$n \cdot AD^2$	$n \cdot AD_{up}^2$	χ^2(p-value)
Log-normal	0.0533	1.3814	14.5717	1.802e+3	296.0444(0.0000)
GJR-GARCH	0.0348	110.9607	3.4462	9.8182	160.6732(0.0038)
Normal GARCH	0.0419	244.2490	5.3795	21.5416	146.2847(0.0139)
NGARCH	0.0307	12.0042	4.1472	53.6825	153.4920(0.0047)
HN-GARCH	0.0347	1.7919	5.7031	1.045e+05	130.7860(0.0389)

11.4   RISK-NEUTRAL ESTIMATION

In this section, we propose a Monte Carlo procedure to estimate parameters by fitting model prices to market prices of options. Option data were obtained from OptionMetrics. The mean between bid and ask prices is used as the market price of the call options. *Moneyness* is defined as the ratio $M = K/S$ of the strike price K over the initial asset price S_0. In the in-sample analysis, we consider liquid European call options traded on September 10, 2008, with prices between \$5 and \$180, maturities 10, 20, 38, 73, 101, 112, 192, 202, 283, and 293 days, and $0.8 \leq M \leq 1.2$ for a total of 98 mid-prices. The same data set will be empirically studied in Chapters 12 and 14.

A popular approach employed to price options with GARCH is to model stock price log returns under the market measure using the equation

$$\log\left(\frac{S_t}{S_{t-1}}\right) = r_t - d_t + \lambda_t \sigma_t - g(\sigma_t) + \sigma_t \varepsilon_t, \quad 1 \leq t \leq T,$$

where the function g denotes the log Laplace transform of the innovation distribution. The conditional variance may have a GARCH(1,1), a GJR-GARCH, a NGARCH or a Heston-Nandi form. If one assumes that the innovation follows a normal distribution, then it is simple to prove that the dynamic becomes

$$\log\left(\frac{S_t}{S_{t-1}}\right) = r_t - d_t + \lambda_t \sigma_t - \frac{\sigma_t^2}{2} + \sigma_t \varepsilon_t, \quad 1 \leq t \leq T, \tag{11.10}$$

where the conditional variance has the form

$$\sigma_t^2 = h(\sigma_{t-1}, \varepsilon_{t-1}, \theta)$$

A possible risk-neutral dynamic, as proposed by Duan (1995), is

$$\log\left(\frac{S_t}{S_{t-1}}\right) = r_t - d_t + -\frac{\sigma_t^2}{2} + \sigma_t \xi_t, \quad 1 \leq t \leq T,$$

where the conditional variance has the form

$$\sigma_t^2 = h(\sigma_{t-1}, \xi_{t-1} - \lambda, \theta).$$

where for simplicity λ is considered constant and ξ_t is standard normally distributed. If one wants to price options with only information about the underlying (i.e., using only the estimated stock market parameters), as will be shown later in this chapter, such a model does not perform well. For this reason, we also estimate risk-neutral parameters by using only information obtained from the option market and we assess option pricing out-of-sample performance in the next section. We note that the initial value for volatility is given by the market estimation in section 11.3. The dynamic described in equation (11.10) allows one to choose a conditional volatility, which has a GARCH(1,1), a GJR-GARCH, or a NGARCH form.

In the Heston and Nandi case together with equation (11.10), we have to consider the following expression:

$$\sigma_t^2 = \alpha_0 + \alpha_1(\xi_{t-1} - \omega\sigma_{t-1})^2 + \beta_1\sigma_{t-1}^2, \quad t \in \mathbb{N},$$

where

$$\omega = \gamma + \lambda + \frac{1}{2}.$$

If a GARCH(1,1) model is used to explain the volatility clustering effect, there are four unknown parameters (together with the initial local volatility estimate using the underlying time series) to be estimated to match model prices to market prices of options.

To obtain the risk-neutral estimates, we find a parameter set $\tilde{\theta}$ that solves the following optimization problem:

$$\min_{\tilde{\theta}} \sum_{i=1}^{N}(C_i(\tau_i, K_i)) - C^{\tilde{\theta}}(\tau_i, K_i))^2, \tag{11.11}$$

where C_i denotes the price of an option as observed in the market and $C_i^{\tilde{\theta}}$ denotes the price computed according to a pricing formula in the above defined GARCH models with a parameter set $\tilde{\theta}$. Figure 11.1 and Tables 11.3 and 11.4 show the option pricing fitting exercise described in equation (11.11) together with the estimated parameter and the pricing errors.

Monte Carlo simulations of the normal innovation are kept fixed during the optimization procedure in order to reduce the variance in the option valuation and increase the computational speed. Furthermore, the same random variates are considered across all different models to obtain a better model comparison. Even though in the Heston-Nandi case one may use a

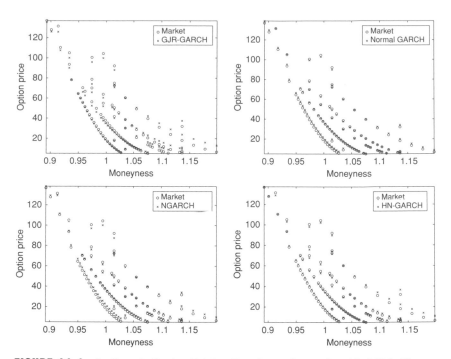

FIGURE 11.1 In-Sample Option Pricing Results on September 10, 2008: The GJR-GARCH, the Normal GARCH, the NGARCH, and the Heston-Nandi GARCH Model

recursive formula,[8] we prefer to consider the same simulation algorithm for all five models in order to have a more precise model comparison that is not influenced by numerical issues. In particular, the random variates are kept fixed in both the first approach, in which one considers only market parameters extracted from the underlying, and in the second one, in which one consider the parameters fitted by matching model prices to market prices of options.

As already noted, the value of the initial conditional variance is obtained by time-series estimation. Thus the set of GARCH parameters is estimated by numerically solving the optimization problem defined in equation (11.11). Also in this case, the MATLAB `fmincon` function together with a suitable selection of the starting value and of the constraints have been used to minimize the objective function. For example, the estimated market parameters may be used as the initial point of the optimization. Note that any numerical

---

[8]See Heston and Nandi (2000).

TABLE 11.3 Risk-Neutral Parameter Estimation

	σ				
Log-normal	0.0132				
	β	α_1	α_0	γ	μ
GJR-GARCH	0.9517	0.0247	4.9174e-7	0.0411	-6.4551e-4
	β	α_1	α_0	λ	γ
Normal GARCH	0.7500	0.0498	7.7946e-6	1.7667	
NGARCH	0.7500	0.0840	1.3103e-5	0.7166	0.2709
HN-GARCH	0.8083	1.9895e-5	1.000e-8	10.000	50.000

TABLE 11.4 In-Sample European Call Option Pricing Pricing Errors on September 10, 2008[a]

	APE	AAE	RMSE	ARPE
	Market-Based Pricing			
Black-Scholes	0.1238	4.5682	5.7035	0.1500
GJR-GARCH	0.0820	3.0251	3.9404	0.1009
Normal GARCH	0.2126	7.8414	9.4308	0.4831
NGARCH	0.0867	3.1990	3.2656	0.1939
HN-GARCH	0.0662	2.4429	3.6530	0.0739
	Risk-Neutral Estimation			
Black-Scholes	0.0614	2.2635	2.7841	0.1196
GJR-GARCH	0.0580	2.1379	2.7445	0.1151
Normal GARCH	0.0314	1.1567	1.4145	0.0544
NGARCH	0.0517	1.9084	2.1868	0.1073
HN-GARCH	0.0365	1.3452	1.6603	0.0717

[a] $S_0 = 1,232.04$ and $r_0 = 6.4800e\text{-}05$, with prices between \$5 and \$180; maturities 10, 20, 38, 73, 101, 112, 192, 202, 283, and 293 days; and $0.8 \leq M \leq 1.2$ for a total of 98 options.

algorithm to find an optimal point involves the choice of initial values. A more complex optimization procedure may be used in order to obtain a more precise and fast algorithm to find the minimum point.[9] In most of the cases that we have to deal with, we do not have a unique solution and the minimum point is only a local one. Consequently, there is no simple numerical procedures.

For completeness we report in Table 11.4 the pricing errors when using the estimated market parameter of section 11.3 to find the fair value of the

---

[9] See Cont and Tankov (2004).

European call option we investigated and compare the pricing errors to those obtained from the risk-neutral approach. Pricing using the estimated market parameter clearly underperforms the pricing obtained using the risk-neutral approach. Furthermore, in the constant volatility case, we obtain the worst market assessment and the largest pricing error. By comparing Tables 11.1 and 11.3 we note that risk-neutral parameters are usually different from the market ones. This empirical finding shows that the risk-neutral parameters are different from the market parameters, and thus the risk-neutral probability measure is not the same as the market measure. The pricing error obtained by the derivative evaluation based on the market parameter estimation, as shown in Table 11.4, is larger in comparison to the pricing error obtained by matching model prices to the market price of options. Though this findings is easily understandable from a purely computational point of view, this also has a financial interpretation. First, there is difference between the *trader approach* and the *fundamental approach*. This means that the trader approach, also referred to as the option-based approach, considers only information given by the option market itself, while the fundamental approach, also referred to as the market-based approach, uses only information contained in the underlying. Second, from a practical point of view, the risk-neutral estimation is obtained by matching model prices to market prices of options by solving the optimization problem minimizing the distance defined in equation (11.11), while with the market-based approach one prices options by using only parameters based on log-returns MLE.

The models allowing for volatility clustering exhibit a similar performance in matching market prices of options: The HN-GARCH and the classical normal GARCH model seem to be the best performers, at least for call options examined here.

11.4.1   Out-of-Sample Performance

In this section, we analyze the out-of-sample performance of the different normal GARCH models under a particular market scenario. We consider liquid European call options traded between Thursday, September 11, 2008, and Wednesday, September 17, 2008. Recall that we specifically used the latter day because of the dramatic market movement on that trading day. On that trading day, Bloomberg reported:

> *U.S. Treasury three-month bill rates dropped to the lowest since World War II as a loss of confidence in credit markets worldwide prompted investors to abandon higher-yielding assets for the safety of the shortest-term government securities.*

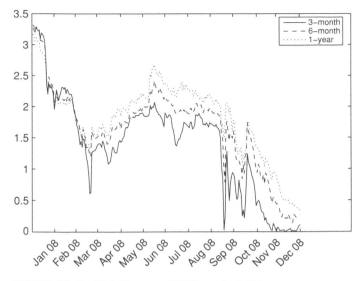

FIGURE 11.2   U.S. Treasury Bill Rates in 2008

Two days before, Lehman Brothers filed for Chapter 11 bankruptcy protection (September 15, 2008). The failure of this investment bank, one of the largest U.S. bankruptcies, caused an unprecedented market turmoil and this motivated our empirical study. Figure 11.2 reports the 3-month, 6-month, and 1-year U.S. Treasury bill rates[10] in 2008. Note that in September 2008 the 3-month Treasury was almost zero. We will show that the estimated parameters on September 10, 2008, do not sufficiently explain the market turmoil resulting from the Lehman Brothers bankruptcy announcement. In particular, considering a risk-free rate not far from zero gives an option price that is far from being realistic.

In the analysis, we consider options with prices between $5 and $180, maturities less than 450 days, and moneyness $0.8 \leq M \leq 1.2$. There is a total of 613 mid-prices.[11] Risk-neutral parameters estimated in section 11.4 on September 10, 2008, are used to evaluate the prices of European call options traded on each trading day until September 17, 2008, by considering the corresponding information for the index value, time to maturity, and interest rate between September 11 and September 17, 2008. The spot variances for the out-of-sample analysis for a given day are computed by applying

---

[10]Data source: U.S. Department of the Treasury, www.ustreas.gov/.
[11]We will consider the same data set in Chapters 12 and 14.

TABLE 11.5   Out-of-Sample European Call Option Pricing Errors between
September 11 to September 17, 2008[a]

	APE	AAE	RMSE	ARPE
	September 11, 2008			
Black-Scholes	0.1001	4.2616	5.3203	0.1210
GJR-GARCH	0.0830	3.5316	4.1051	0.1313
Normal GARCH	0.0349	1.4846	1.8351	0.0373
NGARCH	0.0462	1.9643	2.5478	0.0576
HN-GARCH	0.0554	2.3575	2.8395	0.0704
	September 12, 2008			
Black-Scholes	0.1166	5.0103	6.1785	0.1434
GJR-GARCH	0.1016	4.3643	4.9857	0.1527
Normal GARCH	0.0568	2.4387	2.7557	0.0853
NGARCH	0.0658	2.8249	3.5728	0.0764
HN-GARCH	0.0817	3.5096	3.9703	0.1178
	September 15, 2008			
Black-Scholes	0.2577	10.3184	11.5342	0.3484
GJR-GARCH	0.2355	9.4296	10.6136	0.3138
Normal GARCH	0.2463	9.8600	10.4407	0.3736
NGARCH	0.2532	10.1387	10.9621	0.3638
HN-GARCH	0.2522	10.0959	10.8686	0.3715
	September 16, 2008			
Black-Scholes	0.1564	7.8242	9.1852	0.2123
GJR-GARCH	0.1402	7.0154	8.2684	0.1906
Normal GARCH	0.0755	3.7760	4.3944	0.1124
NGARCH	0.0912	4.5639	5.6898	0.1136
HN-GARCH	0.1468	7.3441	8.2498	0.2318
	September 17, 2008			
Black-Scholes	0.3053	11.8214	13.2724	0.4059
GJR-GARCH	0.3038	11.7630	13.3330	0.3934
Normal GARCH	0.2589	10.0251	11.0552	0.3622
NGARCH	0.2756	10.6687	12.0242	0.3649
HN-GARCH	0.3372	13.0537	14.3124	0.4731

[a]Option prices between $5 and $180, maturities less than 450 days, and moneyness
$0.8 \leq M \leq 1.2$ for a total of 613 mid-prices.

the GARCH filter to the S&P 500 log-return, the risk-free rate, and the
historical estimation of GARCH parameters. This means that the value of
the spot volatility is updated according to the selected GARCH model.

The standard normal random variate together with the variance reduction technique explained in section 11.4 are employed to evaluate the option

value. The use of the same random numbers is of minor concern since the simulation of a matrix of standard normal random variables with 20,000 rows and 300 columns takes only few seconds: We use it only to reduce the variance across models and times. The out-of-sample pricing performance is acceptable only for options traded on September 11 and 12 as shown in Table 11.5. The pricing exercise gives an unsatisfactory result once the distance between the estimation date (September 10, 2008) and the option trading date increases.

11.5 SUMMARY

In this chapter, we reviewed some classical models to explain that stock price returns move in clusters. The performance of these models is compared to the market standard log-normal approach with constant volatility.

First, we estimated five models under the market measure and analyzed different goodness-of-fit statistics. The log-normal model is clearly outperformed by those models that consider a time-varying volatility. Then, we extracted the risk-neutral parameters by using the spot variance estimate from the GARCH stock price log-returns fit, and examined the error in option pricing. The so-called trader approach, based on information given in the option market, was compared with the fundamental approach, based only on the information given in the stock market. The former approach clearly outperformed the latter approach.

By taking into consideration the risk-neutral parameter estimate, we calculated the prices of options traded in the days that followed. In the out-of-sample analysis, we showed that the forecasting power decreases as the distance between the estimation day and the option trading day increases. In particular, under the stressed scenario between September 15 and September 17, 2008, the pricing errors become large, mostly due to the decline in the short-term interest rate on those days.

REFERENCES

Barone-Adesi, G., Engle, R., & Mancini, L. (2008). A GARCH option pricing model with filtered historical simulation. *Review of Financial Studies*, *21*(3), 1223–1258.

Cont, R. & Tankov, P. (2004). *Financial modelling with jump processes*. Boca Raton, FL: CRC Press.

Duan, J. (1995). The GARCH Option Pricing Model. *Mathematical Finance*, *5*(1), 13–32.

Engle, R. & Ng, V. (1993). Measuring and testing the impact of news on volatility. *Journal of Finance*, 48(5), 1749–1778.

Heston, S. & Nandi, S. (2000). A closed-form GARCH option valuation model. *Review of Financial Studies*, 13(3), 585–625.

Hsieh, K. & Ritchken, P. (2005). An empirical comparison of GARCH option pricing models. *Review of Derivatives Research*, 8(3), 129–150.

CHAPTER 12

Smoothly Truncated Stable GARCH Models

12.1   INTRODUCTION

In Chapter 3, we considered two ways of tempering heavy tails, leading to two different families of distributions with tempered heavy tails. The tails of a random variable can be tempered in a delicate way; that is, tempered stable (TS) or tempered infinitely divisible (TID) random variables can be obtained by tempering at the level of Lévy measures. These random variables are still infinitely divisible (ID) as is the α-stable.[1]

Furthermore, the tempered stable distribution can be obtained by following the more crude idea of tail truncation. By using this approach, one can obtain the so-called smoothly truncated stable (STS) random variable.[2] STS distributions are obtained by smoothly replacing the upper and lower tails of an arbitrary stable cumulative distribution function by two appropriately chosen normal tails. Consequently, the density of a smoothly truncated stable distribution consists of three parts. Left of some lower truncation level a and right of some upper truncation level b, it is described by two possibly different normal densities. In the center, the density is equal to that of a stable distribution. As a result, STS distributions lie in the domain of attraction of the normal distribution and possess even a finite-moment generating function while offering at the same time a flexible tool to model extreme events.

This chapter draws in part from Menn and Rachev (2009) but uses more recent data for the empirical analysis.

[1] See Chapter 3 for the construction of such distributions.

[2] This distribution has been introduced in Menn and Rachev (2009) and reviewed in Chapter 3.

As a consequence, the speed of convergence to the normal distribution is extremely slow.[3]

In this chapter, we show how to build a nonlinear asymmetric GARCH (NGARCH) stock price model allowing for non-normal innovation distributions.[4] Supported by some recent evidence reported in the literature,[5] we enhance a parsimonious nonlinear asymmetric GARCH(1,1) dynamic (NGARCH)[6] for describing the evolution of the conditional variance. For the pricing of derivatives, we will need a risk-neutral version of our time series model. Instead of focusing on the sufficient conditions for investors preferences to motivate the specific form of the change of measure, we provide a general framework that even allows for different residual distributions under the objective and the risk-neutral measure.

We test the STS-NGARCH model along two different dimensions. As already done in Chapter 11, we investigate the model's fit to a long history of S&P 500 log-returns. Then we compare the impact of the model specification and the distributional assumption on the ability to explain market prices of S&P 500 index options. We analyze option prices with three different estimation methodologies: (1) based only on time-series information, which we refer to as the *maximum likelihood estimation* (MLE) *methodology*; (2) based on time-series information but seeking to eliminate its deficiencies, which we refer to as the *MLE/fitted methodology*; and (3) a slight variation of the Heston-Nandi approach, which we refer to as the *nonlinear least squares* (NLS) *methodology*. For the third methodology, all GARCH parameters, including the spot variance, are determined from the market prices of options through a NLS optimization with respect to the sum of squared pricing errors. To assess the overall pricing performance of the STS-NGARCH variants, we adopt common practice and compare the different models with the normal-GARCH model and the normal-NGARCH model.

12.2 A GENERALIZED NGARCH OPTION PRICING MODEL

We begin by introducing a general option pricing model containing most of the GARCH stock price models proposed in the literature as particular

---

[3]This phenomenon was empirically observed by Mantegna and Stanley (1994).
[4]The model is mainly inspired by the Duan (1995) framework.
[5]See Christoffersen and Jacobs (2004b).
[6]See Engle and Ng (1993).

cases. We enhance the existing models so as to allow for alternative non-normal distributions in the innovation process while keeping the intuitive decomposition of the expected rate of return into risk-free rate plus risk-proportional risk premium.

Formally, the log-returns of the underlying are assumed to follow the following dynamic under the objective probability measure P:

$$\log\left(\frac{S_t}{S_{t-1}}\right) = r_t - d_t + \lambda_t\sigma_t - g(\sigma_t;\theta) + \sigma_t\varepsilon_t, \quad t \in \mathbb{N}, \tag{12.1}$$

S_t denotes the adjusted closing price of the underlying at date t and r_t and d_t denote the continuously compounded risk-free rate of return and dividend rate respectively for the period $[t-1,t]$. Both quantities as well as λ_t are assumed to be predictable, but can in general be modeled by separate stochastic processes. The innovation ε_t, with parameters θ, is a random variable with zero mean and unit variance, and the function $g(x;\theta)$ is the *log-Laplace-transform* of ε_t; that is, $g_{\varepsilon_t}(x) = \log(E[e^{x\varepsilon_t}])$, which is defined on some finite interval of the real line (eventually on the whole real line).[7] The conditional variance σ_t^2 is assumed to follow an asymmetric NGARCH(1, 1)-process:

$$\sigma_t^2 = \alpha_0 + \alpha_1\sigma_{t-1}^2(\varepsilon_{t-1} - \gamma)^2 + \beta_1\sigma_{t-1}^2, \quad t \in \mathbb{N}, \tag{12.2}$$

where we assume $\alpha_1(1 + \gamma^2) + \beta_1 < 1$ in order to guarantee the existence of a strong stationary solution with finite unconditional mean.[8] The choice of this particular GARCH specification is motivated by empirical findings.[9] The restriction to the case $p = q = 1$ has mainly been made for practical reasons, it seems sufficient for our purposes, and it simplifies the exposition.[10]

We note that if the distribution of the innovations equals the standard normal distribution and if we assume constant r, and λ then equation (12.1)

---

[7]If the distribution has all exponential moments finite, the Laplace transform is defined on the entire real line. This is the case of the normal and rapidly decreasing tempered stable distribution (RDTS).

[8]This is a natural extension of the classical condition obtained by Nelson (1990) for the GARCH(1,1) and by Bougerol and Picard (1992) for the GARCH(p, q) model; see, for example, Duan (1997) for details.

[9]See Ritchken and Trevor (1999) and Christoffersen and Jacobs (2004b).

[10]The generalization to the NGARCH(p, q) case or different GARCH variants is straightforward.

reduces to Duan's option pricing model.[11] For $\alpha_1 = \beta_1 = 0$ the model boils down to the discrete-time Black-Scholes log-normal model with constant volatility.

For the pricing of derivatives we will need a risk-neutral version of the model specification (12.1). A simple left-shift by the amount of the market price of risk applied to the distribution of the innovations at every time step enables us to formulate the dynamic of model (12.1) in one possible risk-neutral world.[12]

Now we present the natural generalization of this basic idea. For any standardized probability distribution ξ_t, with parameters $\tilde{\theta}$, which is equivalent to the marginal distribution of the innovations ε_t, the distribution of the following process is equivalent to the NGARCH stock price model described in equations (12.1) and (12.2)

$$\log\left(\frac{S_t}{S_{t-1}}\right) = r_t - d_t - g(\sigma_t; \tilde{\theta}) + \sigma_t \xi_t,$$

and the conditional variance has the form

$$\sigma_t^2 = \alpha_0 + \alpha_1 \sigma_{t-1}^2 \left(\xi_{t-1} - \lambda_t + \frac{1}{\sigma_{t-1}}\left(g(\sigma_{t-1}; \tilde{\theta}) - g(\sigma_{t-1}; \theta)\right) - \gamma\right)^2 + \beta_1 \sigma_{t-1}^2.$$

The importance of this fact is that it allows for different innovation distributions under the objective measure and the risk-neutral measure. In the case where efficient calibration procedures and reliable market prices of derivatives are available, it is possible to estimate the model parameters and the objective distribution from time-series data, whereas the risk-neutral distribution can be retrieved from market prices.

The above equation shows a way to obtain a risk-neutral version of the pricing process for the STS-GARCH model without actually getting into the option-theoretical intricacies. We emphasize the fact that the suggested change of measure is actually nothing more than a left shift of the innovation distribution and no economic argument has been given.

Furthermore, we are not interested in proving that the risk-neutral distribution we obtain is indeed the *right* one for pricing derivatives. It is just a

---

[11]For $\gamma = 0$ we obtain the model introduced in Duan (1995) and in the general case the one treated in Wei and Duan (1999).

[12]This fact follows from the equivalence between random variables with density. This means that if we have two random variables X and Y with density, it can be proved that the null measure sets of X are also null measure sets for Y, and the converse is true as well.

possible risk-neutral measure to be used to price derivatives. A discrete-time financial market with a continuous distribution for the returns is inevitably incomplete. Put differently, there are an infinite number of possible pricing measures and further assumptions about investors' preferences have to be made in order to obtain a unique pricing measure. Indeed, for every choice of the risk-neutral innovation satisfying the condition above, we obtain a different risk-neutral pricing measure and as a direct consequence also different option prices. In this sense, the suggested type of change of measure is not comparable to the *risk-neutral valuation relationship* (RNVR), *locally risk-neutral valuation relationship* (LRNVR), and its generalization to heavy-tailed returns.[13] The only claim we make is that for every choice of the random variable ξ_t, the resulting measure is a valid pricing measure in the sense that derivative prices calculated as discounted expected payoffs under the chosen measure will preclude arbitrage.

We see that the absence of restrictive assumptions provides new flexibility. We investigate the usefulness of the change of measure presented: We will check the quality of the model under the objective probability measure and then verify whether the option prices obtained with the help of the risk-neutral dynamic are able to explain the observed prices. In this context, this more general form of change of measure can then be seen as a first step toward an internally consistent option pricing framework where the risk-neutral distribution as well as the objective distribution of the probabilistic model is able to provide an acceptable fit to the empirically observed time-series and option market data.

12.3   EMPIRICAL ANALYSIS

We test the option pricing model presented in this chapter on the S&P 500 index market using options written on this index. We are particularly interested to see if the use of the STS distribution affects the statistical fit and the forecasting properties of the asymmetric NGARCH stock price model. Therefore, we divide our statistical analysis into two parts: In the first part, we investigate the statistical properties under the objective probability measure P, while in the second part we examine the model's ability to explain observed market prices of liquid options under the risk-neutral measure Q. As already done in Chapter 11, we empirically study the S&P 500 index in the period between 1998 and 2008 by analyzing both index log-returns and option prices.

---

[13]See Wei and Duan (1999) and references therein.

12.3.1 Results Under the Objective Probability Measure

We are interested in answering the following question: To what extent can the use of an appropriate probability distribution for the innovation process improve the statistical fit and the forecasting properties of popular GARCH models for stock-returns? We perform a comparative analysis, where the model candidates differ by their innovation distribution as well as by the specific GARCH form. Due to the general structure of the generalized NGARCH model, [14] all models can be expressed as a special subtype of the generalized NGARCH model. To simplify the estimation procedure, we impose a constant market price of risk λ. As candidates for the innovation distribution under the market measure, we will consider the normal, the Student-t, the α-stable, and the class of STS distribution. For all models, the conditional variance of the log-returns is assumed to follow a subtype of the asymmetric NGARCH model as introduced in equation (12.2).

Based on the model previously described, if we assume that ε_t is t distributed with parameter v and scale parameter $c = 1$, then a t-GARCH model can be defined. Furthermore, GARCH models with α-stable distribution can be considered. As explained in Chapter 3, an α-stable random variable is characterized by an index of stability α, a skewness parameter β, a scale parameter σ, and a location parameter μ, which we denote by $S_\alpha(\sigma, \beta, \mu)$. Thus, one can define two specific subclasses in order to draw a non-normal GARCH model with heavy tails (actually, very fat tails):

- A symmetric α-stable distribution $S_\alpha S(\sigma)$, with $\beta = \mu = 0$, and $1 < \alpha \leq 2$.
- An asymmetric α-stable distribution $S_{\alpha\beta}$, with $\sigma = 0.65$, $\mu = 0$, and and $1 < \alpha \leq 2$.

The assumption on α is not very restrictive in practice because most of the financial time series have finite mean. For $\alpha = 2$, one obtains the classical normal GARCH model. Thus, if we assume that ε_t is a symmetric α-stable distribution $S_\alpha S$ with parameter α and σ or an asymmetric α-stable distribution with parameters α, β, and σ, we define the $S_\alpha S(\sigma)$-GARCH and the $S_{\alpha\beta}$-GARCH models. We assess the model performance of these models in the next section.

To emphasize the importance of the GARCH components (α_1, β_1) and especially the asymmetric GARCH component γ on the statistical fit, we will consider the constant conditional variance (CCV) case $\alpha_1 = \beta_1 = 0$ and

---

[14]See equations (12.1) and (12.2) in section 12.2, and Chapter 11.

the symmetric GARCH model with $\gamma = 0$. In summary, we examine and compare the six models shown in Table 12.1.

All models are estimated by a numerical maximum likelihood routine. Assume for a moment that the parameters of the standardized distribution governing the innovation process are known. This is only the case when we assume standard normally distributed innovations. If we denote by f the corresponding density function, then a standard argument leads to the following conditional log-likelihood function for the NGARCH stock price model with innovation distribution

$$
\log L(\theta) = - \sum_{t=1}^{T} \log f\left(\frac{y_t - r_t + d_t - \lambda_t \sigma_t + \frac{\sigma_t^2}{2}}{\sigma_t}\right). \tag{12.3}
$$

The conditional variance is recursively obtained from

$$
\sigma_t^2 = \alpha_0 + \alpha_1 \sigma_{t-1}^2 (\varepsilon_{t-1} - \gamma)^2 + \beta_1 \sigma_{t-1}^2,
$$

and

$$
y_t = \frac{S_t}{S_{t-1}}
$$

denotes a series of log-returns, r_t a corresponding series of risk-free returns, and d_t the corresponding dividend yields.

As usual, the conditional likelihood function depends on the choice of the starting values ε_0 and σ_0, but for increasing sample size, the impact of the starting values on the estimation results is negligible. Maximizing the conditional likelihood function leads to estimates for the unknown model parameters θ. From these estimates, we can recursively recover the time series of empirical residuals $(\varepsilon_t)_{t=1,\dots,T}$. The empirical distribution of these residuals is used to estimate the parameters under the non-normal approaches.[15]

Table 12.2 summarizes the estimation results for the six variants of the generic generalized NGARCH model. Judged purely on the log-likelihood,

---

[15]We emphasize the fact that normal quasi-maximum likelihood methods are not applicable as the distributional assumption enters the dynamic of the conditional mean in the form of its logarithmic moment-generating function (Rachev et al. 2007). For this reason, Menn and Rachev (2009) propose an iterative procedure in which, after each iteration step, one calculates the Kolmogorov-Smirnov (KS) distance between the distributional assumption and the empirical distribution of the residuals. The iterations end as soon as this distance stops decreasing.

TABLE 12.1 Models Considered in the Empirical Analysis

Model	Description
CCV	The model as given by equations (12.1) and (12.2) with constant market price of risk λ, standard normally distributed innovations, and constant conditional variance ($\alpha_1 = \beta_1 = 0$).
Normal-GARCH	The model as given by equations (12.1) and (12.2) with constant market price of risk λ, with standard normally distributed innovations, and symmetric GARCH conditional variance ($\gamma = 0$).
Normal-NGARCH	The model as given by equations (12.1) and (12.2) with constant market price of risk λ, with standard normally distributed innovations, and asymmetric NGARCH conditional variance.
t-NGARCH	The model as given by equations (12.1) and (12.2) with constant market price of risk λ, standardized skewed t distributed innovations, and asymmetric NGARCH conditional variance. The logarithmic moment generating function in (12.1) is replaced by the one of a standard normal distribution, since the t distribution has no finite exponential moment.
α-stable-NGARCH	The model as given by equations (12.1) and (12.2) with constant market price of risk λ, symmetric and asymmetric α-stable distributed innovations, and asymmetric NGARCH conditional variance. The logarithmic moment generating function in equation (12.1) is replaced by the one of a standard normal distribution, since the α-stable distribution has no finite exponential moment.
STS-NGARCH	The model as given by equations (12.1),(12.2) with constant market price of risk λ, standard STS distributed innovations, and asymmetric NGARCH conditional variance. This case is subdivided into two variants: First, we estimate the model with a fixed STS distribution (STS-NGARCH fixed), where the predetermined STS distribution has reasonably chosen parameter values. Second, we estimate a standardized STS distribution (STS-NGARCH estimated).

TABLE 12.2 Market Models Comparison: Estimated S&P 500 Market Parameters and Goodness of Fit Statistics Using the Recursive Two-Step MLE Approach (September 10, 1998, to September 10, 2008)

Model	KS	AD	$n \cdot AD^2$	$n \cdot AD^2_{up}$	χ^2(p-value)	LL
CCV	0.0534	1.2815	14.571	1802	296.0(0.000)	−3680.7
	β 8.0802e-5	α_1 0.0115				
Normal-GARCH N(0,1)	0.0375	1.7108	5.1975	102.5	239.4(0.000)	−3665.1
	β 0.9482	α_1 0.0500	α_0 5.0740e-7	λ 0.0307		
Normal-NGARCH N(0,1)	0.0307	12.004	4.1472	53.68	153.5(0.004)	−3524.6
	β 0.8866	α_1 0.0733	α_0 1.8852e-6	λ 1.0000e-6	γ 0.6415	
t-GARCH t(10.2239,-0.0936)	0.0209	0.0544	0.8400	6.309	131.7(0.110)	−3495.4
$S_\alpha S$-GARCH $S_{1.9465}(0.6719, 0, 0)$	0.0264	0.0542	2.2286	9.985	137.7(0.024)	−3502.6
α-stable-GARCH $S_{1.9257}(0.65, -0.2, 0)$	0.0257	0.0548	2.2989	8.362	144.3(0.006)	−3502.8
STS-GARCH^{fixed} $S\|^{-0.6196,19.9964}\|(0.65, -0.2, 0)_{1.9}$	0.0266	39.179	2.9787	10.87	159.6(0.000)	−3527.3
STS-GARCH $S\|^{-3.9749,2.2906\|}(0.6658, -0.2, 0.0190)_{1.9197}$	0.0207	0.0452	1.6634	10.36	135.1(0.029)	−3499.7

Note: All non-normal models use as a starting point the estimation of the NGARCH parameters, which are based on the normal distributional assumption.

the second variant of the STS-NGARCH-model performs best. A completely unsatisfactory fit occurs for the three models based on the standard normally distributed innovations (i.e., CCV, normal GARCH, and NGARCH) and these models are rejected by the goodness-of-fit statistics we have considered. At the same time, the results show that the NGARCH model is superior to its classical counterpart, a finding that is consistent with other studies. The difference in performance between GARCH and NGARCH decreases for the cases where the innovation distribution admits skewness. The reason is that in these cases, the residual distribution is able to explain part of the leverage effect that can be explained by the parameter γ in the NGARCH model.

Judged on the distance between the empirical and the theoretical distribution of the residuals, the picture changes slightly. The KS and AD statistics allow us to reject all normal models, while all non-normal models present a good performance. Models based on the STS distribution outperform all other normal-based models. Summarizing the results and repeating findings in other studies, we can state the following: Albeit GARCH models are well known to be one of the best-performing models to describe the evolution of volatility, a satisfactory statistical fit can only be provided when the distribution of the innovation is non-normal.[16] As we have shown, the STS distributions are able to capture all important properties of the empirical residual distribution and can therefore help in building a consistent model where the model's assumptions coincide with the empirical distribution of the filtered residuals. Due to its modeling flexibility, the class of STS distributions turns out to be a viable alternative to other popular heavy-tailed distributions.

12.3.2   Explaining S&P 500 Option Prices

Next we take a closer look at the pricing performance of the STS-NGARCH option pricing model. For convenience, the following two equations recapitulate the specific dynamic under the objective probability measure P, which we assume throughout this section:

$$\log\left(\frac{S_t}{S_{t-1}}\right) = r_t - d_t + \lambda\sigma_t - g(\sigma_t; \theta) + \sigma_t\varepsilon_t,$$

$$\sigma_t^2 = \alpha_0 + \alpha_1\sigma_{t-1}^2(\varepsilon_{t-1} - \gamma)^2 + \beta_1\sigma_{t-1}^2,$$

---

[16]In a recent study by Barone-Adesi et al. (2008), the authors try to circumvent alternative distributional assumptions by applying a methodology called *filtering historical simulation* (FHS), by using the empirical distribution of the filtered historical residuals for simulation purposes.

where

$$\varepsilon_t \overset{iid}{\sim} S_\alpha^{[a,b]}(\sigma, \beta, \mu).$$

This specific version differs from the general model by assuming a constant market price of risk λ and the special choice for the innovation distribution. The meaning of the different parameters is the same as in section 12.2. Throughout the remainder of this chapter, we impose the especially simple form of the risk-neutral measure Q, which leads to the following process dynamic under Q:

$$\log\left(\frac{S_t}{S_{t-1}}\right) = r_t - d_t - g(\sigma_t; \tilde{\theta}) + \sigma_t \xi_t,$$

$$\sigma_t^2 = \alpha_0 + \alpha_1 \sigma_{t-1}^2 (\xi_{t-1} - \tilde{\gamma})^2 + \beta_1 \sigma_{t-1}^2,$$

where

$$\xi_t \overset{iid}{\sim} S_\alpha^{[a,b]}(\sigma, \beta, \mu),$$

meaning that we consider the same distribution for residuals in both market measure and risk-neutral measure, and where $\tilde{\gamma} = \gamma + \lambda$ is the asymmetry parameter under the risk-neutral measure.[17] This dynamic can be used to price any derivative instrument with underlying the stock price S by means of Monte Carlo simulation. The set of parameters that is needed to simulate paths of the STS-NGARCH model under Q consists of the six STS distribution parameters, the four risk-neutral model parameters, and the spot variance σ_0. We analyze the following three estimation methodologies:

- *MLE.* The STS distribution and the model parameters under the objective probability measure are estimated from a history of log-returns, dividend, and interest rates by the same iterative maximum-likelihood procedure that we already described and applied in the section 12.3.1. The spot variance σ_0 is obtained as a by-product of the time-series estimation, and the risk-neutral asymmetry parameter $\tilde{\gamma}$ is obtained as $\tilde{\gamma} = \gamma + \lambda$.
- *MLE/fitted.* As in MLE, all distribution and model parameters are estimated from past information. In a second step, we determine new values of $\tilde{\gamma}$ and σ_0 by fitting the model prices to the available market prices of

---

[17]We consider the same random variable under both market and risk-neutral, noting that it is even possible to use a random variable under the market measure and a different one under the risk-neutral measure.

liquid options. This is done by minimizing the sum of squared pricing errors over these two parameters.

- *NLS.* This approach can be seen as complementary to the MLE/fitted approach. All GARCH parameter values are obtained by minimizing the sum of squared pricing errors between model and market prices, except the spot variance σ_0, which is taken by the previous *MLE/fitted* estimation. The STS distribution parameters are exogenously set to the values, which were obtained by approach *MLE*.[18]

Because it is only based on time-series information, the advantage of the *MLE* methodology is that it can even be applied in situations where no reliable market data of derivatives are available. The *MLE/fitted* approach is motivated by two empirical findings. First, the market price of risk parameter λ, which is known to be time varying in reality, is difficult to estimate and very likely to be different for the lifetime of some derivative instrument than for the estimation window. This reduces confidence in the estimated value based on past information and therefore it seems plausible to rely on an estimate, which is based on the forward-looking information provided by option prices. Note that determining $\tilde{\gamma} = \gamma + \lambda$ from option prices is actually equivalent to determining λ, if the value of γ is considered to be given.

Second, the option prices generated with the NGARCH model are highly sensitive to the value of spot volatility. The question is whether the right value can be better revealed from the time-series information or from the option market. Filtering of the spot variance requires a long data history in order to minimize the starting value bias. Therefore, one could argue that current option prices contain more information on the current level of volatility than a return from five years ago. The underlying idea for this approach is that GARCH models are well known as being excellent in describing the dynamic of volatility. The disadvantage of this approach is that from the option prices only risk-neutral parameters can be determined, whereas the available data are supposed to be generated from the objective distribution. Because the values of the objective parameters cannot be retrieved from the risk-neutral ones (in the risk-neutral world, γ and λ are only observed through their sum as $\tilde{\gamma}$), the filtering of volatility will lead to a biased estimate for the spot variance. In our application, we solve the identifiability problem by setting the market price of risk parameter equal to its time-series estimate.

---

[18]This methodology is similar to the approach of Heston and Nandi (2000) who enhanced the pure NLS-methodologies as applied in Bakshi et al. (1997) by estimating all model parameters from the market prices but filtering the spot variance from a series of past log-returns.

Regarding the *NLS* approach, since the simulation of STS random variates is not particularly time consuming, it would also be possible to estimate the risk-neutral distribution of residuals from the option prices. However, we do not consider this approach since we have enough parameters to obtain a small error in the calibration of option prices observed in the market. If a larger set of option prices is available, it could be useful to consider this additional flexibility of the model.

The three estimation techniques are compared with respect to their in-sample and out-of-sample pricing performance. The 2,506 data points of the daily log-return, dividend, and interest rate series, the closing prices of all 98 options on September 10, 2008, are available for the estimation. The model option prices are determined by Monte Carlo simulation with 20,000 paths[19] and the empirical martingale simulation is applied to reduce the variance.[20] Because we use this technique, and the difference between the logarithm of the Laplace transform of the standard normal distribution and STS distribution is small, we consider the function $g(\sigma_t)$ of equation (12.4) as in the normal GARCH case. This means that, since the logarithm of the Laplace transform of a standard normal random variable is equal to $\sigma_t^2/2$, we use this quadratic function also in the STS-NGARCH model. We adopt this simplification because in the STS case we do not have a closed-form formula for this function, and therefore has to be evaluated with a Monte Carlo integration procedure.

In Figure 12.1, we display the behavior of the logarithm of the Laplace transform for the standard normal and for the STS case evaluated by means of 200,000 random numbers.

As empirical experiments have shown,[21] the convergence of the option prices is slower than for the classical normal GARCH model. For this reason, we consider 20,000 paths per simulation in order to account for the STS distributed innovations.

Figure 12.2 reports the behavior of the S&P 500 index between September 11 and 17, 2008. The results of the in-sample estimation are reported in Tables 12.3, 12.4, and 12.5. The MLE/fitted approach only differs from the MLE approach in the estimates for σ_0 and $\tilde{\gamma}$.

Table 12.3 reports the estimation results for the STS-NGARCH model with different estimation techniques. α_0, α_1, and β_1 are the parameters of the NGARCH(1,1) process. The asymmetry parameter under the risk-neutral

---

[19]The computational time for simulating a matrix 20,000 × 310 of STS random numbers is 10 seconds. The authors are grateful to Christian Menn of DZ Bank AG for providing the MATLAB code for the STS distribution.

[20]This method, introduced by Duan and Simonato (1998), is described in Chapter 8.

[21]See Menn and Rachev (2009).

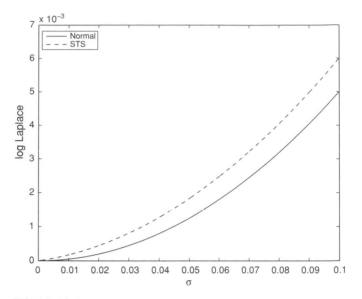

FIGURE 12.1 Shape of the Log Laplace Transform of the Standard Normal Distribution and of the STS Distribution $S_{1.9197}^{[-3.9749, 2.2906]}(0.6658, -0.2, 0.0190)$

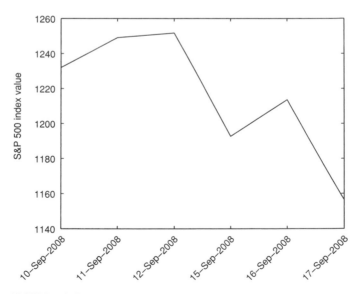

FIGURE 12.2 S&P 500 Index Values between September 10 and September 17, 2008

TABLE 12.3 Risk-Neutral Parameters Estimation[a]

Model	β	α_1	α_0	λ	γ
Normal-GARCH (MLE/fitted)				0.1297	
Normal-GARCH (NLS)	0.9025	0.0524	1.7911e-6	0.8668	
Normal-NGARCH (MLE/fitted)					0.6595
Normal-NGARCH (NLS)	0.9155	0.0405	5.2218e-7	0.7166	0.2709
STS-NGARCH (MLE/fitted)					0.2330
STS-NGARCH (NLS)	0.9084	0.0335	1.2776e-6	1.0643	0.2321

[a]We assume the $N(0, 1)$ distribution for the normal model, and the $S_{1.9197}^{[-3.9749, 2.2906]}$ (0.6658, −0.2, 0.0190) for the STS model.

measure Q is denoted by γ, and the market price of risk parameter is denoted by λ. In Table 12.4, we denote by σ_0^P the annualized estimated spot variance under the market measure, and by σ_0^Q the annualized estimated spot variance under the risk-neutral measure. The spot variances for the out-of-sample analysis at a given day are computed by applying the GARCH filter by using the S&P 500 log-return, the risk-free rate, and the estimated GARCH parameters. This means that the value of the spot volatility is updated according to the GARCH models.

So far we have only discussed different estimation techniques for one model. Obviously, we also need an objective benchmark, which allows us

TABLE 12.4 Estimated Annualized Volatilities

	Sep 10		Sep 11	Sep 12	Sep 15	Sep 16	Sep 17
Model	σ_0^P	σ_0^Q					
CCV (NLS)	0.1817	0.2082	0.2082	0.2082	0.2082	0.2082	0.2082
Normal-GARCH (NLS)	0.2494	0.1890	0.1888	0.1810	0.1755	0.2687	0.2563
Normal-NGARCH (NLS)	0.2819	0.2215	0.2090	0.2003	0.1951	0.2694	0.2580
STS-NGARCH (MLE)	0.2819		0.2708	0.2562	0.2447	0.3399	0.3212
STS-NGARCH (MLE/fitted)	0.2819	0.2263	0.2189	0.2078	0.1994	0.3103	0.2933
STS-NGARCH (NLS)	0.2819	0.2263	0.2167	0.2076	0.2033	0.2705	0.2588

TABLE 12.5 In-sample European Call Option Pricing Pricing Errors on September 10, 2008[a]

Model	APE	AAE	RMSE	ARPE
	In Sample			
CCV (NLS)	0.0459	2.9685	3.6373	0.1026
Normal-GARCH (MLE)	0.2126	7.8414	9.4308	0.4831
Normal-GARCH (MLE/fitted)	0.0563	2.0760	2.7369	0.1085
Normal-GARCH (NLS)	0.0341	1.2569	1.5563	0.0530
Normal-NGARCH (MLE)	0.0867	3.1990	3.2656	0.1939
Normal-NGARCH (MLE/fitted)	0.0207	0.7654	0.8752	0.0463
Normal-NGARCH (NLS)	0.0154	0.5676	0.6891	0.3958
STS-NGARCH (MLE)	0.0911	3.3625	3.9029	0.2016
STS-NGARCH (MLE/fitted)	0.0168	0.6198	0.7262	0.0290
STS-NGARCH (NLS)	0.0134	0.4954	0.6186	0.0287

[a] $S_0 = 1,232.04\$$ and $r_0 = 6.4800e\text{-}05$, with prices between \$5 and \$180, maturities 10, 20, 38, 73, 101, 112, 192, 202, 283, and 293 days, and $0.8 \leq M \leq 1.2$ for a total of 98 options.

to judge the absolute performance of the STS-NGARCH option pricing model. For this reason, we show the performance of an option pricing model measured by the four statistics discussed in Chapter 7: the average prediction error (APE), average absolute error (AAE), root mean-square error (RMSE), and average relative pricing error (ARPE). The values are reported in Table 12.5. The greater values of the absolute RMSE of all models compared to similar studies can be explained by our specific data set, which contains options with different maturities, included long maturities. In Figure 12.3 we show the in-sample option pricing results on September 10, 2008 for four different models.

For the out-of-sample comparison, the model parameter estimates are used to price the option contracts between September 11 and 17, 2008. The models are only allowed to use the estimation result on September 10, 2008, plus the observations of the index value and interest rate series on each day between September 11 and 17, 2008. Table 12.6 reports the model performance of the CCV model, the two normal GARCH models based on the NLS estimation, and the three STS models.

The absolute valuation errors for options with greater prices tend to be greater. This explains the increased values of the RSME. However, the numbers reported for the relative RSME are in accordance with similar studies. It can be seen that in-sample, the normal-GARCH models outperforms all

TABLE 12.6 Out-of-sample European Call Option Pricing Errors between September 11 and September 17, 2008[a]

Model	APE	AAE	RMSE	ARPE
	September 11, 2008			
CCV (NLS)	0.1001	4.2616	5.3203	0.1210
Normal-GARCH (NLS)	0.0873	3.7163	4.1391	0.1258
Normal-NGARCH (NLS)	0.0595	2.5330	2.8651	0.0704
STS-NGARCH (MLE)	0.0436	1.8557	2.4508	0.1036
STS-NGARCH (MLE/fitted)	0.0516	2.1973	2.4693	0.0662
STS-NGARCH (NLS)	0.0554	2.3590	2.6098	0.0711
	September 12, 2008			
CCV (NLS)	0.1166	5.0103	6.1785	0.1434
Normal-GARCH (NLS)	0.1242	5.3362	5.8142	0.2076
Normal-NGARCH (NLS)	0.1076	4.6240	4.9732	0.1715
STS-NGARCH (MLE)	0.0540	2.3185	3.6039	0.0576
STS-NGARCH (MLE/fitted)	0.0988	4.2423	4.5653	0.1645
STS-NGARCH (NLS)	0.1009	4.3354	4.6186	0.1673
	September 15, 2008			
CCV (NLS)	0.2577	10.3184	11.5342	0.3484
Normal-GARCH (NLS)	0.3106	12.4374	13.1878	0.4727
Normal-NGARCH (NLS)	0.3066	12.2766	13.0833	0.4547
STS-NGARCH (MLE)	0.2667	10.6760	11.8607	0.3702
STS-NGARCH (MLE/fitted)	0.2992	11.9799	12.6900	0.4519
STS-NGARCH (NLS)	0.2943	11.7841	12.4689	0.4445
	September 16, 2008			
CCV (NLS)	0.1564	7.8242	9.1852	0.2123
Normal-GARCH (NLS)	0.0512	2.5632	3.1236	0.1056
Normal-NGARCH (NLS)	0.0502	2.5090	2.8868	0.1026
STS-NGARCH (MLE)	0.0618	3.0914	3.6111	0.1560
STS-NGARCH (MLE/fitted)	0.0652	3.2603	3.8909	0.1468
STS-NGARCH (NLS)	0.0267	1.3335	1.7168	0.0510
	September 17, 2008			
CCV (NLS)	0.3053	11.8214	13.2724	0.4059
Normal-GARCH (NLS)	0.1739	6.7319	7.4849	0.2386
Normal-NGARCH (NLS)	0.1769	6.8492	7.5436	0.2418
STS-NGARCH (MLE)	0.1570	6.0780	7.6925	0.1749
STS-NGARCH (MLE/fitted)	0.1395	5.4020	6.0729	0.1817
STS-NGARCH (NLS)	0.2197	8.5067	9.2354	0.3108

[a]Option prices between $5 and $180, maturities less than 450 days, and moneyness $0.8 \leq M \leq 1.2$ for a total of 613 mid-prices.

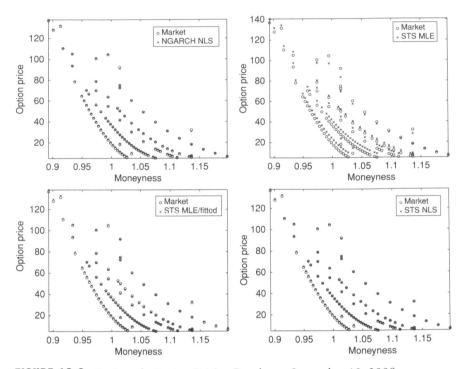

FIGURE 12.3 In-Sample Option Pricing Results on September 10, 2008: Normal-NGARCH and the Three STS-NGARCH Models

three variants of the STS-NGARCH model. However, out-of-sample, the STS models perform best. Interestingly, the NLS approach is similar to those of the MLE/fitted approach for the in-sample as well as out-of-sample data.

Furthermore, the pricing performance results are that the ordering of the different models in the out-of-sample comparison depends on the performance criteria. Given the fact that the NLS parameters are determined by minimizing the absolute RSME, these results are not too surprising, at least in the in-sample analysis. The problem with the NLS approach is that the estimated parameter values depend significantly on the loss function used for the minimization procedure. Furthermore, the loss function has an impact not only on the estimation but also on the out-of-sample performance.[22] Given

---

[22]See the recent studies of Ritchken and Trevor (1999) and Christoffersen and Jacobs (2004a).

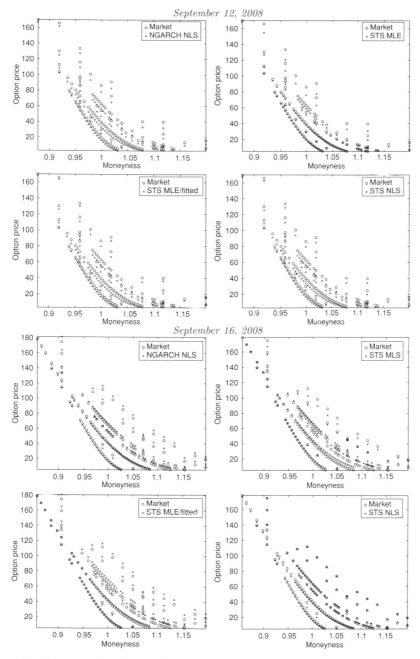

FIGURE 12.4 Out-of-Sample Option Pricing Results on September 12 and September 16, 2008: Normal-NGARCH and the Three STS-NGARCH Models

the satisfactory out-of-sample performance of the *MLE/fitted* approach and even the pure MLE approach, we believe that these are competitive approaches.

Figure 12.4 shows the out-of-sample prices of the NGARCH model based on the normal distributional assumption and the three STS-GARCH models on September 12 and 16, 2008. On both days, the STS models are the best performers: on September 12 the *MLE/fitted* performance is the best performer, while on September 16 the *NLS* approach outperforms all others.

12.4   SUMMARY

In this chapter we introduce an application of the class of smoothly truncated stable (STS) distribution that is well suited to meet the needs of modeling financial data. STS distributions combine the modeling power of stable distributions with the appealing property of finite moments of arbitrary order. This model enhances the classical NGARCH option pricing model so as to allow for non-normal innovation distributions. In this sense, we create a time-series model, which combines the three major characteristics observed for financial data: volatility clustering, leverage effect, and conditionally leptokurtic returns. The pricing measure is constructed in a canonical way and is only driven by dynamic of the market price of risk. In its most general case, the model allows for a different innovation distribution under the risk-neutral and the objective probability measure, a property that could be helpful on the way toward an internally consistent option pricing model. These types of models will be considered in Chapter 13.

The empirical investigation of the STS model leads to encouraging results. First, we show that the use of non-normal innovation distributions significantly improves the statistical fit of the NGARCH model under the objective probability measure. The second part of the empirical study is dedicated to the analysis of the model's ability to explain market prices of S&P 500 index options. We compare three variants of the STS-NGARCH option pricing model with normal GARCH models. We find that the STS-NGARCH model, where the model parameters are estimated from time-series information and only the market price of risk and the spot variance are inverted from option prices, performs best on an out-of-sample basis. These findings provide the motivation for Chapters 13 and 14. In those chapter we use the family of tempered stable distributions and different non-normal GARCH models to investigate the information content provided by historical time series for pricing options traded in the market.

REFERENCES

Bakshi, G., Cao, C., & Chen, Z. (1997). Empirical performance of alternative option pricing models. *Journal of Finance, 52*(5), 2003–2049.

Barone-Adesi, G., Engle, R., & Mancini, L. (2008). A GARCH option pricing model with filtered historical simulation. *Review of Financial Studies, 21*(3), 1223–1258.

Bougerol, P. & Picard, N. (1992). Stationarity of GARCH processes and of some nonnegative time series. *Journal of Econometrics, 52*, 115–127.

Christoffersen, P. & Jacobs, K. (2004a). The importance of the loss function in option valuation. *Journal of Financial Economics, 72*(2), 291–318.

Christoffersen, P. & Jacobs, K. (2004b). Which GARCH model for option valuation? *Management Science, 50*(9), 1204–1221.

Duan, J. (1995). The GARCH option pricing model. *Mathematical Finance, 5*(1), 13–32.

Duan, J. (1997). Augmented GARCH (p,q) process and its diffusion limit. *Journal of Econometrics, 79*(1), 97–127.

Duan, J. & Simonato, J. (1998). Empirical martingale simulation for asset prices. *Management Science, 44*(9), 1218–1233.

Engle, R. & Ng, V. (1993). Measuring and testing the impact of news on volatility. *Journal of Finance, 48*(5), 1749–1778.

Heston, S. & Nandi, S. (2000). A closed-form GARCH option valuation model. *Review of Financial Studies, 13*(3), 585–625.

Mantegna, R. & Stanley, H. (1994). Stochastic process with ultraslow convergence to a Gaussian: The truncated Lévy flight. *Physical Review Letters, 73*(22), 2946–2949.

Menn, C. & Rachev, S. (2009). Smoothly truncated stable distributions, GARCH-models, and option pricing. *Mathematical Methods of Operations Research, 63*(3), 411–438.

Nelson, D. (1990). Stationarity and persistence in the GARCH (1, 1) model. *Econometric Theory, 6*, 318–334.

Rachev, S., Mittnik, S., Fabozzi, F., Focardi, S., & Jašić, T. (2007). *Financial econometrics: From basics to advanced modeling techniques.* Hoboken, NJ: John Wiley & Sons.

Ritchken, P. & Trevor, R. (1999). Pricing options under generalized GARCH and stochastic volatility processes. *Journal of Finance, 54*(1), 377–402.

Wei, J. & Duan, J. (1999). Pricing foreign currency and cross-currency options under GARCH. *Journal of Derivatives, 7*(1), 51–63.

CHAPTER 13

Infinitely Divisible GARCH Models

In the last 30 years, an enormous number of papers identifying the problems with option pricing have been published. As Emanuel Derman (2005), a well-known market practitioner, wrote:

The history of quants on Wall Street is the history of the ways in which practitioners and academics have refined and extended the Black-Scholes model. (p. 8)

The homoskedasticity and the lognormality assumptions made in the Black-Scholes framework cannot deal effectively with stylized facts about the volatility clustering and the leptokurtosis found for asset prices. In Figure 13.1, the S&P 500 index log-returns are shown. As can be seen, the distribution is asymmetric, has fat tails, and exhibits volatility clustering. Although asset return distributions are known to be conditionally leptokurtic, only a few studies consider non-normal innovations in the GARCH model literature.

A general opinion is that, for the purpose of option valuation, parameters estimated from option prices are preferable to parameters estimated from the underlying returns.[1] Alternatively, the most recent results are based on a different approach. Both historical asset prices and option prices are considered to assess the model performance. Parametric and nonparametric models have been proposed by connecting the statistical with the risk-neutral measure. In general, the asset return model is specified under the historical measure $\mathbb{P}$ and cannot be directly used to price options. One possibility is to specify a change of measure between $\mathbb{P}$ and possible risk-neutral measure $\mathbb{Q}$. This approach is particularly attractive because the GARCH parameters can be easily estimated using historical asset returns and used for pricing purposes.

---

[1]See, for instance, Chernov and Ghysels (2000).

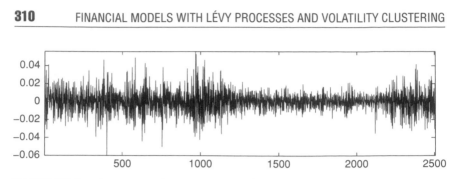

FIGURE 13.1   S&P 500 Index Log-Returns from September 10, 1998, to September 10, 2008

Unfortunately, the failure to explain observed option prices only by considering time series information is well known. This approach leads to a rather poor pricing performance and it is largely dominated by option pricing models estimated only using option prices. To overcome this drawback, the dynamic of the logarithmic stock price can be driven by a GARCH(1,1) process where the standardized innovations are governed by an infinitely divisible (ID) distribution with zero mean and unit variance and finite moment generating function. In this chapter, and in the following chapter, we compare the performances of some non-normal GARCH models recently proposed in the literature. In particular, some non-normal GARCH models are considered, such as the *normal inverse Gaussian* (NIG), *skewed variance gamma* (SVG), *inverse gaussian* (IG), *classical tempered stable* (CTS), and *rapidly decreasing tempered stable* (RDTS) models with volatility clustering. These, in turn, are compared with the nonparametric FHS-GARCH model.

Since discrete-time markets with continuous return distribution fail to be complete, the problem of the appropriate choice of the equivalent, respective martingale pricing measure for the discounted asset price process will be solved, while considering a density transformation between ID distributions. Instead of imposing unrealistic conditions on investors' preferences or the Esscher transform, a suitable change of measure will allow us to choose an equivalent martingale measure and to perform a joint estimation of objective and risk-neutral measures.

By following the literature on option pricing with GARCH, we consider European options written on the S&P 500, pointing out that our approach could be applied to over-the-counter markets since the risk-neutral dynamics are calculated with a pure mathematical argument and without assuming any economic reason.

We begin by reviewing GARCH models with non-normal ID distributed innovations. In particular, ID asymmetric distributions with tails fatter than the normal distribution are considered. Because asset return distributions are known to be asymmetric and conditionally leptokurtic, different distributional assumptions are taken into consideration in order to address these facts, which are rarely considered in the recent GARCH model literature.

13.1   STOCK PRICE DYNAMIC

In this section, we present a GARCH model with an ID distributed innovation process. The GARCH stock price model is defined over a filtered probability space $(\Omega, \mathcal{F}, (\mathcal{F}_t)_{t\in\mathbb{N}}, \mathbb{P})$, which is constructed as follows. Consider a sequence $(\varepsilon_t)_{t\in\mathbb{N}}$ of independent and identically distributed (i.i.d) real random variables on a sequence of probability spaces $(\Omega_t, \mathbb{P}_t)_{t\in\mathbb{N}}$, such that ε_t is an ID distributed random variable with zero mean and unit variance on $(\Omega_t, \mathbb{P}_t)$, and assume that $E[e^{x\varepsilon_t}] < \infty$ where $x \in (-a, b)$ for some $a, b > 0$.

In order to construct this model, the distribution of the random variable ε_t must have exponential moments of some or any order.[2] Now we define

$$\Omega := \prod_{t\in\mathbb{N}} \Omega_t,$$

$$\mathcal{F}_t := \otimes_{k=1}^{t}\sigma(\varepsilon_k) \otimes \mathcal{F}_0 \otimes \mathcal{F}_0 \cdots,$$

$$\mathcal{F} := \sigma\left(\cup_{t\in\mathbb{N}}\mathcal{F}_t\right),$$

$$\mathbb{P} := \otimes_{t\in\mathbb{N}}\mathbb{P}_t,$$

where $\mathcal{F}_0 = \{\emptyset, \Omega\}$ and $\sigma(\varepsilon_k)$ means the σ-algebra generated by ε_k on Ω_k.

We first propose the following stock price dynamics:

$$\log\left(\frac{S_t}{S_{t-1}}\right) = r_t - d_t + \lambda_t\sigma_t - g_{\varepsilon_t}(\sigma_t) + \sigma_t\varepsilon_t, \quad t \in \mathbb{N}, \qquad (13.1)$$

where S_t is the stock price at time t, r_t and d_t denote the risk-free and dividend rate for the period $[t-1, t]$, respectively, and λ_t is a $\mathcal{F}_{t-1}$ measurable random variable. S_0 is the present observed price and $\hat{S}_t = S_t \exp(\sum_{k=1}^{t} d_k)$ is the stock price considering reinvestment of the dividends. The function $g_{\varepsilon_t}(x)$ is the *log-Laplace-transform* of ε_t, that is, $g_{\varepsilon_t}(x) = \log(E[e^{x\varepsilon_t}])$, which is defined on the interval $(-a, b)$. The one-period-ahead conditional variance

---

[2]A similar condition is necessary for the construction of exponential Lévy models; see Cont and Tankov (2004).

σ_t^2 follows a GARCH(1,1) process with a restriction $0 < \sigma_t < b$, that is,

$$\sigma_t^2 = (\alpha_0 + \alpha_1 \sigma_{t-1}^2 \varepsilon_{t-1}^2 + \beta_1 \sigma_{t-1}^2) \wedge \rho, \quad t \in \mathbb{N}, \ \varepsilon_0 = 0, \tag{13.2}$$

where α_0, α_1, and β_1 are non negative, $\alpha_1 + \beta_1 < 1, \alpha_0 > 0$, and $0 < \rho < b^2$. Clearly, the process $(\sigma_t)_{t \in \mathbb{N}}$ is predictable. Any ID distribution with exponential moments of some order is suitable for constructing a GARCH model having ID distributed innovation. The stock price dynamics defined as (13.1) with the conditional variance, defined as (13.2) over the probability space $(\Omega, \mathcal{F}, (\mathcal{F}_t)_{t \in \mathbb{N}}, \mathbb{P})$ where $(\varepsilon_t)_{t \in \mathbb{N}}$ is the ID distributed i.i.d. real random variables, is called the ID-GARCH model. If ε_t equals the standard normal distributed random variable for all $t \in \mathbb{N}$, then $g_{\varepsilon_t}(x)$ is defined on the whole real line. This can be proven by considering the fact that the characteristic function of the normal distribution is an entire function, indeed, it is analytic at all finite points of the complex plane $\mathbb{C}$. Consequently, we can ignore the restriction $\sigma_t < b$ since the normal distribution has exponential moments of any order, and hence the model becomes the normal-GARCH model.[3] In section 13.3, we see that a similar argument is also true in the RDTS case.

13.2   RISK-NEUTRAL DYNAMIC

In order to price options, we cannot use the physical measure $\mathbb{P}$ defined above. The objective in this section is to find a measure equivalent to the physical measure $\mathbb{P}$ that makes the price of the stock discounted by the risk-free rate a martingale. A proper change of measure between zero mean and unit variance distributions allows one to derive the process dynamic of the log-returns under an equivalent measure. By construction, the new measure $\mathbb{Q}$ makes the discounted stock price process a martingale. This result allows one to obtain the distribution of the stock return under an *equivalent martingale measure* (EMM) and to calculate option prices.

The change of measures between the class of ID distributions has been widely used in continuous-time modeling.[4] We will see how the structure of the problem in the discrete-time case is different in comparison with the continuous one. The risk-neutral distribution is not always the same for the entire time window, but on each time step it is governed by different

---

[3]As introduced by Duan (1995).
[4]It takes its origin in the work of Sato (1999).

parameters.[5] This comes from the discrete-time nature of this setting. Unfortunately, this approach does not provide analytical solutions to price European options and hence numerical procedures have to be considered. The use of non-normal GARCH models combined with Monte Carlo simulation methods allows one to obtain small pricing errors. Technics for simulating some ID distributions, proposed in Chapter 8, is used to obtain option prices.

The model (13.1) defines an incomplete market, where the set of all possible EMMs is infinite. Among the elements of this set, we select those for which the distribution of the innovation process remains the same in both a market and risk-neutral measure. At least theoretically, the great flexibility offered by the ID family allows one to use a given zero mean and unit variance ID random variable to model the innovation ε_t under a market measure and a different zero mean and unit variance ID random variable to model the innovation ε_t under a risk-neutral measure, by considering the equivalence relation within the ID family. In the following, we do not take into consideration such measure change, but we focus on models with the same random variable for the stock market and for the risk-neutral ones. That is, we consider the same parametric distribution in both the stock market and risk-neutral world. In the following, the notation *std* before the name of a distribution means that we are considering a distribution with zero mean and unit variance. We consider random variables with some or possibly any finite exponential moments.[6] One cannot use this model with an α-stable distributed innovation because it does not have a finite second moment even if ID distributed. In particular, one cannot apply this approach to an infinite variance model.

Now, we briefly describe the behavior of the stock price process under a risk-neutral measure.[7] Let $\mathbb{P}_t$ be a measure under which ε_t is stdID distributed with parameters θ, and $\mathbb{Q}_t$ be a measure under which $\xi_t = \varepsilon_t + k_t$ is stdID distributed with parameters $\tilde{\theta}_t$, for each $1 \leq t \leq T$, where k_t is defined as

$$k_t := \lambda_t + \frac{1}{\sigma_t}(g_{ID}(\sigma_t; \tilde{\theta}_t) - g_{ID}(\sigma_t; \theta)) \qquad (13.3)$$

and $T \in \mathbb{N}$ be the time horizon. Define a measure $\mathbb{Q}$ on $\mathbb{F}_T$ equivalent to the measure $\mathbb{P}$, with Radon-Nikodym derivative $\frac{d\mathbb{Q}}{d\mathbb{P}} = Z_T$ where the density

---

[5]As already figured out in Christoffersen et al. (2010).
[6]We remind the reader that the finiteness of some exponential moment implies that all moments are finite.
[7]See Kim et al. (2008a), Kim et al. (2009), and Bianchi et al. (2010) for further details.

process $(Z_t)_{0 \le t \le T}$ is defined according to

$$Z_0 \equiv 1,$$

$$Z_t := \frac{d(\mathbb{P}_1 \otimes \cdots \mathbb{P}_{t-1} \otimes \mathbb{Q}_t \otimes \mathbb{P}_{t+1} \otimes \cdots \mathbb{P}_T)}{d\mathbb{P}} Z_{t-1}, t = 1, \ldots, T. \tag{13.4}$$

Then the measure $\mathbb{Q}$ satisfies the following properties:

(i) The stock price dynamics under $\mathbb{Q}$ can be written as

$$\log\left(\frac{S_t}{S_{t-1}}\right) = r_t - d_t - g_{ID}(\sigma_t; \tilde{\theta}_t) + \sigma_t \xi_t, \quad 1 \le t \le T$$

and the variance process has the form

$$\sigma_t^2 = (\alpha_0 + \alpha_1 \sigma_{t-1}^2 (\xi_{t-1} - k_t)^2 + \beta_1 \sigma_{t-1}^2) \wedge \rho,^8 \quad 1 \le t \le T, \quad \xi_0 = 0.$$

(ii) The discount stock price process $(e^{-r_t} \hat{S}_t)_{1 \le t \le T}$ is a $\mathbb{Q}$-martingale with respect to the filtration $\mathbb{F}_{0 \le t \le T}$, and, therefore, the following equation holds for all

$$E_{\mathbb{Q}}[\hat{S}_t | \mathbb{F}_{t-1}] = e^{r_t} \hat{S}_{t-1}$$

for all $1 \le t \le T$.

(iii) We have

$$Var_{\mathbb{Q}}\left(\log\left(\frac{S_t}{S_{t-1}}\right) \middle| \mathbb{F}_{t-1}\right) \overset{a.s.}{=} Var_{\mathbb{P}}\left(\log\left(\frac{S_t}{S_{t-1}}\right) \middle| \mathbb{F}_{t-1}\right), \quad 1 \le t \le T.$$

Now we are in the position to find the fair price of European call options. Under the risk-neutral measure $\mathbb{Q}$, the arbitrage-free price of a call option with strike price K and maturity T is given by

$$C_t = \exp\left(-\sum_{i=t+1}^{T} r_i\right) E_{\mathbb{Q}}[\max(S_T - K, 0) | \mathbb{F}_T],$$

---

[8]The constant ρ disappears in the RDTS-GARCH model since the RDTS distribution has exponential moment of any order.

where the stock price at maturity T can be calculated iteratively using the following formula:

$$S_T = S_t \left(\sum_{i=t+1}^{T} (r_i - d_i - g_{ID}(\sigma_i; \tilde{\theta}_i)) + \sigma_i \xi_i \right)$$

and on each step the conditional variance is evaluated through the equation

$$\sigma_i^2 = (\alpha_0 + \alpha_1 \sigma_{i-1}^2 (\xi_{i-1} - k_i)^2 + \beta_1 \sigma_{i-1}^2) \wedge \rho, \quad t + 1 \leq i \leq T.$$

We note the dependence of k_t on the time t, which gives at each step a different set of parameters for the stdID distribution that we are considering. Of course, one could evaluate prices for options with a more complex pay off. Such models address three different features of the dynamics of log-returns: asymmetry, fat tails, and volatility clustering.

13.3 NON-NORMAL INFINITELY DIVISIBLE GARCH

Here we consider different parametric examples in the ID distribution class. We develop financial market models based on these distributions with finite moment of any order and exponential moments of some or any order. We also consider parametric examples introduced in Chapter 3. With the purpose of pricing options, all models considered can be simulated with the algorithms described in Chapter 8. We also take into consideration the results that were described in Chapter 5 and focused on the change of measures that allow one to find a feasible density transformation and the risk-neutral dynamic for all different distributional assumptions.

13.3.1 Classical Tempered Stable Model

Among the class of TS distributions introduced by Rosiński,[9] the *classical tempered stable* (CTS) model is one of the better-known parametric examples.[10] Here we follow the approach of Kim et al. (2008a). Let X be a CTS random variable with parameter $(C, \lambda_-, \lambda_+, \alpha, m)$, where we define

$$C = \frac{(\lambda_+^{\alpha-2} + \lambda_-^{\alpha-2})^{-1}}{\Gamma(2 - \alpha)}$$

---

[9]See the seminal work of Rosiński (2007).
[10]See Schoutens (2003).

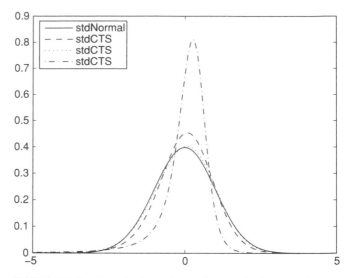

FIGURE 13.2   Density Functions of a Standard Normal
Distribution and Different stdCTS

and

$$m = 0.$$

Then we call this distribution *stdCTS* with parameter $(\lambda_-, \lambda_+, \alpha)$. In this case, the function $g_{CTS}(u)$ is of the form

$$g_{CTS}(u) = \frac{(\lambda_+ - u)^\alpha - \lambda_+^\alpha + u\alpha\lambda_+^{\alpha-1} + (\lambda_- + u)^\alpha - \lambda_-^\alpha - u\alpha\lambda_+^{\alpha-1}}{\alpha(\alpha - 1)(\lambda_+^{\alpha-2} + \lambda_-^{\alpha-2})}.$$

In Figure 13.2, we show the different shapes of the stdCTS densities with respect to the standard normal density.

Consider the ID GARCH model with the sequence $(\varepsilon_t)_{t\in\mathbb{N}}$ of i.i.d. random variables with $\varepsilon_t \sim \text{stdCTS}(\lambda_-, \lambda_+, \alpha)$ for all $t \in \mathbb{N}$. We refer to this model as the CTS-GARCH model. Since $E[e^{x\varepsilon_t}] < \infty$ if $x \in (-\lambda_-, \lambda_+)$, ρ has to be in the interval $(0, \lambda_+^2)$.

Thus, we consider the CTS-GARCH model.[11] Let $T \in \mathbb{N}$ be a time horizon and fix a natural number $t \leq T$. Suppose $\tilde{\lambda}_-(t)$ and $\tilde{\lambda}_+(t)$ satisfy the

---

[11]We can make use of Theorem 4.1 of Rosiński (2007) or Corollary 3 of Kim and Lee (2007) to find a suitable density transformation, as described in Chapter 5.

following conditions:

$$
\begin{cases}
\tilde{\lambda}_+^2 > \rho \\[2mm]
\tilde{\lambda}_+(t)^{\alpha-2} + \tilde{\lambda}_-(t)^{\alpha-2} = \lambda_+^{\alpha-2} + \lambda_-^{\alpha-2} \\[2mm]
\dfrac{\lambda_+^{\alpha-1} - \lambda_-^{\alpha-1} - \tilde{\lambda}_+(t)^{\alpha-1} + \tilde{\lambda}_-(t)^{\alpha-1}}{(1-\alpha)(\lambda_+^{\alpha-2} + \lambda_-^{\alpha-2})} \\[3mm]
\qquad = \lambda_t + \dfrac{1}{\sigma_t}(g_{CTS}(\sigma_t; \tilde{\lambda}_-(t), \tilde{\lambda}_+(t), \alpha) - g_{CTS}(\sigma_t; \lambda_-, \lambda_+, \alpha)).
\end{cases}
\tag{13.5}
$$

Then there is a measure $\mathbb{Q}_t$ equivalent to $\mathbb{P}_t$ such that

$$
\varepsilon_t + k_t \sim \mathrm{stdCTS}(\tilde{\lambda}_-(t), \tilde{\lambda}_+(t), \alpha)
$$

on the measure $\mathbb{Q}_t$ where

$$
k_t = \lambda_t + \frac{1}{\sigma_t}(g_{CTS}(\sigma_t; \tilde{\lambda}_-(t), \tilde{\lambda}_+(t), \alpha) - g_{CTS}(\sigma_t; \lambda_-, \lambda_+, \alpha)).
\tag{13.6}
$$

In order to generate a random variate from this distribution, we consider the general shot-noise representation,[12] as described in Chapter 8.

13.3.2 Generalized Tempered Stable Model

Before considering the GTS-GARCH model, let's define the stdGTS distribution, that is, a GTS distribution with zero mean and unit variance. Let X be a GTS random variable with parameter $(C_+, C_-, \lambda_-, \lambda_+, \alpha_+, \alpha_-, m)$, where we define

$$
C_+ = \frac{p\lambda_+^{2-\alpha_+}}{\Gamma(2-\alpha_+)},
$$

$$
C_- = \frac{(1-p)\lambda_-^{2-\alpha_-}}{\Gamma(2-\alpha_-)},
$$

---

[12]The shot-noise representation of proper TS laws has been presented in Rosiński (2007).

where $p \in (0, 1)$ and

$$m = 0.$$

We call this distribution $stdGTS$ with parameter $(\lambda_-, \lambda_+, \alpha_+, \alpha_-, \mathbb{P})$. In this case, the function $g_{GTS}(u)$ is of the form

$$g_{GTS}(u) = p\frac{(\lambda_+ - u)^{\alpha_+} - \lambda_+^{\alpha} + u\alpha\lambda_+^{\alpha_+-1}}{\alpha_+(\alpha_+ - 1)\lambda_+^{\alpha_+-2}} + (1 - p)\frac{(\lambda_- + u)^{\alpha_-} - \lambda_-^{\alpha} - u\alpha\lambda_+^{\alpha_--1}}{\alpha_-(\alpha_- - 1)\lambda_-^{\alpha_--2}}.$$

In Figure 13.3, we show the different shapes of the stdGTS densities with respect to the standard normal density.

Consider the ID-GARCH model with the sequence $(\varepsilon_t)_{t\in\mathbb{N}}$ of i.i.d. random variables with $\varepsilon_t \sim stdGTS(\lambda_-, \lambda_+, \alpha_+, \alpha_-)$ for all $t \in \mathbb{N}$. We call this model the GTS-GARCH model. Since $E[e^{x\varepsilon_t}] < \infty$ if $x \in (-\lambda_-, \lambda_+)$, ρ has to be in the interval $(0, \lambda_+^2)$.

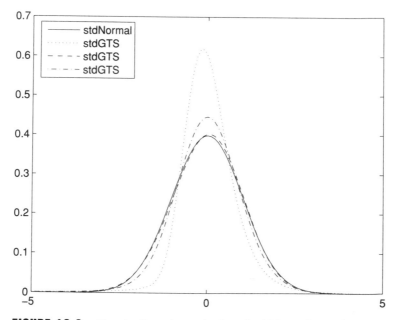

FIGURE 13.3   Density Functions of a Standard Normal Distribution and Different stdGTS

The change of measure problem solved in Chapter 5 allows one to obtain the risk-neutral process. Let $T \in \mathbb{N}$ be a time horizon and fix a natural number $t \leq T$. Suppose $\tilde{\lambda}_-(t)$, $\tilde{\lambda}_+(t)$, and $\tilde{p}(t)$ satisfy the following conditions:

$$
\begin{cases}
\tilde{\lambda}_+(t)^2 > \rho \\[2mm]
\tilde{p}(t)\tilde{\lambda}_+(t)^{2-\alpha_+} = p\lambda_+^{2-\alpha_+} \\[2mm]
(1 - \tilde{p}(t))\tilde{\lambda}_-(t)^{\alpha_- - 2} = (1 - p)\lambda_-^{\alpha_- - 2} \\[2mm]
p\dfrac{\lambda_+^{\alpha_+ - 1} - \tilde{\lambda}_+(t)^{\alpha_+ - 1}}{(1 - \alpha_+)\lambda_+^{\alpha_+ - 2}} + (1 - p)\dfrac{\tilde{\lambda}_-(t)^{\alpha_- - 1} - \lambda_-^{\alpha_- - 1}}{(1 - \alpha)\lambda_-^{\alpha_- - 2}} \\[4mm]
\qquad = \lambda_t + \dfrac{1}{\sigma_t}(g_{GTS}(\sigma_t; \tilde{\lambda}_-(t), \tilde{\lambda}_+(t), \alpha_+, \alpha_-, \tilde{p}(t)) - g_{GTS}(\sigma_t; \lambda_-, \lambda_+, \alpha_+, \alpha_-, p)).
\end{cases}
$$
$$(13.7)$$

Then there is a measure $\mathbb{Q}_t$ equivalent to $\mathbb{P}_t$ such that

$$
\varepsilon_t + k_t \sim \text{stdGTS}(\tilde{\lambda}_-(t), \tilde{\lambda}_+(t), \alpha_+, \alpha_-, \tilde{p}(t))
$$

on the measure $\mathbb{Q}_t$ where

$$
k_t = \lambda_t + \frac{1}{\sigma_t}(g_{GTS}(\sigma_t; \tilde{\lambda}_-(t), \tilde{\lambda}_+(t), \alpha_+, \alpha_-, \tilde{p}(t)) - g_{GTS}(\sigma_t; \lambda_-, \lambda_+, \alpha_+, \alpha_-, p)).
$$
$$(13.8)$$

13.3.3 Kim-Rachev Model

The example we present here demonstrates the flexibility of the Kim-Rachev (KR) distribution. In the previous examples, the parameters under the measure $\mathbb{P}$ together with conditions to find risk-neutral parameters under the measure $\mathbb{Q}$ do not leave any degree of freedom. The change of measure determines univocally risk-neutral parameters, if a solution of the system (13.5), in the CTS-GARCH case, or of the system (13.7), in the GTS-GARCH case, exists. Even though in the KR-GARCH we have a similar system to solve, we still have a parameter free. Theoretically, we could find the parameter that better fits the cross-sectional option data in order to reduce the distance between observed prices and model ones.

Here we go into this model. Letting X be a KR random variable with parameter $(r_+, r_-, k_+, k_-, p_+, p_-, \alpha, m)$, where we define

$$c = \frac{1}{\Gamma(2-\alpha)} \left(\frac{\alpha+p_+}{2+p_+} r_+^{2-\alpha} + \frac{\alpha+p_-}{2+p_-} r_-^{2-\alpha} \right)^{-1}$$

$$k_+ = c \frac{\alpha+p_+}{r_+^\alpha},$$

$$k_- = c \frac{\alpha+p_-}{r_-^\alpha},$$

$$m = 0,$$

then we call this distribution $stdKR$ with parameter $(r_+, r_-, p_+, p_-, \alpha)$. In this case, the function $g_X(u)$ is defined in $u \in (-1/r_-, 1/r_+)$ and is of the form

$$g_{KR}(u) = c\Gamma(-\alpha) \frac{\alpha+p_+}{p_+ r_+^\alpha} (_2F_1(p_+, \alpha; 1+p_+; r_+ u) - 1)$$

$$+ c\Gamma(-\alpha) \frac{\alpha+p_-}{p_- r_-^\alpha} (_2F_1(p_-, \alpha; 1+p_-; -r_- u) - 1)$$

$$- u\Gamma(1-\alpha) \left(c \frac{\alpha+p_+}{p_++1} r_+^{1-\alpha} - c \frac{\alpha+p_-}{p_-+1} r_-^{1-\alpha} \right).$$

In Figure 13.4, we show the different shapes of the stdKR densities with respect to the standard normal density.

Consider the ID-GARCH model with the sequence $(\varepsilon_t)_{t \in \mathbb{N}}$ of i.i.d. random variables with $\varepsilon_t \sim stdKR(r_+, r_-, p_+, p_-, \alpha)$ for all $t \in \mathbb{N}$. We call this model the KR-GARCH model. Since $E[e^{x\varepsilon_t}] < \infty$ if $x \in (-1/r_-, 1/r_+)$, ρ has to be in the interval $(0, 1/r_+^2)$. Consider the KR-GARCH model. Let $T \in \mathbb{N}$ be a time horizon and fix a natural number $t \leq T$. Suppose $\tilde{r}_+(t)$, $\tilde{r}_-(t)$, $\tilde{p}_+(t)$, and $\tilde{p}_-(t)$ satisfy the following conditions:

$$\begin{cases} \tilde{r}_+(t)^{-2} > \rho \\[2mm] \dfrac{\alpha+p_+}{2+p_+} r_+^{2-\alpha} + \dfrac{\alpha+p_-}{2+p_-} r_-^{2-\alpha} = \dfrac{\alpha+\tilde{p}_+}{2+\tilde{p}_+} \tilde{r}_+^{2-\alpha} + \dfrac{\alpha+\tilde{p}_-}{2+\tilde{p}_-} \tilde{r}_-^{2-\alpha}, \\[3mm] \Gamma(1-\alpha) \left(c \left(\dfrac{\alpha+p_+}{p_++1} r_+^{1-\alpha} - \dfrac{\alpha+p_-}{p_-+1} r_-^{1-\alpha} \right) - \tilde{c} \left(\dfrac{\alpha+\tilde{p}_+}{\tilde{p}_++1} \tilde{r}_+^{1-\alpha} - \dfrac{\alpha+\tilde{p}_-}{\tilde{p}_-+1} r_-^{1-\alpha} \right) \right) \\[3mm] \quad = \lambda_t + \dfrac{1}{\sigma_t} (g_{KR}(\sigma_t; \tilde{r}_+(t), \tilde{r}_-(t), \tilde{p}_+(t), \tilde{p}_-(t), \alpha) \\[2mm] \quad - g_{KR}(\sigma_t; r_+(t), r_-(t), p_+(t), p_-(t), \alpha)). \end{cases}$$

$\qquad\qquad\qquad\qquad\qquad\qquad\qquad\qquad\qquad\qquad\qquad\qquad\qquad (13.9)$

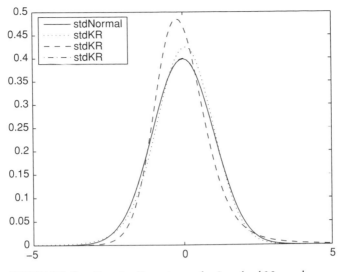

FIGURE 13.4 Density Functions of a Standard Normal Distribution and Different stdKR

Then there is a measure $\mathbb{Q}_t$ equivalent to $\mathbb{P}_t$ such that

$$\varepsilon_t + k_t \sim \text{stdKR}(\tilde{r}_+(t), \tilde{r}_-(t), \tilde{p}_+(t), \tilde{p}_-(t), \alpha)$$

on the measure $\mathbb{Q}_t$ where

$$k_t = \lambda_t + \frac{1}{\sigma_t}(g_{KR}(\sigma_t; \tilde{r}_+(t), \tilde{r}_-(t), \tilde{p}_+(t), \tilde{p}_-(t), \alpha) - g_{KR}(\sigma_t; r_+, r_-, p_+, p_-, \alpha)).$$
(13.10)

In this algorithm, we have to find the solution with four parameters satisfying the condition in equation (13.9). The solution is not unique. There are many ways to select one of them. One way is to select one solution that minimizes the square-root error between the market option prices and the simulated option prices. Another way is by fixing the parameter $\tilde{r}_+(t) = r_+$. Then, since $\rho < r_+$, the first condition in equation (13.9) is naturally satisfied.

13.3.4   Rapidly Decreasing Tempered Stable Model

The random variable we introduce here is an example in the tempered infinitely divisible (TID) class.[13] Now it easy to understand how to construct a discrete-time model with TID distributed innovation. Before considering the RDTS-GARCH model, we are going to define the stdRDTS distribution, that is a RDTS distribution with zero mean and unit variance. We recall that, at least theoretically, the RDTS distribution has similar statistical properties to the CTS distribution, even if the former has exponential moment of any order, while the latter does not. The finiteness of exponential moments of any order for the RDTS random variable is given by the fact that its characteristic exponent is a combination of Kummer's or confluent hypergeometric functions M, which are entire functions, that is, extendible to an analytical function on the complex plane $\mathbb{C}$.

Let X be a $RDTS$ random variable with parameter $(C, \lambda_-, \lambda_+, \alpha, m)$, where we define

$$C = \frac{2^{\alpha/2}(\lambda_+^{\alpha-2} + \lambda_-^{\alpha-2})^{-1}}{\Gamma(1 - \frac{\alpha}{2})}$$

and

$$m = 0.$$

Then we call this distribution the $stdRDTS$ with parameter $(\lambda_-, \lambda_+, \alpha)$. In this case, the function $g_{RDTS}(u)$ is of the form

$$g_{RDTS}(u) = CG(u; \alpha, C, \lambda_+) + CG(-u; \alpha, C, \lambda_-)$$

where the function G is defined in Chapter 3.

In Figure 13.5, we show the different shapes of the stdRDTS densities with respect to the standard normal density.

Consider the ID-GARCH model with the sequence $(\varepsilon_t)_{t \in \mathbb{N}}$ of i.i.d. random variables with $\varepsilon_t \sim$ stdRDTS$(\lambda_-, \lambda_+, \alpha)$ for all $t \in \mathbb{N}$. We call this model the RDTS-GARCH model. The inequality $E[e^{x\varepsilon_t}] < \infty$ is satisfied for each $x \in \mathbb{R}$. By similar argument as in the examples above, now we consider the RDTS-GARCH model. Let $T \in \mathbb{N}$ be a time horizon and fix a natural

---

[13]This class has been introduced in Bianchi et al. (2010) and considered for option pricing in Kim et al. (2010).

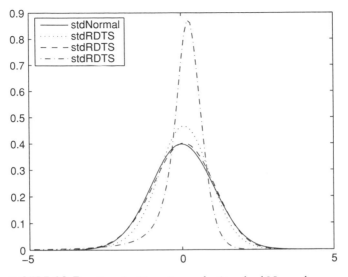

FIGURE 13.5 Density Functions of a Standard Normal Distribution and Different stdRDTS

number $t \leq T$. Suppose $\tilde{\lambda}_-(t)$ and $\tilde{\lambda}_+(t)$ satisfy the following conditions:

$$\begin{cases} \tilde{\lambda}_+(t)^{\alpha-2} + \tilde{\lambda}_-(t)^{\alpha-2} = \lambda_+^{\alpha-2} + \lambda_-^{\alpha-2} \\[2ex] \Gamma(\dfrac{1-\alpha}{2}) \dfrac{\lambda_+^{\alpha-1} - \lambda_-^{\alpha-1} - \tilde{\lambda}_+(t)^{\alpha-1} + \tilde{\lambda}_-(t)^{\alpha-1}}{\sqrt{2}\Gamma(1-\frac{\alpha}{2})(\lambda_+^{\alpha-2} + \lambda_-^{\alpha-2})} \\[2ex] \quad = \lambda_t + \dfrac{1}{\sigma_t}(g_{RDTS}(\sigma_t; \tilde{\lambda}_-(t), \tilde{\lambda}_+(t), \alpha) - g_{RDTS}(\sigma_t; \lambda_-, \lambda_+, \alpha)). \end{cases}$$

$$(13.11)$$

Then there is a measure $\mathbb{Q}_t$ equivalent to $\mathbb{P}_t$ such that

$$\varepsilon_t + k_t \sim \text{stdRDTS}(\tilde{\lambda}_-(t), \tilde{\lambda}_+(t), \alpha)$$

on the measure $\mathbb{Q}_t$ where

$$k_t = \lambda_t + \frac{1}{\sigma_t}(g_{RDTS}(\sigma_t; \tilde{\lambda}_-(t), \tilde{\lambda}_+(t), \alpha) - g_{RDTS}(\sigma_t; \lambda_-, \lambda_+, \alpha)). \quad (13.12)$$

As in the CTS case, to simulate random variates from the RDTS distribution, we consider the series representation.[14]

---

[14]See Bianchi et al. (2010) and Kim et al. (2010).

13.3.5   Inverse Gaussian Model

For the sake of completeness, we review some GARCH models with non-normal innovations.[15] These models can be viewed as examples of TS-GARCH models, even though a more strict assumption on the change of measure has been made in the literature. A particular choice of the GARCH specification allows one to calculate the characteristic function by means of a recursive procedure. Moreover, options prices are found through the characteristic function[16] without having recourse to Monte Carlo simulation. Let X be a IG random variable with parameters (a, b, m) with characteristic exponent of the form

$$\psi(u) = iu\left(m - \frac{a}{b}\right) - a(\sqrt{b^2 - 2iu} - b)$$

Let y_t be a IG random variable with parameter $(\sigma_t^2/\eta^2, 1, 0)$, then the random variable $X \sim \eta y_t$ has zero mean and variance σ_t^2. In this case, the function $g_{IG}(u)$ is of the form

$$g_{IG}(u) = \left(-u + \frac{1 - \sqrt{1 - 2u\eta}}{\eta}\right)\frac{\sigma_t^2}{\eta}.$$

Defining the innovation ε_t as

$$\varepsilon_t = \eta y_t + \frac{\sigma_t^2}{\eta}, \tag{13.13}$$

then return dynamic is of the form

$$\log\left(\frac{S_t}{S_{t-1}}\right) = r_t - d_t + \lambda\sigma_t^2 + \varepsilon_t, \tag{13.14}$$

where the conditional variance[17] σ_t^2 is of the following form

$$\sigma_t^2 = \alpha_0 + \beta_1\sigma_{t-1}^2 + \alpha_1 y_{t-1} + \gamma\sigma_{t-1}^4/y_{t-1}. \tag{13.15}$$

---

[15]These models have been proposed in Christoffersen et al. (2006, 2010). An innovation IG distributed is considered in Christoffersen et al. (2006) together with a conditional variance of the Heston and Nandi (2000) type.
[16]See, in particular, Bakshi et al. (2000).
[17]See Christoffersen et al. (2010).

We call the model given by (13.14) and (13.15) the IG-GARCH model. In order to obtain the return dynamic under the risk-neutral measure, the Esscher transform is considered.

Proposition 1. *Fix $t \in \mathbb{N}$ and let*

$$\varepsilon_t = \eta y_t + \frac{\sigma_t^2}{\eta}$$

define as above and let

$$\xi_t = \eta y_t + \frac{\sigma_t^2}{\eta \sqrt{1 - 2\theta\eta}} + k$$

be the equivalent random variable obtained by the Esscher transform of parameter θ. Then the following equality

$$k = 0 \qquad\qquad (13.16)$$

holds.

Proof. The following equation has to be fulfilled:[18]

$$\tilde{a} - a = \int_{\mathbb{R}} x(e^{\theta x} - 1)v(dx).$$

In this particular case, we have

$$\tilde{a} = \frac{\sigma_t^2}{\eta \sqrt{1 - 2\theta\eta}} + k$$

$$a = \frac{\sigma_t^2}{\eta}$$

and the last integral is

$$\int_{\mathbb{R}} x(e^{\theta x} - 1)v(dx) = \frac{\sigma_t^2}{\eta \sqrt{1 - 2\theta\eta}} - \frac{\sigma_t^2}{\eta}.$$

Hence, equation (13.16) is satisfied.

---

[18]The equation comes from Theorem 33.1, Sato (1999), where the truncation function $h(x) = x$ is chosen in the Lévy-Khinchin formula. See the Appendix to this chapter for further details.

Consider the IG-GARCH model. Let $T \in \mathbb{N}$ be a time horizon and fix a natural number $t \le T$. Suppose $\theta(t)$ satisfies the following conditions:

$$\begin{cases} \dfrac{1}{\eta} - 2\theta(t) > 2\rho \\[2mm] \theta(t) < \dfrac{1}{2\eta} - 1 \\[2mm] \lambda_t \sigma_t^2 + g_{IG}(1; \sigma_t^2/\eta^{3/2}, \sqrt{1/\eta}, \sigma_t^2/\eta\sqrt{1 - 2\theta(t)\eta}) = 0. \end{cases} \tag{13.17}$$

Then there is a measure $\mathbb{Q}_t$ equivalent to $\mathbb{P}_t$ such that

$$\xi_t = \eta y_t + \frac{\sigma_t^2}{\eta\sqrt{1 - 2\theta(t)\eta}} + k_t \sim IG(\sigma_t^2/\eta^{3/2}, \sqrt{1/\eta - 2\theta(t)}, \sigma_t^2/\eta\sqrt{1 - 2\theta(t)\eta})$$

on the measure $\mathbb{Q}_t$ and

$$k_t = \lambda_t \sigma_t^2 + g_{IG}(1; \sigma_t^2/\eta^{3/2}, \sqrt{1/\eta - 2\theta(t)}, \sigma_t^2/\eta\sqrt{1 - 2\theta(t)\eta}). \tag{13.18}$$

Furthermore, the conditional variance under the measure $\mathbb{Q}_t$ satisfies the following property

$$\tilde{\sigma}_t^2 = \sigma_t^2/(1 - 2\theta v)^{3/2}. \tag{13.19}$$

The value of $\theta(t)$ can be explicitly calculated. To do so, it is enough to find the value of θ, which satisfies the equation

$$\lambda \sigma_t^2 - \frac{\sigma_t^2}{\eta^2}\left(\sqrt{1 - 2\eta(\theta(t) + 1)} - \sqrt{1 - 2\eta\theta(t)}\right) = 0.$$

Therefore, $\theta(t)$ does not depend on t and has the form

$$\theta(t) = \theta = \frac{1}{2\eta}\left(1 - \eta - \frac{1}{\eta^2\lambda^2} - \frac{1}{4}\eta^4\lambda^2\right). \tag{13.20}$$

13.3.6   Skewed Variance Gamma Model

Here we review the discrete-time model, where the skewed variance gamma (SVG) distribution is taken into consideration to drive the dynamic of the stock price.[19] The risk-neutral probability is found by means of the Esscher

---

[19]The model has been proposed by Christoffersen et al. (2010).

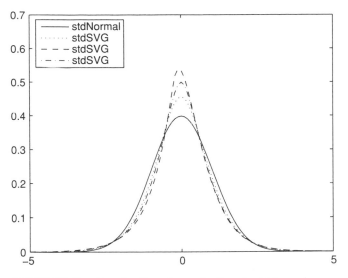

FIGURE 13.6 Density Functions of a Standard Normal Distribution and Different stdSVG

transform. This approach is close to that proposed by Kim et al. (2008a), even if the change of measure problem is solved in a more general way[20] and not with the Esscher transform. The distribution considered to drive the stock return dynamic is the SVG distribution.[21]

Parameters of the SVG distribution are chosen as follows. Let Z_+ and Z_- be independent gamma distributions

$$Z_\pm \sim \Gamma(4/\tau_\pm^2, 1),$$

where τ_+ and τ_- are defined as

$$\tau_+ = -\sqrt{2}\left(s - \sqrt{\tfrac{2}{3}k - s^2}\right) \text{ and } \tau_- = -\sqrt{2}\left(s + \sqrt{\tfrac{2}{3}k - s^2}\right).$$

In Figure 13.6, we show the different shapes of the stdSVG densities with respect to the standard normal density.

---

[20]The Theorem 33.1 in Sato (1999) is considered instead. The Esscher trasform change of measure is a particular case of such theorem.
[21]This is a particular case of the BΓ distribution Küchler and Tappe (2008).

Let us now construct the bilateral gamma (BΓ) random variable[22] from the two gamma variables as

$$Z = \frac{1}{2\sqrt{2}}\left(\tau_+ Z_+ - \tau_- Z_-\right) - \sqrt{2}\left(\frac{1}{\tau_+} - \frac{1}{\tau_-}\right).$$

By the definition of BΓ, there are Z parameters $(C_+, C_-, \lambda_+, \lambda_-, m)$ defined as follows

$$\lambda_\pm = \frac{2\sqrt{2}}{\tau_\pm}$$

$$C_\pm = \frac{\lambda_\pm^2}{2}$$

$$m = 0.$$

Thus, Z has zero mean, unit variance, skewness equal to s, and kurtosis equal to k.[23] The log Laplace transform $g_{SVG}(u)$ is

$$g_{SVG}(u) = \sqrt{2}\left(\frac{1}{\tau_+} - \frac{1}{\tau_-}\right)u - 4\tau_+^{-2}\log\left(1 - \frac{1}{2\sqrt{2}}\tau_+ u\right)$$

$$-4\tau_-^{-2}\log\left(1 + \frac{1}{2\sqrt{2}}\tau_- u\right). \tag{13.21}$$

By Proposition 5 in the Appendix to this chapter, the following results hold.

Proposition 2. *Let X be a random variable $X \sim B\Gamma(C_+, C_-, \lambda_+, \lambda_-, 0)$ under a measure P and $\tilde{X}$ be the random variable obtained by the Esscher transform of X with parameter θ. If $\theta < \lambda_+$ and the equality*

$$k = \frac{C_+}{\lambda_+} - \frac{C_-}{\lambda_-} - \frac{C_+}{\lambda_+ - \theta} + \frac{C_-}{\lambda_- + \theta}, \tag{13.22}$$

then $\tilde{X} = X + k$ is a random variable $\tilde{X} \sim B\Gamma(C_+, C_-, \lambda_+ - \theta, \lambda_- + \theta, 0)$ under the measure Q obtained by the Esscher transform.

---

[22]See Küchler and Tappe (2008).
[23]By equations (2.9)–(2.12) of Küchler and Tappe (2008).

By Proposition 2, it follows that the corresponding parameters of the stdSVG random variable under the Esscher transform become

$$\tilde{\tau}_{\pm} = \frac{2\sqrt{2}\tau_{\pm}}{2\sqrt{2} \pm \theta\tau_{\pm}}.$$

Consider the ID GARCH model with the sequence $(\varepsilon_t)_{t\in\mathbb{N}}$ of i.i.d. random variables with $\varepsilon_t \sim \text{stdSVG}(\tau_+, \tau_-)$ for all $t \in \mathbb{N}$. We refer to this model as the SVG-GARCH model. Let $T \in \mathbb{N}$ be a time horizon and fix a natural number $t \leq T$. Suppose $\theta(t)$ satisfies the following conditions:

$$\left(\frac{\sqrt{2}}{\tau_+} - \frac{\sqrt{2}}{\tau_-} - \frac{\sqrt{2}}{\tilde{\tau}_+} + \frac{\sqrt{2}}{\tilde{\tau}_-} \right.$$
$$= \lambda_t + \frac{1}{\sigma_t}(g_{SVG}(\sigma_t; \tau_+, \tau_-) - g_{SVG}(\sigma_t; \tilde{\tau}_+, \tilde{\tau}_-)). \tag{13.23}$$

Then there is a measure $\mathbb{Q}_t$ equivalent to $\mathbb{P}_t$ such that

$$\varepsilon_t + k_t \sim \text{stdSVG}(\tilde{\tau}_+, \tilde{\tau}_-)$$

on the measure $\mathbb{Q}_t$ where

$$k_t = \lambda_t + \frac{1}{\sigma_t}(g_{SVG}(\sigma_t; \tau_+, \tau_-) - g_{SVG}(\sigma_t; \tilde{\tau}_+, \tilde{\tau}_-)). \tag{13.24}$$

By Küchler and Tappe (2008), the BΓ distribution is the convolution of two independent gamma distributions; thus, it is particularly easy to simulate.

13.3.7 Normal Inverse Gaussian Model

The normal inverse Gaussian (NIG) distribution[24] can be obtained as an inverse Gaussian time-changed Brownian motion[25] or by the exponential tilting of a symmetric *modified tempered stable* (MTS) distribution.[26] Let X be a NIG random variable with parameter $(\delta, \lambda\ \beta, m)$, where we define

$$\delta = \lambda^{-2}(\lambda^2 - \beta^2)^{3/2}$$

---

[24]This distribution was introduced by Barndorff-Nielsen (1995) and applied to GARCH models by Stentoft (2008).
[25]This is proven in Schoutens (2003).
[26]This result was proven in Kim et al. (2008b).

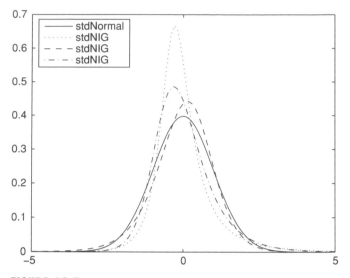

FIGURE 13.7   Density Functions of a Standard Normal
Distribution and Different stdNIG

and $m = 0$. Then we call this distribution *stdNIG* with parameter (λ, β). In
this case the function $g_{NIG}(u)$ is of the form

$$g_{NIG}(u) = -\beta^2(1 - \beta^2\lambda^{-2})u - \lambda^{-2}(\lambda^2 - \beta^2)^{3/2}(\sqrt{\lambda^2 - (\beta + u)^2} - \sqrt{\lambda^2 - \beta^2}).$$

In Figure 13.7, we show the different shapes of the stdNIG densities
with respect to the standard normal density.

We can make use of the following proposition to find a density transformation.

Proposition 3.

(a) *Suppose X is a NIG distribution with parameters $(\delta, \lambda, \beta, m)$ under $\mathbb{P}$
and a NIG distribution with parameters $(\tilde{\delta}, \tilde{\lambda}, \tilde{\beta}, \tilde{m})$ under $\mathbb{Q}$. Then $\mathbb{P}$
and $\mathbb{Q}$ are equivalent if and only if $\delta = \tilde{\delta}$, and*

$$\tilde{m} - m = -\delta(\tilde{\beta}(\tilde{\lambda}^2 - \tilde{\beta}^2)^{-1/2} - \beta(\lambda^2 - \beta^2)^{-1/2}).$$

(b) *Suppose $X \sim \text{stdNIG}(\lambda, \beta)$ under a measure $\mathbb{P}$, and $(X + k) \sim \text{stdNIG}(\tilde{\lambda},
\tilde{\beta})$ under a measure $\mathbb{Q}$ for a constant $k \in \mathbb{R}$. Then $\mathbb{P}$ and $\mathbb{Q}$ are equivalent*

if and only if

$$
\begin{cases}
\lambda^2(\lambda^2 - \beta^2)^{3/2} = \tilde{\lambda}^2(\tilde{\lambda}^2 - \tilde{\beta}^2)^{3/2}, \\[2mm]
k = \lambda^{-2}\left(\beta(\lambda^2 - \beta^2)^{-1/2} - \tilde{\beta}(\tilde{\lambda}^2 - \tilde{\beta}^2)^{-1/2}\right)(\lambda^2 - \beta^2)^{3/2}.
\end{cases}
\tag{13.25}
$$

Consider the ID GARCH model with the sequence $(\varepsilon_t)_{t\in\mathbb{N}}$ of i.i.d. random variables with $\varepsilon_t \sim \mathrm{stdNIG}(\lambda, \beta)$ for all $t \in \mathbb{N}$. We label this model the NIG-GARCH model. Let $T \in \mathbb{N}$ be a time horizon and fix a natural number $t \leq T$. Suppose $\theta(t)$ satisfies the following conditions:

$$
\begin{cases}
\lambda^2(\lambda^2 - \beta^2)^{3/2} = \tilde{\lambda}(t)^2(\tilde{\lambda}(t)^2 - \tilde{\beta}(t)^2)^{3/2}, \\[3mm]
\lambda^{-2}\left(\beta(\lambda^2 - \beta^2)^{-1/2} - \tilde{\beta}(t)(\tilde{\lambda}(t)^2 - \tilde{\beta}(t)^2)^{-1/2}\right)(\lambda^2 - \beta^2)^{3/2} \\[2mm]
\quad = \lambda_t + \dfrac{1}{\sigma_t}(g_{NIG}(\sigma_t; \tilde{\lambda}(t), \tilde{\beta}(t)) - g_{NIG}(\sigma_t; \lambda, \beta)).
\end{cases}
\tag{13.26}
$$

Then there is a measure $\mathbb{Q}_t$ equivalent to $\mathbb{P}_t$ such that

$$
\varepsilon_t + k_t \sim \mathrm{stdNIG}(\lambda, \beta)
$$

on the measure $\mathbb{Q}_t$ where

$$
k_t = \lambda_t + \frac{1}{\sigma_t}(g_{NIG}(\sigma_t; \tilde{\lambda}(t), \tilde{\beta}(t)) - g_{NIG}(\sigma_t; \lambda, \beta)).
\tag{13.27}
$$

Simulation algorithms for such distributions have become standard in statistical toolboxes. In particular, a stochastic representation[27] allows one to generate both univariate and multivariate random variates from a NIG distribution.

13.4 SIMULATE INFINITELY DIVISIBLE GARCH

By following the approach considered in Kim et al. (2008a), we can now construct an algorithm to simulate sample paths by following the approach described in section 13.2. Suppose for a moment that we have a set of market estimated parameters θ for a given parametric distribution, say, CTS, GTS, KR, RDTS, SVG, or NIG, and let $\tilde{\theta}_t$ be the set of transformed parameters at time t.

---

[27]See McNeil et al. (2005).

Simulation of ID-GARCH paths

1. Initialize $t := t_0$.
2. Let $k = k_t$, where k is defined in equation (13.6) (13.8, 13.10, 13.12, 13.18, 13.24, or 13.27) and k_t is defined by equation 13.3.
3. Find parameters $\tilde{\theta}_t$ by considering estimated parameters θ and the non-linear system given by (13.5) (13.7, 13.9, 13.11, 13.17, 13.23, or 13.26).
4. Generate random number $\xi_t \sim \text{stdID}(\tilde{\theta}_t)$.
5. Let

$$\log\left(\frac{S_t}{S_{t-1}}\right) = r_t - d_t - g_{ID}(\sigma_t; \tilde{\theta}_t) + \sigma_t \xi_t, \quad 1 \leq t \leq T.$$

6. Set $t = t + 1$ and then substitute

$$\sigma_t^2 = (\alpha_0 + \alpha_1 \sigma_{t-1}^2 (\xi_{t-1} - k_{t-1})^2 + \beta_1 \sigma_{t-1}^2) \wedge \rho.$$

7. Repeat 2 through 6 until $t > T$ to simulate a sample path.

We apply these algorithms in the next chapter in order to price European call options.

APPENDIX

The Esscher Transform

Before explaining the density transformation via the Esscher transform, the following well-known result must be reviewed:[28]

Theorem 1 (Lévy-Khinchin formula). *A real valued random variable X is infinitely divisible with characteristic exponent $\psi(u)$, that is,*

$$E[e^{iuX}] = e^{\psi(u)}$$

with $u \in \mathbb{R}$, if and only if there exists a triple (a_h, σ, v) where $a_h \in \mathbb{R}$, $\sigma \geq 0$, h is a given truncation function, v is a measure on $\mathbb{R}\setminus\{0\}$ satisfying

$$\int_{\mathbb{R}\setminus\{0\}} (1 \wedge x^2) v(dx) < \infty$$

---

[28]See Sato (1999).

and

$$\psi(u) = ia_h\theta - \frac{1}{2}\sigma^2 u^2 + \int_{\mathbb{R}\setminus\{0\}} (e^{iux} - 1 - iuh(x))\nu(dx) \tag{13.28}$$

for every $u \in \mathbb{R}$.

The procedure of tilting to obtain a density transformation is also related to the Esscher transform. Let ν be a Lévy measure of a ID distribution X such that

$$\int_{|x|\geq 1} e^{\theta x}\nu(dx) < \infty,$$

which is X and has exponential moment of order θ. Then the measure $\tilde{\nu}(dx) = e^{\theta x}\nu(dx)$ is also a Lévy measure.[29] In some cases, the initial and the transformed distribution have the same form, as for example if one considers the BΓ distribution. This means that if a BΓ distribution is transformed via the Esscher change of measure, the transformed distribution is still BΓ distributed. Before proving this fact, we show a useful proposition.

Proposition 4. *Let $\phi(u)$ and $\tilde{\phi}(u)$ be the characteristic functions for the infinitely divisible distributions with Lévy triples $(a, 0, \nu)$ and $(\tilde{a}, 0, \tilde{\nu})$, respectively, where $\tilde{\nu}(dx) = e^{\theta x}\nu(dx)$ and condition*

$$\int_{|x|\geq 1} e^{\theta x}\nu(dx) < \infty.$$

Then assuming a truncation function $h(x) = x$ in the Lévy-Khinchin representation, the following relation[30] holds

$$\log\tilde{\phi}(u) = \log\phi(u - i\theta) - \log\phi(-i\theta) + iu\left(\tilde{a} - a - \int_{\mathbb{R}} x(e^{\theta x} - 1)\nu(dx)\right) \tag{13.29}$$

The result above gives an easy procedure to find the characteristic function of the transformed random variable in the BΓ case.

---

[29]Of course this measure change is only a particular case of Theorem 33.1 of Sato (1999), but it is widely used in finance as well as in actuarial mathematics. See Gerber and Shiu (1994).
[30]The result is proved by Theorem 33.1 of Sato (1999).

Proposition 5. *Let X be a random variable $X \sim B\Gamma(C_+, C_-, \lambda_+, \lambda_-, m)$ and $\tilde{X}$ be the random variable obtained by the Esscher transform of X. If $\theta < \lambda_+$, then $\tilde{X}$ is a random variable $X \sim B\Gamma(C_+, C_-, \lambda_+ - \theta, \lambda_- + \theta, m)$.*

Proof. A $X \sim B\Gamma(C_+, C_-, \lambda_+, \lambda_-, m)$ random variable has Lévy measure

$$\nu(dx) = C_+ x^{-1} e^{-\lambda_+ x} I_{\{x>0\}} + C_- |x|^{-1} e^{-\lambda_- |x|} I_{\{x<0\}} dx$$

and the characteristic exponent is given by

$$\psi(u) = ium + C_+ \left(\log \left(\frac{\lambda_+}{\lambda_+ - iu} \right) - \frac{iu}{\lambda_+} \right) + C_- \left(\log \left(\frac{\lambda_-}{\lambda_- + iu} \right) + \frac{iu}{\lambda_-} \right)$$

We evaluate the integral of the last term of equation (13.29),

$$\int_{\mathbb{R}} x(e^{\theta x} - 1)\nu(dx) = C_+ \int_0^{+\infty} (e^{(\theta - \lambda_+)x} - e^{-\lambda_+ x})dx - C_- \int_{-\infty}^0 e^{\theta x - \lambda_- |x|} - e^{-\lambda_- |x|})dx$$

$$= C_+ \int_0^{+\infty} (e^{(\theta - \lambda_+)x} - e^{-\lambda_+ x})dx - C_- \int_{-\infty}^0 e^{\theta x - \lambda_- |x|} - e^{-\lambda_- |x|})dx$$

$$= C_+ \int_0^{+\infty} (e^{(\theta - \lambda_+)x} - e^{-\lambda_+ x})dx - C_- \int_0^{+\infty} (e^{-(\theta + \lambda_-)x} - e^{-\lambda_- x})dx$$

$$= \frac{C_+}{\lambda_+ - \theta} - \frac{C_+}{\lambda_+} - \frac{C_-}{\lambda_- + \theta} + \frac{C_-}{\lambda_-},$$

Therefore, by considering the integral above, the evaluation of equation (13.29) gives the desired result.

REFERENCES

Bakshi, G., Cao, C., & Chen, Z. (2000). Pricing and hedging long-term options. *Journal of Econometrics*, 94(1-2), 277–318.

Barndorff-Nielsen, O.E. (1995). Normal inverse Gaussian distributions and the modeling of stock returns. Research Report no. 300, Department of Theoretical Statistics, Aarhus University.

Bianchi, M. L., Rachev, S. T., Kim, Y. S., & Fabozzi, F. J. (2010). Tempered infinitely divisible distributions and processes. *Theory of Probability and Its Applications (TVP), Society for Industrial and Applied Mathematics (SIAM)*, 55(1), 59–86.

Chernov, M. & Ghysels, E. (2000). A study towards a unified approach to the joint estimation of objective and risk neutral measures for the purpose of options valuation. *Journal of Financial Economics*, 56(3), 407–458.

Christoffersen, P., Elkamhi, R., Feunou, B., & Jacobs, K. (2010). Option valuation with conditional heteroskedasticity and nonnormality. *Review of Financial Studies, 23*(5), 2139–2183.

Christoffersen, P., Heston, S., & Jacobs, K. (2006). Option valuation with conditional skewness. *Journal of Econometrics, 131*(1-2), 253–284.

Cont, R. & Tankov, P. (2004). *Financial modelling with jump processes.* Boca Raton, FL CRC Press.

Derman, E. (2005). *My life as a quant: Reflections on physics and finance.* Hoboken, NJ: John Wiley & Sons.

Duan, J. (1995). The GARCH option pricing model. *Mathematical Finance, 5*(1), 13–32.

Gerber, H. & Shiu, E. (1994). Option pricing by Esscher transforms. *Transactions of the Society of Actuaries, 46*, 99–140.

Heston, S. & Nandi, S. (2000). A closed-form GARCH option valuation model. *Review of Financial Studies, 13*(3), 585–625.

Kim, Y. & Lee, J. (2007). The relative entropy in CGMY processes and its applications to finance. *Mathematical Methods of Operations Research, 66*(2), 327–338.

Kim, Y., Rachev, S., Bianchi, M., & Fabozzi, F. (2008a). Financial market models with Lévy processes and time-varying volatility. *Journal of Banking and Finance, 32*(7), 1363–1378.

Kim, Y., Rachev, S., Bianchi, M., & Fabozzi, F. (2010). Tempered stable and tempered infinitely divisible GARCH models. *Journal of Banking and Finance, 34*(9), 2096–2109.

Kim, Y., Rachev, S., Chung, D., & Bianchi, M. (2008b). A modified tempered stable distribution with volatility clustering. In J. O. Soares, J. P. Pina, & M. Catalaõ-Lopes (Eds.), *New developments in financial modelling* (pp. 344–365). Cambridge, UK: Cambridge Scholars Publishing.

Kim, Y., Rachev, S., Chung, D., & Bianchi, M. (2009). The modified tempered stable distribution, GARCH models and option pricing. *Probability and Mathematical Statistics, 29*(1), 91–117.

Küchler, U. & Tappe, S. (2008). Bilateral gamma distributions and processes in financial mathematics. *Stochastic Processes and Their Applications, 118*(2), 261–283.

McNeil, A., Frey, R., & Embrechts, P. (2005). *Quantitative risk management.* Princeton, NJ: Princeton University Press.

Rosiński, J. (2007). Tempering stable processes. *Stochastic Processes and Their Applications, 117*(6), 677–707.

Sato, K. (1999). *Lévy processes and infinitely divisible distributions.* Cambridge: Cambridge University Press.

Schoutens, W. (2003). *Lévy processes in finance: Pricing financial derivatives.* Hoboken, NJ: John Wiley & Sons.

Stentoft, L. (2008). American option pricing using GARCH models and the normal inverse Gaussian distribution. *Journal of Financial Econometrics, 6*(4), 540–582.

CHAPTER 14

Option Pricing with Monte Carlo Methods

14.1 INTRODUCTION

In this chapter, we report the results of a Monte Carlo exercise based on non-normal infinitely divisible (ID) distributions and a GARCH model for the volatility. The algorithms described in Chapters 8 and 13 about simulation of non-normal ID distributions and GARCH models are empirically studied in this chapter. Furthermore, if one wants to value over-the-counter (OTC) options and has a historical time series for the underlying with a large number of observations, say 10 years of daily data, this pricing framework becomes much more interesting. In fact, one may select an ID-GARCH model to fit parameters from the underlying by using a two-step maximum likelihood estimation (MLE) method, as explained in section 14.2.1. Then, by changing the probability measure, one can find a suitable stock price dynamic in the so-called risk-neutral world, simulate random numbers, and finally evaluate option prices with the help of some variance-reduction technique by taking into consideration the algorithms described in Chapter 8.

As already done in previous chapters, in order to test our pricing models, we consider a popular stock market index option, the S&P 500 index. Even though the pricing framework we provide can be used to price OTC options, we will focus on European call options written on the S&P 500 index in order to compare observed prices of these options traded in the market with model-generated prices. For the purpose of option valuation, there is a general consensus to prefer parameters estimated from option prices with respect to parameters estimated from stock returns of the underlying asset. In general, the informational set given by the time-series estimation of a normal GARCH model is not enough to explain option prices. The heavy-tailed innovations, together with the volatility clustering effect, that we consider in our empirical tests will be enough to obtain suitable results for the purposes of both historical estimation and option valuation. That is, we are able to obtain a small pricing error even if we consider only parameters estimated from the underlying combined with a pure mathematical measure change.

It should be noted that only historical data on the underlying and on the risk-free rate are considered in obtaining the parameters that are used in option valuation. Instead to consider a *trader approach*, in which one wants to estimate parameters by using only option prices, the so called *fundamental approach* can be used. Using this approach, option prices are calculated using parameters estimated by fitting the underlying asset process together with a suitable change of measure. In this chapter, we assess the performance of various models, by considering the goodness of fit under the market measure and analyzing the option pricing errors. We show the importance of non-normal ID random variables in fitting the log-returns of stock prices. Such distributions are flexible enough to explain the market behavior of log-returns, at least from an ex-post perspective. Furthermore, we see that there is a small pricing error in applying ID distributions to option pricing, which is a performance measure from an *ex-ante* perspective. In particular, we focus on the behavior of the pricing error depending on the option's maturity and moneyness.

The chapter is organized as follows. In the next section we describe the data we use in this chapter. Then we review the normal GARCH and non-normal ID GARCH estimation based on the underlying log-returns and study the option pricing performance under this framework, which merges volatility clustering and non-normal ID distributions.

14.2 DATA SET

It is well known that a large sample of observations is needed to estimate a GARCH time-series model—at least 10 years of daily data to obtain a suitable estimate. For this reason, as already done in Chapters 11 and 12, we use 10 years of daily data. The dividend yield will not be used since adjusted closing index values are taken into account; that is, $d_t = 0$, for each t in our sample. For the daily interest rate we take the time series of the above time window of the 3-month Treasury rate.

We divide the option data into several categories according to either time to maturity or moneyness,[1] where moneyness is defined as the

---

[1] We consider similar categories as in Barone-Adesi et al. (2008).

ratio $M = K/S$ of the strike price K over the initial asset price S_0. In the in-sample analysis, we consider the set of 98 mid-prices analyzed in Chapters 11 and 12. Then we analyzed *deep-in-the-money* (DITM) *options* with $M < 0.9$, *in-the-money* (ITM) options with $0.9 \leq M < 1$, *out-of-the-money* (OTM) options with $1 \leq M < 1.15$, and *deep-out-of-the-money* (DOTM) *options* with $M \geq 1.15$. In classifying an option contract based on the time to maturity, we use the following classifications: short maturity (≤ 70 days), medium maturity (between 70 and 150 days), and long maturity (> 150 days). In both cases, we consider a total of 179 mid-prices.

In the out-of-sample analysis, we consider European call options traded on Wednesday September 17, 2008, with prices between $5 and $180, maturities 3, 13, 31, 66, 94, 105 and 185, 195, and 276 days, and $0.8 \leq M \leq 1.2$ for a total of 118 prices.

Note that the model's performance could be affected by the choice of the trading day, at least for all models we analyze in this chapter. That is, the goodness of market estimations, as well as the pricing errors, could be unstable with respect to a different data set. This means that the model parameters may be different as the time period changes. However, during tranquil periods the model's performance is unaffected by the choice of the trading day, at least for the CTS-GARCH and RDTS-GARCH models.[2] Estimation and options pricing errors for different underliers or at different times in history seem to favor such ID-GARCH models relative to the normal GARCH model.

14.2.1   Market Estimation

The time window between Thursday, September 10, 1998, and Wednesday, September 10, 2008, is considered for the in-sample market estimation. First we estimate the set of parameters $\theta = \{\alpha_0, \alpha_1, \beta_1, \lambda_t\}$ of the normal-GARCH model using the MLE approach. In this setting, stock log-returns are defined as

$$\log\left(\frac{S_t}{S_{t-1}}\right) = r_t - d_t + \lambda_t \sigma_t - \frac{\sigma_t^2}{2} + \sigma_t \varepsilon_t, \quad 1 \leq t \leq T$$

and the conditional variance process has the form

$$\sigma_t^2 = \alpha_0 + \alpha_1 \sigma_{t-1}^2 \varepsilon_{t-1}^2 + \beta_1 \sigma_{t-1}^2, \quad 1 \leq t \leq T, \quad \varepsilon_0 = 0.$$

---

[2] This fact has been noted in Kim et al. (2010).

The parameter $\lambda_t \equiv \lambda$, which can be viewed as the market price of risk, is considered constant under the pure *fundamental* framework. An alternative approach is to estimate λ by using option data since it is difficult to estimate and is very likely to be different for the lifetime of some derivative contract than for the estimation window.[3] In this case, the log-likelihood can be easily written in analytic form as

$$
\log L(\theta) = -\sum_{t=1}^{T} \left(\frac{1}{2} \log(2\pi) + \log(\sigma_t) + \frac{1}{2} \frac{\left(y_t - r_t + d_t - \lambda_t \sigma_t + \frac{\sigma_t^2}{2} \right)^2}{\sigma_t^2} \right),
$$

(14.1)

where we define

$$
y_t = \frac{S_t}{S_{t-1}}.
$$

In order to find the model's parameters with volatility clustering, we have to maximize the likelihood function. In the optimization problem, the log-likelihood function could be evaluated using a recursive method described as follows:

1. Set a starting point θ_0 for parameters α_0, α_1, β_1, and λ. Let us consider $t = 1$.
2. Calculate $\sigma_0 = \frac{\alpha_0}{1 - \alpha_1 - \beta_1}$ and set $\varepsilon_0 = 0$.
3. Calculate $\varepsilon_t = \frac{y_{t-1} - r_{t-1} + d_{t-1} - \lambda_{t-1}\sigma_{t-1} + \frac{\sigma_{t-1}^2}{2}}{\sigma_{t-1}}$.
4. Calculate $\sigma_t^2 = \alpha_0 + \alpha_1 \sigma_{t-1}^2 \varepsilon_{t-1}^2 + \beta_1 \sigma_{t-1}^2$ and the sum in equation (14.1) until t.
5. If $t = T$, return $\log L(\theta)$; otherwise, go to the next step.
6. Set $t = t + 1$ and return to step 3.

The optimization procedure will move the starting point in a suitable direction until it reaches the optimal solution of the problem.

Any optimization package, for example, MATLAB, is able to solve this kind of problem in a few seconds. Then, the estimated innovations $\hat{\varepsilon}_t$ as well as the estimated GARCH parameters $\hat{\theta}$ are taken into account in the two-step

---

[3]See Menn and Rachev (2009).

MLE estimation for the non-normal models. This is a classical procedure to estimate parameters when the distribution of the innovation is not normal.[4] Note that the estimated $\hat{\sigma}_t$ and $\hat{\varepsilon}_t$ are not equal for all GARCH models we consider, even if $\hat{\theta}$ is fixed. This is attributable to the fact that the log-Laplace transform depends on the distribution of the innovation. Numerical procedures are needed for tempered stable and tempered infinitely divisible MLE estimation, together with a recursive method, which takes into account the discrete nature of the GARCH approach. The density function of non-normal ID random variable, in general, is not given in closed form. Since only the characteristic function is known, a discrete evaluation of the density function together with an interpolation algorithm is used. That is, by means of the classical fast Fourier transform procedure, the characteristic function is inverted[5] to calculate the density function.

The classical MLE procedure, which estimates both GARCH parameters and innovation parameters at the same time, is a complex optimization problem. This is because the log-likelihood function to be maximized is of the form

$$\log L(\theta) = -\sum_{t=1}^{T} \log f \left(\frac{y_t - r_t + d_t - \lambda_t \sigma_t + \frac{\sigma_t^2}{2}}{\sigma_t} \right), \qquad (14.2)$$

where f is the density function of the innovation. Such function can be easily written in the normal case as we have seen above, but in general it has a complex structure or cannot be written in analytic form. The two-step MLE method gives one the possibility to skip this cumbersome optimization problem. At least in theory, one may fit all market parameters by directly maximizing the likelihood function. In all non-normal cases, this approach will be quite difficult from a computational perspective. Let's think about the CTS-GARCH model in which we have three parameters given by the GARCH specification, a constant parameter λ, and three parameters given by the stdCTS distribution, for a total of seven free parameters to estimate. Such an estimate is a solution of a nonlinear optimization problem. In practice, an optimization problem with seven dimensions that involves complex non linear functions, could be quite difficult to solve numerically if no other hypothesis on the likelihood function is available.

A suitable way to proceed is as follows. In the first optimization step the normal-GARCH parameters (α_0, α_1, β_1, and λ) are found by MLE. In the

---

[4]For details of this approach, see Rachev et al. (2007) and the references therein.
[5]Here we are referring to a Fourier inversion. See Chapter 6 for more details.

second step, the innovation process and parameters of an ID distribution are estimated. Regarding the innovation process, we note that it depends on the model considered, even if the differences between different models are quite small (of the order of 10^{-5}).

A modified version of the normal GARCH model can be considered for modeling returns in the nonparametric *filtering historical simulation* (FHS) GARCH model[6], that is,

$$r_t = \mu + \eta_t \quad \eta_t \sim N(0, \sigma_t^2)$$
$$\sigma_t^2 = \alpha_0 + \alpha_1 \eta_{t-1}^2 + \gamma I_{t-1} \eta_{t-1}^2 + \beta \sigma_{t-1}^2, \tag{14.3}$$

where η_t is the residual and $I_{t-1} = 1$ for a positive residual; otherwise, it is zero. In the market estimation of the model, one considers a similar MLE approach as described before. The volatility definition, however, is different. An asymmetric Glosten-Jagannathan-Runkle (GJR) model is considered instead. The model considers the leverage effect, that is, bad news raises the future volatility more than good news.[7] Then, the innovation η_t process is estimated and used to price options, as described in section 14.3.1.

In Table 14.1 we provide the market parameter estimates. The Kolmogorov-Smirnov (KS), the Anderson-Darling (AD, AD^2, and AD_{up}^2), and the χ^2 statistics are given in Table 14.2. These tests are described in Chapter 6. The values of the KS statistic show the better fit performances of non-normal models while the AD family of statistics captures the leptokurtic shape of the innovation distribution. Furthermore, the estimated quantile versus empirical quantile (QQ) plots for the innovation fitting are also shown in Figure 14.1. The error between the empirical and the fitted density is smaller in those cases where the asymmetry and the leptokurtosis are captured. This means that kurtosis and skewness can be better approximated by ID non-normal distributions. The normal-GARCH model clearly underperforms all non-normal models, at least for the time series investigated here. According to Table 14.2, for all competitor models, the values of the goodness-of-fit statistics are smaller than those of the normal-GARCH model. This means a larger p-value for such statistics. In particular, we can see that the values of the AD statistics for the standard non-normal ID case are significantly smaller than those of the standard normal case. That means these models explain the extreme event of the real innovation process better than the normal-GARCH model does. Figure 14.1 shows that the empirical

---

[6]The model was introduced by Barone-Adesi et al. (2008) and is reviewed in Chapter 8.

[7]This fact is illustrated in Barone-Adesi et al. (2008).

TABLE 14.1 S&P 500 Market Parameters Estimated using the MLE Approach on the Time Series from September 10, 1998, to September 10, 2008

	β	α_1	α_0	λ		
stdNormal	0.9482	0.05	5.0742e-7	0.0307		
	C	λ_-	λ_+	α		
stdCTS	0.1181	0.3534	0.8582	1.7500		
	C_+	C_-	λ_-	λ_+	α_+	α_-
stdGTS	0.1389	0.1031	0.3127	1.0299	1.7500	1.7500
	c_+	c_-	λ_+	λ_-		
stdSVG	3.3058	2.4538	2.5713	2.2153		
	k_+	k_-	r_+	r_-	p_+	p_- $\quad\alpha$
stdKRTS	0.4246	0.0315	1.4266	5.8200	10.0125	10.0288 1.8500
	C	λ_+	λ_-	α		
stdRDTS	0.1015	0.8204	0.3881	1.7500		
	α	β	δ			
stdNIG	1.8077	−0.1991	1.7749			
	β	α_1	α_0	γ	mu	
FHS	0.9377	0	1.0176e−6	0.1098	−4.1376e − 5	

Note: Normal-GARCH parameters are used in the estimation of non-normal ID models, which are excluded in the FHS-GARCH model where an MLE procedure is implemented. The parameter m is always equal to zero.

density more or less deviates from the normal density and this deviation almost disappears when one uses a non-normal ID distributed innovation.

It has to be noted that the fat-tail property of the distribution of the innovation process is really necessary to obtain a suitable fit. Furthermore, let's recall the definition of volatility clustering. As stated by (McNeil et al.,

TABLE 14.2 Goodness of Fi Statistics on the Time Series from September 10, 1998, to September 10, 2008

	KS	AD	$n \cdot AD^2$	$n \cdot AD_{up}^2$	χ^2(p-value)
Normal-GARCH	0.0419	224.2490	5.3795	21.5417	146.2847(0.0139)
CTS-GARCH	0.0371	0.0809	3.2740	12.9594	136.9576(0.0313)
GTS GARCH	0.0369	0.0804	3.3220	12.8556	128.1980(0.0702)
SVG-GARCH	0.0216	0.2672	1.6350	18.9516	124.7806(0.1588)
KR-GARCH	0.0363	0.0790	3.1459	11.6818	126.1484(0.0783)
RDTS-GARCH	0.0367	0.0799	3.3329	18.6587	135.8244(0.0313)
NIG-GARCH	0.0315	0.1740	2.4237	13.3699	127.8733(0.1305)

Note: The FHS-GARCH model cannot be tested with this approach because it is a nonparametric approach.

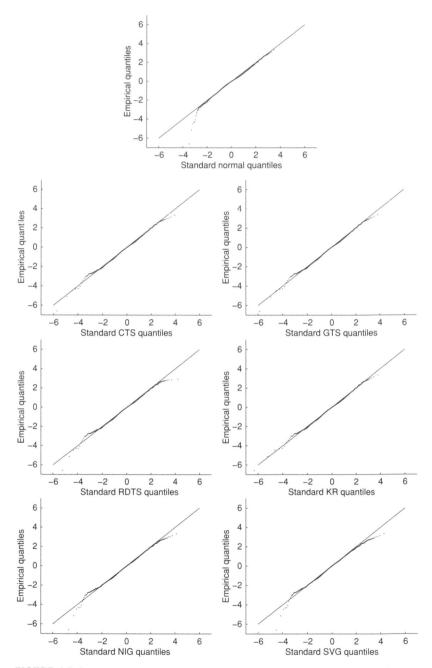

FIGURE 14.1 QQplots Obtained by the Innovation Process under Different Distributional Assumptions

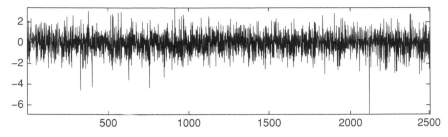

FIGURE 14.2 Estimated Standard Normal Innovation Process from September 10, 1998, to September 10, 2008

2005, p. 118), "Volatility clustering is the tendency for extreme returns to be followed by other extreme returns, although not necessarily with the same sign."

Understanding the behavior of the variance of the return process is important for forecasting as well as pricing option-type derivative instruments since the variance is a proxy for risk. High volatilities in the stock market may be described by GARCH models. Using non-normal distributions allows one to obtain an improvement in the estimation exercise. Summarizing the results and repeating findings of various other researchers, we can state the following: Albeit normal-GARCH models are well known to be one of the best-performing models to describe the evolution of volatility, a satisfactory statistical fit can only be provided when the distribution of the innovation is non-normal. Furthermore, there is a temporal dependence in asset returns: This means that they are not even close to being independent and identically distributed.

In Figures 14.2 and 14.3, the relative estimated innovation ε_t and the σ_t processes are shown. As can be seen, the innovation process presents

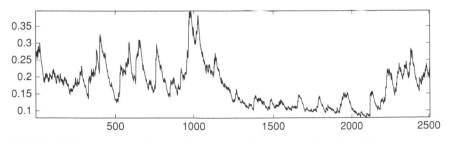

FIGURE 14.3 Estimated Annual σ_t Process from September 10, 1998, to September 10, 2008

frequent extreme negative events; in particular, the innovation is not symmetric around zero. This justifies the consideration of a fat-tailed and skewed distribution. Furthermore, as can be clearly seen in Figure 14.3, the discrete volatility process is not constant: Low volatile market follows high volatile market. From a statistical point of view, a suitable fitting exercise is needed to obtain a small pricing error, as we are going to describe in section 14.2.1.

The results in Table 14.2 show that all non-normal distributions present a better performance fit. This fact is supported by the AD statistics, which have a much lower value in the non-normal cases. By looking at the innovations shown in Figure 14.2, this fact is not surprising since we have extreme events not explainable with a standard normal random variable. The GARCH structure for the volatility is enough to explain the volatility clustering effect. A fat-tailed modeling of the innovation process captures some other stylized facts such as the possibility of dealing with extreme events and asymmetric returns. Both ingredients seem to give a more realistic picture of the time series of log-returns that are otherwise not explainable with a normal distributed approach.

14.3 PERFORMANCE OF OPTION PRICING MODELS

14.3.1 In-Sample

In the second part of the in-sample analysis, we evaluate option prices with different strikes and maturities, considering the European call prices described in the section 14.2 for September 10, 2008. The Monte Carlo procedure is based on the algorithms developed in Chapter 8 and an empirical martingale simulation is performed.[8] This last simulation technique is a simple way to reduce the variance of the simulated sample paths and to preserve the martingale property of the simulated risk-neutral process as well, which is in general lost with a crude Monte Carlo method.

Let us consider a given market model and observed prices C_i of call options with maturities τ_i and strikes $K_i, i \in \{1, \ldots, N\}$, where N is the number of options on September 10, 2008. The FHS-GARCH model, described in the section 14.2 and in Chapter 8, is fitted by matching model prices to market prices using nonlinear least squares. Hence, to obtain a practical solution to the calibration problem, our purpose is to find a parameter set

---

[8]This method has been introduced by Duan and Simonato (1998) and is described in Chapter 8.

$\tilde{\theta}$, such that the optimization problem

$$\min_{\tilde{\theta}} \sum_{i=1}^{N} (C_i(\tau_i, K_i)) - C^{\tilde{\theta}}(\tau_i, K_i))^2 \qquad (14.4)$$

is solved, where C_i denotes the price of an option as observed in the market and $C_i^{\tilde{\theta}}$ denotes the price computed according to a pricing formula in the FHS-GARCH model with a parameter set $\tilde{\theta}$.

The FHS simulation method was introduced in Chapter 8 with a view toward option pricing. The FHS-GARCH works as follows. The dynamic under the risk-neutral measure is

$$\begin{aligned} r_t &= \tilde{\mu} + \eta_t \\ \sigma_t^2 &= \tilde{\alpha}_0 + \tilde{\alpha}_1 \eta_{t-1}^2 + \gamma I_{t-1} \eta_{t-1}^2 + \tilde{\beta} \sigma_{t-1}^2, \end{aligned} \qquad (14.5)$$

where η_t is the residual and $I_{t-1} = 1$ for positive residual; otherwise, it is zero. Note that η_t is the same under both the market and risk-neutral measure. This means that the set of parameters to be estimated is $\tilde{\theta} = \{\tilde{\alpha}_0, \tilde{\alpha}_1, \gamma, \tilde{\beta}\}$, by solving the optimization problem given by equation (14.4). We note that the log-returns of the market price of the underlying asset are considered to estimate parameters of the risk-neutral model. Then, as a second step, random choices of the estimated innovation process are considered to simulate the underlying stock price process under the risk-neutral measure. Thus, risk-neutral GARCH parameters are estimated by fitting model prices to the market prices of options. The computational effort of this approach is negligible in practice since one only needs asymmetric GJR-GARCH model fitting procedures, a random choice algorithm, and a good optimization package.[9]

This nonparametric model seems to be the best competitor model for assessing the performance of our non-normal GARCH model. The model benefits with respect to the Heston and Nandi (2000) models, and other competitors are widely studied in Barone-Adesi et al. (2008). The FHS-GARCH model has a larger informational source for both underlying asset and market prices of options, while our non-normal GARCH models are flexible enough to explain market prices of options using only information about the underlying.

The performance of an option pricing model is measured by four statistics described in Chapter 7, namely, the average prediction error (APE),

---

[9]MATLAB as well as C++ financial libraries can do this job.

average absolute error (AAE), root mean-square error (RMSE), and average relative pricing error (ARPE).

Normal innovations are simulated with the normrnd command of MATLAB, based on the Marsaglia and Tsang (2000) ziggurat method, and tempered stable (TS) innovations are simulated by series representation as described in Chapter 8. The *skewed variance gamma* (SVG) innovation can be faster simulated by the gamrnd function of Matlab since it is by definition the difference between two independent gamma random variables. Furthermore, in the FHS-GARCH model, the random choice is performed by the randint function of MATLAB together with the garchsim function. Due to the structure of algorithms for non-normal innovations, the risk neutral simulation is much more slower than in the normal and in the FHS-GARCH.

We point out that for each time step and for each simulated path, we have to solve an optimization problem to find the risk-neutral parameters,[10] that is, each random number may have different parameters for each time step, which does not occur in the normal or in the FHS case.

The risk-neutral parameters for the ID-GARCH models are not reported since, for each time step, different parameters are considered in the scenario generation, while the risk-neutral estimated parameters of the FHS-GARCH model are $\tilde{\beta} = 0.8647$, $\tilde{\alpha}_1 = 0.0252$, $\tilde{\alpha}_0 = 5.4978e - 6$, and $\tilde{\gamma} = 0.1430$.

The running time ranges from a few minutes for the normal case to 62 hours for the RDTS case to simulate 20,000 paths by using MATLAB R2007b on a Xeon Precision at 3.0 GHz with 3GB RAM. In any case, if one can compute with a cluster (or with a multicore processor), the running time is of minor concern since the structure of the problem allows one to simulate paths separately.[11]

Thus, Table 14.3 shows the performance of different option pricing models. The normal-GARCH model is based on Duan (1995), while the FHS-GARCH is a nonparametric model. The normal-GARCH performs the worst in comparison with the CTS-GARCH, the RDTS-GARCH, and the FHS-GARCH models, and the FHS-GARCH outperforms all other models.

This result is not surprising since the FHS-GARCH model uses both historical and options information, while all ID-GARCH models take into account only historical information. In Figure 14.4 we show the in-sample option pricing results on September 10, 2008 for four different models. To

---

[10]See the algorithm Simulation of ID-GARCH paths in Chapter 13.

[11]The speed of such pricing procedure can be largely improved, but this argument is beyond the scope of this book.

TABLE 14.3 In-Sample European Call Option Pricing Results on September 10, 2008[a]

	APE	AAE	RMSE	ARPE
FHS-GARCH	0.0540	1.9923	2.5474	0.1087
Normal-GARCH	0.2126	7.8414	9.4308	0.4831
CTS-GARCH	0.0836	3.0857	5.0316	0.1411
RDTS-GARCH	0.0748	2.7595	4.0984	0.1417
SVG-GARCH	0.2799	10.3240	12.0903	0.6077
NIG-GARCH	0.2708	9.9906	11.5239	0.5784

[a]$(S_0 = 1,232.04\$$ and $r_0 = 6.4800e\text{-}5$) with prices between \$5 and \$180, maturities maturities 10, 20, 38, 73, 101, 112, 192, 202, 283, and 293 days and $0.8 \leq M \leq 1.2$, for a total of 98 options.

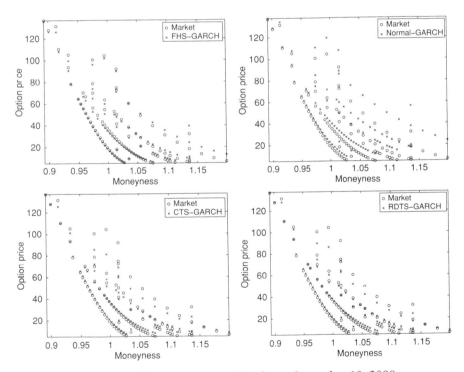

FIGURE 14.4 In-Sample Option Pricing Results on September 10, 2008: Nonparametric FHS-GARCH, normal-GARCH, CTS-GARCH, and RDTS-GARCH Models

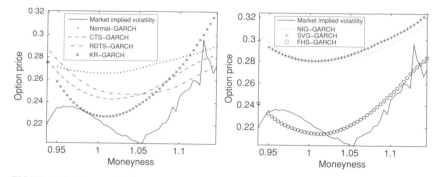

FIGURE 14.5   Implied Volatility of European Call Options on September 10, 2008, written on the S&P 500 Index with Maturity September 20, 2008

assess the benefit of our model, we also show the implied volatility curve corresponding to the shortest maturity. It is well known that the volatility surface becomes flat as soon as the maturity increases. For this reason it is important to test only the model's short maturity-implied volatilities. Figure 14.5 shows the short-term implied volatility for all models previously defined. In particular (1) the KR-GARCH model seems to approximate well the short-term implied volatility, (2) the CTS-GARCH and the RDTS-GARCH offer a volatility smile more pronounced than that of the normal-GARCH model, and (3) other models are quite far from the market-implied volatility. Even if we take into consideration only historical data, the short-term implied volatility given by our models is very close to the real one. This result provides additional proof that the classical Black-Scholes model that assumes constant volatility cannot give a complete picture of real options markets. The normal distribution assumption is rejected by the empirical evidence for both stocks and options markets.

At least for the data set investigated, option prices based on NIG-GARCH and SVG-GARCH models are quite far from market values. These pricing errors may be attributable to the fact that the tail properties of the innovation distribution under the risk-neutral measure are different with respect to the CTS and RDTS random variables and NIG, and SVG-based models are not suitable for pricing short-term and long-term maturity at the same time. Figure 14.5 shows that for short-term maturities, pricing error is not as bad as for medium- and long-term maturities. Note that the CTS and RDTS models for volatility clustering, even if not the best model for the shortest maturity, are remarkably good if one wants to price all maturities at the same time. The behavior of the right tail of the density under both the market and risk-neutral measure allows one to improve market fitting and pricing error with respect to the normal models. Remember that the normal classical model gives the same weights on the right tail (representing losses) as on the left tail (representing gains). This fact is emphasized in Figure 14.1, where, as can be seen, not all models provide good performance in tail fitting, in particular on the "loss" tail.

At least for daily log-returns of financial time series, a more flexible distribution is needed to correct estimation of the stock market behavior and correct valuation of derivatives. A suitable parameter estimation is necessary for correct risk management. These findings for asset returns and option pricing are not mere academic conclusions that hold little interest for practitioners. Rather, they have important implications for asset managers and risk managers. Not properly accounting for these stylized facts can result in models that result in inferior investment performance by asset managers and disastrous financial consequences for financial institutions that rely upon them for risk management.

TABLE 14.4 European Call Options Pricing Performances on September 10, 2008, for Different Maturities and Moneyness

		APE	AAE	RMSE	ARPE
Short	Normal-GARCH	0.1747	3.0763	3.7537	1.7662
	CTS-GARCH	0.0734	1.2925	1.5853	0.8330
	RDTS-GARCH	0.0801	1.4102	1.7165	0.7528
Medium	Normal-GARCH	0.3401	8.4931	9.0848	2.6010
	CTS-GARCH	0.1048	2.6173	2.9607	0.7861
	RDTS-GARCH	0.0862	2.1528	2.3660	0.6573
Long	Normal-GARCH	0.3994	16.3491	16.6665	1.6790
	CTS-GARCH	0.1927	7.8898	10.5712	0.3244
	RDTS-GARCH	0.1530	6.2625	8.3732	0.2444
DITM	Normal-GARCH	0.0104	1.9366	2.0856	0.0100
	CTS-GARCH	0.0057	1.0561	1.3018	0.0049
	RDTS-GARCH	0.0085	1.5850	1.7537	0.0080
ITM	Normal-GARCH	0.0567	3.5580	4.5897	0.0674
	CTS-GARCH	0.0452	2.8390	5.4113	0.0414
	RDTS-GARCH	0.0370	2.3221	4.1276	0.0396
OTM	Normal-GARCH	0.5058	6.5144	8.2248	1.5256
	CTS-GARCH	0.1885	2.4275	3.8152	0.6857
	RDTS-GARCH	0.1765	2.2731	3.2736	0.6156
DOTM	Normal-GARCH	3.3925	6.8447	8.9493	6.5110
	CTS-GARCH	0.7269	1.4667	1.7557	2.0467
	RDTS-GARCH	0.5998	1.2102	1.4698	1.7298

Table 14.4 shows the model performance for all categories previously defined (we refer to short, medium, and long maturities as well as DITM, ITM, OTM, and DOTM options). We compare the CTS and RDTS model with volatility clustering with the classical normal GARCH model. In all cases, the GARCH model based on the normal distribution is outperformed by both models based on the CTS and the RDTS distribution. OTM and DOTM options are better approximated through non-normal GARCH models in comparison to ITM and DITM. The performance of the models decreases when the call option maturity increases. Even this finding is not surprising since it is well known that GARCH models' forecasting performance decreases as the maturity increases. The large pricing errors for in-the-money options occur because we are considering moneyness with different maturities.[12] Most important, a small pricing error for at-the-money options is necessary since the implied volatility may be used as the forecasted future volatility of the underlying. This can be quite interesting in the OTC market, where an option market may not exist at all and a correct option price is needed to calculate implied volatility.

Figure 14.5 shows the estimated short-term implied volatilities with respect to the market implied volatility in the interval containing at-the-money options, that is, $0.94 \leq M \leq 1.15$. The so-called volatility smirk (smile) can be observed.

14.3.2   Out-of-Sample

In this section, we analyze the out-of-sample performance of our models. Market parameters are estimated from the same data set previously considered, that is, from September 10, 1998, to September 10, 2008, for a total of 2,501 observations. We consider European call options on September 17, 2008, with prices between $5 and $180, maturities 3, 13, 31, 66, 94, 105, 185, 195, and 276 days, and $0.8 \leq M \leq 1.2$, for a total of 118 prices.

Estimated parameters on September 10, 2008, are used to evaluate European call options prices traded one week ahead[13] by considering index level, times to maturity, and interest rates on September 17, 2008. The spot variance for the out-of-sample analysis is computed by applying the GARCH filter using the S&P 500 log return, the risk-free rates, and the historical estimation of GARCH parameters. This means that the value of the spot volatility is updated according to the selected GARCH models.

---

[12]See Menn and Rachev (2009).
[13]We adopt the approach of Dumas et al. (1998), Heston and Nandi (2000), and Barone-Adesi et al. (2008).

TABLE 14.5 Out-of-Sample European Call Option Pricing Results on September 17, 2008[a]

	APE	AAE	RMSE	ARPE
FHS-GARCH	0.3061	11.8512	13.3535	0.4038
Normal-GARCH	0.1315	5.0924	6.5914	0.2354
CTS-GARCH	0.2204	8.5317	10.9184	0.2316
RDTS-GARCH	0.2068	8.0060	10.0651	0.2237

[a] $S_0 = \$1,309.9$ and $r_0 = 8e\text{-}7$, prices between \$5 and \$180, maturities 3, 13, 31, 66, 94, 105 and 185, 195, and 276 days, and $0.8 \leq M \leq 1.2$ for a total of 118 options.

As in section 14.2.1, the same Monte Carlo approach is used to price options. In this exercise, by looking at the in-sample analysis in addition to the normal-GARCH, we consider only the best performing models, that is, the FHS, the CTS, and the RDTS based models.

In the FHS case, we consider the risk-neutral GARCH parameters estimated in section 14.2.1 by fitting the FHS model prices to market prices of options on September 10, 2008. For all other models, we run a Monte Carlo algorithm based on market parameters estimated on September 10, 2008, and we consider the initial index value and the initial risk-free rate one week ahead (September 17, 2008).

In Table 14.5 we provide the out-of-sample pricing error. The results in Figure 14.6 indicate poor model performance for all models. It is important to note that our ID-GARCH models have a similar performance in comparison to the nonparametric FHS-GARCH model. The normal model overestimates the prices observed for traded options, while all non-normal models underestimate those prices. The large differences between model prices and observed market prices occur for options with longer maturities. Furthermore, as observed in Chapter 11, in September 2008, the 3-month Treasury rate was almost zero.

However, all non-normal pricing models show good short-term performance, in particular the KR model. Figure 14.7 shows the estimated short-term implied volatilities with respect to the market-implied volatility in the interval $0.78 \leq M \leq 1.16$. The so-called volatility smile can be observed. The normal-GARCH model is incapable of explaining some DOTM prices. The smile is well explained by all non-normal models investigated in this chapter. Since the FHS-GARCH model uses a different dynamic for volatility (i.e., the GJR-GARCH model), even if it has good in-sample performance, it does not show a satisfactory out-of-sample performance, at least for the data analyzed here.

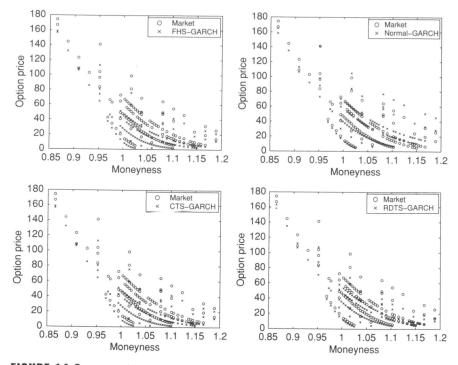

FIGURE 14.6   Out-of-Sample Option Pricing Results on September 17, 2008:
Nonparametric FHS-GARCH, Normal-GARCH, CTS-GARCH, and
RDTS-GARCH Models

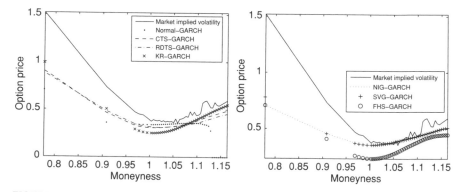

FIGURE 14.7   Implied Volatility of European Call Options on September 17,
2008, Written on the S&P 500 Index with Maturity September 20, 2008

14.4   SUMMARY

In this chapter, we present an empirical study based on the so-called fundamental approach applied to a volatility clustering model with non-normal ID innovation. Our distributional assumptions allows one to price derivatives using only a statistical fit of the underlying. The discrete time nature of our setting and an algorithm principally based on scenario generation, make this framework simple to apply.

The defined discrete-time market is incomplete, therefore, a suitable change of measure is needed in order to obtain a risk-neutral dynamic. In Chapter 12, we proposed a model in which one can use the same parameters under both the market and the risk-neutral measure.[14] In this chapter, we use a change principally inspired by the theory of the absolute continuity of measure between tempered stable and tempered infinitely divisible processes. Note that, in general, under a discrete-time setting based on ID distributions, there is not a unique change of measure. In the models proposed in Chapter 13, we assumed a possible density transformation that implies conditions to be satisfied in order to obtain a risk-neutral dynamic. We have empirically tested this approach and shown its performance in comparison to competitive models.

The idea of considering information given by the stock market to price options is not new in finance. In the case where a liquid market for options does not exist, the well-known Black-Scholes log-normal approach was considered. In that case, the historical volatility may be used in the Black-Scholes formula to price plain vanilla as well as more complex options. In our case, the GARCH framework with ID distributions allows one to obtain very promising results for both the stock market (under the market measure) and options market (under the risk-neutral measure). In particular, we show the benefits of applying models with volatility clustering based on fat-tailed and skewed random variables.

We do not compare discrete-time models with continuous-time stochastic volatility models since usually they are motivated by a different application. Usually model prices are matched to market prices of European options in order to obtain risk-neutral parameters to be used to price more complex options, while in our study we want to understand the stock market behavior in order to price plain vanilla options. Although our focus is on European call options, a similar framework may be used to price more complex path-dependent and American options.

---

[14]In the smoothly truncated stable (STS) case, with the only use of a left shift one can obtain a possible risk-neutral dynamic.

To conclude, we have identified a pricing model that fits market prices of European call options, and this model can be easily applied by a trader to evaluate a portfolio of options. At the same time, we provided a relation between market and risk-neutral parameters, thereby developing an integrated stock and options market model.

REFERENCES

Barone-Adesi, G., Engle, R., & Mancini, L. (2008). A GARCH option pricing model with filtered historical simulation. *Review of Financial Studies, 21*(3), 1223–1258.

Duan, J. (1995). The GARCH option pricing model. *Mathematical Finance, 5*(1), 13–32.

Duan, J. & Simonato, J. (1998). Empirical martingale simulation for asset prices. *Management Science, 44*(9), 1218–1233.

Dumas, B., Fleming, J., & Whaley, R. (1998). Implied volatility functions: Empirical tests. *Journal of Finance, 53*(6), 2059–2106.

Heston, S. & Nandi, S. (2000). A closed-form GARCH option valuation model. *Review of Financial Studies, 13*(3), 585–625.

Kim, Y., Rachev, S., Bianchi, M., & Fabozzi, F. (2010). Tempered stable and tempered infinitely divisible GARCH models. *Journal of Banking and Finance, 34*(9), 2096–2109.

Marsaglia, G. & Tsang, W. (2000). The ziggurat method for generating random variables. *Journal of Statistical Software, 5*(8), 1–7.

McNeil, A., Frey, R., & Embrechts, P. (2005). *Quantitative risk management*. Princeton, NJ: Princeton University Press.

Menn, C. & Rachev, S. (2009). Smoothly truncated stable distributions, GARCH-models, and option pricing. *Mathematical Methods of Operations Research, 63*(3), 411–438.

Rachev, S., Mittnik, S., Fabozzi, F., Focardi, S., & Jašić, T. (2007). *Financial econometrics: From basics to advanced modeling techniques*. Hoboken, NJ: John Wiley & Sons.

CHAPTER 15

American Option Pricing with Monte Carlo Methods

In this chapter, we price American options using Monte Carlo simulation by considering GARCH models with both normal and tempered stable innovation. In the tempered stable case we use a suitable change of measure that allows one to price options with the use of parameters estimated on the historical time series of the underlying.[1]

The key difference between American and European options relates to when the options can be exercised. American options may be exercised at any time before the expiration date. Typically, under the same payoff function, the American option price is more expensive than the European one due to the early exercise feature. However, early exercise is never optimal for American call options on non-dividend-paying stock.[2]

Consider a long position in an in-the-money American call option with non-dividend-paying underlying stock. If we exercise the call when the current stock price S_t at time t is larger than the strike price K, then we obtain $S_t - K$. The price of American call options is more expensive than that of European call options with same strike price and maturity. Furthermore, the price of in-the-money European call option is larger than $S_t - Ke^{-r(T-t)}$ as we have seen in equation (7.2) of Chapter 7, where $r > 0$ is the risk-free rate of return. Since we have $S_t - Ke^{-r(T-t)} \geq S_t - K$, the value of an American call option is greater than the income received by exercising the option at time t. Therefore it is not convenient to exercise the call earlier than the maturity date. It is better to sell the American call in the option market.

Except for the call option case with non-dividend-paying underlying stock, we have to find the optimal time to exercise our option. Suppose we have an American put option. The current price p_t of an American put

---

[1]See Menn and Rachev (2009) for further details.
[2]See Hull (2006) for additional details.

option at time t has to be larger than the exercising payoff $(K - S_t)^+$ at time t. If it is not so, that is, if the put price is less than the exercising payoff, then one can buy the option and exercise it immediately, realizing the arbitrage profit. Hence, a deep in-the-money put option price is approximately the same as the exercise payoff $(K - S_t)^+$. However, if our option is not deep in-the-money option, then we must decide whether to exercise the option. In next section, we will discuss that decision making process for American options in a discrete time market model.

15.1 AMERICAN OPTION PRICING IN DISCRETE TIME

Suppose $(S_t)_{t \geq 0}$ is a risk-neutral stock price process underlying an American option with maturity $T > 0$. Let H be the payoff function of this option. For example, $H(x) = (x - K)^+$ is the payoff function of a call option with exercise price K, and $H(x) = (K - x)^+$ is the payoff function of a put option with exercise price K.

Assume that we can exercise the option in discrete-time steps $0 = t_0 < t_1 < \cdots < t_N = T$. Then we can obtain the option price in utilizing backward induction. Let $(Z_t)_{t \in \{t_0, t_1, \ldots, t_N\}}$ be the discrete process of the value of the option. The value Z_T at the maturity T is equal to $Z_T = H(S_T)$. At time t_{N-1}, the option holder must decide between holding and exercising the option. The current value of the conditional expectation for the option under the σ-filed $\mathcal{F}_{t_{N-1}}$, which is the information until time t_{N-1}, can be defined by

$$E\left[e^{-r(T-t_{N-1})} Z_T | \mathcal{F}_{t_{N-1}}\right], \tag{15.1}$$

where r is the risk-free rate. If the value given by equation (15.1) is less than the value of exercising the option at time t_{N-1}, then the holder should exercise the option. Otherwise, the holder should continue to hold the option. Hence the value of option $Z_{t_{N-1}}$ at time t_{N-1} is

$$Z_{t_{N-1}} = \max\left\{E\left[e^{-r(T-t_{N-1})} Z_T | \mathcal{F}_{t_{N-1}}\right], H(S_{t_{N-1}})\right\}.$$

By a similar argument, the value of option at time t_{N-2} is

$$Z_{t_{N-2}} = \max\left\{E\left[e^{-r(t_{N-1}-t_{N-2})} Z_{t_{N-1}} | \mathcal{F}_{t_{N-2}}\right], H(S_{t_{N-2}})\right\}.$$

By backward iteration, the American option price is obtained by

$$Z_{t_{n-1}} = \max\left\{ E\left[e^{-r(t_n - t_{n-1})} Z_{t_n} | \mathcal{F}_{t_{n-1}} \right], H(S_{t_{n-1}}) \right\}. \tag{15.2}$$

for $n = 1, 2, \ldots, N$. In the following section we will see how this conditional expectation can be defined.

15.2 THE LEAST SQUARES MONTE CARLO METHOD

As the name suggests, the *least squares Monte Carlo* (LSM) method is designed to price American options via Monte Carlo simulation. The method can be applied to various type of options that have an early exercise feature, including Bermuda options.[3]

The owner of an American option must decide between holding and exercising the option at each discrete time until the option's maturity. If the cash flow that would result from exercising exceeds the conditional expectation of the payoff by not doing so, then the option owner should exercise the option immediately. In contrast, if the cash flow from exercising is less than the conditional expectation of payoff from not exercising, owning the option is more convenient than not exercising it. In the LSM method, the conditional expectation of the payoff is estimated by a cross-sectional regression based on the sample paths of stock prices.

Here is an example to explain the LSM method. We consider an American put on a non-dividend-paying underlying stock S_t. That is, we have:

- Payoff function is equal to $H(S_t) = (K - S_t)^+$.
- Exercise price K is 1.05.
- Time to maturity T is 3.

Assume that the current stock price S_0 and the risk-free interest rate r are equal to 1.00 and 0.01, respectively. To simplify the problem, we consider three time steps with the time interval $\Delta t = 1$, and generate eight sample paths for risk-neutral stock prices presented in Table 15.1. The general case can be treated similarly.

In Table 15.2 we report the cash flows generated by the payoff function of the put contract at the maturity time $T = 3$, that is, $\Pi(S_3) = (1.05 - S_3)^+$.

---

[3]Longstaff and Schwartz (2001) introduced the LSM method. A similar algorithm was independently developed by Tsitsiklis and Roy (2001). Convergence of the LSM method was proven by Protter et al. (2002).

TABLE 15.1 Sample Path of Stock Prices

Path	S_0	S_1	S_2	S_3
1	1.00	1.13	1.12	1.37
2	1.00	1.24	1.37	1.56
3	1.00	1.04	1.01	1.03
4	1.00	0.90	0.91	0.80
5	1.00	1.16	1.87	1.84
6	1.00	0.68	0.69	0.87
7	1.00	0.97	0.78	1.01
8	1.00	0.84	1.32	1.79

At time $T = 2$, if $S_2 < K$, then the option holder must decide whether to exercise the option immediately or continue to hold the option until the maturity date $T = 3$. Let Y_3 be discounted cash flow received at time $T = 3$ if the put is not exercised at time $T = 2$. Then, in Table 15.3, we report the values of Y_3, that is defined as follows:

$$Y_3 = e^{-r \Delta t} H(S_3) = e^{-r \Delta t}(1.05 - S_3)^+.$$

The value $E[Y_3|S_2]$ is the current value of the conditional expectation of the option if we continue to hold the option at time $T = 2$, which is the same as equation (15.1). We estimate $E[Y_3|S_2]$ by the regression method, since, as we will see in section 15.3, the equality (15.5) is fulfilled. That is, we write Y_3 as a linear combination of a constant term, S_2, and S_2^2. In the regression, we use only in-the-money stock prices, where $S_2 < K$, to allow more efficient

TABLE 15.2 Cash Flow at Time 3

Path	S_3	$(1.05 - S_3)^+$
1	1.37	0.00
2	1.56	0.00
3	1.03	0.02
4	0.80	0.25
5	1.84	0.00
6	0.87	0.18
7	1.01	0.04
8	1.79	0.00

TABLE 15.3 In-the-Money Stock Prices and Discounted Cash Flows at Time 2

Path	S_2	$Y_3 = e^{-r\Delta t}(1.05 - S_3)^+$
1	1.12	—
2	1.37	—
3	1.01	0.0198
4	0.91	0.2475
5	1.87	—
6	0.69	0.1782
7	0.78	0.0396
8	1.32	—

estimation for the conditional expectation. The regression estimates are as follows:

$$E[Y_3|S_2] \approx f_3(S_2) = -2.3690S_2^2 + 3.8262S_2 - 1.3845. \qquad (15.3)$$

Using equation (15.3), we can decide whether to exercise the option at time $T = 2$. That is, if $(K - S_2)^+ > f_3(S_2)$, then we exercise it; and if $(K - S_2)^+ \leq f_3(S_2)$, then we would rather continue to hold it. The results are presented in Table 15.4.

According to Table 15.4, path 3 is in-the-money at time $T = 2$, but we will not exercise the option. The options are exercised for paths 4, 6, and 7, and the cash flows of the option are changed. For example, the cash flow of path 4 becomes 0.14 at time 2.

TABLE 15.4 Exercise or Continue to Hold

Path	S_2	$(K - S_2)^+$	$f_3(S_2)$	Exercise	Cash Flow $t = 2$	Cash Flow $t = 3$
1	1.12	0.00	—	—	0.00	0.00
2	1.37	0.00	—	—	0.00	0.00
3	1.01	0.04	0.0633	NO	0.00	0.02
4	0.91	0.14	0.1355	YES	0.14	0.25
5	1.87	0.00	—	—	0.00	0.00
6	0.69	0.36	0.1277	YES	0.36	0.18
7	0.78	0.27	0.1586	YES	0.27	0.04
8	1.32	0.00	—	—	0.00	0.00

TABLE 15.5 In-the-Money Stock Prices and Discounted Cash Flows at Time 1

Path	S_1	Y_2
1	1.13	–
2	1.24	–
3	1.04	$0.02e^{-2r\Delta t} = 0.0196$
4	0.90	$0.14e^{-r\Delta t} = 0.1386$
5	1.16	–
6	0.68	$0.36e^{-r\Delta t} = 0.3564$
7	0.97	$0.27e^{-r\Delta t} = 0.2673$
8	0.84	$0.00e^{-r\Delta t} = 0.0000$

At time $T = 1$, let S_1 be the stock prices at time $T = 2$ for which the option is in-the-money and Y_2 be the discounted cash flow received at time $T = 2$ if the put is not exercised at time 1. Since the option can be exercised at time $T = 2$ or time $T = 3$, values of Y_2 presented in Table 15.5 are different from each other. According to the results reported in the table, the value of Y_2 for path 3 is equal to $0.02e^{-2r\Delta t}$ since the option will be exercised at time 3 and the cash flow is 0.02 if the option is not exercised at time 1. Moreover, the value of Y_2 for path 4 is equal to $0.14e^{-r\Delta t}$ since, if the option is not exercised at time $T = 1$, then the option will be exercised at time $T = 2$ and the cash flow is 0.14. That is the same for paths 6 and 7. Paths 1, 2, and 4 are ignored since they are not in-the-money at time $T = 1$. Since path 8 is in-the-money at time $T = 1$, we calculate the value for Y_2 and obtain $0e^{-r\Delta t} = 0$.

Then we estimate again the regression by considering Y_2 as a linear combination of a constant term, S_1, and S_1^2, where $S_1 < K$. As we will see in section 15.3, the equality (15.5) is fulfilled and thereby allows such approximation. We obtain

$$E[Y_2|S_1] \approx f_2(S_1) = 2.9021S_1^2 - 5.5752S_1 + 2.7741. \tag{15.4}$$

By applying equation (15.4) we can decide whether to exercise the option at time $t = 1$. The results are presented in Table 15.6. Paths 3 and 7 are not exercised for $(K - S_1)^+ < f_2(S_1)$, but paths 4, 6, and 8 are exercised for $(K - S_1)^+ > f_2(S_1)$.

Finally, the estimated price of the American put option P is

$$P = \frac{1}{8}\left(0.02e^{-3r\Delta t} + 0.15e^{-r\Delta t} + 0.37e^{-r\Delta t} + 0.27e^{-2r\Delta t} + 0.21e^{-r\Delta t}\right).$$

TABLE 15.6 Exercise or Continue to Hold

Path	S_1	$(K - S_1)^+$	$f_2(S_1)$	Exercise	Cash Flow $t = 1$	$t = 2$	$t = 3$
1	1.13	0.00	–	–	0.00	0.00	0.00
2	1.24	0.00	–	–	0.00	0.00	0.00
3	1.04	0.01	0.1147	NO	0.00	0.00	0.02
4	0.90	0.15	0.1071	YES	0.15	0.14	0.25
5	1.16	0.00	–	–	0.00	0.00	0.00
6	0.68	0.37	0.3249	YES	0.37	0.36	0.18
7	0.97	0.08	0.0967	NO	0.00	0.27	0.04
8	0.84	0.21	0.1386	YES	0.21	0.00	0.00

Generalizing the example, the LSM method can be described by the following algorithm:

Step 1. Simulate M sample paths of risk-neutral stock prices for N time steps $0 = t_0 < t_1 < \cdots < t_N = T$, where T is the time to maturity, and let $(S_{t_n}^{(m)})_{n=0,1,\dots,N}$ be the mth sample path. Let $\Delta t_n = t_{n+1} - t_n$ for $n = 0, 1, \dots, N$.

Step 2. $C^{(m)}(t_N) = H(S_{t_N}^{(m)})$ and $\tau^{(m)}(t_N) = T$, $m = 1, 2, \dots, M$.

Step 3. $n = N - 1$.

Step 4. $Y^{(m)} = e^{-r \Delta t_n} C^{(m)}(t_{n+1})$.

Step 5. Find $a_0, a_1, \dots, a_d$ that minimizes the error

$$\left(\sum_{m=1}^{M} \left(f_n(S_{t_n}^{(m)}) - Y^{(m)} \right)^2 \right)^{\frac{1}{2}},$$

where $f_n(x) = \sum_{j=0}^{d} a_j x^j$.[4]

---

[4]More generally, the function f_n can be defined by $f_n(x) = \sum_{j=0}^{d} a_j \varphi_j(x)$ and φ_j is an orthogonal basis. One possible choice of the orthogonal basis suggested by Longstaff and Schwartz (2001) is a weighted Laguerre polynomials, that is,

$$\varphi_j(x) = e^{-x/2} \left(\frac{e^x}{j!} \frac{d^j}{dx^j} (x^j e^{-x}) \right).$$

Step 6. For $m = 1, 2, \ldots, M$, calculate the cash flow by

$$
C^{(m)}(t_n) = \begin{cases} H(S_{t_n}^{(m)}) & \text{if } e^{-r \Delta t_n} f(S_{t_n}^{(m)}) \leq H(S_{t_n}^{(m)}) \\ e^{-r \Delta t_n} C^{(m)}(t_{n+1}) & \text{if } e^{-r \Delta t_n} f(S_{t_n}^{(m)}) > H(S_{t_n}^{(m)}) \end{cases}.
$$

Step 7. $n = n - 1$

Step 8. Go to Step 4 until $n = 0$.

Step 9. Option price is obtained by

$$
\frac{1}{M} \sum_{m=1}^{M} e^{-r \Delta t_0} C^{(m)}(t_1).
$$

15.3   LSM METHOD IN GARCH OPTION PRICING MODEL

The LSM method is designed for models based on Markov processes. For these processes the conditional expectation $E[e^{-r(t_n - t_{n-1})} Z_{t_n} | \mathcal{F}_{t_{n-1}}]$ in equation (15.2) can be approximated as follows:

$$
E[e^{-r(t_n - t_{n-1})} Z_{t_n} | \mathcal{F}_{t_{n-1}}] = E[e^{-r(t_n - t_{n-1})} Z_{t_n} | S_{t_{n-1}}] \approx \sum_{j=0}^{d} a_j S_{t_{n-1}}^j, \qquad (15.5)
$$

where d is some positive integer, $n = 1, 2, \ldots, N$ and $t_N = T$. However, in general, GARCH models are not Markovian, that is

$$
E[e^{-r(t_n - t_{n-1})} Z_{t_n} | \mathcal{F}_{t_{n-1}}] \neq E[e^{-r(t_n - t_{n-1})} Z_{t_n} | S_{t_{n-1}}].
$$

Therefore, we need to enhance the LSM method as described in the following.[5]

To obtain precise results for non-Markovian GARCH models, the least square regression should be applied not only to the stock price $S_{t_{n-1}}$ but also to the volatility σ_{t_n} which is $\mathcal{F}_{t_{n-1}}$ measurable. That is, we can approximate

---

[5]Stentoft (2005, 2008) discussed American option pricing with the LSM method under GARCH models with the normal innovation and the normal inverse Gaussian (NIG) innovation.

the conditional expectation by

$$E[e^{-r(t_n-t_{n-1})}Z_{t_n}|\mathcal{F}_{t_{n-1}}] \approx \sum_{i=0}^{d}\sum_{j=0}^{e} a_{i,j} S_{t_{n-1}}^{i} \sigma_{t_n}^{j},$$

for some positive integers d and e. We can extend the the LSM method for the GARCH option pricing model by modifying Step 6 of the above algorithm as follows:

Step 6'. Find $a_{i,j}, i = 1, 2, \ldots, d$ and $j = 1, 2, \ldots, e$ such that minimizes the error

$$\left(\sum_{m=1}^{M} \left(f_n(S_{t_n}^{(m)}, \sigma_{t_{n+1}}^{(m)}) - Y^m \right)^2 \right)^{\frac{1}{2}},$$

where $f_n(x, y) = \sum_{i=0}^{d}\sum_{j=0}^{e} a_{i,j} x^i y^j$.

15.4 EMPIRICAL ILLUSTRATION

In this section, we compute American put option prices by using the LSM method for both the Black-Scholes option pricing model and GARCH option pricing models with normal and tempered stable innovations. We consider four tempered stable distributions to model the residual distribution: the *classical tempered stable* (CTS), modified tempered stable (MTS), *normal tempered stable* (NTS), and *rapidly decreasing tempered stable* (RDTS) distributions.

We briefly recall that the GARCH option pricing model was presented in Chapter 13 without dividends. We consider a sequence $(\varepsilon_t)_{t\in\mathbb{N}}$ of independent and identically distributed (i.i.d.) real random variables with zero mean and unit variance.[6] The market price dynamic is modeled by the following:

$$\log\left(\frac{S_t}{S_{t-1}}\right) = r_t + \lambda_t\sigma_t - g_{\varepsilon_t}(\sigma_t) + \sigma_t\varepsilon_t, \quad t \in \mathbb{N}, \tag{15.6}$$

where S_t is the stock price at time t, r_t denotes the risk-free rate for the period $[t - 1, t]$, and λ_t is the market price of risk. S_0 is the price observed

---

[6]$\mathbb{N}$ is the set of natural numbers.

at time $t = 0$. The function $g_{\varepsilon_t}(x)$ is the *log-Laplace-transform* of ε_t, that is, $g_{\varepsilon_t}(x) = \log(E[e^{x\varepsilon_t}])$. If $g_{\varepsilon_t}(x) < \infty$ on a real interval $(-a, b)$ with $a, b > 0$, then σ_t^2 follows a GARCH(1,1) process with a restriction $0 < \sigma_t^2 < b^2$, that is,

$$\sigma_t^2 = (\alpha_0 + \alpha_1 \sigma_{t-1}^2 \varepsilon_{t-1}^2 + \beta_1 \sigma_{t-1}^2) \wedge \rho, \quad t \in \mathbb{N}, \quad \varepsilon_0 = 0, \tag{15.7}$$

where $p \wedge q = \min\{p, q\}$ and $0 < \rho < b^2$. In case $g_{\varepsilon_t}(x)$ is defined on the whole real line, for example ε_t follows the standard normal or standard RDTS distribution, then equation (15.7) is equal to

$$\sigma_t^2 = (\alpha_0 + \alpha_1 \sigma_{t-1}^2 \varepsilon_{t-1}^2 + \beta_1 \sigma_{t-1}^2), \quad t \in \mathbb{N}, \quad \varepsilon_0 = 0. \tag{15.8}$$

The risk-neutral price dynamic is modeled by

$$\log\left(\frac{S_t}{S_{t-1}}\right) = r_t - g_{\xi_t}(\sigma_t) + \sigma_t \xi_t, \quad t \in \mathbb{N}, \tag{15.9}$$

where $(\xi_t)_{t \in \mathbb{N}}$ is a sequence of i.i.d. real random variables with zero mean and unit variance and $g_{\xi_t} = \log(E[e^{x\xi_t}])$. If $g_{\xi_t}(x) < \infty$ for another real interval $(-c, d)$ with $c, d > 0$, then the variance process in the risk-neutral dynamic is equal to

$$\sigma_t^2 = (\alpha_0 + \alpha_1 \sigma_{t-1}^2 (\xi_{t-1} - k_{t-1})^2 + \beta_1 \sigma_{t-1}^2) \wedge \rho, \tag{15.10}$$

where $\rho < d^2$. If $\rho = \infty$ then equation (15.10) is equal to

$$\sigma_t^2 = \alpha_0 + \alpha_1 \sigma_{t-1}^2 (\xi_{t-1} - k_{t-1})^2 + \beta_1 \sigma_{t-1}^2. \tag{15.11}$$

If ε_t and ξ_t are standard normal distributed, then we referred to the GARCH option pricing model as the *Normal-GARCH* model. Moreover, when ε_t and ξ_t are standard tempered stable distributed, then we referred to the GARCH option pricing model as the *Tempered-Stable-GARCH (TS-GARCH) option pricing* model or simply the TS-GARCH model. Each TS-GARCH option pricing model is referred to by the name of that tempered stable distribution (e.g., CTS-GARCH option price model) or simply process name followed by model (e.g., CTS-GARCH model). One method to find the equivalent martingale measure (EMM) in TS-GARCH option pricing models is discussed in Chapter 13.

In this section, we consider the finite time horizon $T < \infty$ and the finite discrete stock price process $(S_t)_{0 \leq t \leq T}$. That is, we consider two finite sequences of i.i.d. random variables $(\varepsilon_t)_{t\in\{1,2,\ldots,T\}}$ and $(\xi_t)_{t\in\{1,2,\ldots,T\}}$ for a positive integer T instead of infinite sequences $(\varepsilon_t)_{t\in\mathbb{N}}$ and $(\xi_t)_{t\in\mathbb{N}}$. By doing this, we can use a simplified method to find the EMM, as was done in Chapter 12.

We assume that the market price of risk λ_t is equal to a constant λ and that $k_t = \lambda$. Moreover, we assume that ε_t and ξ_t have the same distribution. For example, if we consider the CTS-GARCH option pricing model with the market measure $\mathbb{P}$ and the risk-neutral measure $\mathbb{Q}$, we have that ε_t and ξ_t have the same distribution. That is,

$$(\varepsilon_t)_{t\in\{1,2,\ldots,T\}} \text{ is i.i.d. with } \varepsilon_t \sim stdCTS(\alpha, \lambda_+, \lambda_-) \text{ under } \mathbb{P}$$

and

$$(\xi_t)_{t\in\{1,2,\ldots,T\}} \text{ is i.i.d. with } \xi_t \sim stdCTS(\alpha, \lambda_+, \lambda_-) \text{ under } \mathbb{Q}.$$

Since $(\varepsilon_t)_{t\in\{1,2,\ldots,T\}}$ and $(\xi_t)_{t\in\{1,2,\ldots,T\}}$ are finite sequences of random variables, the equivalence of $\mathbb{P}$ and $\mathbb{Q}$ for the CTS-GARCH model is proved by using the arguments in section 5.3.1 as follows.

Suppose $(\varepsilon_t)_{t\in\{1,2,\ldots,T\}}$ is a sequence of i.i.d. random variables such that $\varepsilon_t \sim stdCTS(\alpha, \lambda_+, \lambda_-)$ on $\mathbb{P}$ and $\varepsilon_t \stackrel{d}{=} \xi_t - \lambda$ where $\xi_t \sim stdCTS(\alpha, \lambda_+, \lambda_-)$ on $\mathbb{Q}$. Let the probability density functions of ε_t be given by $f_t(x)$ and $h_t(x)$ on probability measures $\mathbb{P}$ and $\mathbb{Q}$, respectively. Since ε_t's are identically distributed, we have $f_t(x) = f_s(x)$ and $h_t(x) = h_s(x)$ for all $t, s \in \{1, 2, \ldots, T\}$. Let $f(x) = f_t(x)$ and $h(x) = h_t(x)$, then we have

$$f(x) = \frac{\partial}{\partial x}\mathbb{P}[\varepsilon_t < x]$$

and

$$h(x) = \frac{\partial}{\partial x}\mathbb{Q}[\varepsilon_t < x].$$

Since the domain of the function f is the same as the domain of the function h, $\mathbb{P}$ and $\mathbb{Q}$ are equivalent and the Radon-Nikodym derivative is equal to

$$\frac{d\mathbb{Q}}{d\mathbb{P}} = \frac{h(\varepsilon_1)h(\varepsilon_2)\cdots h(\varepsilon_T)}{f(\varepsilon_1)f(\varepsilon_2)\cdots f(\varepsilon_T)}.$$

TABLE 15.7 Innovation Distribution for the Four TS-GARCH Models

Model	Distribution of ε_t under the Market Measure $\mathbb{P}$	Distribution of ξ_t under the Risk-Neutral Measure $\mathbb{Q}$
CTS-GARCH	$\varepsilon_t \sim stdCTS(\alpha, \lambda_+, \lambda_-)$	$\xi_t \sim stdCTS(\alpha, \lambda_+, \lambda_-)$
MTS-GARCH	$\varepsilon_t \sim stdMTS(\alpha, \lambda_+, \lambda_-)$	$\xi_t \sim stdMTS(\alpha, \lambda_+, \lambda_-)$
NTS-GARCH	$\varepsilon_t \sim stdNTS(\alpha, \lambda, \beta)$	$\xi_t \sim stdNTS(\alpha, \lambda, \beta)$
RDTS-GARCH	$\varepsilon_t \sim stdRDTS(\alpha, \lambda_+, \lambda_-)$	$\xi_t \sim stdRDTS(\alpha, \lambda_+, \lambda_-)$

The distribution of ε_t and ξ_t for the other TS-GARCH option pricing models are given in Table 15.7. The equivalence for the other TS-GARCH option pricing models can be proved by the same argument.

In this empirical investigation, we will consider the S&P 100 index (OEX) and the option when the underlying is the index (OEX option). These derivatives are American-style options. We ignore the dividends for S&P 100 index, since we consider adjusted closing prices. Time-series data for the period September 10, 1998, to September 10, 2008, are used to estimate historical market parameters for the GARCH models. The option data for September 10, 2008, will be used for the in-sample analysis; data for September 11, 2008, will be used for the out-of-sample analysis. The quotes for the S&P 100 index on September 10 and September 11, 2008, are 571.73 and 578.88, respectively. The 13-week Treasury bill indexes (IRX) are 1.62% and 1.58% on the two considered days, respectively. We consider put options having moneyness between 0.8 and 1.2. We consider 10 and 9 days to maturity[7] for the in-sample analysis and the out-of-sample analysis, respectively.

In Table 15.8 we report historical parameter estimates obtained from an analysis of the S&P100 index. The parameters are estimated using the following three-step method:[8] (1) estimate GARCH parameters ($\beta_1, \alpha_1, \alpha_0$, and λ) of the normal-GARCH model by maximum likelihood estimation (MLE), (2) extract residuals using the GARCH historical parameter estimates, and (3) estimate parameters of the four standard tempered stable (standard CTS, standard MTS, standard NTS, and standard RDTS) distributions by the MLE using the extracted residuals. Here we assume that $\sigma_0^2 = \alpha_0/(1 - \alpha_1 - \beta_1)$ and $\rho = \max\{\sigma_t^2 : t$ is the observed date$\}$.

The results of the goodness-of-fit test are presented in Table 15.9. Based on the p-values of the Kolmogorov-Smirnov distance statistic (KS-statistic) reported in the table, the Normal-GARCH model is rejected but the four

---

[7]When we simulate, we remove weekends since American options cannot be exercised on weekend days.

[8]This is a simplified version of the *quasi-maximum likelihood estimation* (QMLE) method.

TABLE 15.8 Estimated Parameters

GARCH Parameters and the Market Price of Risk			
$\beta_1 = 0.9329$	$\alpha_1 = 0.0663$	$\alpha_0 = 4.2841 \cdot 10^{-7}$	$\lambda = 0.0353$

Distribution	Tempered Stable Parameters		
CTS	$\alpha = 1.8679$	$\lambda_+ = 0.4196$	$\lambda_- = 0.1219$
MTS	$\alpha = 1.8850$	$\lambda_+ = 0.7233$	$\lambda_- = 0.2151$
NTS	$\alpha = 1.9010$	$\lambda = 0.2882$	$\beta = -0.0281$
RDTS	$\alpha = 1.9043$	$\lambda_+ = 0.1826$	$\lambda_- = 0.1826$

TS-GARCH models are not rejected at the 1% confidence level. Based on the Anderson-Darling statistic (AD-statistic), the Normal-GARCH model has a value that is greater than the four TS-GARCH models.

To price options, we generate 10,000 sample paths for each of the models taken into consideration. Risk-neutral paths can be simulated by considering historical parameter estimates of the normal and of the four tempered stable innovations as reported in Table 15.8. Those generated sample paths are used for pricing American options by the LSM method. The regression step of the LSM method (i.e., modified Step 6) considers the following independent variables $\{1, S_{t_n}, S_{t_n}^2, \sigma_{t_{n+1}}, \sigma_{t_{n+1}} S_{t_n}, \sigma_{t_{n+1}} S_{t_n}^2\}$ for all the GARCH models investigated. There are several reasonable ways to choose the initial variance σ_0^2, which strongly influences the model's behavior. We take the last volatility in the estimated series for the in-sample analysis. For out-of-sample analysis, we choose

$$\sigma_0 = \sqrt{\alpha_0 + \alpha_1 \sigma_t^2 (\xi_t - \lambda)^2 + \beta_1 \sigma_t^2},$$

where σ_t and ξ_t are the last volatility and the last innovation in the estimated series.

TABLE 15.9 Goodness-of-Fit Test for the Estimated Parameters

Model	KS (p-value)	AD
Normal-GARCH	0.0333(0.0081)	85.7259
CTS-GARCH	0.0278(0.0395)	0.0666
MTS-GARCH	0.0274(0.0441)	0.0658
NTS-GARCH	0.0257(0.0702)	0.0646
RDTS-GARCH	0.0277(0.0414)	0.0890

TABLE 15.10   Error Estimators: OEX Put Option

Date	Model	APE	AAE	RMSE	ARPE
Sep. 10, 2008	Black-Scholes	1.6619	0.1187	0.4924	1.8668
($\tau = 10, N = 23$)	Normal-GARCH	0.8091	0.0578	0.2908	0.8785
	CTS-GARCH	0.6304	0.0450	0.2306	0.6805
	MTS-GARCH	0.6288	0.0449	**0.2286**	0.6806
	NTS-GARCH	**0.6191**	**0.0442**	0.2454	**0.6630**
	RDTS-GARCH	0.6760	0.0483	0.2601	0.7228
Sep. 11, 2008	Black-Scholes	1.5245	0.1238	0.5604	1.7658
($\tau = 9, N = 23$)	Normal-GARCH	0.8695	0.0706	0.4202	0.9437
	CTS-GARCH	0.8206	0.0666	0.3825	0.9025
	MTS-GARCH	0.8136	0.0661	**0.3797**	0.8945
	NTS-GARCH	**0.8047**	**0.0654**	0.3947	**0.8838**
	RDTS-GARCH	0.8438	0.0685	0.4096	0.9246

Notes: τ = Days to maturity. N = Number of options.
The smallest error is indicated with bold type.

The Black-Scholes model is used as the benchmark in this investigation. We generate 10,000 sample paths for the Black-Scholes option pricing model. The constant volatility of the model is estimated by the sample standard deviation of the more recent 252 daily returns until September 10 and September 11, 2009, for in-sample and out-of-sample analysis, respectively. The regression step of the LSM method considers the independent variables $\{1, S_{t_n}, S_{t_n}^2\}$ for the Black-Scholes model.

In Table 15.10, the relevant values of four error estimators are given for the in-sample analysis and the out-of-sample analysis. The four error estimators are the *average prediction error* (APE), *average absolute error* (AAE), *root mean-square error* (RMSE), and *average relative pricing error* (ARPE), which are defined in Chapter 7. Implied volatility curves of four TS-GARCH model prices and market prices are presented in Figure 15.1. Based on Table 15.10, we conclude the following. In both the in-sample analysis and the out-of-sample analysis, the NTS-GARCH model has the smallest APE, AAE, and ARPE, and the MTS-GARCH model has the smallest RMSE. Moreover, based on Figure 15.1, we can find that the normal-GARCH model and the four TS-GARCH option pricing models explain the implied volatility curves. While the model implied volatility curves are not exactly the same as the market implied volatility curve, the four TS-GARCH model implied volatility curves have greater curvature than the implied volatility curve for the Normal-GARCH model.

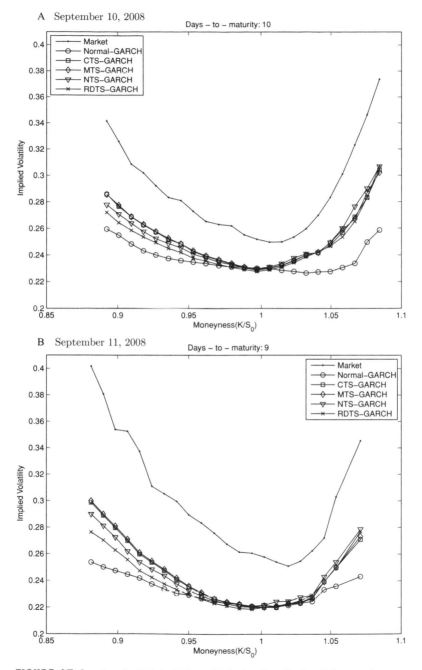

FIGURE 15.1 Implied Volatilities of Market Put Option Prices and Model Prices for the OEX Put on September 10 and September 11, 2008

15.5 SUMMARY

In this chapter, we analyzed American option pricing under tempered stable GARCH models using the least squares Monte Carlo method. We also provide an empirical analysis for the S&P 100 index option. Market parameters are estimated using the maximum likelihood estimator applied to the historical data of the S&P 100 index and the risk-neutral parameters are obtained by a suitable measure change base on the historical estimates of the underlying. We find that the four TS-GARCH models are more realistic than the Normal-GARCH model in estimating the historical parameters, and hence those TS-GARCH models perform better than the Normal-GARCH model for the American put options analyzed.

REFERENCES

Hull, J. C. (2006). *Options, futures and other derivatives* (6th ed.). Upper Saddle River, NJ: Prentice-Hall.

Longstaff, F. A. & Schwartz, E. S. (2001). Valuing American options by simulation: A simple least-squares approach. *Review of Financial Studies, 14*(1), 113–147.

Menn, C. & Rachev, S. (2009). Smoothly truncated stable distributions, GARCH-models, and option pricing. *Mathematical Methods of Operations Research, 63*(3), 411–438.

Protter, P., Clément, E., & Lamberton, D. (2002). An analysis of a least squares regression method for American option pricing. *Finance and Stochastics, 6*(4), 449–471.

Stentoft, L. (2005). Pricing American options when the underlying asset follows GARCH processes. *Journal of Empirical Finance, 12*(4), 576–611.

Stentoft, L. (2008). American option pricing using GARCH models and the normal inverse Gaussian distribution. *Journal of Financial Econometrics, 6*(4), 540–582.

Tsitsiklis, J. N. & Roy, B. V. (2001). Regression methods for pricing complex American-style options. *IEEE Transactions on Neural Networks, 12*, 694–703.

Index